INSIDE THE TERRIFYING WORLD OF
JAISH-E-MOHAMMED

INSIDE THE TERRIFYING WORLD OF JAISH-E-MOHAMMED

ABHINAV PANDYA

HarperCollins *Publishers* India

First published in India by HarperCollins *Publishers* 2024
4th Floor, Tower A, Building No. 10, DLF Cyber City,
DLF Phase II, Gurugram, Haryana – 122002
www.harpercollins.co.in

2 4 6 8 10 9 7 5 3 1

Copyright © Abhinav Pandya 2024

P-ISBN: 978-93-6569-480-2
E-ISBN: 978-93-6569-974-6

The views and opinions expressed in this book are the author's own and the facts are as reported by him and the publishers are not in any way liable for the same.

Abhinav Pandya asserts the moral right
to be identified as the author of this work.

All rights reserved. No part of this publication may be reproduced, stored in a retrieval system, or transmitted, in any form or by any means, electronic, mechanical, photocopying, recording or otherwise, without the prior permission of the publishers.

Typeset in 11/15.2 Berling LT Std at
HarperCollins *Publishers* India

Printed and bound in India by
Manipal Technologies Limited

This book is produced from independently certified FSC® paper to ensure responsible forest management.

To
the forty bravehearts of Pulwama who laid down their lives for the country

Contents

Foreword by Rohan Gunaratna	ix
Foreword by Michael Rubin	xv
Preface	xix
1. The Master of Fidayeen Attacks	1
2. The Origins of JeM and Pakistan's Deobandi Ecosystems	15
3. Masood Azhar and JeM's Dark Ideological Alleyways	54
4. JeM's Organizational Evolution and India Operations	115
5. JeM and Its Fidayeen Missions: Training and Tactics	197
6. Militant Profiles	275
7. Pathankot and Pulwama: Obsession with the Pleasures of Jannat	338
Acknowledgements	393
Abbreviations	395
Notes	401
Index	473

Foreword

INSIDE THE TERRIFYING WORLD OF JAISH-E-MOHAMMED BY Abhinav Pandya is a tour de force. The book maps the origins, development and the future of a threat entity least understood by counterterrorism practitioners and scholars. Abhinav has meticulously researched the Deobandi ecosystem and the ideological alleyways that form the outfit's foundation and drivers. Before mapping the contours of the threat, Abhinav delineates its indoctrination, training, tactics and operations. After profiling its leadership, membership and support base, the book provides a comprehensive account of its cascading attacks.

An Al Qaeda affiliate, Jaish-e-Mohammed also forged ties with the Islamic State (IS), especially its branch in Afghanistan and Pakistan. The book assesses the impact and influence of JeM on geopolitics. The confrontation brought the two nuclear powers India and Pakistan to the brink of war. Similarly, with its attacks in Pathankot and Mazar-i-Sharif in 2016, the Indo-Pakistan peace-building process was dismantled.

Like the catastrophic attack by JeM, Hamas launched a cascading attack on 7 October 2024, precipitating a war between Iran and Israel, two regional powers. Like the JeM attack derailed the peace process in the subcontinent, the Hamas attack disrupted the peace in the region following the Abraham Accords, the bilateral agreements on Arab–Israeli normalization. Abhinav's book provides insight and foresight into how certain non-state armed attacks can bring powers to the brink of war and precipitate a war between actual and aspiring nuclear weapon states. JeM's ties with IS and its ecosystem extending to the West, especially Europe, are serious concerns. To mitigate this insidious threat, this book is a must-read by both national security leaders, and concerned citizens.

In an age where information is both a weapon and a shield, the responsibility of understanding and combating extremism falls not just on governments and security agencies, but also on scholars, analysts and informed citizens. The book you hold in your hands is a testament to this responsibility—a diligent, insightful exploration of one of the most notorious regional terror organizations.

JeM, since its inception, has been a subject of intense scrutiny and concern, both for its ideological motivations and its operational reach. Understanding such a complex and dangerous entity requires not only deep knowledge of global and regional geopolitics, but also a nuanced understanding of the sociopolitical factors that give rise to such groups. This book, written by my esteemed student and colleague Abhinav Pandya, delves into these complexities with a rigour and dedication that is both commendable and necessary.

Abhinav's exploration of JeM is not just an academic exercise—it is a vital contribution to our understanding of extremism and its implications for regional and global security. Such a detailed examination of the group's origins, ideology and operations provides readers with a comprehensive understanding that is crucial for policymakers, researchers and anyone interested in the dynamics of modern terrorism.

The foundation of JeM is intricately linked with the history and rise of the Deobandi movement, which played a pivotal role in shaping the ideological landscape of South Asia. The author traces this history with precision, offering readers a clear understanding of how religious movements can evolve into potent forces that influence regional stability. This exploration is not just a recounting of events, but an analysis that connects the dots between ideology and its eventual militarization, shedding light on the pathways that lead from theological discourse to armed struggle.

Delving into the actors behind JeM, the book addresses the controversial and often clandestine role of Pakistan's Inter-Services Intelligence (ISI) in nurturing and supporting regional terror entities. By meticulously documenting the relationship between state actors and non-state militants, Abhinav tactfully brings to light the complex web of alliances that has fuelled the rise of outfits such as JeM. This analysis is particularly crucial for understanding the broader geopolitical implications of state-sponsored terrorism, especially in a region as volatile as South Asia.

A key figure in the JeM narrative is Masood Azhar, whose life and actions are explored in depth in these pages. Abhinav provides a comprehensive account of Azhar's rise, his strategic vision and the impact of his leadership on the trajectory of the organization. This biographical exploration is coupled with an examination of how individual actors can significantly influence the course of extremist movements, making it a valuable case study for scholars and practitioners alike. A deep analysis of Azhar, including his personal background, rise to power, detention, release in exchange for a hijacked aircraft and relationships to other major groups and leaders, enable the reader to acquire a deep understanding of this character.

The book also delves into the greater geopolitical implications of the India-Pakistan rivalry, a conflict that has had far-reaching consequences for the rise of terror entities in the region. The author expertly navigates the complex dynamics of this rivalry, illustrating how national interests, regional power plays and global alliances have contributed to the proliferation of militant groups. This analysis is essential for anyone seeking to understand the broader security challenges that arise from one of the world's longest and most perilous conflicts.

Lastly, the relationship of JeM with other threat groups is thoroughly examined, highlighting the interconnected nature of modern terrorism. In contemporary discourse, it is essential for practitioners and academics to understand the links between various terror entities. Abhinav explores this brilliantly. His insights into these alliances and rivalries within the extremist ecosystem offer readers a nuanced understanding of how these groups operate, both independently and collaboratively, to achieve their goals. This examination not only enhances the readers' understanding of JeM, but also provides a broader perspective on the global network of terror that continues to challenge international peace and security.

This work is a culmination of years of research, analysis and a steadfast commitment to uncovering the truth in a world often clouded by misinformation. This book stands as a significant scholarly achievement and an important resource for those seeking to understand the mechanisms of terror that continue to challenge global peace. It is a work that is both timely and timeless, addressing the urgent needs of today while contributing to the broader discourse on security and extremism.

I am honoured to have been asked to write this foreword, and I do so with great pride in the author's accomplishments. This book is a reflection of not just the author's intellectual rigour, but also his unwavering commitment to making the world a safer, more informed place.

It is my sincere hope that this work will serve as a valuable resource and inspire further research and dialogue in the fight against terrorism.

—**Professor Rohan Gunaratna** is a threat specialist of the global security environment, and professor of security studies at the S. Rajaratnam School of International Studies, Nanyang Technology University, Singapore

Foreword

ACROSS INDIA AND THE WORLD, AL QAEDA IS A household name. Lashkar-e-Taiba also has a global reputation, largely due to its 2008 attack on Mumbai. Counterterrorism experts and intelligence analysts know and understand Jaish-e-Mohammed to be just as lethal, though the group's activities often fall below the public radar. This is unfortunate. While a 2004 crackdown in Pakistan and successful Indian counterterror operations in Kashmir undermined JeM, the group came back with a vengeance in 2016, culminating in the Pulwama massacre.

As academic and analyst Abhinav Pandya writes, JeM is, in many ways, more dangerous now, because, in sharp contrast to other Islamist terrorist groups, it shifts operational strategies, tends to flout the ISI's dictats and lacks a clear chain of command, except in its top brass. In effect, for many counterterror and security services, it remains a puzzle—and an increasingly lethal one. The group is not just an Indian problem. As Pandya notes, 'JeM also shares Al Qaeda's pan-Islamist vision.'

This is why Pandya's book is so important. As those of us who have worked in national security know, fresh information is often hard to come by. Safety concerns often insulate analysts from the topics they cover. Security parameters restrain diplomats from roaming freely. Intelligence operatives receive information remotely and even traditional spies seldom analyse their own work. No matter how much generals promote 'winning hearts and minds', the very nature of military operations distorts relationships and creates distance between it and the civilian population, especially during counterterror operations. No civilian is going to knock on the bulletproof window of an armoured personnel carrier and share a cigarette with a soldier. Pandya, however, fills a gap. As an academic, he spent years in Kashmir assessing security and radicalization. He had an eye for and a deep knowledge about security, could speak to ordinary people without pretence and hear unvarnished ground truth. This is why both the governor and Indian commanders often solicited his opinion and treated him as an important, if informal, adviser. Few analysts can access both soldiers on the front lines, and prisoners and their supporters.

Inside the Terrifying World of Jaish-e-Mohammed is a masterclass on the terrorist group, which journalists, diplomats, think-tank scholars and intelligence professionals must read. Pandya has a historian's touch. He traces Pakistan's strategy sponsoring insurgency and embracing proxy terror groups to the late 1950s, just a decade after Partition, and traces Pakistan's terror support and nuclear embrace in the decades after. He shows how Pakistan used that nuclear capability not just for defence, as its diplomats and politicians claimed, but also to provide cover for terrorism as Pakistani leaders believed they could act without consequence. It is no coincidence, as Pandya notes, that JeM exploded in Kashmir shortly after Pakistan overtly demonstrated its nuclear capability.

Alongside Lashkar-e-Taiba, JeM began conducting attacks across India, sometimes under its own name, but also under the guise of various front groups it established to both exaggerate supposed grassroots opposition to India and eschew direct accountability. Here, Pandya rolls back the curtain to show definitively what Western analysts should have recognized all along. He also shows how Pakistani intervention and intelligence-sharing helped blunt even token Western efforts to neuter JeM finances.

Too often, academics, diplomats and counterterror experts view terror through the lens of grievance. Robert Pape, the University of Chicago political scientist who penned the influential *Dying to Win: The Strategic Logic of Suicide Terrorism*, which argued that fighting occupation motivates most suicide bombers, is perhaps the most famous of these. In reality, however, ideology matters perhaps even more. Pandya's strength is that he does not succumb to either political correctness or polemic. He treats religion with respect, but does not shy away from its internal debates. Hence, he delves deep into the Deobandi ecosystem of both Pakistan and JeM.

He also fills in the blanks that have so often confounded intelligence agencies with multibillion-dollar budgets. Charts illustrate the narrative and show the ever-shifting alphabet soup of groups as they evolve, merge, marry and divorce, all leading to JeM's rise. He delves into not only top-tier personalities, but also their deputies and significant underlings. His mastery and exhaustive research not only details their careers in Pakistan, but also manages to trace their foreign travel across Africa, the Middle East and Europe. This alone should give pause to anyone prone to dismissing JeM as a group limited in its operations and influence to Kashmir or South Asia. In these pages, he provides a veritable encyclopaedia of the group.

Military analysts, at least in the United States, often speak of the DIME model, in which every strategy should have a diplomatic, informational, military and economic component. Academics speak of hard power and soft power, which more often intertwine than remain distinct. Diplomats, meanwhile, may speak of a 'whole of government' approach. Whatever the framework, this book checks all the boxes. Alongside the attacks that gain headlines, Pandya allows readers to delve deep into the group's economy, its media amplification and strategy, and its outreach. This holistic approach is not only a credit to Pandya's scholarship, but also highlights the threat and sophistication of the adversary JeM has become. But Pandya does not simply provide a snapshot—rather, his approach is four-dimensional, carefully tracing the group's evolution on all fronts as it now spans generations.

JeM is not just a front group for Pakistan any more; and neither was it ever a legitimate grassroots group of Kashmir. Its links with Al Qaeda rightly make it a terror group of global reach that the world ignores at its peril. Pandya has done a service, and the knowledge chronicled in this book will save lives, not only in India but worldwide. Terrorism studies is a new field that too often has attracted journalists whose expertise is skin-deep and academics who prioritize their own theories over fieldwork and reality. Too many former government officials who turn to writing, meanwhile, remain constrained by the narrow confines of their own government pigeonhole. They describe trees but fail to identify the forest. Pandya falls into neither of these traps, and sets a new standard for terror analysis and has become a leader in the field. India should be proud, and the world grateful.

—**Dr Michael Rubin** is a senior fellow at the American Enterprise Institute and the director of policy analysis at the Middle East Forum

Preface

MY ACADEMIC QUEST ON JAISH-E-MOHAMMED (JEM) began right after destiny made me witness the horrors of the brutal Pulwama fidayeen attack (14 February 2019). In those days, I was a field researcher in Kashmir, occasionally advising the governor on security, radicalization and other militancy-related issues in an informal capacity. In the second half of 2018, the security forces (SF) successfully led its counterterrorism efforts, neutralizing a record number of militants and dismantling the over-ground workers (OGW) network of terror groups and their finance modules. The parallel political efforts to unleash a new narrative of peace and development, and the crusade against corruption, made us all feel that—finally—militancy was losing its sheen and tottering towards a slow death. However, the improvised explosive device (IED) blast of 14 February 2019, brutally killing forty-two Indian soldiers, shook all of us. It felt as if the entire effort of the state and civil society over the three years since Hizbul Mujahideen (HM) commander Burhan Wani's encounter death in 2016 had come to naught.

Additionally, the Pulwama tragedy brought India and Pakistan once again to the verge of a full-fledged war. It was not the first time. In 2016, JeM shattered the India–Pakistan peacebuilding process with its lethal Pathankot and Mazar-i-Sharif fidayeen attacks. In 2001, the organization had left the two nuclear adversaries only a step short of a full-fledged war—with the potential of nuclear escalation—when it attacked the Indian Parliament.

Post-Pulwama, India's retaliation through the Balakot strikes has changed the geopolitical dynamics of South Asia. Gone are the days when Pakistan's nuclear blackmail worked. In the future, if JeM or any other Pakistan-supported terror group orchestrates a large-scale attack leading to casualties in double digits, then India's Hindu-nationalist government is most likely to respond with strikes surpassing the Balakot ones, both in magnitude and intensity. Hence, with Pulwama, India and Pakistan become more vulnerable to a full-fledged war-like situation resulting from a spectacular terror attack.

Among the SFs and the intelligence community, I have encountered a deep-rooted sense of ambiguity regarding JeM, its secretive nature, modus operandi, recruitment, ideology and radicalization tactics. In the past, on several occasions, security experts had written JeM's obituary. Post-2004, when the group faced a state crackdown in Pakistan after its name figured in the Pervez Musharraf assassination plots, it seemed that its time was over. However, it continued to operate in Kashmir. By 2011–12, JeM had become almost non-existent in Kashmir, with merely two or three militants dying in the encounters. However, it made a comeback in early 2016. It commenced a journey upwards—this time majorly focusing on recruiting local boys as fidayeen attackers and executing large-scale IED attacks, which culminated in the Pulwama fidayeen attack. Yet, the lack of pattern in its operational strategies and tactics, and a systematic organizational chain of command, explicit in other groups like the Lashkar-e-Taiba (LeT), made it even more elusive for the intelligence community.

The return of the Taliban has made JeM more relevant and robust. JeM believes in the fundamentalist Deobandi ideology of Islam, to which the Taliban also subscribes. Many senior JeM leaders, including Masood Azhar, have studied with the senior members of the Taliban hierarchy at Madrasa Binoria in Karachi. JeM fighters have fought alongside the Taliban against the US forces. In the Taliban regime, JeM members will find safe havens and other kinds of support in Afghanistan, which can potentially enhance its operational capabilities. Besides, JeM has strong ties with the Al Qaeda (AQ), the transnational terrorist group (TTG). To an ordinary observer, JeM's ties with AQ are not much known; however, any keen observer knows well that AQ played a vital role in the formation of JeM. JeM also shares AQ's pan-Islamist vision. Apart from this, AQ has always looked beyond Kashmir and maintained a keen interest in the pan-India Islamist agenda, the result of which is known to the world in the form of AQ in the Indian Subcontinent (AQIS). AQ finds India's current social and political scenario congenial for its expansion in the Indian hinterland. The Narendra Modi government's decisions in domains of terror funding, radicalization and refugee rehabilitation have dealt a massive blow to terror infrastructure. Along with this, the proposed measures like the uniform civil code and population control bill will likely check the ghettoization of Muslims and help their mainstreaming. However, many of these decisions have purportedly alienated a section of the Muslim minority, as they are being perceived as anti-Muslim and anti-Islam. Groups like AQ want to harness this polarization and communal fault lines. JeM becomes critical here because it can facilitate the expansion and penetration of AQ in the Indian hinterland. Deobandi pockets are spread nationwide, where JeM can find support and shelter. Also, Inter-Service Intelligence's (ISI) relatively weaker control over JeM vis-à-vis

Lashkar-e-Taiba, Hizbul Mujahideen and other groups makes it an even more serious concern for the security establishment.

Lastly, whereas other groups like Lashkar-e-Taiba are being watched by counterterrorism experts and scholars in the West, JeM more or less remains under the radar, carrying an image of a Kashmir-centric South Asian terror outfit. However, the world needs to know that JeM always had pan-Islamist ambitions. It has had a role in Western terror plots like the transatlantic 'shoe bomber' among others. Through its ties with a widespread network of Deobandi mosques in the US and Europe, JeM has the potential to stage spectacular terror attacks in the West. On top of it, its ties with the Taliban, Islamic State–Khorasan Province (ISKP) and the Tehreek-e-Taliban Pakistan (TTP) make it even more dangerous for the West. In the light of this organization's unique capabilities to launch strikes with a long-lasting geopolitical impact, I felt JeM needed an intense and detailed investigation.

In this book, I explore and investigate JeM's origins, evolution, organizational structure, ideology, strategy, tactics, training, infiltration, recruitment, militant profiles, ties with Deobandi institutions and other transnational and Kashmir-centric terrorist groups, finances, fidayeen attacks, madrasa networks, and indoctrination techniques.

During my assignment, I had close interactions with members of the security forces, terror-financing networks, journalists, OGWs and intelligence community members. The insights I gleaned were a gold mine on terrorism and counterterrorism. It would have been challenging for an outsider to gain access to such critical sources on the covert subject of militancy and start afresh with a research-based book on JeM. This was not an impossible task for me since I had been working in Kashmir since 2016 and had already finished the manuscript of my book on terror financing. So, in a way, it was relatively convenient for me to embark upon a book on JeM. Having acquired a robust field-level knowledge of the organization and its operations, I felt that not writing this book would have tormented me.

Three years of challenging research, including extensive field tours, interactions with intelligence and SF personnel, surrendered militants and OGWs of JeM opened up an entirely different world of human existence to me. To collect the data, I had to visit areas where I felt umpteen threats at every stage in the form of hidden IEDs planted by terrorists, abduction, being followed by the OGWs of terrorist groups, or being surveilled by undercover agents of the state intelligence apparatus. However, it was this in-depth learning of the domain of terrorism and counterterrorism that equipped me with a robust academic and field-based foundation to pursue my career in terrorism studies.

When I remember the sleepless nights spent reading interrogation reports (IRs), open-source documents, intelligence dossiers, interview manuscripts and journal articles, I feel that the journey was worth its while. It does not come to an end today. Instead, it transforms into a new journey of executing the lessons learned in policy planning and implementation.

1

The Master of Fidayeen Attacks

ON 14 FEBRUARY 2019, THE WORLD WITNESSED THE horror of an unprecedented and brutal suicide attack in Indian-administered Kashmir. Jaish-e-Mohammed, a Pakistan-sponsored terrorist group, killed forty Indian soldiers in a spectacular fidayeen attack on the Central Reserve Police Force (CRPF) convoy[1] at Lethpura on the Jammu–Srinagar highway (Pulwama district), which was ferrying Indian paramilitary soldiers. At 3.15 p.m. IST (Indian Standard Time), JeM fidayeen commando Adil Ahmed Dar—a local boy from the Pulwama district of Indian-administered Jammu and Kashmir—rammed 300 kgs of vehicle-borne explosives, including 80 kgs of high-grade RDX, into the CRPF convoy.[2] Thirty minutes later, his video owning up to the attack went viral on social media, where he says, 'By the time it reaches you, I will be in Jannat.'

The mayhem resulted in nationwide anger and protests. Over the next few days, South Asia witnessed an agitated security situation and intense geopolitical activity, including backchannel talks and high-profile diplomacy. India revoked Pakistan's MFN (Most Favoured Nation) status[3] and doubled its efforts to get the Financial Action Task Force (FATF) to blacklist Pakistan.[4] Finally, on 26 February, India retaliated with airstrikes at Balakot, the JeM training camp in Khyber–Pakhtunkhwa, reportedly neutralizing 300 Jaish militants.[5] A day after the Balakot strikes, the Indian Air Force foiled Pakistan's air attack.[6] While shooting down a Pakistani F-16 from his MiG-21, Wing Commander Abhinandan Varthaman was captured alive.[7] The Modi government's formidable posturing and non-relenting attitude, coupled with the US's timely intervention, compelled Pakistan to return the captured pilot and defuse the crisis. Nevertheless, JeM had once again brought the two South Asian rivals to the verge of a full-blown war after the 2001 Parliament attack.

Pakistan's Proxy War Strategy

In Pakistan's sabotage toolkit, proxy war has always been the most effective strategy and force multiplier against numerically, militarily and economically far superior India. Pakistan remains an octopus executing sabotage missions through its proxy terrorist groups, which function as the sucker-bearing arms. Through these proxies, Pakistan has kept thousands of Indian soldiers engaged in quelling a localized insurgency and the Indian security agencies grappling with domestic security challenges. However, the question that intrigues any student of geopolitics in South Asia is how Pakistan, a power much weaker than India in military and economic terms, and facing severe internal fault lines, could successfully use proxy war with surprising impunity and inflict damage without inviting any strong reprisals from India. C. Christine Fair, an eminent expert on South Asia, argues that Pakistan has used its nuclear programme to shield itself from reprisals for its proxy insurgency and terrorism strategy.[8] She suggests that the history of Pakistan's nuclear program and strategy of proxy warfare are inextricably linked together.[9] Further, she argues that to strengthen its capabilities and advances in irregular/proxy war, i.e., at 'the lower end of the conflict spectrum', Pakistan innovated at the strategic level through the acquisition of nuclear weapons.[10]

In academic and security circles, though, there is a general tendency to acknowledge the beginnings of Pakistan's proxy war strategy in 1990. The country had realized the importance of using non-state actors in a proxy war/insurgency in the 1947 war with India, in which it supported the Pathan Kabaili raiders, who were invading Kashmir. However, the formalization of using non-state actors to pursue state goals as a strategy began in 1954, when the US formally allied with Pakistan against communist threats from China and Russia.[11] The US wanted to strengthen the Pakistan army to counter these countries. Senior Pakistan army generals felt that Islamabad could develop its 'People's Army' as the second line of defence against India. In 1957, the *Pakistan Army Journal* republished an article from the Australian Army journal titled 'Guerilla Warfare', which suggested that mountainous areas with forest cover, swampy flat areas and flat forest areas could form an ideal terrain for a successful guerilla war.[12] Throughout the 1960s, *Pakistan Army Journal* published several articles analysing the need of the People's Army for offensive and defensive missions against India. Even the civilian members of the Pakistani government supported the idea of proxy war by infiltrating irregulars in the Indian territory. Zulfikar Ali Bhutto strongly backed Operation Gibraltar (1965) in which troops were disguised as civilians.[13] Aslam Siddique, a civilian bureaucrat in Ayub Khan's Bureau of National Reconstruction, quoted instances from the Prophet's life to justify irregular warfare against India with religious arguments.[14] He said that the Prophet used irregular warfare against enemies because of his small army; likewise, to counter India's conventional superiority, every non-disabled person of Pakistan should volunteer for its defence and offense against India.[15] The embarrassing defeat of 1971 further heightened the need for employing irregular warfare against India.

However, Pakistan needed a shield to guard itself against global reprisal and that could come only from a nuclear arsenal. By 1979, Pakistan was importing critical components for setting up a uranium enrichment facility.[16] When Muhammad Zia-ul-Haq, then the president of Pakistan, confirmed this, the US imposed the Symington sanctions[17] in April 1979. In 1979, US intelligence suggested that Pakistan would have a single device (plutonium) by 1982 and, with Chinese help,[18] Islamabad would have a nuclear bomb with highly enriched uranium by 1985.[19] Pakistani authorities' statements also confirmed the intelligence inputs.[20] In 1987, the head of Pakistan's nuclear programme, Abdul Qadeer Khan, stated in an interview with the Indian journalist Kuldip Nayar that Pakistan had nuclear weapons capability that could be used to defend against India.[21] Zia also confirmed Khan's claim and said, 'Pakistan can build a bomb whenever it wishes.'[22]

Finally, after the 1998 nuclear tests, Pakistan acquired an overt atomic capability. After that, Islamabad's security establishment was more emboldened to aggravate low-intensity conflict against India. Pakistan was confident that its nuclear capability would restrain New Delhi's options for punitive actions. It was its atomic arsenal that gave the country the confidence and audacity to indulge in the Kargil misadventure, orchestrate the hijacking of Indian airliner IC-814, and support foreign terrorist groups (FTG) like LeT and Jaish.

The formation and launch of the JeM in Kashmir coincided with Pakistan's formal acquisition of nuclear capabilities, which majorly upset the power balance in the subcontinent by severely limiting India's retaliatory options. With its nuclear capability,

Pakistan could sanction attacks beyond Kashmir on India's Parliament, Mumbai and various other parts of India.

Post-1998, terrorist groups like the LeT and JeM conducted terror attacks in different parts of India. They also developed sleeper cells and front groups like the Students Islamic Movement of India (SIMI) and Indian Mujahideen (IM). The nuclear blackmail let Rawalpindi[23] go unscathed after a series of attacks in major Indian cities like Jaipur, Ahmedabad, Pune and Delhi.

After the LeT-orchestrated attack on Mumbai's Taj Mahal Palace (2008), popularly known as the 26/11 attacks, India planned to launch airstrikes inside Pakistani territory, according to Khurshid Kasuri, Pakistan's former foreign minister.[24] A former Research and Analysis Wing (R&AW), India's external intelligence organization, chief—also an expert on Afghanistan-Pakistan issues—told me on the condition of anonymity[25] that India's intelligence czars had recommended airstrikes at Balakot. He said that the Indian Air Force (IAF) leadership, in its assessment, informed the United Progressive Alliance (UPA) government—led by Manmohan Singh—that the 'IAF can take a calibrated airstrike action ... though there is a possibility of a few casualties, the action will significantly damage the terror camps and the outcome will be in India's favour'.[26] Corroborating this, former Indian Air Force pilot, Group Captain (Retd) Mohonto Panging claimed in a media interview after the Balakot strikes of 2019 that he was to lead a Sukhoi squadron to attack Pakistani territory at Muzaffarabad[27] after the attacks; however, the government did not give its nod.

Once again, ambiguity about Pakistan's response clouded India's security establishment and political leadership's decision-making, and fearing nuclear retaliation, it rejected the airstrike proposals. The former R&AW chief also told me that the UPA government was a 'much weaker government as compared to the Modi-government because the PM had hardly any say in the decision-making, which was mostly controlled by the Gandhis ... only in the case of the India–US nuclear deal issue, PM Manmohan Singh took a stand and even threatened to resign if the deal were to be cancelled by [the] Gandhis, who wielded the real authority in the UPA government ... The UPA government could not withstand the intense international pressure to avoid escalation by taking any major retaliatory action.'[28]

Pakistan's nuclear arsenal also helped internationalize the Kashmir issue, which has always been Islamabad's objective. Any major terrorist attack by a Pakistan-supported terrorist group and India's toughening posture against it would immediately bring the global powers to defuse the crisis. The international powers also felt the need to continuously engage with Pakistan, as its isolation could lead to the terrorist groups getting hold of nuclear weapons. Pakistan's nuclear blackmail lasted from 1998 till 2019, when, after the Pulwama fidayeen attack, the Modi government crossed the Rubicon and retaliated with airstrikes at the JeM training camp in Balakot, deep inside Pakistani territory. The 2019 Balakot airstrikes finally nailed Pakistan's nuclear bluff and steeply raised the costs of any large-scale terror attack on Indian soil. The airstrikes marked the end of the era of 'strategic restraint'. They signalled that any future terror attack resulting in double-digit casualty figures is likely to invite harsh retaliation from Delhi.[29] Since then, Pakistan has modified its strategy and tactics.[30] It continues to support terror groups but makes sure that any major Pulwama-scale terror attack does not happen, as it is likely to invite an Indian retaliation. It is even expected that the Indian response could be stronger in scale and intensity than the Balakot airstrikes. Hence, terror groups now indulge in several minor and scattered attacks on SFs and targeted killings of individuals to keep the brutality and intensity below the Pulwama threshold. In addition, Pakistan operates through several front organizations of the LeT and JeM, with secular-sounding names like The Resistance Front (TRF), Pir Panjal Peace Forum, etc., thus creating a third layer to claim plausible deniability.

Other important reasons that strengthened Pakistan's position vis-à-vis using proxy terrorist groups in Kashmir are the establishment of the Taliban rule in Afghanistan in 1996, and the US's dependence on Pakistan after the emergence of Al Qaeda as a major threat to its interests and AQ's entrenchment in Afghanistan under the Taliban and Inter-Services Intelligence (ISI) shelter (1996 onwards). After the onset of the Taliban rule, Pakistan shifted terror-training camps from Pakistan-administered Kashmir to Afghanistan, where terrorist groups were patronized under a protective environment in the India-hating Taliban regime. Quality training and the arranging of logistics for terrorist groups became much easier under the friendly Taliban regime. Besides, all these activities could carry on smoothly without international scrutiny. In the event of a terror attack on Indian territory, Pakistan could always claim plausible deniability as the terror training camps were in Afghanistan, another sovereign territory.

After the Taliban rule, Al Qaeda became firmly entrenched in Afghanistan. It had cultivated strong functional, ideological and operational links with ISI-backed Deobandi terrorist groups (discussed in detail in the next chapter). From its safe haven in Afghanistan, AQ was targeting US assets in Africa. After the AQ's US embassy bombings in Africa (1998), its presence in Afghanistan became a major security concern for the US.

The US conducted retaliatory strikes in Afghanistan in which about twenty-one Harkat-ul-Mujahideen (HuM) militants and five ISI trainers were killed.[31] In Afghan operations, Pakistan's support was crucial, something that the US had realized during the Afghan jihad of the 1980s when Washington worked with Islamabad, arming mujahideens against the Soviets. After the 11 September 2001 attacks (9/11), the US launched its Global War on Terror (GWoT), in which Pakistan's support was critical. Pakistan's then president, Pervez Musharraf decided to support the US effort to overthrow the Taliban regime and uproot AQ. He thought that Pakistan could exploit the US dependence on Pakistan's support in its war against Taliban and Al Qaeda in Afghanistan, as a bargaining chip with Washington to give them a free run in Kashmir.[32] Since the US was deeply involved in Afghan operations, and was entirely dependent on Pakistan for supply routes and operational assistance, Rawalpindi could use that leverage to force India into negotiations by ramping up terrorist attacks in the country.

Following the release of Masood Azhar in December 1999 and the formation of JeM in January 2000, India witnessed a spate of lethal suicide bombings and terrorist attacks in Jammu and Kashmir (J&K) conducted by the outfit. The situation became alarming for India when JeM attacked the J&K legislative assembly in October 2001 and the Indian Parliament in December 2001. New Delhi took these as an attack on its sovereignty and, in response, ordered massive troop mobilization on the Pakistan border, raising fears of a full-fledged war situation. The US, fearing that Pakistan would transfer its troops from the Afghanistan border to the Indian borders, which would hurt the US's Afghan operations against AQ and the Taliban, pressurized Musharraf to stop supporting Kashmiri terrorist groups.[33] Reportedly, Musharraf wanted to leverage the US's dependence on Pakistan and expected Washington to pressure India. He was reluctant to give a formal commitment to withdraw the country's support for Kashmir's terror outfits. However, after much persuasion from Washington, Musharraf declared on 12 January 2002, that 'Pakistan rejects and condemns terrorism in all its forms and manifestations. Pakistan will not allow its territory to be used for terrorist attacks anywhere in the world … No organization will be allowed to indulge in terrorism in the name of Kashmir.'[34] However, he continued to delay the fulfilment of his 12 January promises. Terror attacks intensified in Kashmir in July 2002, making it amply clear that Pakistan was repeatedly shunning the US's request to stop its support of terror groups. Leveraging the US's dependence on Pakistan, Islamabad was confident that it could step up attacks as Washington would prevent India from taking any harsh retaliatory measures.

The Sinister Trinity of LeT, JeM and Hizbul Mujahideen

The Pakistan-supported terror ecosystem in Kashmir runs on the three pillars of aggressive jihadist radicalization, political separatism and, most importantly, the violent terrorist movement. A vast network of organizations constitutes the backbone of the terror infrastructure in Kashmir. Pakistan's three most potent terrorist groups, active in Kashmir, are Lashkar-e-Taiba, Jaish-e-Mohammed and Hizbul Mujahideen. After the encounter death of HM commander Burhan Wani—who became the poster boy of new-age militancy in Kashmir—in 2016, militancy was revived with the strong participation of local youth. Many new outfits, such as the Islamic State of Jammu and Kashmir (ISJK) and Ansar Ghazwat-ul-Hind (AGuH), emerged, claiming to be the local affiliates of Islamic State (IS) and Al Qaeda, respectively. Post the abrogation of Article 370, new outfits came up with secular-sounding names, such as

The Resistance Front. However, investigations revealed TRF[35] to be a front organization for LeT—apparently a part of Pakistan's strategy to project Kashmir's militancy as a secular movement for a separate homeland and evade the global terror watchdog Financial Action Task Force's pressure. Likewise, JeM also came up with front organizations, reportedly Kashmir Tigers[36] and Lashkar-i-Mustapha[37]. However, these new entities remain fluid, with cadres from the various parent groups joining one organization or the other. LeT, JeM and HM still occupy the core of Kashmir's militancy.

Hizbul Mujahideen has a robust base with many local youths joining it; hence, the easy availability of sources facilitates its sufficient coverage in academic research, intelligence investigations and media reporting. The LeT orchestrated the Mumbai suburban railway bombing (2006) and 26/11 attacks (2008), in which scores of foreign nationals died, twenty-two and twenty-six, respectively.[38] Hence, it received the attention of Western terrorism researchers. Following these attacks, many experts from the Western world, such as C. Christine Fair and Stephen Tankel, studied LeT in detail and came out with seminal works, *In Their Own Words: Understanding Lashkar-e-Tayyaba* (2018) and *Storming the World Stage: The Story of Lashkar-e-Taiba* (2014), respectively.

Founded in 2000, after the release of Maulana Masood Azhar in exchange for setting free more than 150 hostages of the hijacked Air India flight IC-814, JeM continues to be one of the most lethal terrorist organizations in South Asia. Its strong emphasis on religious indoctrination and future pan-India ambitions are likely to present the most challenging threat to India among all the other terrorist groups, including the transnational ones such as Al Qaeda and Islamic State. Further, the strengthening presence of Deobandi networks across the length and breadth of India—an ideology to which the outfit subscribes—provides a favourable religious milieu to expand and penetrate vigorously. It has conducted some of the deadliest fidayeen attacks in India, including the 2001 attacks on the legislative assembly in Kashmir and the Indian Parliament,[39] Pathankot airbase in Punjab (2016),[40] Uri in J&K (2016)[41] and, most recently, the Pulwama fidayeen attack (2019). In the Kashmir assembly attack, twenty-nine people died;[42] the Parliament attack left six dead. In the Uri attack, seventeen soldiers died, and in Pulwama, forty-six soldiers died.[43] Amongst all the groups active in Kashmir, JeM specializes in lethal fidayeen attacks and has some of the most well-trained, most-indoctrinated and battle-hardened terrorist cadres.

The US has recognized JeM as a Foreign Terrorist Organization (FTO) along with the LeT in 2001 and has banned it—however, the move was primarily to placate India for New Delhi had ordered a massive military build-up on the Pakistan border and threatened a full-scale war in response to the Parliament attack (2001). To address Indian concerns, the US banned JeM. Nevertheless, the ban turned out to be an eyewash as Pakistan's security establishment informed most of these terror groups about it beforehand. Thus, they could transfer their money and assets before being seized. Later, they resurfaced under different names. Hence, JeM continues to evade the attention of the global strategic and academic community.

The Scope of Research and Its Limitations

This project studies JeM in detail, exploring diverse aspects of its organization, tactics, strategy, ideology, funding sources and critical interest areas from an academic standpoint. It is a clandestine subject—and therefore, this project had enormous challenges. However, my five-year-long research and field experience in dealing with terrorism challenges in Kashmir enabled me to produce substantial research work on JeM based on the amalgamation of findings derived from field studies, my sources and the information available in open-domain sources. Through this work, I do not claim to replace the work done by professional intelligence agencies; I intend to study the organization and its diverse aspects from an academic perspective. In India, terrorism studies are generally considered the forte of the intelligence set-up and not encouraged in educational research because of the lack of data.

The clandestine nature of the subject matter of this research project made it challenging to approach the subject within the rigorous framework of qualitative and quantitative research methods. The methodology was thus primarily qualitative and I employed historical discourse analysis techniques. In the historical discourse analysis, I investigated how the discourse on JeM has evolved over the last twenty-one years.

Since there is not much material available in the public domain, the backbone of this study is made up of field research. I conducted field visits in Delhi, Jammu and Kashmir. Due to the sensitive security situation, I did not conduct field visits to Pakistan and Afghanistan. To compensate for that, I referred to the works of Pakistani scholars on terrorism/Islamic radicalization and JeM.

In the field study, I conducted the following types of interviews:

a) In-depth one-on-one interviews

b) Focus group interviews

Most of the critical information needed for terrorism studies is with the National Investigation Agency (NIA), law enforcement and intelligence agencies. Their investigation and interrogation reports are confidential and unavailable to academic researchers. However, during my field inquiry, I successfully got access to several crucial Interrogation Reports. These IRs opened the floodgates of information about the JeM's origins, ideology, motives, strategy and tactics, counter-JeM operations, radicalization techniques, training programmes, infiltration routes, finances, psychology, and the socio-economic and geographic background of the JeM cadres and commanders.

In addition, due to my years of fieldwork in Jammu and Kashmir, I could get access to some insiders in the JeM's broader organizational ecosystem, state security and intelligence machinery. Hence, this project's novelty comes from the in-depth interviews of stakeholders who provided 'insider information'. The expression 'insider information' tends to tread on a slippery slope. What I mean when I say this is that the information, analysis, forecast, narratives and stories I have here are not found in open-domain journalistic or institutional academic sources.

Such information, derived from current and former cadres and commanders of the organization, OGWs, hawala coordinators, journalists and members of security forces, always suffers from a lack of accuracy and also runs the risk of biases arising from the interests, beliefs and ideologies of the interviewee. In my rigorous and lengthy experience in studying Kashmir militancy over the last five years, I have attempted to identify the right stakeholders and ensure authenticity to the best possible limit. Nevertheless, the twin problems of accuracy and subjective bias remain; still, this approach satisfies the objectives of an academic study by providing a reasonably precise picture of the broad trends of the JeM. I believe that this approach gives vital insights into the nature and activities of a terrorist organization, and can provide nuanced information to enable better counterterrorism policymaking and strategic forecasting of terror attacks.

Taking this approach is fraught with risks. Suppose one ventures out as a researcher on such sensitive subjects in Kashmir. He quickly comes under the scanner of Indian security and intelligence agencies, terrorist groups and foreign intelligence agencies. The terrorist groups maintain a vast network of OGWs who gather intelligence about such researchers and other relevant entities, and report them to the group's leadership. In these circumstances, lay researchers cannot go on random visits to remote areas as there is a strong chance of them getting abducted or even killed. Thus, for future researchers, it is advised that this approach should be resorted to at their own risk and after careful consideration of the safety-related aspects.

Lastly, due to the sensitive nature of the research topic, maintaining the anonymity of the interviewees is a critical concern. In a conflict zone like Kashmir, due to the terrorist threats and surveillance exercised by an array of intelligence agencies, the subjects prefer to keep their identity confidential. I have not disclosed the identities of many sources—human or otherwise—and have often changed the names of sources and interviewees.

Through this work, I believe I have provided an objective and evidence-based study of JeM, which can be immensely useful for scholars and policymakers.

2

The Origins of JeM and Pakistan's Deobandi Ecosystems

IN 1979, IRSHAD AHMED—A STUDENT OF NIZAMUDDIN Shamzai, the hardliner Deobandi vice-chancellor of Karachi's Binoria Town mosque—founded Harkat-ul-Jihad-al-Islami (HuJI) to fight armed jihad in Afghanistan.[1] HuJI split in 1984 when Fazlur Rehman Khalil, a Pashtun commander, set up a splinter group, Harkat-ul-Mujahideen, defying Qari Saifullah Akhtar's leadership of HuJI.[2] However, in 1993, HuM reunited with HuJI after a group of Deobandi clerics persuaded Khalil to merge the two entities to put up a united front in Kashmir jihad. The merger produced Harkat-ul-Ansar (HuA). Masood Azhar also played a vital role in this merger,[3] after which he was sent to Kashmir. HuA was deeply involved in the Afghanistan jihad; thirty-nine out of 113 jihadis caught in Afghanistan in 1997 belonged to HuA.[4] The merger lasted for four years. HuA's links with Arab–Afghans and Osama bin Laden led to the end of this nominal merger. In 1997, the US State Department banned HuA. Bypassing the ban a year later, it re-emerged as HuM. Following its embargo in 2001 by the Musharraf government, it reappeared as Jamaat-ul-Ansar, which was again banned. Then, it either split or resurfaced—experts are divided—

as Harkat-ul-Mujahideen Al-Alami (HuMA). JeM emerged as a splinter group from HuM, its parent organization.[5,6] Based on the chronology given above, it would seem that in Pakistan's Deobandi ecosystem, of which JeM is a part, splintering was not a static but a fluid phenomenon.

Masood Azhar was a member of HuM when he was arrested in Kashmir (1994), where he was sent to unite the opposing factions of HuA and HuM, and revitalize the jihad against India. After his release following the Kandahar hijack episode (December 1999), he toured Afghanistan, and reportedly met Taliban chief, Mullah Omar, and Al Qaeda chief, Osama bin Laden.[7] Muhammad Amir Rana,[8] Pakistan's expert voice on terrorist organizations, reported that Masood Azhar,[9] after his release following the Kandahar hijacking, was upset with the infighting in HuM.[10]

Finally, he formed a separate outfit, Jaish-e-Mohammed, literally meaning 'Army of the Prophet Mohammed', on 4 February 2000, at Karachi's Masjid Falal. Many other senior leaders also joined him. His personality clash and ideological differences over Kashmir jihad with Maulana Fazlur Rehman Khalil, chief of HuM and the 'grand old man' of Pakistan's Deobandi nexus, played a crucial role in the emergence of JeM. Khalil was not very enthusiastic about supporting the Kashmir jihad because most Kashmiri Muslims were Barelwis.

About three-quarters of the members of HuM moved to JeM. Most Punjabis joined Masood Azhar and the Pathans stayed with Fazlur Rehman Khalil, a Pashtun himself.[11] It reportedly led to a violent clash between JeM and HuM. Khalil was adamantly against Masood's decision and wanted to keep HuM united. He even offered to resign and give his post to Masood; however, the latter was unrelenting, which was least expected from someone who had just come out of jail, and was trying to rebuild a career of his own and looking for support. Security experts from Pakistan told me in informal communications that Masood was an ambitious man and, with JeM, he aspired to become the most powerful leader of the entire Deobandi Islamist movement—which could have been difficult with the association of a tall leader like Fazlur Rehman Khalil. JeM's rivalry with HuM continued over the distribution of assets, ultimately leading to the assassination of Maulana Ludhianvi, JeM's ardent supporter. However, Masood continued with his new organization.

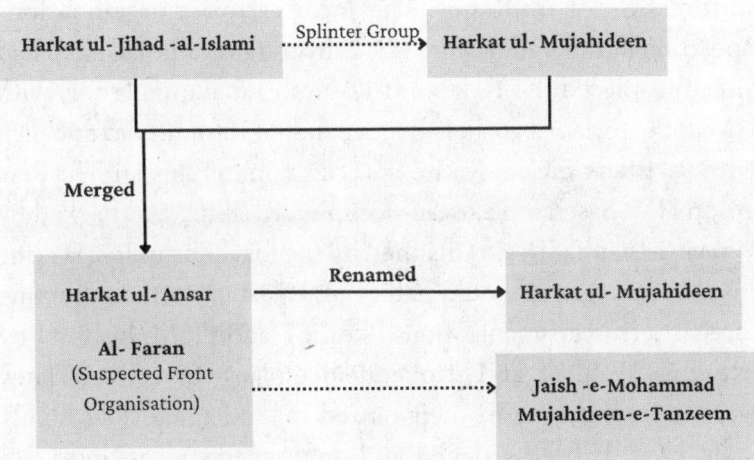

Source: Author; Figure 1: Jaish Splintering from HuJI

The Role of Pakistan's Intelligence and Al Qaeda

The most pertinent question about the origins of JeM is the role of the ISI in its formation. In the case of other terror outfits like LeT and Hizbul Mujahideen, it is asserted quite conveniently that the ISI is the main force behind it. In Indian intelligence circles, it is believed that JeM was formed to capitalize on the high-pitched propaganda unleashed by Pakistan's electronic and print media to glorify jihad, and to boost the sagging morale of the terrorists in the Kashmir Valley. However, there are many smokescreens about the ISI's role in the creation of the outfit. The most critical question is why the ISI would create JeM when it already had robust outfits like HM and LeT.

By the mid-nineties, India had majorly crushed militancy in Kashmir. PM Narasimha Rao's government followed a tough line against terror groups. The Indian SFs also successfully created divisions within the militant organizations, and the renegades formed Ikhwan, which played a major role in the forceful suppression of militancy. The local terrorist organizations operating in the Valley were not delivering results. Pakistan had already replaced JKLF (Jammu-Kashmir Liberation Front) with HM as the former's goal of an independent Kashmir did not align with Pakistan's idea of Kashmir's accession to Pakistan. The new group HM, based in Pakistan-occupied Kashmir, and backed by Jamaat-i-Islami (JI), was manned by the local Kashmiris. Fearing that the insurgency would peter out, Pakistan started inducting foreign terrorist organizations like LeT and HuM, inspired by extremist Wahhabi and Deobandi ideologies, respectively. They were more extreme in their hatred for India, and had highly radicalized, battle-hardened and disciplined cadres, and were more willing and suited to do ISI's bidding. Islamabad could exercise far more control over the FTOs in strategic and tactical matters, and they were more reliable in the sense that they were less likely to betray Pakistan and work with Indian SFs as compared to Kashmiri groups.

Unleashing FTOs linked with AQ and the Taliban could be immensely helpful in internationalizing the Kashmir jihad. In its fifteen years of involvement in the Afghan jihad, Pakistan had realized that supporting Wahhabi and Deobandi extremist groups in Kashmir would elicit more jihad funds from Saudi

Arabia's donors, and support from transnational terrorist groups (TTGs) like AQ and Taliban. Raising jihad funds through donations from West Asia and drug smuggling has also become a rich source of revenue for the Pakistan Army over the years. In addition to sustaining and escalating militancy and radicalization in Kashmir, there was another incentive to get more jihad funds—i.e., embezzlement and misappropriation by the Pakistan Army and the deep state, which has almost become a vital practice that is less known and discussed.[12]

The creation of JeM was a part of the more extensive process of inducting FTOs in Kashmir that had already begun in the mid-1990s. Pakistan's rout in the Kargil War (1999) had shaken the Kashmiri people's faith in Islamabad's ability and determination to get their freedom. Local groups like Jamaat-i-Islami and its militant wing HM were also going through internal disputes as a significant segment of their cadres wanted a ceasefire with India and were in constant communication with Indian intelligence.[13] Hence, for Pakistan, a highly radicalized and religious organization like JeM could serve as a potent instrument in restoring its credibility in the eyes of Kashmiris and its domestic constituency.

The next question that arises is why the ISI would risk sabotaging its robust Nepal set-up by hijacking an Indian plane from Kathmandu. By the early 1990s, the ISI had established a strong presence in Nepal with a vast network of agents.[14] The ISI ran training camps in the country, and frequently used Nepal routes for routing hawala funds and sending trained jihadis to India.[15] Mr Mota (name changed),[16] a Srinagar-based separatist journalist, raised the question as to why the ISI would plan the IC-814 hijack when it was bound to bring colossal embarrassment to Pakistan—for, in the diplomatic community, the country's ties with terrorist groups were an open secret.

Further, he suggested that the IC-814 hijack alarmed India about the ISI's robust base, and compelled New Delhi to focus on Nepal to drive the ISI out and regain its foothold, which it did. Hence, the ISI could not have shot itself in the foot. In Mr Mota's analysis, the IC-814 hijack was the HuM's operation to get Masood released and he believes that the ISI might not have had much knowledge of the plan.[17]

Meanwhile, Farzan (name changed), my informed interlocutor with deep connections in the ISI and its jihadist ecosystem, told me that though it sounds counterintuitive, the fact is that the ISI could go to any lengths—including sacrificing its Nepal base—to get Masood released. Masood was like a lifeline to the intelligence body. He had already built a formidable reputation as a motivator in the Afghan jihad. A man like him could unleash a cataclysmic revolution in the religious radicalization of Kashmiris and infuse them with violent jihadist fervour, which was seen as much needed in the Valley's historically liberal society bred on Sufi Islam. He further said that Pakistan had attempted three times to get Masood released—twice by kidnapping foreign nationals in Delhi and Srinagar (1994–95), and a third time by orchestrating a jailbreak. However, the Indian government did not realize the importance of Masood Azhar in Pakistan's jihadist design. As for the IC-814 hijack, Farzan said that the entire operation was done in Nepal, in which HuM was kept as a façade behind which HM cadres were used. Their fake Indian passports were procured from the Bombay regional passport office through forged documents and bribes.[18] The idea behind keeping HuM as the face was to expose and destroy it, and raise a new organization to replace it—for the ISI masterminds were not satisfied with its leadership. HuM chief Maulana Fazlur Rehman Khalil also played a crucial role in arranging logistics.[19] The arrest of Pakistani diplomat

Mohammad Arshad Cheema, alias 'Mac', who was posted in Nepal and allegedly an ISI man, with 16 kg of RDX, also lends credibility to Farzan's claim that the ISI played a crucial role in the hijack.[20] Reportedly, Cheema and his deputy at the embassy, Zia Ansari, and a Nepali citizen, Abdul Rias Khan, travelled in the Pakistani official embassy car to meet the hijackers at the Tribhuvan International Airport on 24 December 1999, shortly before the plane took off.[21] They also handed over a piece of baggage to the hijackers, which could escape security checks because of diplomatic immunity. Allegedly, the bag contained arms and ammunition. The airport log entries showed the car's registration number. According to Indian intelligence sources, Cheema was an ISI agent who was also involved in supplying counterfeit Indian currency, particularly fake 500-rupee notes.[22] Yakeer Singh, a Khalistani militant who was arrested in 1998 in Kathmandu with 20 kgs of RDX, told the police that Arshad Cheema had given him the explosives.[23] Later, Cheema was declared persona non grata and deported by the Nepal government to Pakistan at India's request.[24]

While discussing the IC-814 saga and India's botched-up rescue operation, my interlocutors from the Indian Foreign Service, who served in senior positions and closely watched the IC-814 developments, said that the rescue could have been executed successfully at Amritsar, where the plane landed for refuelling. However, a relative of two powerful bureaucrats posted in the country's topmost office objected to the commando action in Amritsar. It isn't easy to verify these claims and furnish concrete evidence. However, former R&AW officer R.K. Yadav, in his book *Mission R&AW*,[25] mentioned that Shashi Bhushan Singh Tomar, R&AW's Kathmandu station chief, was on board the plane as passenger number 162 on seat number 16C. He was a relative of N.K. Singh, principal secretary to the PM, and Nikhil Kumar, director general of the National Security Guards (NSG). Both were Crisis Management Group members, which dealt with the hijack drama. Yadav writes that the 'critical delay at Amritsar occurred because Kumar and N.K. Singh feared for their relative's life and allowed the plane to take off.'[26] However, A.S. Dulat, the then R&AW chief, denied these allegations.

Another contributing factor to the hijacking was that the ISI was disappointed with Fazlur Rehman Khalil, as, under his leadership, Harkat groups in Kashmir were going through a lot of infighting.[27] The ISI's tilt towards Masood was implicit when he was initially sent to Kashmir in 1994 to unify these warring groups. According to a classified Indian intelligence report, Brigadier Ijaz Ahmed Shah, a close confidante of Musharraf, was Masood Azhar's handler in the ISI. He monitored and calibrated his every move, and played a crucial role in the IC-814 saga for his release. During the hijack, Brigadier Shah was the chief of ISI in Punjab.[28]

Khalil was a battle-hardened field commander with a characteristic Pashtun ego who often defied the ISI's dictates.[29] Masood was an intellectual, a motivating scholar, an ideologue, and a favourite of Nizamuddin Shamzai (the chancellor of Binoria mosque, Karachi). Hence, the ISI believed he would be more respected as a leader and compliant as an asset than Khalil.[30]

Other evidence of the ISI's role comes from a former chief of R&AW, who had long innings in Kashmir and was also a member of the delegation sent to Kandahar to negotiate the release of the 155 passengers of the hijacked IC-814. He told me that ISI officers were continuously monitoring and guiding the hijackers on how to make demands and deal with the negotiators. Every demand and statement made by the other side was allegedly under the mentorship of the ISI. India's current national security advisor, Ajit Doval, who was also part of the negotiating team with the hijackers, in his interview with Reuters India chief Myra McDonald, said that the ISI actively supported the hijackers.[31]

Further, Doval said that the ISI had already guaranteed safe passage to the hijackers, and if they had not supported them, New Delhi would have got the plane rescued.[32] The claims of both Doval and my source in the intelligence agency are based on evidence.[33] The Indian aircraft that carried the negotiating team had sophisticated listening technology that could intercept all the wireless communication for miles around the area. Indian negotiators realized early on that the ISI handlers were guiding the hijackers. After the negotiations, when one of the hijackers asked Vivek Katju, a 1955-batch Indian diplomat leading the Indian negotiating team, if they could take the plane in possession, a voice speaking in Urdu was heard asking the hijackers to carry their luggage out before handing over the aircraft to Indians. When they realized that it would take time to separate the hijackers' cargo from the baggage of the other passengers, the unknown voice asked the hijackers to tell the Indian negotiators that their bags were full of explosives and, hence, needed to be taken out.[34] Perhaps the anonymous ISI handlers wanted to destroy the evidence that could have emerged from those bags. When Masood Azhar, Omar Sheikh and Mushtaq 'Latram' Zargar got off the Indian chartered plane which brought them from Delhi, ISI officials received them and verified their identities.[35] One of the ISI men leading the team kissed Omar Sheikh's head and said, 'So, back to Kandahar. I am so happy to see you.'[36]

As regards the Taliban's role, Vivek Katju believed that the organization was genuinely interested in resolving the issue soon as they were desperate for international recognition. Taliban's foreign minister Wakil Ahmed Muttawakil, in his official statement, said that he was embarrassed that IC-814 landed in Kandahar. However, the other two negotiators from the Indian team, Ajit Doval from the Intelligence Bureau (IB) and C.D. Sahay from R&AW, were sceptical about the Taliban's role in the entire episode. Later, the Taliban's support and sympathy for the hijackers became evident when they deployed rocket launchers and tanks around the IC-814 to guard against the possibility of any covert Indian attempt to rescue the plane and neutralize the hijackers.[37] Usually, such heavy weaponry is not deployed during hostage negotiations. When the Indians confronted the Taliban about this, they said it was for defence. However, the Taliban's real intent was more than evident. Masood's written records after his release, in which he expressed his love and gratitude for Mullah Omar and Mullah Akhtar Usmani—the Taliban's Kandahar corps commander who received Masood Azhar at the airport—made it amply clear that the outfit was facilitating the hijackers. Later, when the Indian investigating team demanded the airport records to identify who was present that day, it was discovered that the records had been destroyed by the Taliban. It is believed that the information could have revealed the presence of ISI men at the airport.

After his release, Masood was lionized, and the ISI paraded him as a celebrity in a public victory tour across Pakistan, reportedly to collect funds for creating and running a new terrorist group.[38] The grand projection of Masood boosted his popularity and catapulted him into superstar status on the jihadist horizon. Masood went on a lightning tour of the country with ISI officers by his side, giving provocative speeches. In his Karachi speech, he said, 'Marry for jihad, give birth for jihad, and earn money only for jihad till the cruelty of America and

India ends.'³⁹ It laid a fertile ground for the creation of JeM, as it was expected that the old guards and senior leaders of HuM would create hurdles and challenges to forming a separate terrorist group. Ayesha Siddiqa, Pakistan's eminent expert on JeM, says that Masood started the outfit in 1994 as a splinter group of HuM. She claims to have come across 'death certificates for martyrdom of cadres in Kashmir and Af-Pak border, issued by the JeM in 1994, indicating that the organization existed in some premature form even before 2000.'⁴⁰ ISI's prior intent to form and publicly announce JeM after Masood's release cannot be ruled out; however, it needs further investigation.

The Pakistan government's banning of JeM in 2003 also created a smokescreen about the ISI's role in its creation, as it appears counterintuitive to ban an organization just a few years after starting it to serve as a cornerstone of jihad in Kashmir. However, it merits mention that the organization was banned for reasons beyond Pakistan's control. One of the crucial reasons was the involvement of JeM elements in an assassination plot to kill Musharraf. Also, as mentioned in the previous chapter, the ban was to appease the Indians by at least initiating a semblance of action against the outfit. Since the US had already banned it, Islamabad knew it had no choice but to follow suit. Later, when JeM, along with many other Deobandi outfits, went against Musharraf's decision to help the US in its operations against the Taliban in Afghanistan, the relations between the Pakistani state and the terror groups were embittered. It led to an internal split in JeM and two splinter groups were formed—Khuddam-ul-Islam and Jamaat-ul-Furqan. Nevertheless, Masood Azhar, leading the Khuddam-ul-Islam faction, remained loyal to the ISI.

Though officially, JeM remains banned by the US, United Nations Security Council (UNSC) and Pakistan, the ISI has been adamant about protecting and promoting Masood Azhar. Robust operational linkages exist between the ISI and JeM. The ISI has helped the group with financing, weapons and training. It also helped Masood acquire considerable assets in Bahawalpur by funnelling money through dubious trusts. The ISI's relationship with the group will be discussed in detail in the next chapter.

A close aide of Masood, Abbas (name changed),[41] when he was the information secretary of HuA (1994), revealed to a Pakistani news magazine that Masood behaved strangely after his return from India. As per Abbas's testimony, Masood refused to meet the delegation of HuA members and, two weeks later, announced the formation of JeM. The HuM leadership, according to Abbas, could not understand how Masood became so powerful that he could open offices in remote areas and build his headquarters in a building worth billions of rupees in such a short period. Masood's aide's testimony makes it amply clear that the formation of JeM was a pre-planned idea in the minds of Masood and the ISI. Masood could not have garnered the vast finances, material and human resources needed to begin and run an independent terrorist organization in such a short time without the help of the ISI and other benefactors, such as AQ and the Afghan Taliban.

My interview with C.D. Sahay, former chief of R&AW, and an expert voice on terrorism who dealt with Kashmir militancy in the 1990s, also confirms that the ISI supported and nurtured JeM after its formation in every possible way. He said that HM militants working as Indian assets informed Indian agencies that the ISI's new favourite was JeM—and other organizations were relegated to the back-burner. Pakistan was flooding JeM's coffers with huge amounts of money. The organization had become so powerful that one needed high-level recommendations to join it in those days, and the ISI was hand-picking young boys to recruit to JeM.

The ISI's decision to create a rift in HuM (formerly HuA) is an established tradecraft in intelligence—if a proxy terrorist group working as an asset goes out of control, engineering internal friction can be an effective countermeasure. For the ISI, HuA/HuM's activities in Kashmir were becoming increasingly difficult to control. Its Kashmir commanders often acted autonomously of its Pakistan-based leadership and the ISI.[42] Notably, Masood Azhar was initially sent to Kashmir to resolve the internal differences between Harkat factions.[43] HuA/HuM, a Deobandi terrorist outfit, was less dependent on the ISI because it could get financial support from a plethora of other revenue streams such as foreign donations from the Gulf, South Africa and Europe, and a vast Deobandi madrasa and mosque network in Pakistan. They were also linked to a political party, Jamiat Ulema-e-Islam (JuI), a coalition partner in the Benazir Bhutto government after 1993, giving Deobandi groups robust political clout. Strategically, creating a splinter group centred on the leadership of a loyal leader like Masood Azhar appears intuitive and rational. To do that, Masood had to be projected as a hero, a militant celebrity and a paramount religious leader who could bring India to its knees, and compel Delhi to set him free. Victory parades following his release after the IC-814 saga helped in projecting Masood as a hero in the jihadist world.

Emboldened by the generous financial and organizational support from the mighty ISI, JeM dared to challenge state institutions and the local administration. In one such case in 2000, JeM clashed with the local administration in Bahawalpur over the imprisonment of some of its cadres accused of harassing a local transporter.[44] JeM's armed militants cordoned off the local town hall that day. Masood Azhar threatened that 'rivers of blood would flow if the state of Pakistan shifted its attention away from Kashmir.'[45] Eventually, the local police released most of its members and the senior police superintendent who initiated the action against JeM was transferred out.[46] Similarly, the police also ignored the murder of Al-Furqan (also known as Jamaat Al-Furqan) militant Rab Nawaz, who died in a shootout between JeM and an Al-Furqan cadre in Bahawalpur in 2000.[47]

Eminent scholars on Islamist terrorism in South Asia, like Ayesha Siddiqa, C. Christine Fair and Bruce Riedel,[48] have all suggest that the ISI played a crucial role in forming JeM. Ayesha Siddiqa writes:[49]

> Masood Azhar and his party have a long-standing relationship with the intelligence agencies who have, on several occasions, come to his rescue, even helping to free him in 2002/2003. Sources claim that Maulana Tahir Ashrafi, who was close to both the Shujaat Hussain/Pervaiz Elahi government and the secret agencies, was instrumental in the release, which went through despite the opposition of the district police. The ISI was also allegedly instrumental in building up the JeM.

She also mentions common ideological links between JeM and other Deobandi organizations like Sipah-e-Sahaba Pakistan (SSP), Lashkar-e-Jhangvi (LeJ) and the Afghan Taliban. In addition to common Deobandi beliefs, all three had close operational ties with the ISI. After its formation, the SSP became JeM's patron and its chief, Azam Tariq, became Masood's *muqqalid* or follower, putting his party's resources and workforce at JeM's disposal.[50] JeM provided training and shelter to SSP and LeJ activists involved in sectarian killings. In the local law-enforcement and administrative circles, the three organizations are known as the three wings of the same party.[51] SSP assumed the role of the umbrella organization, while JeM and LeJ were the foreign and domestic militant jihadist wings. Masood and Azam Tariq jointly addressed many public processions in Bahawalpur. In one of them, Masood defended LeJ's leader Malik Ishaq, who was arrested in Faisalabad (1998) for his involvement in sectarian killings—including an attack on an Iranian cultural centre that left seven dead, including an Iranian diplomat—as a 'holy warrior'.[52] Masood supported the hijacking of another plane to get Ishaq released. JeM's involvement in SSP/LeJ-styled sectarian killings came to light after one of its workers was arrested for his involvement in an attack on a religious congregation in the village of Malhowali, Pindi Gheb (10 April 2000). The attack left seventeen people dead and thirty others critically injured.[53]

Reportedly, Osama bin Laden and the Afghan Taliban encouraged Masood Azhar to start a separate outfit, and provided seed funding to buy offices, madrasas and training camps.[54] Nasir-al-Bahri, bin Laden's bodyguard in the late 1990s, said that the Al Qaeda chief planned the IC-814 hijack as a joint AQ and HuM operation as he wanted Azhar freed.[55] India's former external affairs minister Jaswant Singh, who led the Indian delegation that released Masood Azhar, Omar Sheikh and Mushtaq 'Latram' Zargar in Kandahar, and Pakistan's terrorism expert Ahmed Rashid also suggest that bin Laden planned the plane hijack. However, that does not absolve the ISI of its role. It makes a fundamental question even more critical—i.e., how deep are, or were, the relations between the ISI and Al Qaeda/ Osama bin Laden?

Masood, after his release, met with Osama bin Laden, Taliban chief Mullah Omar, and other senior Taliban leaders. Afghan

Taliban and several Deobandi Islamist groups of Pakistan lent their support to Masood Azhar.[56] Al Qaeda under Osama bin Laden compensated the HuM for its assets taken over by JeM during its formation in 2000, as it had created a rift between HuM and JeM, and AQ provided substantial financial support to JeM.[57] All negotiations between the HuM leadership, Masood Azhar, the Afghan Taliban and AQ representatives took place in the Binoria mosque of Karachi, where the state provided logistical support and kept the local law-enforcement agencies away.

Further, three prominent Deobandi religious chiefs supported Masood: Mufti Nizamuddin Shamzai of the Majlis-e-Tawan-e-Islami, Maulana Mufti Rasheed Ahmed Ludhianvi of the Darul-Ifta-e-wal-Irshad, and Maulana Sher Ali of the Sheikh-ul-Hadith Dar-ul Haqqania.[58] Such strong support from influential religious leaders and the humongous organizational split, revamping and manipulation would not have been possible for Masood without the ISI's strong backing and assistance, as he had been away from the power corridors of the terror world of Afghanistan and Pakistan for about five years since his arrest in 1994.

Bruce Reidel, a CIA veteran and an expert on South Asia, bringing an insider perspective on the Pakistan Army's policy, suggests that Pakistan's defence forces continue to differentiate between the so-called 'good terrorists' like LeT, JeM and Afghan Taliban, and the 'bad terrorists' like TTP who oppose the army. This, according to Reidel, is in order to justify its nuclear weapons programme, and maintain its strict control over the national security policy and the security budget.[59] Reidel further confirms that the JeM received weapons and training from the ISI, and worked closely with AQ. Christine Fair also confirms Reidel and Siddiqa's assessment, writing, 'Pakistan's Inter-

Service Intelligence Directorate (ISI) created Jaish by working with several Deobandi terrorists associated with Harkat-ul-Mujahideen to hijack Delhi-bound Indian Airlines flight 814 after it departed [from] Kathmandu in late 1999.'[60] Further, in an exciting observation, Fair also claims that JeM was created as a competitor to LeT, to 'escalate violence in Kashmir.'[61] While the LeT was to take on 'high-risk missions', JeM was to gain expertise in suicide attacks.

Avinash Mohananey, former joint director of the IB, India's most influential intelligence agency in Kashmir with a robust grassroots network, also suggests that JeM was established to counter LeT.[62] However, Fair and Mohananey's claims cannot be the concrete basis on which to conclusively argue that LeT was slipping out of the ISI's control; or that they brought JeM to keep LeT in check. Based on my field research in Kashmir, I argue that it has been ISI's strategy to create and maintain multiple terror fronts to ensure checks and balances, create smokescreens, prevent any particular group from gaining ascendency, minimize dependence on one single group and maintain firm control over various terrorist outfits. Hence, it appears reasonable to suggest that the ISI might have thought of creating JeM as a competitor, even if LeT was not challenging its control or creating any roadblocks to its mission in Kashmir.

It is prudent to consider JeM as an ISI-engineered splinter terrorist group. More like an extension of HuM—its natural ideological and material origins go back to the Afghan jihad of the 1980s when, under Zia's Islamization process, the ISI created many Deobandi extremist outfits. The announcement of the new entity, JeM, in 2000, was merely a tactical decision. The organization is primarily rooted in Pakistan's Deobandi terrorist landscape and, therefore, it is necessary we understand the broader context.

The Deobandi Movement: The Fountainhead of Jihadism in South Asia

The decline of the Mughals and the onset of the British empire threatened the status of the Ulama—teachers and interpreters of religious laws and theologians—as state functionaries. As a result, their political and economic fortunes underwent a massive decline. The downfall of the Mughals also led to the rise of revivalist instincts among many Islamic clerics, who felt the corruption of puritanical Islamic practices due to intermingling with Hindus was the primary cause of the end of Muslim rule.[63] Islamic scholar Shah Waliullah Dehlawi (1703–62) was one of the most ardent voices of Islamic revivalism who inspired the Deoband movement.

Deoband is a revivalist movement within Sunni (primarily Hanafi) Islam.[64] Centred in India, Pakistan, Afghanistan and Bangladesh, it has also spread to the United Kingdom, France and the US, and has a presence in South Africa as well. The movement was founded in 1867 in the wake of the failed uprising of 1857 in north India. A group of Indian Islamic scholars—comprising Rashid Ahmad Gangohi, Muhammad Yaqub Nanautai, Shah Rafi al-Din, Syed Muhammad Abid, Zulfiqar Ali, Fadhl al-Rahman Usmani and Muhammad Qasim Nanotwi—were the pioneers of the early Deoband movement. They developed it to counter the British rule as they perceived colonialism to be corrupting Islam. The group founded an Islamic seminary known as Darul Uloom Deoband (1867)—and the movement derives its name from the place where the school is located—where the Islamic revivalist and anti-imperialist ideology of the Deobandis began to develop. Over time, Darul Uloom Deoband became the second-most significant[65] centre of Islamic teaching and research after Al Azhar University of Cairo. The Deoband ideology began to spread through organizations such as Jamiat Ulema-e-Hind and Tablighi Jamaat.

During India's independence movement, the Deobandis advocated composite nationalism. In this, Hindus and Muslims were seen as one nation, and asked to be united in the struggle against the British. In 1919, a large group of Deobandi scholars formed their political party, Jamiat Ulema-e-Hind. Later, they opposed the Pakistan Movement. A minority group joined Muhammad Ali Jinnah's Muslim League, starting the Jamiat Ulema-e-Islam in 1945.

The Deobandi school of thought is generally regarded as a South Asian cousin of Wahhabism. Like Wahhabism, the Deobandi school of thought is also against the worship of shrines and tombs, and the celebration of the Prophet's birthday. Their attitude towards Shias and infidels is closer to that of Wahhabis. In social and religious domains, they are very conservative. Though they opposed the Partition of India,[66] the reasons were not entirely secular. They believed that carving an already Muslim-dominant Pakistan out of India would strongly hinder the spread of Islam in the entire Indian Hindu hinterland.[67] The Deobandi school, unlike the Wahhabis,[68] believes in taqleed (which means traditions and, in this context, interpretations of Islamic laws by the eminent Islamic scholars)[69] and follows the Hanafi school of Islamic jurisprudence. The Taliban, SSP, LeJ and JeM subscribe to the Deobandi school of thought.

In India, the Deobandis have shunned jihadi violence and have issued strong fatwas against terrorism—but they continue to adhere to extremist and orthodox Islamic teachings. Hence, despite the outer trappings of nationalism, the security agencies remain sceptical of their ideology and long-term vision. They constitute 20 per cent of India's Muslim population and are often at odds with the majority Barelwis' school of thought.

Furthermore, ideologically they (India's Deobandis) also oppose Wahhabis or Salafis, a relatively new entrant in India, though they are closer to Deobandis in beliefs than the Barelwis.

As mentioned above, Deobandis are present in South Africa and the Western world too. Masood's outreach to the Deobandi diaspora in the West and in Africa was critical in raising funds for HuM and JeM.

Tablighi Jamaat

Tablighi Jamaat (TJ),[70] Deoband's missionary offshoot, is the largest Islamic network, with around seventy to eighty million followers in 150 countries[71] worldwide[72]. Its members in Europe are estimated to be in the range of 1,50,000.[73] TJ engages in religious proselytization. Its *ijtemas* (religious congregations) in India, Pakistan and Bangladesh attract the largest number of Muslims after the Haj. Though in popular perception it is an apolitical and religious organization, in many quarters, it is believed that TJ plays an indirect role in jihadi radicalization. Arguably, it preaches a conservative and fundamentalist Deobandi strain of Islam which prepares a fertile ground for jihadi radicalization. French TJ expert Mark Gaboriau has suggested that the organization's aim is nothing short of a 'planned conquest of the world'.[74]

TJ has an extensive and robust network in the West, which has been operational since 1945. The group was guarded and careful about its activities and spread in the West, as a result of which it was not under the scrutiny of law enforcement and intelligence agencies for a very long time. In the West, TJ primarily operates through its strong Deobandi networks. Darul Uloom Bury, the most important Deobandi institution in Europe, was established under the guidance of Indian Deobandi leader Muhammad Zakariyya, who also wrote the famous Deobandi text *Fazail-*

i-Amaal.[75] In the 1970s, Darul Uloom Dewsbury, the second Deobandi institution, was established, which over time became the Deobandi headquarters in Europe.[76] Interestingly, in the UK, Deobandis are 3 per cent of the total Muslim population; however, they control 40 per cent [77] of the mosques.[78]

TJ/Deobandis have attracted thousands of Muslims from North African backgrounds in France. French intelligence claims that 80 per cent of its own jihadis once may have been members of TJ, referring to it as the 'ante-chamber of fundamentalists.'[79] In the US, it is estimated there are 15,000 active TJ members, of which only 60 per cent are South Asian.[80] In early 2000, Pakistan's intelligence claimed that 400 American terrorist recruits in Pakistan and Afghanistan emerged from American TJ groups. Some of the famous Western TJ-tied terrorists[81] include Richard Reid, the transatlantic 'shoe bomber'; Mohammed Siddique Khan, mastermind of the 7/7 terror attacks in London; and Abu Qatada,[82] a leading Jordanian jihadist preacher and an Al Qaeda contact.

Tablighi Jamaat and Terror Groups in Pakistan

In Pakistan, General Zia-ul-Haq's regime offered a friendly environment for the work of Deobandi and Tablighi extremists. Since then, Tablighi cadres have played influential roles in Pakistan, including holding positions as powerful as the director general of the ISI.[83] In Pakistan, TJ has proven connections with terror groups. Top-level recruiters from terror outfits have visited TJ cadres in Raiwind[84] and motivated individual Tablighis to enrol with terror groups. Reportedly, in 1995, TJ's military arm, Jihad-bi-Al Saif,[85] was accused of conspiring to assassinate Benazir Bhutto, Pakistan's former Prime Minister.

Harkat-ul-Mujahideen, founded in 1980, recruited all of its original members from Tablighi Jamaat. HuM hijacked Indian

Airlines flight IC-814 in 1998 and murdered French engineers in Karachi in 2002. Approximately 6,000 Tablighis were trained in HuM camps. Many of them fought in Afghanistan and joined Al Qaeda after the defeat of the Soviets. Another violent wing of TJ, HuJI, is active in Kashmir and Gujarat.[86] HuJI staged an attack on an American cultural centre in 2002 and, in 2004, attempted to assassinate Sheikh Hasina Wajid, then the leader of the moderate Awami League and the former Prime Minister of Bangladesh.[87]

TJ's Indian members, on their Pakistan tours for ijtemas and preaching work, are reportedly lured by terror groups like Al Qaeda, LeT and Harkat-ul-Mujahideen.

Deobandi Spread in Pakistan

In the colonial era, Sufi Islam, premised on the *pir-murid* (spiritual master–follower) relationship, dominated Pakistan's Islamic spread. Sufi Islam, mostly followed by the Barelwis, has been relatively syncretic and tolerant towards other faiths, vis-à-vis the Ahl-i-Hadith and Deobandis, which preach a literalist and extremist interpretation of Islamic texts.

In the medieval and colonial era of Punjab, there were numerous mosques and maulanas; however, Sufi Islam, with its pirs and shrines (dargah), had an overwhelming influence over the Muslim masses. The most influential Sufi orders were Chishti, Qadri, Naqshbandi and Suhrawardy.[88] Naqshbandi was the most orthodox and puritanical one, followed and preached by Sheikh Ahmad Sarhindi, who hailed from Sirhind. Sarhindi (1564-1625) was the contemporary of Mughal kings Akbar and Jehangir. Known as Mujaddid, i.e., reviver, for his extremist views, he was extremely critical of heterodox liberal movements like Akbar's Din-e-Elahi.[89] The Deobandi sect holds him in great reverence. The dominance of pirs was not merely confined to the religious theatre. They also exercised massive social and political clout because of their vast landholdings. The shrines had been the beneficiaries of land grants by various rulers since the eleventh century, including the Sultanate kings, Mughals and Sikhs. Initially, the British passed a legal statute disallowing direct land grants to Sufi shrines and pirs.[90] However, over time, the British bureaucracy came close to the Sajdanasheen (pirs) and shrines as the latter exercised tremendous social and political influence by which they could control the restive and rebellious population. This relationship was particularly useful after the Revolt of 1857.[91] The Sufi pirs acted as mediators/troubleshooters between the government and the people. They even joined the British administration as honorary judges, zamindars and land revenue officers.

However, towards the closing years of the nineteenth century, the Deobandis started gaining influence in Punjab, and challenged the traditional Sufi structures dominated by pirs and shrines. In today's Pakistan, Deobandis form the most significant part of the Muslim population, exercising an overwhelming influence on the Madaris. Roughly 65 per cent of the Madaris follow Deobandi Islam, and preach and practice a highly militant form of Islam.[92]

Deobandis played an instrumental role in the anti-Ahmadiyya movement, which ultimately led Pakistan to declare them as non-Muslims. Since the 1980s, Deobandis have perpetrated sectarian violence against Shia Muslims. Deobandi terrorist organizations have been active in sectarian violence in Pakistan and Afghanistan, and jihadist militancy in Kashmir. They have also challenged the Pakistani state by orchestrating an unsuccessful assassination plot to kill the then-president Musharraf and carrying out an armed resistance from the ramparts of Lal Masjid (2007) in the capital city of Islamabad.

Historical Background

In the second half of the nineteenth century, the Deobandi movement started spreading in Punjab. Initially, as per Gilmartin,[93] an expert voice on South Asian history, the support came from the urban centres where the influence of Sufi saints and shrines was weaker than in the rural areas. Towards the end of the nineteenth century, Darul Uloom–affiliated madaris appeared in Peshawar, Gujranwala and Lahore. Some of the earliest Darul Uloom madaris include Madrasa-i-Rashidiya at Jalandhar (1897) and Madrasa-i-Numaniya (1907).[94] Hussain Ali (1866–1943) of Mianwali (Punjab) was the first recorded scholar to study at Darul Uloom, Deoband.[95] Gangohi and Nanotwi taught him. After returning, he preached absolute faith in Tauhid (monism) and the Quran as the ultimate source of truth.[96] His disciple Ghulam Ullah Khan (1909–80) founded the famous madrasa of Talim-ul-Quran in northern Punjab.

In the early twentieth century, Abdul Rahim Raipuri (1853–1919), a Naqshbandi pir, and Maulana Ashraf Thanwi (1863–1943), a Sunni scholar from Darul Uloom Deoband, commanded robust influence in Deobandi circles in Punjab. His successors started several madaris in Sargodha and Lahore named Idara Rahimiya Ulum-i-Qurania.[97]

The next prominent figure in the Deobandi circuit was Ubaidullah Sindhi,[98] who laid the foundation of Deobandi activism in Punjab. At Deoband, he was a student of Maulana Mahmud-ul-Hasan, known for catapulting the movement into political activism. Ubaidullah Sindhi established the madrasas Darul Irshad (1901) in Sind and Nazarath-ul-Maarif in Delhi (1912). Besides, his name figures as an operational chief in the 'silk-letter conspiracy'—a plan hatched with Afghanistan's ruler, Amanullah Khan, and Turkey to oust the British from India.

However, the British intelligence learned of the plan and its ring leaders were arrested before it could take off.

In 1919, in the shadows of the Khilafat Movement led by Mahatma Gandhi against the dismemberment of the Ottoman caliphate, the Deobandis formed a political group, Jamiat-ul-Ulema-e-Hind.[99] Maulana Abul Kalam Azad and Mahmud-ul-Hasan were the principal figures in that group. The Khilafat Movement and Non-Cooperation Movement made a tremendous impact on the masses in north India. Punjab, Lahore, Sialkot and Gujranwala became hotbeds of anti-British resentment in the 1920s. During this time, Deobandi leaders like Ubaidullah Sindhi, Ahmed Ali Lahori, Habib-ur-Rahman Ludhianvi and Ata Ullah Shah Bokhari started their careers preaching an exclusionary and extremist strain of Islam. The idea of Khatm-e-Nabuwat (end of prophethood after Mohammed), mainly directed against the Ahmadiyya sect of Muslims, which disagreed with Mohammed being the last Prophet, was central to their teachings since the 1890s when the Ahmadiyya movement began.[100]

In 1929, Majlis-e-Ahrar-e Islam[101] was formed, comprising the dissidents from the Punjab Khilafat committee. Maulana Zafar Ali Khan, Maulana Daud Ghaznavi, Syed Ata Ullah Shah Bokhari, Chaudhry Afzal Haq, Maulana Mazhar Ali Azhar, Khwaja Abdul Rehman Ghazi, Sheikh Hissam-ud-din and Maulana Habib-ur-Rehman Ludhianvi constituted the core leadership of the Ahrar. Though it represented all the Muslim segments, its core ideology and prominent leaders, including Maulana Ahmed Ali Lahori, Maulana Qazi Ahsan Ahmed Shuja Abadi and Ata Ullah Shah Bokhari, were Deobandi. They adopted puritanical and agitational activism in 1930s politics. The Ahrar Movement gained an immense following among the urban lower-middle-class Muslims, mainly among artisans in

Amritsar, Lahore and Sialkot. Ahrar's agitation (1931) against the alleged oppressive rule of Kashmir's Hindu king, Maharaja Hari Singh, (in a state with majority local Muslim population) made them hugely popular in urban Punjab.[102] Later, they organized a similar agitation in favour of the Muslim subjects of Kapurthala against the maharaja of Kapurthala. Ahrar activists also courted arrests in the Madeh-i-Sahaba movement in the United Provinces (1937–39), which widened the rift between the Shias and Sunnis. However, the sectarian differences were brushed under the carpet during the Partition. They resurfaced in Pakistan after Partition and intensified to the extent that it led to the formation of SSP in 1985. SSP leaders like Haq Nawaz Jhangvi and Zia-ur-Rahman Farooqi held the legacy of Ahrar stalwarts like Bokhari in great reverence. The main fruits of the Ahrar Movement was its idea of Khatme Nabuwwat and its impact on the Deobandi clerics, which finally resulted in a strong anti-Ahmadiyya movement in the 1970s, ultimately leading to the sect no longer being recognized under the umbrella of Islam.

Leading Deobandi Ulemas and Madaris Leaving a Legacy

Maulana Ahmed Ali Lahori (1886–1962)[103] was held in great esteem as he rose to the status of Sheikh-ul-Tafsir. His exegesis of the Quran is considered the most authentic and comprehensive in the Deobandi school. He laid the foundation of institutions like Anjuman-i-Khuddam-ud-Din and Qasim-ul-Uloom and actively participated in the anti-British resistance, for which he was jailed several times.

In his teachings, he emphasized the ultimacy of the Quran and Sunnat (the tradition of the Prophet). He propagated a literalist interpretation, giving primacy to scriptures, and rejecting the shrine and Sufi traditions as heresy (bid'ah). He was also closely associated with the Ahrar agitation against Kashmir's maharaja (1931). After the Partition, Ahmed Ali volunteered to collect funds for jihad in Kashmir and even went to Muzaffarabad with his son Ubaidullah Anwar to donate the funds.[104] Ahmed Ali was also active in Jamiat Ulema-e-Hind (JuH). He was elected its emir in 1956. His son continued his association with the JuH. Ahmed Ali and his institutions contributed to the religious realm, and left a legacy of political activism through their association with JuH, majorly contributing to the cause of political Islam.

Apart from Lahore, Ludhiana and Jalandhar also emerged as thriving centres of Deobandi Islam. In Ludhiana, Maulana Muhammad and Maulana Muhammad Abdullah staunchly condemned Murza Ghulam Ahmed, founder of the Ahmadiyya sect, as a 'kafir'.[105] Abdullah established Madrasa Darul Uloom Numaniya in the region. Habib-ur-Rehman was the most prominent Deobandi leader from Ludhiana, also mentioned above. Interestingly, in Punjab, the Deobandi school initially attracted the Muslims from lower middle and lower classes such as the agrarian community of *Arains*. In Jalandhar, Maulana Faqirullah Raipuri Jullunduri (1878–1963) and Maulana Khair Muhammad Jullunduri (1891–1970) who emerged as stellar figures in Deobandi leadership, were both from the *Arain* community. After graduating from Deoband, Maulana Faqirullah Raipuri returned to Jalandhar, where he taught eminent future Deobandi leaders such as Rashid Ahmed Salfi, Habib-ur-Rehman Ludhianvi, Muhammad Ali Jullunduri, Abdul Jabbar Hissarvi and Maulana Khair Muhammad Jullunduri at his alma mater Jamia Rashidiya.[106] After Partition, he migrated to Pakistan and revived Jamia Rashidiya at Sahiwal, transforming it into one of the leading Deobandi institutions.

Maulana Khair Muhammad Jullunduri established Madrasa-i-Khair-ul-Madaris in Jalandhar. After Partition, he relocated to Pakistan and settled in Multan. Though an apolitical man by taste, Jullunduri supported the Pakistan movement. He was elected as president of JuH, but he lost interest in politics after a brief stint.

The Proliferation of Madaris after Partition

In the 1940s, the separatist movement to carve out an Islamic state of Pakistan created a rift among top-level Deobandi leaders, with Hussain Ahmed Madni, Abul Kalam Azad and Habib-ur-Rehman Ludhianvi choosing the nationalist line of the Indian National Congress and Jamiat Ulema-e-Hind, and a small segment treading the separatist course. Finally, in 1945, the separatist faction under the leadership of Shabbir Ahmed Usmani, Ehtisham-ul-Hassan Thanvi, Zafar Ahmed Usmani and Mufti Muhammad Shafi broke away and founded Jamiat Ulema-i-Islam (JuI), which supported Jinnah's Muslim League.[107] After Partition, Deobandi institutions progressed by leaps and bounds, and their madaris registered a multi-fold growth in numbers. All this strengthened JuI's political profile. Since most of the JuI leadership came from madaris, where the majority was from lower and middle-class backgrounds, the camaraderie in the Deobandi JuI strengthened.

In 1947, Pakistan had 245 religious schools; in 2001, their number increased to 6,870.[108] In Punjab, the rise in the number of seminaries was the most significant—i.e., 'three and a half times between 1975 and 1996, from over 700 to 2,463, and out of these, 750 were "aggressively sectarian".'[109]

Table 1: Madaris of Various Sects (1988)

Province/Region	Deobandi	Barelwi	Ahl-i-Hadith	Shia	Others	Total
Punjab	590	548	118	21	43	1,320
NWFP	631	32	5	2	8	678
Sind	208	61	6	10	6	291
Balochistan	278	34	3	1	31	347
Pakistan-administered Kashmir	51	20	2	0	3	76
Islamabad	22	20	--	2	3	47
Northern Areas	60	02	27	11	2	102
Total	1,840	717	161	47	96	2,861

Source: Ministry of Education, Islamabad, 1988.[110]

The reasons for the mushrooming of Deobandi madaris:

1) The massive inflow of petrodollars from the Arab countries, mainly Saudi Arabia, as the Arab nations were alarmed at the growth of left-wing thought in the 1970s in Pakistan, and wanted Islam as a bulwark against communism.[111] Over time, the relations between Islamist institutions and charities in the Gulf countries became stronger, and operated independently of official control. The Pakistani ulema and madaris were the biggest beneficiaries of these 'religious and intellectual bonds that became embedded in institutional contacts and networks of patronage'.[112]

2) The Afghan jihad also led to the growth of madaris and later resulted in the militarization of madaris with financial largesse from Saudi Arabia and the US.[113]

3) General Zia-ul-Haq, Pakistan's dictator, was himself a Deobandi and a grand champion of the Islamization of Pakistan. Under his patronage, Deobandi madaris were given massive aid that helped them flourish. After 1980, madaris also received zakat,[114] and the state policy to appoint madrasa students to higher administrative positions elevated their social and political status, resulting in many students joining madrasas.

Table 2: Evolution of Madaris in Pakistan

Province/Region	1947	1960	1980	1988	2000
Punjab	121	195	1,012	1,320	3,153
NWFP	50	87	426	678	1,281
Sind	21	87	380	291	905
Balochistan	28	70	135	347	692
Pakistan-Administered Kashmir	4	8	29	76	151
Islamabad	0	1	27	47	94
Northern Areas	12	16	47	102	185
FATA	0				300
Total	245	464	2,056	2,861	6,761

Source: Ministry of Religious Affairs, Islamabad, 1988, 2000.[115]

The two most influential Deobandi seminaries of Lahore are Jamia Ashrafia and Jamia Madina. These two institutions have a strong influence on the urban class of Lahore. Though, officially, they avoid politics and refrain from jihad, their students and members are actively involved with many jihadist organizations.

Most of the Deobandi expansion is concentrated in the southern districts of Pakistani Punjab. In 1988, the number of Deobandi madaris in Punjab was 590 out of 1,320. It rose to 972, with 80,120 students in 1996.[116] Interestingly, 595 out of 972 madaris were in the three southern districts of Multan—Dera Ghazi Khan, Bahawalpur and Rahim Yar Khan. Similarly, Wifaq-ul Madaris-ul-Arabia (established in 1959), a regulatory body of Deobandi Madaris, is also situated in Multan. South Punjab was an active Deobandi centre even in pre-Partition days, and after the establishment of Khair-ul-Madaris (Multan), Deobandis expanded rapidly in south Punjab. This extraordinary growth of Deobandi seminaries in south Punjab can be attributed to poverty, a feudal socio-cultural setup, lack of infrastructure and social development, lack of secular educational institutions, and the pervasive shrine and pir culture. This culture in an illiterate and poor society makes the masses very vulnerable to the teachings of the learned Islamic scholars of Deoband, who project themselves as the representatives of authentic Islam and the illiterate shrine-worshipping Muslims as ignorant apostates. Some of the powerful Deobandi seminaries of south Punjab are Jamia Abbasia, Bahawalpur; Qasim-ul Uloom, Multan; Darul Uloom, Kabirwala; Madrasa Qasim-ul Uloom, Faqirwali; Madrasa Ashraful Uloom, Rahim Yar Khan and Makhzanul Uloom, Khanpur.

South Punjab is one of the most fertile recruiting grounds for Deobandi Sunni terrorist organizations like LeJ, SSP, and those operating in Kashmir and Afghanistan, like JeM. Ayesha Siddiqa, an expert on jihad in Pakistan, in her vast research on jihadism in Pakistan, rightly suggests that Bahawalpur (the JeM headquarters) is one of the few districts contributing as much to jihad as some in the frontier districts. Deobandi terrorist commanders and clerics like Masood Azhar (JeM) and Abdul Rashid Ghazi (Lal Masjid's Naib Khatib, killed in action in 2007) come from south Punjab—Bahawalpur and Rajanpur, respectively.

Deobandi Militant Organizations

According to historian Tahir Kamran[117], the two major developments that transformed the Deobandis into a militant force were:

1) The anti-Ahmadiyya agitation by the Deobandis (1953) in which Ahraris played a crucial role. The army violently suppressed the movement. Later, the agitation surfaced again in 1973, and Zulfiqar Ali Bhutto declared Ahmadiyyas non-Muslims. This victory was a great morale-booster for the Deobandis; as a result, they continued their extremist agenda and militant tactics with more vigour.
2) Afghan jihad further galvanized them into a militant, fanatic movement. It resulted in the emergence of an array of sectarian and extremist Deobandi terrorist groups.

The main Deobandi terrorist groups[118] are HuJI, HuM, HuA, JeM, Taliban, TTP, SSP and LeJ. Among these, SSP and LeJ mostly operate within Pakistan, targeting Shias. They now operate under the umbrella organization Ahl-i-Sunnat Wal Jamaat (ASWJ).[119]

Sipah-e-Sahaba Pakistan

Established in 1985 in Jhang by four anti-Shia clerics—Maulana Haq Nawaz Jhangvi, Maulana Zia-ur-Rahman Farooqi, Maulana

Isar-ul-Haq Qasmi and Maulana Azam Tariq, the Sipah-e-Sahaba Pakistan, or SSP, originated from the Anjuman-e-Sipah-e-Sahaba.[120] General Zia's military regime and the Saudi monarchy were the main pillars behind it.[121] The purpose behind raising an anti-Shia extremist group was to deal with the Iranian threat. The eminent scholar on Iran and Shia Islam, Vali Nasr, has suggested that raising the SSP was a key element of Zia's strategy to downsize the sect in Pakistan, which, in his orthodox Sunni vision, was a major stumbling block in the Islamization of state and society.[122] Reportedly, the ISI backed such extremist outfits and was hence involved in sectarian killings. The systematic campaign against Shia-based militant outfits and their elimination after 1989 is clearly suggestive of the ISI's robust support for Sunni extremist groups.

Khaled Ahmed, an expert on Pakistan's sectarian militancy, opines that the SSP secured financial support from both domestic and foreign sources.[123] The internal sources primarily included the local trader-merchant class in Jhang. The foreign funding came from Arab rulers of the Gulf, who frequented Rahim Yar Khan for hunting expeditions. Further, he says that Maulana Jhangvi also enriched himself through these linkages. Since most of its leaders were from south Punjab, the SSP saw a meteoric rise in this region, resulting in an alarming rise in sectarian violence in south Punjab, especially during the 1980s and the 1990s.

Riaz Basra, an SSP terrorist, had committed 300 murders before he was finally neutralized in 2002.[124] The outfit was also involved in a tussle with the Sharif family—one of Pakistan's pre-eminent political families. This was due to the Shahbaz Sharif government in Punjab targeting the group and killing many of its militants. In 1997–98, the SSP staged an attack on the country's Prime Minister Nawaz Sharif, but he managed to escape. The PML-N (Pakistan Muslim League-Nawaz), the SSP and LeJ managed to resolve their disputes through dialogue. The PML-N Punjab government assured job quotas for SSP members in exchange for the withdrawal of the LeJ candidate contesting against Shahbaz Sharif in Bhakkar.

The SSP has been involved in sectarian violence and war—first against the Soviet Union and later the US. Ramzi Yusuf, the mastermind of the World Trade Centre bombing[125] in 1993, was associated with this militant outfit. The SSP was a pioneer in sending its jihadis to join Al Qaeda. It has fought alongside the Taliban since 1988.

In Pakistan, SSP unleashed a series of Shia killings—particularly targeting Shia doctors in Karachi in 2001. It also started making inroads in electoral politics. Some of its prominent members contested elections. For instance, Maulana Azam Tariq, one of its founding members, contested elections in 1990, 1993 and 2002. Over time, it became difficult to differentiate between the political and militant wings of the organization.

Though the SSP's top leadership—Zia-ur-Rahman Farooqi, Isar-ul-Haq Qasmi and Azam Tariq—was neutralized by 2000, the organization has more or less been revived by cultivating strong ties with other outfits, such as JeM. Reportedly, in October 2008, JeM chief Masood Azhar officiated the dastaarbandi of SSP's Maulana Zia-ul-Haq Qasmi, who was made the chairman of the supreme council of the SSP.

Lashkar-e-Jhangvi

Lashkar-e-Jhangvi[126] is a splinter group of the SSP.[127] SSP leaders like Akram Lahori, Malik Ishaq (from Khanewal) and Riaz Basra (from Sargodha) formed LeJ in 1996 in Bhakkar, south Punjab, because they believed that the SSP had moved astray from its course and ideology.[128] Malik Ishaq served a jail term in Sahiwal jail till 2014.[129] Detained again in 2015, he was killed in police firing while his supporters fired at the police convoy to free him. Riaz Basra was killed in a police encounter in 2002. However, this happened only after a long phase during which the state authorities turned a blind eye to his activities.[130] In one such instance, in 1994, allegedly, the Benazir government allowed Basra to escape from police custody after her government and the LeJ's parent outfit—the SSP—clinched an election collaboration.[131]

LeJ, one of the most clandestine terror groups in the world, aspires to transform Pakistan into an orthodox Sunni state, thereby completely marginalizing Shias. LeJ has been involved in several attacks on Western assets and institutions, in the murders of ethnic minorities, Shias, Sufi Muslims and non-Muslims. In the beginning, LeJ pursued its sectarian anti-Shiite agenda through violent means, including suicide bombings, assassination attempts, armed assaults and kidnappings. After a military coup in Pakistan in 1999, sectarian violence declined for a brief period. Reportedly, Qari Abdul Hai, LeJ's advisory council chief, was against reviving anti-Shiite attacks because he argued they would be harmful to national solidarity within Pakistan and could lead to a massive government crackdown that could negatively affect the outfit. Basra disagreed with him. In 2001, due to a widening rift between its leaders, LeJ split into a faction led by Basra with a Punjabi militant majority and another led by Abdul Hai based in Karachi. LeJ remained under the leadership of Basra.

Following the ban on LeJ in 2001, a substantial section of its cadres moved to Afghanistan, where they found shelter in the Taliban regime. Operating from there, they continued to orchestrate attacks inside Pakistan. Post 9/11, LeJ was involved in fighting against the US in the latter's War on Terror. The LeJ was allegedly one of the first Sunni terrorist groups to send cadres to Al Qaeda. Its long association with Arab rulers frequenting south Punjab to take part in hunts, enabled the group to cultivate deep ties with the AQ and nurture its commitment to the Afghan war. Stanford University's terrorism database says that LeJ's relationship with AQ began in early 2000 and these collaborative ties developed throughout the 2000s. Reportedly, in several cases AQ and LeJ had overlapping memberships. For example, high-profile terrorists like Qari Mohammad Zafar and Qari Hussain Mehsud were members of both the organizations. Later, the LeJ developed ties with prominent AQ leaders such as Khaled Sheikh Mohammad—who allegedly ordered the attack on the Karachi Corps commander in 2004—and Abu Musab Al Zarqawi.[132]

LeJ has orchestrated several terror attacks in Pakistan, particularly in Islamabad and Lahore. It has nurtured strong links with the Taliban, and commands a growing influence in many south Punjab towns and rural areas. This outfit plays a significant role in providing cadres from within Punjab who are used in terrorist activities inside the province. The Islamabad Marriott bombing (2008) and the suicide attack on the police training facility in Quetta[133] (2016) have been linked with men from south Punjab, organized by the LeJ.

The organization has also been involved in sectarian killings, such as the killing of the Iranian diplomat Sadiq Ganji, the murder of a group of Iranian technicians and a group of Iranian Air Force cadets visiting Pakistan. These killings during the 1990s adversely affected relations between Islamabad and Tehran. The main perpetrator, Malik Ishaq, was killed in a police encounter in 2015.[134] The LeJ was also involved in the attacks against the Christian community in Bahawalpur city. The LeJ's Shakeen Anwar, who belonged to Bahawalnagar, was instrumental in the attack on a church in October 2001. LeJ was involved in the 2002 abduction and murder of US reporter Daniel Pearl. In 2003, it carried out an unsuccessful attempt to murder President Musharraf. Four years later, it also attempted an unsuccessful assassination against Prime Minister Benazir Bhutto. In 2012, Pakistan witnessed a revival of sectarian killings at the behest of the LeJ. Even though it was going through a leadership crisis as most of its top leaders had been killed or jailed, the group intensified sectarian killings in Pakistan and Afghanistan. In 2016, the LeJ staged an attack in Quetta with IS-KP. As regards its relations with Kashmir-centric terrorist outfits, in several quarters, it is suggested that the SSP and the LeJ have policy differences with the Kashmir-centric terrorist groups like JeM and LeT; though evidence of a linkage between the two is visible, particularly in south Punjab.

Tehreek-e-Taliban Pakistan

The TTP—the country's largest terrorist umbrella outfit[135]—based in South Waziristan Agency, has strong ties with AQ and the Afghan Taliban. TTP aims to establish Shariah law in the nation, supporting the Afghan Taliban's control in Kabul after the US withdrawal of forces, as well as to orchestrate attacks against Pakistani security forces as defensive jihad.[136] Their final goal is to dislodge the Pakistani government and replace it with an Islamic caliphate. It was established in 2004 by Waziristan-based Deobandi terrorists, who had been fighting alongside the Taliban in Afghanistan. In 2007, a Shura (tribal group) of Pakistan's forty Taliban leaders united under TTP's banner with Baitullah Mehsud as their emir (commander), and Maulana Hafiz Gul Bahadur and Maulana Faqir Mohammed as deputies. Many leaders and terrorists who parted ways from JeM—taking a stand against Pakistan aligning with the US in its War on Terror against the Afghan Taliban—joined TTP. Hence, TTP emerged as an umbrella organization with most Pakistan Taliban groups under it. It is an 'agglomerate of more than 40 Islamist and Pashtun tribal factions from Pakistan's Federally Administered Tribal Areas (FATA) and Khyber Pakhtunkhwa (KPK).'[137] However, the outfit has suffered from a lack of coordination among its various commanders.

With FATA and Khyber-Pakhtunkhwa as its major strongholds, TTP has a Pashtun majority and Punjabi fighters. Its robust ties with Punjabi Taliban and Deobandi groups have ensured a continuous supply of cadres and suicide bombers from south Punjab. The outfit has also leveraged its networks with Punjabi Deobandi groups to orchestrate terror attacks deep inside Pakistan. Ethnic diversity is TTP's hallmark. In addition to a Pashtun majority, it has Uzbek, Arab, Punjabi and Chechen combatants. The Mehsud group and the Punjabi Taliban are the most influential and powerful factions in the TTP. Primarily dedicated to jihad against the Pakistani government, the Mehsud group forms the backbone of the TTP. The Punjabi Taliban, with many sectarian groups, has Kashmiri jihad as its main agenda.

TTP has close relations with AQ and other Deobandi terrorist groups like SSP, LeJ and JeM. TTP has orchestrated some of the most brutal terrorist attacks against the Pakistani state, including the Peshawar army school attack (2014).

From 2014 onwards, the Pakistani government, realizing that the group was the most significant security threat in the nation, launched operation Zarb-e-Azaab to crush TTP.[138] A combined onslaught of US drone strikes, the Pakistani Army's operations and internal financial struggles caused massive damage to the group. TTP's infrastructure was in a shambles in FATA; by 2015, 70 per cent of its cadre had to flee FATA. Some factions led by commanders such as Maulvi Nazir and Baitullah Mahsud have become state allies. Many of its leaders, like Ehsanullah

Ehsan, defected to the Pakistan government, claiming that TTP was defiling Islam. After the establishment of IS-KP, many of its cadres defected to the group. On 15 June 2018, TTP leader Mullah Fazlullah was killed in a US drone strike in Kunar, following which the outfit declared Mufti Noor Wali Mehsud as its chief. The death of Mullah Fazlullah was a setback and the outfit faced challenges in remaining united. However, after the US withdrawal from Afghanistan and the Taliban's return to power in 2021—on account of its historic and kinship ties with the Afghan Taliban—TTP has received much support and strength that is demonstrably revitalizing it. Since then, TTP has once again emerged as the most significant threat to Pakistan, launching several terrorist attacks on the nation's security forces.

The Deobandi ecosystem in Pakistan has a long history of almost 150 years, leading to strong and deeply entrenched roots in Pakistani society. After Partition, Deobandi madrasas and mosques have grown exponentially in various parts of Pakistan, particularly in Punjab—with a massive concentration in south Punjab and KPK, erstwhile NWFP, and the neighbouring FATA regions. This concentration explains why south Punjab is a stronghold for LeJ, JeM and SSP, whereas KPK and FATA are TTP strongholds. Besides, the Deobandis' deep-rooted and robust presence in Pakistani society makes them a mighty social, political and cultural force. For political parties and the security establishment, Deobandis are a force to reckon with. Political parties compete for their support in elections and the Deoband school has a massive following in the Pakistani security forces. Deobandi terrorist and political groups have emerged from this solid historical and social presence; hence, the Pakistani Army is not in a position to fully tame these terrorist outfits.

3

Masood Azhar and JeM's Dark Ideological Alleyways

JAISH-E-MOHAMMED, THE YOUNGEST AMONG THE THREE main terrorist groups of Kashmir, continues to puzzle the Indian state and the counterterrorism community with its lethal fidayeen missions, and highly secretive and layered operational tactics—even twenty-one years after its formation. The group's ability to surprise the SFs and intelligence agencies remains its USP. Over the last twenty-one years, there have been several occasions when the security establishment declared it dead and read its obituaries; however, it has returned each time, more lethal and horrific than ever. In January 2019, when the SFs in Kashmir were jubilant with their extraordinary success in counterterror operations, JeM hit back with Pulwama (February 2019)—an attack that shook the power corridors of New Delhi, Islamabad and Washington DC, almost bringing the two nuclear-armed adversaries to war. With the Taliban's return to power, JeM is likely to feel encouraged to pursue its Kashmir jihad and pan-Islamic agenda with an intensified vigour due to the endemic ties between the two; hence, it is crucial to understand the layered, secretive and complex world of the terror outfit. The ideal beginning of this exercise can be by unravelling Masood Azhar, JeM's founder and emir general.

In His Own Words

Masood Azhar[1] was born to Allah Baksh Sabir, in a Sunni Deobandi middle-class family on 10 July 1968, in his native place, Bahawalpur, in Pakistan. His father, a primary school teacher and a small-time businessman of poultry farms, was a resident of Kausar Colony in Bahawalpur, where JeM later built its lavish and sprawling complex. Masood's mother, Rukaiyah Bibi, was a housewife. His paternal grandfather, Maulana Allah Dittah'Ata, was a conservative and staunch Muslim, and a spiritual mentor of the people. His maternal grandfather, Muhammad Hasan Chughtai, believed in political Islam. He played a crucial role in the Khatme Nabuwwat movement and remained emir of the International Majlis-e-Ahrar till 1992.[2]

He has five brothers and six sisters.[3] His brothers are Mohammad Tahir Anwar and Mohammad Ibrahim Athar Alvi[4] (hereafter referred to as Ibrahim Athar), both in the poultry farm business; Abdul Rauf Azgar, a Deobandi student and later the operational commander of JeM as Mufti Rauf Azgar; Mohammad Jehangir and Mohiuddin Aurangzeb Alamgir alias Ammar Alvi, both madrasa students.[5] His sisters are Zohri Bibi, Abid Bibi, Rabiya Bibi, Sadia, Safia and Sumira Bibi. His uncles, Rahmatullah and Najibullah, were government teachers, and another uncle, Muhammad Iqbal, was a bank officer. His maternal uncles were based in Saudi Arabia, working in a small-time carpenter business. Masood's permanent addresses are:

1) 6-B, 1260/108, Kausar Colony, Model Town, Bahawalpur, Pakistan

2) Flat no. 4, Dadi Mansion, Regal Chowk, Karachi, Pakistan

Physical Appearance, Health and Early Education

He is five-feet and seven-inches tall with a 'sallow complexion, stout build, protruding belly and round face'.[6] He was an obese man with a poor physique at the time of his arrest. He also limped because he sustained a severe bullet wound in Afghanistan.[7] He had stepped out of his tent one night and on his way back, forgot the security code to re-enter the camp. The night guard thought he was a Russian spy and fired at him. Later in his jihadi career, this incident helped build his image of a brave warrior to boost his popularity and appeal. As of now, he is believed to be overweight and sick. In March 2019, Pakistan's foreign minister, Shah Mahmood Qureshi, said, 'He (Masood) is in Pakistan, according to my information. He is unwell to the extent that he can't leave his house, because he's really unwell.'[8] Following that, Indian security officials maintained that he was suffering from renal failure and was getting regular dialysis in the army hospital at Rawalpindi.[9] However, the information at times is deliberately planted by intelligence agencies; hence, it is difficult to find out the exact health status and location of Masood. Physically, he was unsuitable for a combat role. When he went to Afghanistan in 1989, he could not perform well in various physical training activities like the obstacle race and weapons handling.

He knows Urdu, Hindustani, Saraiki and Arabic. His spoken English is broken; however, he can read the language. His formal education was till Grade VIII. He told his interrogators, 'My father had Deobandi influence and was extremely religious.' After finishing Grade VII at a school in Bahawalpur, he moved to Rahim Yar Khan, where his maternal uncle lived. In his school education, he passed with a distinction and actively participated in public speaking events, which became his forte later in life.[10] In Rahim Yar Khan, his father's friend Mufti Sayeed convinced his uncle to send Masood to Jamia Uloom Islamia Seminary in Binoria town, Karachi, popularly known as Binoria mosque seminary. In 1978, he joined Jamia Uloom Islamia at Binoria mosque. Professor Rasheed Ahmed Masood, an Islamic scholar, who translated Masood's seminal work *Fatah-ul-Jawaad*, describes his Binoria mosque days in the following words:[11]

> Soon he became the center of attention of all his teachers due to his God-gifted intelligence, diligence, hard work, devotion to studies, depth of perception, learning everything minutely, fear of Allah and piety. Besides examinations, he actively participated in speech contests and debates and always stood distinctive. As Masood had an inborn love for the reformation of the heart and company of the saints and holy men, during his student life, he pledged allegiance to the Spiritual Guide Hazrat Maulana Mufti Wali Hasan Tonki to reform his 'self.' Besides education and religious training, he learned mysticism and spiritualism from him. He passed all the examinations with distinction and mastered the Arabic and Persian languages. So, after completing the '*Shahadat-ul-'Alimia*,' he was appointed teacher at his Alma Mater.

At Binoria mosque seminary, Masood graduated with an 'Almia degree' in Islamic education in 1989 with an A-1 grade. Then, he joined the same institution as a teacher, where he continued till April 1992.

The Onset of the Jihadist Journey

At Jamia Uloom Islamia, HuM cadres and ideologues had an influential presence, with many leaders having studied there.

Masood was impressed with HuM's work in the Afghan jihad against the Soviets. At Binoria mosque, he interacted and exchanged thoughts on Islam and global jihad with foreign Deobandi students from Sudan, Bangladesh and the Arab world. This international exposure helped him build a perspective and vision of his own about pan-Islamism, which later in his career was explicitly visible in his interest and passion for the global jihadist agenda. Besides, in his earliest inspiration for jihad, his brother Ibrahim Athar, who had participated in the Afghan jihad in the 1980s, played a crucial role by taking Masood to Afghanistan in 1988.[12]

HuM was recruiting many cadres from the Binoria seminary. Masood, already spellbound by their work, met Maulana Fazlur Rehman Khalil, emir of HuM, at Karachi in June–July 1989. Khalil invited him for 'tarbiyat' (training) at Yavar, in Afghanistan. In those days, HuM had three principles for recruitment: Forty days of combat training (arms and physical training) in Afghanistan—waived for ulemas; the recruit should not have affiliations with other groups like Muhajir Qaumi Movement,[13] Jiye Sindh[14] and Saraiki Movement[15]; and the recruit should be a major, as revealed by his beard. Besides, Shias were not enrolled. HuM recruited from Deobandi Muslims only.

At Yavar, Masood underwent a week-long weapons training programme. However, due to his ill health, he failed to finish the forty-day combat training. Next, he was asked by HuM leadership to edit a monthly magazine. It was at this time he met Sajjad Afghani, who later became HuM commander in Kashmir, at the Yavar training camp.

In Karachi, his friend Maulana Zameel, a correspondent of *Jung*, an Urdu daily, arranged the necessary permissions to publish a monthly, *Sada-i-Mujahid*, formally registering himself as the owner of the monthly. In August–September 1989, Masood

Azhar established the magazine, working as its chief editor from Lasbela Chowk near Bilal Mosque in Karachi. Initially, it was priced at PKR 5, and 2,000 copies were printed, 80 per cent of which were distributed free of charge in public meetings, during Friday prayers, and speeches. The magazine published write-ups on HuM's activities in Afghanistan, its new offices in Pakistan and on Islamic teachings. By 1990, HuM had opened offices in almost all of Pakistan's major cities—Karachi, Lahore, Gujranwala and Islamabad. In 1991, *Sada-i-Mujahid*'s office was shifted to a different location in Karachi. In 1992, HuM started another magazine, *Irshad*, with Masood as the chief editor.

Masood's Foreign Travels

Zambia

In his 1994 interrogation, Masood said that during Ramzan, he had visited Mecca every year for Umrah since 1986. His maternal uncle, who has been based in Mecca since 1984, hosted him. After he joined HuM, his foreign visits involved a different objective—fundraising for HuM and disseminating information about its work in Afghanistan. His first visit was in 1990, when he accompanied Fazlur Rehman Khalil to Lusaka and Chipata in Zambia. The visit resulted from an invitation from Ibrahim Lambert, a profoundly religious businessman dealing in fruits, from Zambia. Ibrahim had built many madrasas and mosques in Zambia. His sons, Abu and Yusuf, knew Masood from their days in the Binoria mosque. They convinced Ibrahim to invite Masood and Khalil to Zambia. For Ibrahim, already a motivated man, hosting jihad warriors and maulanas from Binoria mosque was indeed a great honour and religious gratification.

Masood told his interrogators that Zambia had a significant Muslim population from India and Pakistan, who were affiliated with Tablighi Jamaat but not interested in armed jihad. In Zambia, he delivered religious lectures in several mosques and house majlis (gatherings). Impressed with his command over the holy scriptures, attendees donated vast amounts to HuM. In June 1992, he visited Zambia a second time, accompanied by Tahir Hamid, a Pakistani national, who was also the sub-editor of *Sada-i-Mujahid*. On his second visit, Lambert hosted Masood, who once again successfully raised enormous funds for HuM.

The UAE and Saudi Arabia

Once again, in 1990, during Ramzan, Masood visited the UAE with Maulana Farooq of HuM for fundraising. Maulvi Ghazi Marzan, a bureaucrat attached to Hizb-e-Islami's commander, an Afghan minister himself, arranged for his visa. However, their success was much below expectations because of the UAE's strict rules about donations. Masood also tried to get funds from Saudi Arabia by contacting Jamiat-ul-Islah (Ikhwan), an ally of Jamaat-i-Islami (JI).[16] JI of the Pakistan-administered Kashmir, led by Maulana Abdur Rasheed Turabi, was receiving funds from Jamiat-ul-Islah (Ikhwan). However, Masood's requests were turned down because HuM owed allegiance to JuI, the Deobandi political party of Pakistan. When Jamiat-ul-Islah refused, Masood approached Jamiat Amal Khairia, an organization the Sheikh of Sharjah (UAE) started to counter Jamiat-ul-Islah (Ikhwan). However, he failed to get any help because Amal Khairia refused any grant for Kashmir. After all, the UAE had good relations with India. They put the condition that the donation would be used for welfare work for widows and orphans, not for any jihadist agenda in Kashmir.

Sharing his insights about West Asia's Islamist movements, Masood told his interrogators, 'I may state that parties like Tablighi Jamaat, Jamaat-e-Islami are basically those organizations which believe in religious freedom and education to achieve a real Islamic rule in green countries.'[17] Further, with his nuanced understanding of the region, he said that Jamiat-ul-Islah was a splinter of Ikhwan-ul-Musalmeen, which first began its jihad against the secular rule of Anwar Sadat in Egypt because he had turned the nation into a 'European country', pushing Islam to the fringes. Reportedly, Ikhwan lost almost fifty to fifty-five jihadis in Lebanon and Libya. About ten years ago, they suffered massive reverses when their eldest leaders, Syed Qutub and Hassan-ul-bana, were executed. After that, Ikhwan-ul-Musalmeen changed its approach. Some members formed the Jamiat-ul-Islah and decentralized it. Now, Jamiat-ul-Islah is governed by Murshid-ul-Ikhwan in each country. They have devoted their resources to building mosques, madrasas and Islamic education centres.

Masood's interaction with foreign jihadists during his Binoria mosque days laid the foundations of his interest in global Islamic movements. Later, this interest was further strengthened by his foreign visits. Over time, he developed a keen understanding of Islamic organizations, and the movements in West Asia and North Africa, such as Ikhwan-ul-Musalmeen and Jamiat-ul-Islah. His testimony to the interrogators reveals that he knew the internal fault lines of West Asia's Islamic politics. As per his statements, organizations like Jamiat Amal Khairia (Sharjah) and Rabtar-e-Islamia (Saudi Arabia) were formed to counter the influence of Ikhwan, which was a threat to Arab monarchies. These kingdoms were alarmed because Ikhwan, with its egalitarian approach and religious passion, had become a powerful organization collecting enormous funds for jihad in Bosnia, Somalia and other theatres. Further, he said that the Arab nations did not give donations for Kashmir jihad because they had good relations with India.

The UK

On 6 August 1993, Masood visited the UK.[18] He stayed there for forty days and delivered forty lectures. There, he was received by Mufti Ismail, a British Muslim of Gujarati origin. Mufti Ismail had studied at Darul-Ifta-e-wal-Irshad, Nazimabad, in Karachi. Mufti Ismail was introduced to Masood Azhar by an HuM associate, Mufti Abdul Rahman, of the madrasa. He arranged for Masood's British visa with the help of Saudi businessman Khalid Suleiman, who had participated in the Afghan jihad and was a friend of Fazlur Rehman Khalil.[19] Mufti Ismail arranged Masood's stay and lectures in various mosques in the UK. His discussions with Muslim scholars were focused on jihad, its needs and the other related aspects.

He gave his first lecture at the Madina mosque in east London, speaking at length about jihad, which, as per *Sada-i-Mujahid*, moved the audience to tears. After a series of lectures in east London mosques, he moved to the north, giving lectures at Zakariya Mosque in Dewsbury, Madina Masjid in Batley, Jamia Masjid in Blackburn and Jamia Masjid in Burnley. His most remembered lecture was at Darul Uloom, Bury, UK's most important Deobandi seminary and school in Lancashire.[20] He addressed a group of students and teachers, stating that a substantial part of the Quran had been about 'killing for the sake of Allah',[21] and most of the Prophet's sayings were about the importance of jihad. In his lecture at Jamia Milia Islamia mosque at Plaistow, he discussed the 'divine promise of victory for those engaged in jihad'. His British trip proved critical in raising awareness about jihad among British Muslims, so much so that veteran journalist Innes Bowen has written that Masood Azhar was 'first to spread the seeds of modern jihadist militancy in Britain—and it was through South Asian mosques belonging to the Deobandi movement that he did it.'[22]

In the UK, Masood successfully raised an enormous amount of funds with the help of several Muslim scholars. The most prominent among them was Mufti Ismail, a British Muslim of Indian origin, who was engaged in building mosques in liberated parts of Albania and Mongolia. He invited Masood to Albania; however, Masood was hesitant as it was difficult for a Pakistani to get a visa. So, Mufti Ismail arranged a Portuguese passport for him in the name of Vali Adam Issa (a Gujarati Muslim settled in Portugal) through Hafiz Sahi, a cloth merchant of Dewsbury. Hafiz Sahi travelled to Karachi in January 1994 to deliver the Portuguese passport to Masood. Hafiz Sahi also helped him get a visa for India and Bangladesh on his Portuguese passport. Later, Masood used this passport to enter India. During his time in India, he carried that Portuguese passport using the cover of a Gujarati settled in Portugal as it would hardly raise any suspicions.

Kenya

In December 1993, Masood Azhar visited Nairobi to meet the leaders of Al-Ittihad Al-Islamiya, an AQ-linked terrorist group in Somalia, who had requested HuM leaders to provide weapons to them. The groundwork for his Nairobi visit was laid ten months previously when 400 UAE nationals along with militants from other countries were arrested in Peshawar. Due to international pressure, they were later released. However, the UAE refused to accept such citizens with terrorist links, so most of them went to Sudan, from where they moved to Somalia and joined Al-Ittihad Al-Islamiya. They stayed in touch with Masood Azhar and Fazlur Rehman Khalil through letters describing the plight of Muslims in Somalia. They also told them that the Pakistani soldiers working in UN missions in the region were posted in troubled areas where the majority of the population were

Muslims, and the Indians were posted in border areas with a non-Muslim majority. Mostly, Pakistani soldiers guarded American convoys, so Ittihad cadres faced a huge dilemma when they wanted to engage with American soldiers because if they fired, they would be killing fellow Muslim Pakistani soldiers. Masood was disturbed by this development. He vented out his anger in a series of articles in *Sada-i-Mujahid*, stating that Pakistanis were being used to protect 'American infidels' and kill mujahids of Al-Ittihad Al-Islamiya. After that, he was invited by the Peshawar group of militants to Nairobi to talk to Ittihad leaders. In his meeting with them at the Ambassador Hotel (Nairobi), they asked him to put pressure on the Pakistani government to demobilize the country's soldiers in Somalia. To that end, he returned two weeks later to Nairobi with a team of Pakistani journalists, including Mujibur-Rahman Shamsi of *Zindagi* and *Jung*, Altaf Hussain Qureshi of *Urdu Digest*, and Mustapha Sadiq of All Pakistan Newspaper Society. In Nairobi, they met the Arab leaders of Al-Ittihad Al-Islamiya and other members. After their return, they published several stories condemning Pakistan's role in Somalia.

Dhaka

By 1993, Masood had already become a globetrotter—collecting jihad funds and delivering lectures. His subsequent foreign visits were going to sow the seeds of his role in the Kashmir jihad for the next three decades. Between December 1992 and January 1993, he accompanied Khalil to the HuM office in Upper Domel, Muzaffarabad, in Pakistan-occupied Kashmir (PoK). In that visit, Masood organized public meetings in Bagh, Muzaffarabad, Mirpur, Rahim Yar Khan and Abbaspora in PoK to motivate the youth to join jihad in Kashmir and to meet the families of militants killed by Indian security forces. Sajjad Afghani, a

HuM militant commander, who knew Masood from his Yavar days, also joined in these visits. It was during this time that it was decided to send Sajjad to Kashmir as HuM commander; due to the heavy snow along the Line of Control (LoC),[23] he would travel via Bangladesh. Maulana Farooq, emir of HuM's Kashmir chapter, wanted Masood Azhar to accompany Sajjad to induct him in Kashmir and launch him as the new chief. Masood and Sajjad used Pakistani passports to enter Bangladesh. There, they were received by Maulvi Kalimullah, who knew Masood from his Binoria mosque days. Kalimullah ran Al-Madaris-un-Noorani in Mohammadpur in Dhaka. Kalimullah arranged their stay at Hotel Pritam, in Dhaka. From there, they travelled to Jessore, where they met Abdul Khaliq, who escorted Sajjad to the India–Bangladesh border and helped him cross with his trusted men. After that, Masood flew back to Karachi. Masood and HuM also wanted to extend their operations to Bosnia but could not find an entry.

HuJI Split and Masood Azhar's India Visit

Harkat-ul-Jihad Islami[24] was formed in 1980 when some young members of Deobandi groups Jamiat Ulema-i-Islam and Tablighi Jamaat went to Afghanistan to participate in the jihad against the Soviets. The prominent members who constituted the leadership of HuJI included Fazlur Rehman Khalil, Maulana Abdus Samad Sial, Irshad Ahmed, Maulana Masood Kashmiri and Qari Saifullah Akhtar. Over time, HuJI gained strength by recruiting members from the Binoria mosque in Karachi. In 1985, Irshad Ahmed and fifteen other HuJI commanders were killed in Sharana, Afghanistan.[25] After Irshad Ahmed's death, Qari Saifullah Akhtar was appointed as the chief emir. However, Fazlur Rehman Khalil did not accept his leadership, leading to differences between the two. In 1986, Khalil left HuJI and formed HuM, naming himself as its emir. Maulana Masood Kashmiri also defected to HuM; however, he left in 1990 and formed Jamaat-ul-Mujahideen (JuM).

After the end of the Soviet war, HuJI reoriented its focus on the Kashmir jihad against India. Its Kashmir operations began in 1991 with the formation of HuJI's J&K branch, HuJI 111, under Mohammad Ilyas Kashmiri.[26] It operated from Kotli and Muzaffarabad in PoK. By 1993, it had sent 300 jihadis to Kashmir from Saudi Arabia, Turkey and Afghanistan.[27] In 1991, HuJI also appointed Maulana Sadatullah as its emir. HuJI also received financial and logistical support from the ISI for its Kashmir operations. However, its chequered history of internal splits disappointed the ISI and many Deobandi maulanas, prompting them to work for the reunification of HuJI, HuM and the JuM. In October 1993, leading Deobandi ulemas like Maulana Kalimullah Khan, chancellor, Jamia Farooqi; Mufti Rafi Usmani, chancellor, Darul Uloom Karachi; and Mufti Rashid Ahmed, chancellor, Darul-Ifta-e-wal-Irshad, Karachi, initiated the dialogue between HuJI, HuM and JuM. They advised them to unite because the three had no ideological differences. They argued that the three groups were wasting resources in maintaining separate offices, finances, phones and vehicles. Also, it confused people and created a negative image of the Harkat movement. As a result, in November 1993, HuJI and HuM united, and rechristened the new organization as Harkat-ul-Ansar (HuA). In HuA, Maulana Sadatullah was made the emir and Khalil joined as deputy emir with the crucial portfolios of finance, administration and terrorist operations under him. Farooq Kashmiri was made second deputy emir with the critical charge of Kashmir affairs, Tajikistan operations and training activities under him.

By 1993, Masood had already made a name as a motivator, recruiter and fundraiser in the Harkat leadership, so he was given the powerful position of secretary general. As per his testimony, he was not given any official charter of duties; however, he was given a high-profile role because he frequently travelled abroad to collect funds. It was considered practical to project him as a powerful entity in HuA leadership to facilitate him in his fundraising campaigns abroad. After the unification of HuJI and HuM, messages were dispatched to commanders in Kashmir to merge the two groups, but no further communication came until January–February 1994. Therefore, differences between the Kashmir branches of the two groups continued. HuA leadership then decided to send Masood Azhar to Kashmir to resolve the differences, ascertain the ground situation and boost the morale of the militant cadres in the Valley.

On 26 January 1994, Masood boarded a Dhaka-bound flight from Karachi. From Dhaka, he flew to Delhi on a Biman Bangladeshi Airlines flight and reached Delhi on 29 January 1994. For his India journey, he used his Portuguese passport, which gave him the identity of Vali Adam Issa. In Pakistan, Mohammad Maqsood, a HuA worker, used his Karachi airport contacts to illegally affix an entry/arrival stamp on Masood Azhar's Portuguese passport. At Delhi airport, the immigration officer had some reservations about Masood's Portuguese nationality; however, he was convinced when Masood told him that he was born Gujarati. Gujarat is known for its mercantile and business community, travelling and settling down in foreign countries for business. In Delhi, he checked into Ashoka Hotel where Ashraf Dar, originally from Srinagar but staying in New Delhi to manage HuA militants' logistics, came to meet him with Abu Mohammad, emir of HuA in Doda (Jammu region). Then, Masood visited the Darul Uloom, Deoband, with Ashraf

Dar and Abu Mohammad in a Maruti car. They stayed at the seminary for a day, and left the next day, after prayers, to Gangoh and then to Saharanpur.

In Saharanpur, they spent the night in a Tablighi Jamaat mosque. In all these places, Masood did not reveal his true identity. His articles, speeches and books had already reached Deobandi circles worldwide—he, therefore, feared that if he showed his identity, people would easily recognize him, which could endanger his security. On 31 January, they returned to Delhi, where he checked into Janpath Hotel. Two days later, Ashraf Dar informed him that his flight to Kashmir was scheduled for 9 February. During the second leg of his Delhi stay, he met Farooq, Mehmood and Qari Abu Ubeda, Kashmiri militants who were getting their medical treatment in the capital city. All of them were from Punjab (in Pakistan) and stayed in Hotel Usman opposite Jamia mosque. In those days, it was a common practice for Pakistani militants to visit Delhi for medical treatment; however, they were cautious about keeping the identity of their doctors discreet.

On 6 and 7 February, Masood travelled to Lucknow by bus to meet Maulana Hassan Nadwi, aka Ali Mian, India's eminent Islamic scholar who shared Maulana Abul A'la al-Maududi's (the founder of JI and one of the most prominent thinkers on political Islam) vision of an Islamic state. The scholar was not present when Masood arrived; so Masood could only meet Maulana Salman, Ali Mian's student, who later became the dean at Darul Uloom Nadwatul Ulama Madrasa in Lucknow. Masood wanted to meet Maulana Manzoor Numani as well, but could not meet him either. In his Lucknow meetings too, Masood did not reveal his identity. The same day, he returned to Delhi and stayed at Hotel Sheesh Mahal in Karol Bagh. It is evident Masood didn't check into the same hotel twice in a bid to shake off anyone who might be on his tail. On 8 February, he visited the Tablighi Jamaat centre in the Nizamuddin area and he bought twelve compasses to give to militants in the Valley.

On 9 February, he travelled to Srinagar and Ashraf Dar received him there. The two never met again. Sajjad Afghani visited him in the evening at Darul Uloom Qasimiya in the Lal Bazaar area of Srinagar, with his deputy, Amjad Bilal, who was armed. The meeting focused on discussions about the merger of HuJI and HuM. The next day, Masood, along with Sajjad Afghani and Amjad, reached Matigund village, where some nineteen Pakistani militants arrived to meet them. They were all encouraged by the merger of HuJI and HuM and the arrival of Masood Azhar. Masood and Sajjad then left for Anantnag with Farooq, a HuA section commander. After his return from Anantnag, Masood was to meet the leaders of the All Party Hurriyat Conference (APHC), a conglomerate of all the separatist parties in Kashmir. However, destiny had something else in store for him.

Their car broke down due to technical problems, so they hired an autorickshaw to Anantnag. Indian security forces stopped them for a random check. But Farooq panicked, opened fire and escaped. The police promptly arrested Masood and Sajjad Afghani at Khanabal near Anantnag district.

Masood's Jail Life

After his arrest, it took the authorities some time to ascertain his real identity for he was carrying a Portuguese passport. He was interrogated several times by the IB, R&AW and the J&K state police. Later, after five Western backpackers were kidnapped in Kashmir by Al Faran (a splinter group of the HuA) in a bid to release Masood, the FBI also interrogated him. In his interrogations, he displayed a mild and cooperative demeanour.

He gave the impression of a religious scholar and an intellectual. With his long experience in journalism, he was smooth in his interviews with the media too; however, he was not comfortable giving interviews to female journalists. He did not look into their eyes because it was deemed un-Islamic.[28]

Chanchal Singh,[29] the jail superintendent at Kot Bhalwal Jail at the time of Masood's release, said that he was treated like an ordinary terrorist. He was kept in a different cell, separate from HM terrorist Mushtaq Zargar and another Jaish militant Omar Saed Sheikh,[30] his aides, who were also released with him. However, some officers suggest he was addressed as 'Azhar sahab' in the jail.[31] Mostly, the jail staff say, he prayed in his cell and distributed small amulets (taweez) to jail inmates. Sometimes, visitors came to him for spiritual healing—looking for relief in their medical and family issues. It is believed that Masood began sermonizing in jail, and radicalized some of his fellow inmates.[32]

Avinash Mohananey,[33] former ID official, who interrogated Masood, revealed that his initial confessions were about how Deobandi clerics inspired him. He said that Masood was very communicative and forthcoming in sharing knowledge about Pakistan's jihadi groups and their networks, including how they recruited terrorists, their training and the ISI's role.[34] However, he feigned ignorance about Omar Saed Sheikh, who had already led a failed attempt, along with Ilyas Kashmiri, to get Masood released by kidnapping three British and one American national from Delhi in October 1994. Delhi Police arrested Omar Saed Sheikh while Ilyas Kashmiri escaped, becoming one of the most lethal terrorists, masterminding Musharraf's assassination plot later. Omar Saed Sheikh's growing importance and popularity disturbed Masood's inflated ego. Mohananey says Masood feigned ignorance about Omar Saed Sheikh because he might not have actually known him. However, he might have also done it because of his expertise in the tradecraft of terrorism. He shared many generic things about the jihadi landscape but cleverly hid what mattered. During my own field research in Kashmir, I interviewed many militants and OGWs, presently or formerly associated with terrorist groups. I found it a common tendency among them to be liberal in sharing generic information about jihadi organizations' clandestine worlds, which may impress a person who is not an insider. However, they never shared anything substantial about operational details.

Masood was highly disappointed with his organization in Pakistan for providing him with a misleading picture of the ground realities in Kashmir that led to his arrest. He also severely criticized the returning mujahids, called 'ghazis' (victors) in Pakistan, for narrating all kinds of false stories of how Kashmir was on the verge of freedom, and the Indian forces were demoralized and on the back foot. In his interrogations, he said, 'I had imagined an Afghanistan-like situation, where mujahideen groups created a liberated belt, and one could travel to and from Pakistan without much difficulty. On the contrary, I found mujahideens on the continuous run, avoiding security forces.'

Mohananey also said that Masood was aware and boastful about his importance. He apparently claimed that when he landed at Heathrow Airport in London, a massive crowd of followers came to see him, resulting in a two-hour traffic jam. Masood further said that he was too important for Pakistan and that India would not be able to keep him in prison for long. Masood knew that his ability to infuse a highly radical and violent jihadi fervour in Kashmir made him indispensable to the ISI. His ego was hurt when Al Faran, during the second kidnapping attempt (July 1995), demanded the release of HuJI chief Nasrullah Manzoor Langaryal, along with him, in exchange for four foreign nationals. He felt it eroded his stature and importance as Nasrallah was a mere 'foot soldier, a person of low intellect', in his view.[35]

Masood was unfit for a combat role ever since the beginning of his career as a mujahideen. Masood travelled by plane into India using a Portuguese passport because he could not cross into Kashmir from the snowy and mountainous LoC on foot. His physique stopped him from running away and therefore, he was arrested in Anantnag. Initially, after his arrest, Sajjad Afghani told the police that they had nothing to do with each other. However, Masood, not used to handling physical torture, gave away the identity of his colleague in thirty minutes—right after an army soldier slapped him. He allegedly said, 'My father had never slapped me, but for the first time, an army jawan did so even before asking me any question.' Their relations remained strained the entire time they were jailed together because Masood had revealed Sajjad's identity to the Indian Army.

Later, in 1999, another bid was made to release him. Masood's aides dug a tunnel to help him escape, but he got stuck halfway through. Sajjad Afghani died in that escape bid. After he got stuck in the tunnel, Masood had to be dragged back by jail guards who mocked him for his physique, saying that these commando-style operations were not for him. Jail guards allegedly told him that he should dig more tunnels to lose weight.[36] Masood replied, 'I don't need to dig tunnels because, very soon, one day, you will escort me out of these gates with respect.'[37] Among Indian intelligence circles, Masood is still known as 'Mota' (fat).

An insight into Masood's future plans comes from his interactions with Charles Sobhraj,[38] a serial killer who was in Tihar Jail until 1997. For some time, Masood was shifted to Tihar in 1996, where he reportedly became friends with Sobhraj, and the latter claims that he taught Masood English. Masood apparently shared his plans to attack Mumbai, India's

Parliament and major power plants with him. Sobhraj further claims that after the IC-814 hijack, he contacted Masood's organization in Pakistan, and they assured him that they would not harm the passengers for eleven days. Later, he was allegedly asked by the IB to negotiate the release of IC-814 with Masood, which he declined because he knew Masood would disagree. However, it is challenging to verify Sobhraj's claims and, given his criminal record of lying, it is highly likely that such claims are not valid.

Attempts to Rescue Masood Azhar

Masood Azhar was an indispensable ISI asset because he could motivate, indoctrinate and radicalize young Muslims to take up arms for the cause of jihad. According to R.V. Raju, founder of the National Investigation Agency (NIA), India's premier counterterrorism agency, 'Azhar is a strategic asset for Pakistan's ISI. They can afford to get any number of militants killed, but they need someone who can motivate the young to pick up guns to kill or die. They are cannon fodder. He is an ideologue. That's the difference.'[39]

Interestingly, Azhar knew about his importance to the ISI. He told his interrogators, 'You people will not be able to keep me in custody for long. You don't know how important I am to Pakistan and the ISI. You are underestimating my popularity. The ISI would ensure that I am back in Pakistan.'[40] ISI considered Masood Azhar indispensable to sustain jihad in Kashmir in the long term. The Kashmiri temperament is nurtured on Sufi ideals; hence, it is relatively moderate and unsuited to the extremist version of Islam propagated by Deobandi terror groups. Such a pacifist nature is not agreeable to nurturing a long-term terrorism project. The only way to do that is to transform it into an Islamic jihad at large and, for that, extremist motivators like Masood were crucial. Hence, he had to be rescued.

The first attempt was in the summer of 1994 when a HuA district commander abducted two British citizens, Kim Housego and producer David Mackie. However, they were released after Housego's father, a British ex-journalist based in New Delhi, organized a public campaign. In October 1994, Omar Saed Sheikh and Illyas Kashmiri kidnapped three Britons and one American from Delhi. However, they were soon caught and Omar Saed Sheikh was arrested, while Ilyas Kashmiri escaped. Later, much after his release in the IC-814 saga, Omar Saed Sheikh was arrested and convicted for murdering journalist Daniel Pearl, and Ilyas Kashmiri died in a US drone strike in June 2011.[41]

In July 1995, Al Faran kidnapped six foreign nationals—two Americans, two Britons, a German and a Norwegian. In exchange, they demanded the release of Masood Azhar, Sajjad Afghani, Nasrallah Manzoor Langaryal and eighteen other terrorists.[42]

In 1999, Sajjad Afghani orchestrated a jailbreak in Kot Bhalwal Jail, Jammu, by getting his and Masood's aides to dig a tunnel. Masood could not escape because of his poor physique and Sajjad Afghani died trying to make his way out.

Finally, on 24 December 1999, IC-814, a Delhi-bound Indian airliner from Kathmandu, was hijacked by five armed militants of HuM. In the interim, HuA had changed its name to HuM because the US had designated it as a terrorist organization in 1997. The plane was carrying 155 passengers, including the five hijackers and eleven crew members.[43] In exchange for releasing the prisoners, Masood Azhar, Omar Saed Sheikh and Mushtaq Zargar aka 'Latram'—a Kashmiri militant who ran the Al Umar

Mujahideen terror group and had become close to Masood Azhar in prison—were released.

An Asset to Pakistan

After his release, and soon after he set up JeM, the group was declared a foreign terrorist organization by the US. In 2010, the US Treasury Department added his name and the JeM proxy, Al Rahmat Trust, to the Specially Designated National list.[44,45]

Nevertheless, Masood Azhar continues to be an important asset for Pakistan. Islamabad, with China's support, tried its best to block India's proposals in the UN to declare Masood a global terrorist. Over the last ten years, China blocked the proposal to declare him a global terrorist under UNSC resolution 1267, which sanctions global terrorists and terror groups, in 2016, 2017 and in March 2019.[46] Finally, in May 2019, China relented and withdrew its technical hold,[47] after which he was designated a global terrorist by the UNSC 1267 Sanctions Committee.[48]

A Scholar and an Intellectual

The last and the most crucial aspect of Masood's personality is that he remained an intellectual, an ideologue and a man of letters. In the HuM hierarchy, he was known as a profound scholar, extraordinary orator, charismatic motivator and organizer par excellence. In 1989, when HuM opened offices in various cities across Pakistan, including Lahore, Gujranwala, Islamabad and Hyderabad, and commenced a recruitment drive, Masood showed his impressive oratory skills in motivating and indoctrinating young minds to join HuM.[49] He has been a prolific writer, publishing articles in the JeM media outlet *Al Qalam* under the pen name[50] of 'Saadi'. Masood Azhar has written about two dozen books; his seminal work is *Fatah-ul-Jawaad*, a two-volume book[51] dealing with the Quranic concept of jihad. It clearly reflects his obsession with jihad, which will be discussed in the next section. He also authored *Fazail-i-Jihad* (Virtues of Jihad), and *Kamil*—an 850-page commentary on a medieval Islamic work, *Mashāri'al-Ashwāqil'a-Maṣari'al-'Ushshāq* by Ibn Nahhas, student of Ibn Taimiyah, a thirteenth-century extremist Islamic scholar who inspired Muhammad Ibn-Abdul Wahhab, whose revivalist thoughts form the foundations of modern political Islam.[52] His other books[53] include:

1) *Yahūd kī Cālīs bīmāryān* ('Forty Diseases of the Jews'). Middle East Media Research Institute (MEMRI) noted that it may be one of the most anti-Semitic books in the Urdu language.
2) *Muskurāte Zakhm*. Political autobiography.
3) *Khuṭbāt-i-jihād*. It contains Islamic sermons on the eminence of jihad according to the teachings of Islam.
4) *Rang o Nūr*. Collected columns chiefly on jihad and criticizing the Pakistani government for following United States policies.
5) *Jamāl-i-Jamīl*. On the life of Muhammad Jamil Khan, 1953–2004, a noted religious scholar.
6) *Zād-i-Mujāhid: mamaktūbāt-i-khādim*. On the eminence, views, and interpretation of jihad.
7) *7 Din Raushnī ke jazīre par*. A seven-day comprehensive course on Islamic teachings.
8) *Tuḥfah-yi-Sa'ādat* (Gift of Virture)
9) *Ma'arka* (The Struggle).

Jaish-e-Mohammed: Ideology and Objectives

Having explored the enigma of Masood Azhar, the next logical step in unravelling the secretive world of JeM can be understanding its ideology and objectives. The group subscribes to Deobandi Islam. Deobandi groups in Pakistan are committed to establishing a Shariah-governed society. They believe in Khatme Nabuwwat, and adopt a very harsh view against Shias and Ahmadiyyas. As far as generic Deobandi beliefs are concerned, JeM agrees with the larger Deobandi ecosystem. However, the outfit makes some detours and prefers a sharp focus customized to its India-centric operations, particularly in Kashmir. Besides, Masood Azhar and his family remain the central force behind JeM. Masood's ideological obsessions and goals play a critical role in shaping JeM's ideology and objectives.

JeM's political and religious objective is freeing Kashmir from India's control, acceding it to Pakistan and establishing a Shariah rule there. Masood Azhar nurtures a pathological hatred against India, which is deeply rooted in his understanding of Deobandi ideology. Precisely a month after his release, he announced the formation of JeM on 31 January 2000, in Karachi outside the Falal mosque. Addressing a massive gathering of 10,000 armed men, he said:

> I have come here because it is my duty to tell you that Muslims should not rest in peace until we have destroyed America and India. Kashmir has to be liberated from Indian rule. Soldiers of Islam have come from twelve countries to free Kashmir. Our organization has nothing to do with politics. We fight for religion and do not believe in the concept of nations. We want Islam to rule the world ... The ISI tries to use our reputation for its own ends. But its motives

are *siyasi* (political), while ours are purely *mazhabi* (religious) … wherever Muslims need our help, we will be there.[54]

Praveen Swami, India's eminent expert on terrorist groups, told me that Masood's early writings show the influence of Maulana Maududi's thoughts on political Islam. In one of his writings, he discusses how the graves of jihadis has a fragrance to them—a belief which one also finds in bin Laden's mentor and Salafi thought leader Abdullah Azam's writings. He defined JeM in the following words, 'JeM is an international Islamic movement created at this time on the principles of Shariah. The movement brings with it an end to wickedness and an invitation of complete obedience to the Shariah … the motto of this movement, in easy words, is jihad against the infidels and struggle against infidelity to faith.'[55]

JeM's first base, Balakot, was chosen because of its glorious history in the ideological tradition of jihad in South Asia.[56] Syed Ahmad Barelwi and fellow commander-scholar Shah Ismail, and their band of military adventurers, died in Balakot fighting jihad against the Sikh army of Maharaja Ranjit Singh.[57] Barelwi was a true disciple of Shah Waliullah, a revivalist and puritanical Islamic scholar of the 1730s. Shah Waliullah shared some teachers with Abdul Wahab. Syed Ahmad Barelwi had set up an office in Patna modelled on the Islamic Caliphate. He decried Hindu and Sufi influences in Islam, and argued that jihad is like heavenly rain that can bring salvation to Muslims. He called his journey from Bareilly to Balakot 'Hijrat' (Prophet's journey from Mecca to Medina). The shrines of Barelwi and Shah Ismail are held in great reverence by all the modern jihadist organizations—particularly the Deobandis. Initially, the camp was set up in 1995 by Saifur Rahman Saifi,[58] a HuA terrorist from Punjab. As discussed above, Masood was also once a general secretary of HuA. In 2000, Saifi joined JeM and Masood asked him to convert it to a JeM camp.

Masood's Karachi speech reveals that religion is primary in his mission. For him, politics is secondary—nation-states are anti-Islamic, and America and India are the worst enemies because they symbolize infidel religions, i.e., Christianity and Hinduism. During my field research, while interviewing JeM militants and OGWs, they categorically stated that Israel is also their worst enemy, and the trio of India, Israel and the US represents the axis of sin that deserves to be conquered and subjected to Shariah-based rule.

In India's case, it merits mention that amongst the various extremist strains of Islam in Pakistan and, to a large extent, in the entire subcontinent, Deobandis have a much stronger social, demographic, political and cultural presence as compared to Wahhabis or Salafis. Only two states in India follow Wahhabism—one is Kerala, since a large population from the state forms the diaspora in the Arab world where they are exposed to this version of Islam. The other is Kashmir, where it has emerged very strongly over the last two decades.[59] However, Deobandis have a much stronger presence in north India. Barelwi/Sufi Muslims see them as the prominent rival sect due to ideological differences. The Deobandi movement emerged after the downfall of the Mughal empire. In Delhi, Shah Waliullah[60] represented the revivalist trend in the 1730s. He stated that Muslim decline had come because many Hindu influences had defiled Islam. Hence, he strongly advocated keeping distance from Hindus and was a votary of completely ridding Islam of Hindu influences. For Deobandi extremists, since the movement has its origin and history in the crisis that followed the decline of the Mughals—perceived by Muslim aristocracy and clergy as their loss of political power due to the penetration of Hindu influences—Hindus, the largest non-Muslim group in South Asia, are the greatest enemies of Islam, and are kafirs. This situation is significantly different for the Salafi/Wahhabi extremists of West Asia, for whom the Jewish community occupy that place because of a different historical experience.

In the case of JeM, there are some additional peculiarities. Due to its strong links with pan-Islamism, global jihad theatres like Shia Iran, Ahmadiyyas, Jewish Israel and America significantly matter as its targets as well. In addition to its baggage of Deobandi history, JeM nurtures intense hatred for India due to its focus on Kashmir. In India too, due to the organization's Deobandi roots, its ambitions are not confined to Kashmir alone. After reaching Delhi, the first place Masood visited was Deoband in UP, which speaks volumes of his reverence for the historic Deobandi sites, figures and symbols. After that, he visited Lucknow and Ayodhya. In Lucknow, he planned to meet prominent Deobandi revivalists and puritanical scholars like Maulana Nadwi. Since he was not there, he met his disciple, Salman Nadvi. Salman Nadwi became a prominent Deobandi leader who recognized ISIS chief Abu Bakr al-Baghdadi's caliphate.[61] In 2014, he wrote a letter to the Saudi government promising 5,00,000 Indian Sunni youth to become part of the global Islamic army to 'fight Shias and infidels'. Further, Salman Nadwi suggested that terrorists were committed to a noble cause, so they should not be called terrorists and all jihadi organizations should form a global confederation to become a powerful force.

After Lucknow, Masood visited Ayodhya. Pained to see the ruins of Babri mosque, Masood observed, 'I remember the day I was standing there. In front of me lay the Babri Masjid in ruins. Angrily, I was stamping the ground, squashing the Indian soil with my shoes and saying, "O Babri Masjid, we are ashamed, O

Babri Masjid, we are sorry . . . you were a sign of our glorious past, and we will not rest till we restore you to your former glory."'[62] Later, these lines became a central theme in all his speeches, helping recruit and indoctrinate the Harkat cadre. The recorded tapes of these speeches were sold in Lahore, Rawalpindi and other cities in Pakistan. His emotional outburst on the Babri mosque demolition makes it amply evident that for JeM, the battle is for Islam, the jihad is against all the infidels, and Kashmir's independence or accession to Pakistan is primarily a religious issue. Its political dimension is secondary. Kashmir's cause is important because it is a religious war to liberate the Muslim subjects of Kashmir from 'Hindu India'.

Some scholars,[63] former intelligence officials and journalists[64] suggest that had it not been for the Babri mosque demolition, Masood would not have turned his focus to India. They go on to the extent of arguing that he was content with his role as the editor of *Sada-i-Mujahid* and would never have become a terrorist. Their views are either based on short interviews or the abridged and edited interrogations reports of India's intelligence agencies. As regards India's intelligence officials, most of them join the services on deputation from the Indian Police Service, a general police service that recruits officers for law-and-order enforcement and other wings of the police department. Intelligence postings are not the preferred ones. Those who fail their field postings or need to be marginalized are sent to intelligence agencies. Only a tiny segment join the intelligence services out of genuine passion, expertise and interest. As a result, a large majority lacks the interest and in-depth understanding of Islamic terrorist groups and extremist groups. A superficial knowledge of this phenomenon becomes a stumbling block in interrogating high-profile and intellectual global terrorists like Masood Azhar.

On the other side, Masood Azhar, even at the young age of twenty-five when he was arrested, was a mature and widely travelled mujahideen fighter and a profound scholar of pan-Islamist/jihadist ideologies with a vast knowledge of geopolitics and Islamist movements. He was also well trained in the nuances of his clandestine tradecraft, amply evident from the fact that he kept his identity secret during his visits to Deoband and Lucknow. Being a journalist and a global jihadi, he knew the importance of constructing a favourable narrative that could paint India as an oppressor and evoke the sympathies of terrorist groups fighting against 'Indian atrocities'. He knew how to manipulate and tell stories to interrogators and journalists. Also, he might likely have carefully crafted these answers, knowing full well that Pakistan would rescue him soon, and his interviews with Indian journalists and interrogators would continue to be quoted and studied for decades to come.

Factually speaking, HuJI and HuM's Kashmir operations started in 1991, a year before the Babri mosque incident. After the US and Soviet withdrawal, the veterans of the Afghan jihad wanted a new theatre, and Kashmir offered a suitable opportunity. It was a part of ISI's strategy to send FTGs and cadres to Kashmir to induce more violence and radicalize the Valley on Islamist lines. Even if the Babri mosque demolition had not taken place, those operations would have gone on unabated. Also, when Masood was sent to India (in 1994), the purpose was to resolve the disputes between the Harkat factions, motivate the cadres and intensify the militancy. The Babri mosque demolition does not figure anywhere as the primary reason for his visit. He had already been on fundraising and jihadist missions to the UK, Kenya, Saudi Arabia, UAE and Africa. HuM had links with the pan-Islamist AQ, so it was just a matter of time for them to train their guns on Kashmir—it was not a question of ideology. The

Babri mosque incident might have pained Masood individually and, at best, given him an excuse to recruit more militants. However, to say that it triggered him to become a terrorist or start Kashmir operations is a fallacious argument without substantial evidence.

More evidence of JeM's pan-India ambitions comes from its attack patterns. Right after its formation, the organization executed a fidayeen attack on India's Parliament in the national capital city of Delhi. Interestingly, there is not much concrete evidence to conclude that ISI sanctioned this attack, despite its proven role in the IC-814 hijack and facilitating Masood to form JeM. Hypothetically, if, without ISI's sanction, the outfit attacked India's capital city, it speaks volumes of its pan-India ambitions, going beyond ISI's control. Besides, it has conducted many suicide missions beyond Kashmir, mainly in the Jammu region and in Pathankot, Punjab. More recently, in July 2021, JeM's front organization, Lashkar-i-Mustapha's (LeM) commander Hidaytullah Malik, procured weapons from Bihar for carrying out attacks in Jammu.[65] LeM's coordinator and weapon supplier was arrested from Bihar's Chapra district, clearly suggesting the group's linkages beyond Kashmir.

Masood's writings also give insights into JeM's ideology and objectives. The Quranic concept of jihad, Masood's most critical obsession and single-minded focus, has been discussed at length in his three crucial books, i.e., *Ma'arka*, *Fazail-i-Jihad* and *Tuhfah-yi sa'adat*.[66] In *Fazail-i-Jihad*, he praises those who die in Allah's way. He drew inspiration for jihad from Syed Ahmad Barelwi's jihad against the Sikhs and later against the British in the early nineteenth century (1824–62).

Masood's jihadi literature talks at length about the grievances faced by Muslims. The history of jihad in South Asia holds great importance for him. He draws parallels between the persecution of Muslims under British rule and the US domination after the end of the Cold War. Further, he suggests that the global geopolitical developments over the last 200 years have been unkind to Muslims. He laments Israel's rule in Palestine, Indian rule in Kashmir, the Russian conquest of Chechnya and the subjugation of the Muslim population of Manila by the Catholic state. For him, these theatres are religious theatres where Muslims are fighting a jihad against the non-Muslims. He blames the lack of superior military power for their defeat. To address this power imbalance, he offers the solution in his third book, *Tuḥfah-yisa'ādat*, that 'every Muslim must turn to God'. In his 'struggle', he motivates young Muslims to join the jihad against the West and India by citing examples of earlier Muslim conquests over non-believers. He gives the example of the Battle of Badr (623 CE), in which the Prophet and his 313 followers defeated thousands of soldiers of Arabia's pagan tribes.

He is staunchly against Western culture and secularism. His seminal work *Fatah-ul-Jawaad* emphasized the need to fight all colonial powers, and concepts like capitalism and secularism. Also, he suggested that jihad is the duty of every individual Muslim, for which they do not need to get permission from the state. In *Fazail-i-Jihad*, he argues that puritanical Islam faces challenges from the overpowering Western secular culture in the same manner as Islam faced challenges from non-believers in its early days in the seventh century CE. He suggests that Muslims should identify the 'detractors' and enemies of Islam, and fight them in the same way as Prophet Mohammed and his companions fought 1,400 years ago. He discards the changes over the last 1,400 years with a highly revivalist and anti-evolutionary outlook. He has great reverence for Osama bin Laden because of their shared beliefs and Laden's financial contribution to jihad from his inherited wealth. Offering the same theological argument for his fight in Kashmir, which bin Laden stated for his struggle against the US—that the Americans defiled Muslim holy lands—Masood said that the infidels of India cannot rule Muslims in Kashmir. India's military presence is an attack on Muslim sovereignty.

Further, he argued that submission and slavery damage Islam as a faith; hence, sovereignty is an existential issue for Muslims. According to Masood, if Islam is firmly rooted in society and politics—i.e., forming its core—only then the damage done by 'submission and slavery' can be undone. The ultimate quest is for political power to bring back an extremist and puritanical form of Islam, for which the ends justify the means. Hence, there are no moral compunctions about killing innocent non-Muslim civilians, be it in Kashmir or in the World Trade Center.

Masood's focus on jihad is so clear that he never engaged in Takfir (condemning other Muslims as non-Muslims; hence liable to be killed) and confrontation with the state, lest it lead to division in Muslim ranks on sectarian grounds. However, as per Ayesha Siddiqa's research,[67] he did provide men for Musharraf's assassination plot, after which he never got involved in any confrontation with the state. He stayed away from the Lal Masjid episode. Masood refused to raise the issue of un-Islamic practices like drugs and prostitution as it would detract him from his mission of freeing Muslims from the rule of non-Muslims. His passion for jihad even led him to confront a powerful army general in a private meeting[68] when the latter spoke of withdrawing support for the terrorist groups in the wake of Musharraf's decision to support US's GWoT in Afghanistan. His unwavering determination for jihad and its corollary, Ghazwa-i-Hind—the Prophet's prophesy of the reconquest of India by Muslims—makes him an immensely popular and motivating figure among Deobandis. He is seen as someone who has the charisma and gravity to be a central figure and attract followers towards his mission with blind zeal. JeM's values and ideals are shared by a large segment of Pakistan's intelligence and military set-up, giving this alliance ideological strength and a strong foundation.

Exploring Masood's focus on jihad, Ayesha Siddiqa, an expert on JeM, writes:[69]

> JeM's jihad will not end until the entire world converts to Islam. It has focused on developing, among its members, a deeper understanding of an Islamic war, which is why its initial training sessions focus on proselytizing about jihad. Unlike in the past, when jihadi groups randomly picked up people and sent them for military training, Jaish has improvised on the method. Candidates have to go through rigorous ideological training before they are selected for military training and then combat.

Further, she says that JeM primarily recruits from madrasas; however, it also finds mujahideens in government schools. JeM spends about US $10,000 to prepare a trained and committed jihadi.

Masood's fervour for jihad was not merely a dull intellectual exercise. He nurtured an emotional passion bordering on obsession for jihad, which made him much more than an ordinary cleric. His unrestrained passion made him the perfect motivator for young recruits. Describing his meeting with Kashmir's local and foreign terrorists at a remote village in Anantnag (70 km from Srinagar), he wrote:

> About 25 armed mujahideen were gathered at a small house in the village. They greeted us warmly, and soon a religious

discourse began. The young men's chests were decorated with magazines, and within them burned the flame of courage and bravery. All of them were listening to me intently, and their AK-47s lay cradled in their laps like children in their mother's care. Some of them also had carbines and rocket launchers that they must have seized from the army. I picked up a Kalashnikov and, after feeling the weapon in my hands, found that it was ready to talk to the mushrikeen (enemy). The bullet was in the chamber, and it was ready to fire, and I felt ecstatic at the thought of enemy soldiers falling ... my joy knew no bounds as I held the loaded gun in my hands.[70]

Fatah-ul-Jawaad

Though Masood prefers to be addressed as 'maulana', a religious scholar, he was primarily a motivator and a commander who knew how to make the best use of religious discourses to justify armed struggle and terrorist activities. His exposure to mujahideens fighting in Afghanistan and their conditions made him contemplate the need for jihad. The visit to Afghanistan became a revolutionary episode in his life, igniting jihad's fire in him. He became so obsessed with the idea that he made it his routine to go to other maktabs, masjids, and streets and bazaars of Karachi to persuade people to choose a life of jihad through meetings, discussions and speeches. So much so that on holidays, he did not take rest; instead, he would tour other cities like Hyderabad, Sukkur, Khipro and Nawabshah, and ignite the fire of jihad in the hearts of the people.[71] This also inspired Masood's decision to become a journalist. Masood Azhar's biographer Professor Rashid writes:[72]

> At last, the stage came when every moment of his life was spent in Jihad. Therefore, he sacrificed everything at the altar

of Jihad. In order to communicate the message of Jihad to every Muslim, he considered it essential to take up the field of journalism, i.e., print media ... He himself tried to witness the oppressions and cruelties exercised by the Kuffar upon the Muslim Ummah and resolved to bring the actual facts before the world through the medium of Journalism.

Even during his captivity in Indian jails in Anantnag, Tihar, Kot Bhalwal, Budgam and Srinagar, he delivered lectures on Quranic traditions and jihad to his fellow inmates. He is said to have memorized the Quran in a month during his jail period in India. His deep contemplation of jihad and its international applicability during this time further strengthened his commitment to the cause. Professor Rashid continues:[73]

... Hence, no sooner did he get release than he began to conduct training and teaching programs of Jihad verses and washed the layers of dust spread by the false forces, uprooted the new deceptive terms of infidelity and changed the direction of Satanic propaganda with the help of his books and hence he removed the doubts of his own people as well as the foreigners ... that is why; some people call him the 'Revivalist of Jihad'. The authentic Ulama and Jurisconsult of Ummah trust and support him. It is also an admitted fact that the Muslim who listens to his address attentively with a receptive mind or studies his books cannot help feeling inclined to Jihad.

His passion for jihad found an outlet in several booklets, articles and books.[74] However, its most explicit and in-depth expression can be found in his pivotal work *Fatah-ul-Jawaad*. In this, he has provided a detailed description and analysis of all the

Quranic verses about jihad in Surah Al-Baqarah, Surah Al-Imran, Surah Al-Nisa, and Surah Al-Maidah. He also discusses those verses that give clues and symbolic references to jihad. Professor Rashid, who translated his book into English says, 'Hazrat Maulana Muhammad Masood Azhar, since his adolescence, has been thinking of jihad, waging jihad, speaking jihad, writing about jihad and conducting training programs about the jihad verses whether it is day or night, dawn or dusk, journey or stay, captivity or release, fatherland or foreign land.'[75] According to him, *Fatah-ul-Jawaad* has the unique distinction of being the only separate exegesis on jihad verses in the last 1,400 hundred years of Islamic history.

Scrutiny of the work also reveals a lot about the psychological aspects of the text. Though the text discusses jihad as a religious idea, the hidden intent is to explore it as a doctrine of war, strategy and tactics. It reads like a war manual that sees through the enemy's conspiracies, and suggests preventive measures and a response mechanism. Further, it imparts mental, spiritual and emotional training, giving its readers a deep-rooted sense of passion and persuasion for jihad.

Masood Azhar's Quotes about Jihad from *Fatah-ul-Jawaad*

1) Masood's explanation of verse no. 109 of Surah Al-Baqarah, Madiniyah, quoted from the English translation of *Fatah-ul-Jawaad* by Professor Rashid:[76]

    (i) Allah Almighty is cautioning and warning the Muslims that the people of the Scripture (the Jews and the Christians) are always busy in making efforts to apostatize you (Muslims). They are your open and hidden enemies. They do so out of envy.

(ii) At present, Muslims should observe patience, strengthen their relation with Allah through Salat and Zakat, and strengthen their organization with the help of these acts of worship.

(iii) The cure for those who conspire against Islam and the Muslims is going to be revealed in the form of jihad in the way of Allah. In the way of Allah, jihad is a law that brings peace worldwide.

(iv) The Muslims should not worry due to their weakness and the power of the enemy. When the command for jihad is revealed, and the Muslims act upon it, they will not be lonely. Allah is All-Powerful to assist and make them prevail upon the enemy.

(v) Jihad is Allah's dictate.

b) It means the people of Allah in the past carried out jihad against their enemies in the company of their prophets. They were not discouraged or weakened by the troubles and difficult circumstances they faced in jihad, but they stood firm in jihad with perseverance: O Muslims! Show greater courage and perseverance in jihad than they do.

c) No one knows the fixed time of death except Allah. Then why is there so great a fear and hesitation from taking part in war? Death will come when Allah will. It cannot come without Allah's will, however hard the dangers confronting. If we realize these facts, the actual fear of death will not exceed reasonable limits.

Masood uses the Prophet's battles, such as the battle of Uhud, as historical references to motivate, teach strategy and tactics, and project armed jihad as a quintessential element of Islam.

JeM and LeT: A Comparison in Ideological Domains

LeT follows the hard-line Ahl-i-Hadith brand of Islam, which is also against the worship of Sufi saints and Prophets. It is ideologically closer to Deobandis than to Barelwis; however, in Pakistan, Deobandi terrorist groups have serious differences with LeT in ideological and operational matters. Mushtaq (name changed), a former LeT militant jailed in Kashmir for killing a policeman, told me on the condition of anonymity that Deobandi terrorist groups are ideologically more radical and extremist. They are so extreme that they do not consider LeT cadres as sufficiently Muslim. They are willing to take on the Pakistani state, the ISI and the Pakistani armed forces if they perceive them to be going against Islam.

On the other hand, LeT is most loyal and would never revolt against the Pakistani state. Further, explaining the strong ties between the Pakistan Army and LeT, Mushtaq said that in jihadist circles, LeT cadres are sarcastically referred to as Pakistan Army soldiers without uniforms. Though LeT follows the hard-line Wahhabi brand, it never advocates violence inside Pakistan against Shias and other minorities as it functions well within the grip of ISI. Christine Fair also confirms Mushtaq's assessment of LeT refraining from violence inside Pakistan.[77] She writes that LeT is a peaceful organization within the country that maintains absolute loyalty to the state and supports the current economic, political and social order. Unlike Deobandi groups, they do not support Takfiri—branding Pakistanis (mostly Shias and Ahmadiyyas, followed by Barelwis) as non-Muslims and killing them.[78] LeT believes in converting them through social and humanitarian work. Deobandi groups like TTP and LeJ have a close affinity to the Islamic State, whereas LeT calls itself an ideological competitor to the Islamic State. In the case of Deobandi groups, it can be observed that they have strong support from Deobandi clerics, and political and religious leaders. In contrast, most of the Ahl-i-Hadith clerics dislike LeT because they believe that only an Islami Riyasat—i.e., an Islamic state—can wage jihad, and not a non-state actor like LeT.[79] For LeT, ISI and its strategic and tactical directives matter more than the institutional support from the Ahl-i-Hadith clerics.

Unlike LeT, Deobandi terrorist groups have a robust historical presence in Pakistan's cultural, social, political and religious space; hence, they are not entirely dependent on ISI. Deobandi terrorist groups, such as the Harkat movement, have a strong following in the Pakistani Army. Most of their cadres come from Tablighi Jamaat, headquartered in Raiwind. Former DG ISI, Lt Gen. Nasir was from Tablighi Jamaat.[80] Their solid grassroots presence, following and ideological fervour can enable them to challenge the state, which they have repeatedly done when they perceived the country as going against the Islamic cause. Also, their links with pan-Islamist groups[81] operating in the Af-Pak region (Taliban, AQ, TTP, ISK), Philippines (Abu Sayyaf), Uzbekistan, Chechnya, Egypt, Bosnia, Somalia, Kenya and other global jihadist theatres lend them distinct ideological extremism.

In September 1995, a group of forty army officers and ten civilians led by Major General Zahir-ul-Islam Abbasi was arrested for plotting to kill PM Benazir Bhutto and senior army officers to establish an Islamic state. This group was linked to HuM.[82] In 1999–2000, Deobandi groups like JeM and HuM staunchly opposed the India–Pakistan peacebuilding process that began under the Indian Prime Minister, Atal Bihari Vajpayee, and his counterpart, Nawaz Sharif. Masood Azhar addressed Vajpayee as 'Abu Jahil' (ignorant) and vowed to kill him.[83] HuM leader Fazlur Rehman Khalil warned that more bodies of Indian officials would be sent in coffins from Kashmir on the days that Vajpayee visited Lahore to meet Nawaz Sharif.[84] He also observed that

Islam's rivalry with India was ideological and not merely territorial. In 2003, Brigade 313, a cluster of Deobandi terrorist groups, attempted to kill Musharraf with AQ's support (this is discussed in detail in the next chapter). In 2007, Deobandi terrorist groups staged a 'coup' at Lal Masjid, Islamabad, against which Musharraf ordered military action. After the 2016 Pathankot attack, Masood Azhar warned the Pakistani state that any action against JeM would have severe consequences for Pakistan's security, integrity, unity and peace.[85] After the Pulwama fidayeen attack, JeM wanted India and Pakistan to engage in a full-fledged war so that it could infiltrate an army of its cadres into India.[86]

JeM's Pan-Islamist Ambitions and Links to Transnational Terrorist Groups

Though focused on Kashmir jihad, JeM is essentially motivated by an international pan-Islamic agenda that goes far beyond the liberation of Jammu and Kashmir. This agenda is evident in its statements, posters and calendars that have pictures of burning American effigies.[87] After 9/11, JeM, in a joint statement with Al Badr, another terrorist group with a strong presence in the Af-Pak border region, stated, 'American repression and imperialism is a challenge for the entire Muslim world ... linking Osama with the attacks in the US is part of a plan to pave the way for the US's sinister plans to strike against Afghanistan.'[88]

JeM's media mouthpiece, *Zarb-i-Mumin*, has published write-ups denouncing Zionists, America and other alleged oppressors of Muslims like the Pakistani government for supporting the US-led GWoT. In April 2003, it wrote, 'the real war has just started ... After Palestine and Afghanistan, now Iraq will also give birth to holy warriors who will free me from the clutches of the Jews.'[89] Masood Azhar himself has stated on various occasions that 'no Muslim can rest in peace until Israel and America are annihilated and stated the need for Muslim military power from Chechnya to the Philippines'.[90]

JeM's fountainhead, the Pakistan Deobandi Harkat movement's first theatre of jihad, was in Afghanistan against the Soviets, which imparted an international character to it. In Afghanistan, the Harkat movement had strong ties with Al Qaeda. HuM had mujahideens from various parts of the world. Before his arrest in India, Masood's vast international travel also helped him develop a concrete pan-Islamist vision.

JeM has helped recruit Muslim converts and Pakistanis living in the West, often linking them with Al Qaeda. Masood lectured in prominent Deobandi mosques during his UK visit, giving detailed and passionate discourses on jihad, its requirements and the training. Interestingly, Omar Saed Sheikh, who kidnapped foreign nationals in Delhi to get Masood released, was a British national. Omar's family was known to Masood Azhar.[91] After finishing his training in Afghanistan, Masood asked Omar to join him on his India visit; however, he could not because of his dual citizenship.[92]

He was arrested after the foiled kidnapping attempt (discussed previously) and later released with Masood Azhar after the 1999 plane hijack episode. Omar was a close aide of Masood Azhar. He was also reported to have transferred US $100,000 to AQ's Muhammad Atta, the World Trade Center bomber.[93] Due to his AQ connections, and close association with Masood and ISI, he is known as an ISI asset in AQ in some intelligence quarters.[94] Muhammad Bilal, from Birmingham in the UK, was one of the earliest fidayeens of JeM who blew himself up outside the army cantonment in Srinagar in 2000.[95] Masood also provided training and logistical support to British Muslims who wanted to organize terrorist attacks in the UK.

Rashid Rauf, who was reportedly involved in many UK-based terror attacks—like 7/7, 21/7 and the 2006 attempt to smuggle liquid bombs on transatlantic airlines—was married into Masood Azhar's family in Pakistan.[96] During a police interrogation, Rashid Rauf confessed that he arrived in Bahawalpur in 2002, where he met a JeM operative, Amjad Farooqi.[97] After training at Bahawalpur and building ties with AQ, he went to Afghanistan with Amjad Farooqi in mid-2002.[98]

The alleged perpetrator of the July 2005 London bombings, Shehzad Tanvir, visited Pakistan in 2003 and met Osama Nazir, a JeM militant who was reportedly involved in a 2002 church bombing in Islamabad, in which two Americans died.[99] Reportedly, the Australian Muslim convert Shane Kent attended an orientation session organized by JeM at a mujahideen camp near the China border in 2001.[100] Shane was arrested by the police in Melbourne in 2005 and accused of hatching a conspiracy to organize 'violent jihad' in Australia. In August 2004, the US Bureau of Immigration and Customs Enforcement (ICE) deported a Colorado resident, Sajjad Nassar, to Pakistan.[101] Nassar had become enraged after his brother was killed fighting against the US forces in Afghanistan. He had attended a JeM training camp in 2001 during his visit to Pakistan, facilitated by his childhood friend, who had become a JeM recruiter. He received training in rocket launchers, shooting from a pick-up bed and paramilitary tactics. However, he was frustrated with the overload of physical exercises and he quit. Later, the grand jury in the US found Sajjad guilty of immigration fraud and deception as he tried to hide his terrorist links in the polygraph tests.[102]

In May 2009, the FBI unearthed a suspected plot in New York to bomb a Jewish synagogue and Jewish community centre, and shoot stinger missiles at US military planes.[103] Among the four individuals arrested, James Cromite told the FBI that he was upset with the killing of Muslims by the US forces in Afghanistan and Pakistan, and he wanted to join JeM to die as a jihadi.

Aimen Dean,[104] a former AQ member with proximity to bin Laden who was later recruited by the British intelligence, said that before 9/11, the global Deobandi network, including British Deobandis and groups like HuM, supported 'Taliban to the hilt', and even after 9/11, many British Deobandi mosques were adamantly supporting the outfit. British Deobandi extremists like Khaled Muhammad enjoyed close ties with Deobandi terrorist groups like HuM and SSP. During his UK tour, Khaled Muhammad shared a dais on many occasions with SSP's paramount leader, Azam Tariq.[105] Notably, Azam Tariq in turn was also a close associate of Masood Azhar.

Understanding more about JeM's pan-Islamist agenda requires delving deeper into the Harkat movement's links with Al Qaeda.

Pakistan's Harkat Movement and Its Links with AQ

Before 9/11, AQ had a strong presence in Pakistan's urban and rural areas. Pakistan's Harkat movement, comprising a cluster of Deobandi militant outfits—HuM, HuJI, HuA and JeM—provided crucial support to AQ in many ways. The first point of interface began with the Afghan jihad. The battlefields of southeastern Afghanistan were critical to the operational development of Harkat groups and AQ.

HuJI, formed in 1979, had close ties with an Afghan mujahideen party, Harkat-ul-Inqalab Islami, led by Mohammed Nabi Mohammadi;[106] specifically, the outfit had ties to Arsalan Khan Rehmani, a commander of the party.[107] Fazlur Rehman Khalil, who later founded HuM in 1985, had close ties with Jalaluddin Haqqani, a mujahideen commander in the anti-Soviet war and the founder of the Haqqani network, and Maulvi Yunus Khalis, the mujahideen commander of the Hizb-e-Islami during the anti-Soviet war in Afghanistan, and a personal friend of Osama bin Laden.[108] HuM began its jihadist activities under the operational and ideological mentorship of Jalaluddin Haqqani.[109] AQ was formed in 1987; however, a significant chunk of its military commanders had fought under Jalaluddin Haqqani before 1987.[110] Operational collaboration between Haqqani, HuM and small Arab fighting groups was explicitly evident in a twelve-hour-long attack led by Haqqani in March 1988 in Khost province (Afghanistan) on a military outpost defended by the Afghan forces.[111] Haqqani was joined by Egyptian, Saudi and Pakistani fighters. The majority of Pakistani fighters were from HuM. HuM cadres fought with Afghan mujahideens and AQ in the final battle for Khost and Gardez (1991).[112] In the 1990s, AQ and HuM developed robust links with the Taliban, and supported it in operational and tactical matters against its main rival, the Ahmed Shah Masood-led Northern Alliance (NA). In 1999–2000, out of the 113 prisoners of the Taliban interviewed by Jamestown Foundation's terrorism expert Julie Sirrs, 92 per cent were Pakistanis, and the overwhelming majority of them belonged to Harkat groups.[113] Harkat cadres' participation in Taliban battlefronts is also substantiated by the fact that a large number of its cadres died in Taliban battles. Pakistani journalist Imtiaz Gul, who has extensive experience of reporting on terrorist groups, states, 'HuJI lost as many as 340, HuM lost 79, JeM, 36, and LeJ (Laskhar-e-Jhangvi) 27 in the coalition attacks.'[114] An internal document of AQ, cited by US's Combating Terrorism Center's terrorism expert Anne Stenersen also gives insights into Harkat groups' cooperation with AQ in operational, logistical and tactical matters.[115] The document details AQ commander Abd-al-Hadi al-Iraqi's plan to withdraw

Arab fighters from Qal'ah-ye Murad Beg near Kabul and put up a joint front with HuJI cadres at Bagram.

After the withdrawal of Soviet troops in the late 1980s, Harkat groups mainly focused on Kashmir; however, they had a decent extra-regional presence. HuM and HuJI operatives were involved in global theatres of jihad beyond South Asia, such as Bosnia, the Philippines, Chechnya and Tajikistan, and the recruitment and training of foreign jihadists from around the globe, including Westerners.[116] HuJI had commanders for Myanmar and Uzbekistan. In the 1990s, HuM cadres travelled to south Philippines as preachers. They trained the recruits of Abu Sayyaf and Moro Islamic Liberation Front and joined terrorist operations against Filipino SFs.[117] HuM had also hosted Filipino jihadists in Afghanistan. HuM was present at the signing of bin Laden's 'Khost Fatwa of Jihad against Jews and Crusaders' (1998), represented by Fazlur Rehman Khalil.[118] In a parallel development, AQ was also expanding its global footprint and relationships in many of the theatres mentioned above. Though not much substantial evidence is available, strategic and tactical solidarity between AQ and Harkat groups in foreign theatres is highly likely to have taken place. The first concrete evidence of AQ's operational, ideological links with HuM and JeM emerged in August 1998 after the US cruise missile attacks on two AQ camps in Afghanistan—Khalid bin Waleed and Muawiya—in retaliation for the bombings at the US embassies in Kenya and Tanzania.[119] Among the terrorists killed, twenty-one were found to be affiliated with HuM and LeT.

Masood Azhar's Africa Visits and AQ Linkages

Masood Azhar's African engagements and visits suggest deeper links with AQ in African jihad theatres. Interestingly, his Somalia visit happened at the same time when AQ deputed its stalwarts like Saif al-Adl, Abu Hafs al-Masri and Saif al-Islam to Somalia to find safe havens and train local jihadi cadres.[120] Though there is no concrete evidence, the UN report testifying the presence of Afghan and Pakistani advisers with Osama bin Laden at Ali Jihad Base gives ample clues of the cooperation between AQ and Harkat cadres in Somalia. The interrogation reports of Masood Azhar in Indian jails and his diaries tell us that he visited Kenya (1993) on the instructions of Fazlur Rehman Khalil to meet Al-Ittihad Al-Islamiya. HuA, on the requests of Somalis, supported them with men and money.[121] Also, the interrogations suggested that Masood was linked to Yemen-based AQ terrorist Tariq Nasir Fadhli, a suspect in the December 1992 hotel bombings in Yemen that targeted US Marines travelling to Somalia.[122] Ahmed Rashid, a terrorism expert, claims that Masood imparted tactical weapons training to Somalian jihadists; however, given his expertise in oratory and intellectual work, he might have supervised and facilitated tactical weapons training by HuM cadres.

Several sources, though speculative and vague in authenticity, suggest that in the early 1990s, Masood Azhar's relationship and interaction with AQ was far more profound and had objectives extending beyond synergizing their efforts in Afghanistan and Pakistan. Masood Azhar had great admiration and respect for Osama bin Laden. In his 802-pages manual, *Fazail-i-Jihad*, he expressed his gratitude for bin Laden, calling him the, '*Jihad ke sholo ko dobara bhadkanewala* (one who reignited the fire of jihad)' and an inspiration to liberate Islam from the clutches of the morally decadent, secular culture of the West.[123] Muhammad Amir Rana, Pakistan's terrorism expert, talks about two secret meetings between Masood Azhar and bin Laden in 1994 in Kenya and Masjid-e-Nabwi (Prophet's Mosque) in Saudi Arabia.[124] Mariam A. Zahab and Olivier Roy, French political scientists writing on terrorism issues with a keen eye on South Asia, also discuss the 'unsubstantiated rumour about Masood following Laden in Sudan'.[125] My cross-verification from Indian intelligence sources suggested that these meetings discussed the agenda of bringing the HuA cadre directly under the ambit of the AQ network and hierarchy.[126] However, such claims still lack substantial evidence and need further exploration.

Harkat Groups' Global Memberships and Terrorist Operations

Harkat groups' pan-Islamist linkages and extra-regional ambitions also become evident from its cadre profiles and terrorist operations conducted against Western targets. According to Masood's interrogation report (IR), Binoria town mosque, Karachi, served as a critical centre for recruitment in HuM and HuJI. It had a sizable contingent of international Deobandi students from the Arab world, Sudan, Bangladesh, Somalia, Central Asia and the Balkans, who readily joined Harkat groups. For example, as per HuJI's documents, before 2004, at least 650 of its fighters 'were killed in battle against the Indian army: 190 belonged to both sides of Kashmir, nearly 200 belonged to Punjab, 49 to Sindh, 29 to Balochistan, 70 to Afghanistan, 5 to Turkey, and 49 collectively to Uzbekistan, Bangladesh, and the Arab world'.[127] Masood's December 1991 article in *Sada-i-Mujahid*, discussing his Afghanistan visit with his French accomplices, mentioned Umar Farooq as the chief of HuM's French contingent.[128]

A US declassified cable (1995)[129] revealing information about the transnational linkages of HuA mentioned that the organization, though focused on Kashmir, has a mission of 'permanent jihad' in all those places where Muslims were facing persecution. HuA had anywhere between 2,000 and 10,000 members, mostly war veterans from Afghanistan. It had Afghan veterans from Algeria, Tunisia, Sudan, Egypt and Saudi Arabia, besides Afghans and Pakistanis, who constituted the largest segment. HuA had a presence in Burma, Chechnya, the Philippines, Bosnia, Afghanistan and Kashmir. The declassified cable also mentions the presence of ten to sixteen American Muslims as its members, who were following a Pakistani peer (religious authority). Most of the HuA cadres were from Tablighi Jamaat. TJ's global Deobandi network provided ample funding to HuA. UK-based Gujarati Deobandi Muslims constituted the largest donor group.

Omar Saed Sheikh's journey[130] into jihad also offers insights into the Harkat groups' international outreach. Omar Saed Sheikh, a British national, who was arrested after a failed kidnapping attempt in Delhi–Ghaziabad to get Masood released, joined jihad in Bosnia after finishing his university education in the UK. In Bosnia, a Pakistani HuM terrorist, Abdul Rauf, invited him for training in Pakistan.[131] He also suggested Omar get in touch with Deobandi Maulvi Ismail, imam of the Clifton Mosque in north London, to convince his father to allow him to join jihad. Rauf wrote a recommendation letter for him.[132] With his recommendation letter, he reached Miran Shah (Pakistan) and arrived at the AQ training camp at Khalid bin Waleed camp (between Khost and Zhawar Kili) in late 1993. Many of his instructors were from the Pakistan army's elite Special Security Guards.[133] In HuA's failed Delhi kidnapping attempt of three British nationals and one American tourist,[134] Omar was assisted by Ilyas Kashmiri. Ilyas Kashmiri[135] escaped, led HuJI, and functioned as a key connect between AQ and Harkat groups. Omar was released along with Masood Azhar in 1999 and reportedly played a crucial role in raising JeM as an organization in its formative years. Later, after his arrest in the Daniel Pearl murder case, he said in an interview that before his death in November 2001, AQ leader Abu Hafs al-Masri gave him PKR 1 million for a confidential project.[136]

In another terrorist operation targeting Westerners, six tourists were kidnapped in Kashmir in July 1995 by HuA's splinter group, Al Faran. After the US bombings of AQ facilities in retaliation for the outfit's attack on US embassies in Africa (1998), HuM cadres killed an Italian army officer[137] working with the UN. In HuA's hijacking of IC-814 to get Masood released, one of the main hijackers, along with Ibrahim Athar[138] Masood's brother, was Amjad Farooqi,[139] who later served as the 'lynchpin of [the] AQ network in Pakistan'.[140] According to bin Laden's Yemeni bodyguard, Nasir-al-Bahri, the IC-814 hijacking was orchestrated by bin Laden because he admired Masood and wanted him freed as he needed his help.[141]

As mentioned earlier in this section, Masood's UK trip played a crucial role in sowing the seeds of jihad in Britain. JeM's first suicide bomber, Asif Sadiq, aka Muhammad Bilal, was a British national from Birmingham who blew himself up outside the military cantonment in Srinagar. Later, many other British Muslims of Pakistani origin volunteered for suicide missions. Mohammed Siddique Khan, a key figure in the AQ's 7/7 UK attacks, who died in a suicide bombing mission, was trained at a HuM training camp in Afghanistan.[142] Likewise, Tanzanian AQ operative Khalfan Hamis Mohamed, who was involved in the US embassy bombings (1998), learned bomb-making techniques in a HuA training camp in the early 1990s.[143]

Cooperation in Media Management, Ideological Nexus and the Indian Parliament Attack

Harkat groups and their leaders also helped AQ in its public relations work and spreading its jihadist message to the global community. Harkat leaders like Fazlur Rehman Khalil and Maulana Allah Wasaya Qasim,[144] a HuA leader, facilitated Pakistani journalist Hamid Mir's interview with bin Laden in 1997. Harkat cadres and leaders escorted Pakistani journalists across the border in North Waziristan to Khost to attend his press conference in 1998, in which he announced the 'World Islamic Front against Zionists and Crusaders'.[145] HuM and HuJI members were also present at the press conference as organizers and audience.[146] In the US retaliatory bombings after the AQ attacks on the US embassies in Kenya and Tanzania, along with the AQ camps, two HuM camps were also destroyed, in which five ISI agents and about twenty-one HuM militants were killed.[147] Fazlur Rehman Khalil's statement after the US missile attacks carried the distinct imprint of AQ's 1998 fatwa. He said, 'The US has struck us with Tomahawk Cruise missiles at only two places, but we will hit back at them everywhere in the world, wherever we find them. We have started a holy war against the US and they will hardly find a tree to take shelter beneath.'[148] From the statement and the events that followed in the coming years, it appears that Harkat leaders were providing background support to AQ, which also included safe havens and shelters to its cadres after the US invasion of Afghanistan after 9/11.

AQ–Harkat links also exist in the ideological domain. Nizamuddin Shamzai, the Chancellor of Binoria town madrasa, which is regarded as the 'ideological headquarters of the Deobandi extremist movements',[149] provided crucial ideological support to Bin Laden's outfit, agenda and vision. However, after the murder of Shamzai in 2004,[150] these ties declined. Binoria town madrasa has also provided leadership, cadres and the ideological foundation for the Harkat movement. Prominent Harkat stalwarts[151] who graduated from Binoria town madrasa or were affiliated with it include the two founders of HuJI—Maulana Irshad Ahmed and Maulana Abdus Samad Sial; former leader of HuJI—Qari Saifullah Akhtar; the founder of HuM—Maulana Fazlur Rehman Khalil; the founder and leader of JeM—Masood Azhar; the founder of Karachi-based terrorist group Al-Rashid Trust[152]—Maulana Mufti Rasheed Ahmad Ludhianvi[153] and the late leader of AQIS, Asim Umar.[154]

Reportedly, bin Laden met with Taliban chief Mullah Omar under the 'benign gaze of Chancellor Shamzai'.[155] Some sources suggest that bin Laden also used Binoria town madrasa as his base in Karachi for some time.[156] Shamzai endorsed his 1996 and 1998 war fatwas against the Americans and Zionists.[157] In 1999, Shamzai issued a fatwa that mirrored the AQ agenda by validating the murder of Americans. It said 'the shedding of American blood' was permissible because 'Washington was in a "state of war" with Muslims'.[158] Shamzai's language was quite similar to AQ's 1996 and 1998 fatwas.[159]

The chancellor also played mediator in a conflict between Mullah Omar and bin Laden. He had tremendous credibility because he was a highly respected figure in the Taliban hierarchy for he was Mullah Omar's spiritual mentor and advisor.[160] Moreover, Shamzai had excellent standing and trust among the other Deobandi extremist groups such as Al Rashid Trust and Jamiat-e-Ulema Islam. These groups were Taliban's staunch political allies in Pakistan and supported them against their arch-rival, the Northern Alliance.[161] Ayman Al Zawahiri also mentioned in his interviews that Shamzai was bin Laden's friend and advisor.[162] As per Zawahiri's version, Shamzai visited bin Laden in Afghanistan, and had long discussions with him on jihad and how the Western nations were controlling the sea, land and airways, and were dictating terms to the Islamic world. Osama bin Laden's lecture so moved Shamzai that he gave the same lecture to his followers and friends after returning to Karachi. He also attended Osama bin Laden's son's wedding[163] in Kandahar before 9/11. Though on some issues like the 9/11 attacks, Shamzai disagreed with bin Laden, as he said that such attacks led to the killing of innocent people,[164] but on the broader issues of jihad, there always was a strong consensus between the two. For example, after the US invasion of Afghanistan (2001), Shamzai issued a fatwa sanctioning defensive jihad against America.[165] Likewise, after the US invasion of Iraq (2003), Shamzai and other scholars of Binoria town released a joint press statement stating that all Muslims of the world needed to wage jihad against the American forces.[166] After the Pakistan Army's action against the Lal Masjid a radical Deobandi centre, Osama bin Laden gave a call to armed jihad against Musharraf, citing Shamzai's fatwa against Musharraf for siding with the infidels.

JeM's attack on the Indian Parliament in December 2000 led to a minimal number of casualties—twelve—but its timing, target and repercussions make it a highly strategic attack. It coincided with the US's 'hammer operations' against AQ fighters. Musharraf had switched sides to support the US in its War on Terror against the Taliban and AQ. Squeezed between the American forces on the west and Pakistani forces on the east, AQ was staging its last-ditch resistance[167] in the Tora Bora mountain range. Washington wanted the Pakistanis to detain or kill AQ fighters fleeing to Pakistan after being pushed by its 'hammer operations'. However, the Indians considered the attack on its Parliament an act of war by Islamabad—as a result of which New Delhi deployed a massive number of troops on the border, which looked like the 'largest military mobilization in Indian history',[168] bringing the two countries on the verge of war. In return, Pakistan also deployed 70,000 troops and massive equipment on the border.[169] The Americans wanted Pakistan to focus entirely on detaining and killing AQ fighters fleeing into its territory. Still, the Indian mobilization distracted Pakistan's efforts, leading to the shifting of a major chunk of its forces to the eastern border.

Though there is no concrete evidence to prove that the Parliament attack was deliberately orchestrated to divert Pakistan's attention by creating a war-like situation to alleviate pressure on AQ and provide them space to flee, the attack undoubtedly did just that. Given the JeM's deep ties with ISI, it raises many questions about who planned the attack. Was there a small, radical Deobandi segment in the Pakistan Army/ISI that disagreed with Musharraf's official policy of supporting Americans and wanted to help AQ, or was it done entirely by JeM to help AQ without the ISI knowing about it? A third possibility is that the Pakistan Army was not sincere in its commitment to the Americans and intended to help AQ, but wanted to come out looking clean. To do that, they might have secretly agreed to the Parliament attack and feigned ignorance in public and to the Americans, knowing full well that India would react in a limited manner as Pakistan is a nuclear-armed state. India's massive mobilization was bound to look like a genuine reason to divert its troops. Given the way Pakistan helped the Taliban covertly over the last twenty years, finally resulting in the ouster of the Americans and bringing it back into power in 2021, this third possibility cannot be denied.

Thus, despite the lack of sufficient data to prove that AQ and Harkat groups have a well-structured and systematic relationship, it can be concluded that both had deep-rooted, broad-based and robust ideological and operational ties before 9/11 and the period immediately after 9/11 (between the late 1990s–2002). Given that Harkat groups received strong support from Pakistan, it raises questions about Islamabad's support—was it an active participant or a mute spectator to AQ's activities and expansion? The people who played an important role in this relationship from the Harkat side are Masood Azhar, Maulana Fazlul Rehman Khalil, Qari Saifullah Akhtar, Ilyas Kashmiri, Maulana Allah Wasaya Qasim and Omar Saed Sheikh, as well as others. Then there were those who coordinated Al Qaeda's interactions with these groups, including Abd al-Hadi al-Iraqi, Khaled Sheikh Mohammad and Abu Zubaydah. Before 9/11, HuM and HuA were at the forefront; however, after 1999, JeM and Masood Azhar were the leading Harkat allies of AQ.

It is difficult to precisely know the nature of cooperation and the potential issues of competition and friction between the groups since there was a lot of overlap in activities and the areas of operation; however, it can be argued with a considerable degree of certainty that AQ's pan-Islamist vision and agenda had a profound impact on Harkat groups and their leaders' thinking, including JeM and Masood Azhar.

JeM and Other TTGs: Taliban, Tehreek-e-Taliban Pakistan, IS-KP and the Haqqanis

In the Af-Pak region, an array of terrorist groups has flourished, including AQ, Taliban, Harkat groups, Tehreek-e-Taliban Pakistan, Haqqani Network, LeT and, most recently, Islamic State–Khorasan Province. Most of these groups have a parallel existence, constituting a 'combine' or a kind of 'terrorist ecosystem,' with many overlaps and synergies in operational and ideological domains, and a vast range of informal linkages, occasionally beefed up with formal ties. Also, the intergroup dynamics have not always been about cooperation. There have been instances and phases of friction and tensions over ideological and operational matters—for example, Osama bin Laden and Mullah Omar had disputes that Shamzai mediated. Likewise, JeM and LeT had differences as LeT has remained under the firm grip of ISI and has never supported violence inside Pakistan. In contrast, JeM cadres plotted to kill Musharraf and also assisted the Lal Masjid terrorists. Moreover, JeM has maintained strong ties with Sunni extremist groups like SSP and LeJ, which have indulged in bloody violence against Shias inside Pakistan. Even intragroup tensions saw spillover effects on the other groups of this terrorist ecosystem. When Musharraf decided to support the US War on Terror, a significant number of JeM cadres left the organization and, later, these dissidents joined TTP (2007). Likewise, when the Pakistan Army launched harsh operations against TTP after its involvement in the Peshawar army school attack (2014), many of its cadres defected to ISIS-K, now known as IS-KP. Some others entered negotiations with the Pakistani government, and were given the choice of rehabilitation into JeM and commencing terrorist activities in the Kashmir jihad front.[170]

Having discussed its ties with AQ, JeM's ties with other groups merit a brief mention. JeM and Taliban share a long history, subscribing to the same Deobandi ideology. Binoria town mosque has been critical to both Taliban and Harkat groups in their operational and ideological evolution. Chancellor Shamzai was a spiritual guide and a mentor to Mullah Omar. Along with bin Laden, Mullah Omar helped Masood Azhar with men and money to form JeM. HuM terrorists took the hijacked IC-814 plane to Kandahar, where they had a supportive and protective umbrella of the Taliban government. After the plane carrying

Masood reached Kandahar, escorted by Indian minister Jaswant Singh, Masood's description of his journey makes his admiration for the Taliban and immense respect for Mullah Omar amply clear.[171]

> ... The runway flashed by, and I was a mixture of emotions ... The plane was racing towards the airport building, and the sight of the beautiful faces of the thousands of Taliban armed guards was adding joy to my heart ... The land where the plane touched down, everything belonging to it was intensely dear to me. Mullah Omar, the person whose deep love filled my heart, lived here in Kandahar. He, whose presence is a true blessing for the Muslims, had made Islam proud. When I was in prison, I desperately yearned to behold this city and kiss the hand of Mullah Omar ... As soon as my feet touched the ground, my heart was transformed ... Taliban officials greeted us at the foot of the stairs. A storm of emotions washed over me, and tears welled in my eyes ... I couldn't help thinking of one thing: the day my hands had been tied behind my back, and I had been pushed into a truck was a Friday. Today was a Friday, too. Both my hands were free, and I was sitting in a Taliban car heading towards freedom.

Following his release, Masood met Taliban leaders, seeking their support in forming JeM. When Musharraf decided to support the American-led GWoT against the Taliban in Afghanistan, Masood was very upset, though he remained loyal to ISI. However, the organization split into two entities—Khuddam-ul-Islam (KuL), headed by Masood, and Jamaat-ul-Furqan (JuF), led by Abdul Jabbar.[172] Pakistani authorities arrested Jabbar for his alleged role in the Musharraf assassination plot; however, he was released in December 2003. Both KuL and JuF were banned in that year. In 2008, JeM decided to shift its focus to Afghanistan to strengthen the Taliban's fight against the US-led coalition forces.[173]

On 13–14 April 2020, Afghan forces raided a Taliban camp in Mahmund Dara in Nangarhar province in eastern Afghanistan, resulting in a gunfight that cost the lives of four soldiers of the Afghan forces.[174] However, out of the fifteen militants killed, ten were from JeM, who were being trained to fight in Kashmir. Reportedly, the outfit was running three camps in Nangarhar, along with four Taliban camps.[175] The camps were Khogyani I, Khogyani II and Dargah camp in Nangarhar province, which Taliban had lent them in return for the Haqqani network's cadre being trained in JeM's camps in Pakistan. Indian intelligence reports[176] also indicated that Wali Azhar, son of Mufti Abdul Rauf Azgar,[177] Masood's brother and the de facto head of JeM, was undergoing training in these camps. In total, the outfit trained 400 militants in these camps set up after the February 2020 deal reached between the US and the Taliban.[178] Former Afghan war veteran and HuM leader Mufti Asghar Kashmiri was heading these camps, and his deputy at these camps was the JeM's Kashmir infiltration specialist Abdullah aka Asadullah. According to the UN Sanctions Monitoring Team's mid-2020 report,[179] 6,500 Pakistani terrorists from LeT, JeM, and other terrorist groups like TTP, Lashkar-i-Islam, Lashkar-e-Jhangvi, Jamaat-ul-Ahrar and Al Badr, were fighting alongside the Taliban against the US forces. The report stated that JeM and LeT were the main groups bringing foreign fighters to Afghanistan.

After the Pulwama fidayeen attack, Pakistan was facing intense FATF pressure to act against terror groups. JeM and LeT started sending hundreds of its fighters from 2019 onwards to Afghanistan—perhaps under the ISI's direction, to evade the FATF scrutiny, which was focused more on their Kashmir operations.[180] Most LeT and JeM fighters were concentrated in Kunar and Nangarhar in eastern Afghanistan, and Helmand in south eastern Afghanistan. All these provinces share borders with Pakistan. Besides, Pakistani terrorists were also present in Ghazni, Khost, Logar, Paktia and Paktika provinces in south and southeast Afghanistan. In field operations, JeM and LeT cadres were deployed in groups of 200, with five to eight suicide bombers in each group. Mullah Muhammad Yakub, Mullah Omar's son, worked closely with JeM and LeT, and appointed their commanders as advisers and administrators in many areas.[181] Taliban's return led to the release of many JeM cadres imprisoned in Afghanistan jails.[182] JeM celebrated the Taliban victory, writing in its publication that 'Taliban victory in Afghanistan will inspire mujahideen to continue their struggle for Islam'.[183] Most recently, after the Taliban returned to power, Masood Azhar met Taliban leader Abdul Ghani Baradar in Kandahar in the third week of August 2021 and asked him to support JeM operations in Kashmir.[184] In my interview with Rahul (name changed upon request), a Kashmir-based intelligence operative working on JeM–Taliban linkages, he said that according to the latest inputs, Nasrullah Manzoor Langaryal[185]—a veteran terrorist commander of HuJI—and his associate, Shahid Sajjad, a HuM member, are mediating and moderating the discussions between Taliban and JeM, to achieve a better synergy and coordination in the Kashmir operations. Having supported the Taliban against the Americans, JeM expects the Taliban to return the favour in Kashmir. Langaryal hails from Poonch district in PoK and was active as a HuJI commander in Kashmir in the 1990s, where he was arrested in 1993 in Doda. Notably, JeM ties with the Taliban had soured after the Musharraf assassination plot. However, by 2008, JeM's outreach to the Taliban restarted and continued after that.

JeM is also linked to TTP, a terror outfit formed in 2007 and known for its brutal terror attacks, like the 2014 attack on the Peshawar army school, killing 145 people—most of whom were children—the assassination of Benazir Bhutto (2008), the Dera Ismail Khan suicide bombing (2008), the suicide bombing at Camp Chapman, a CIA base in Khost (2009), the failed car-bomb attempt at Times Square, NYC (2010) and the suicide bombing at the army compound at Mardan (2011). Many former JeM cadres who defected from the organization after Musharraf's decision to support the US-led GWoT later joined TTP. For example, TTP's Punjab Taliban faction was once led by a former JeM commander, Asmatullah Muawiya. It maintains strong ties with AQ. In fact, AQ has openly expressed its confidence in TTP.[186] TTP chief Mufti Noor Wali Mehsud publicly pledged its allegiance to Afghan Taliban leader Maulvi Hibatullah Akhunzada, stating that TTP is Taliban's branch in Pakistan.[187] TTP also fought alongside the Taliban in Afghanistan. Despite Pakistan's repeated requests to the Taliban to crack down on TTP, it continues to maintain its ties with the terror group and has not taken any action so far. Instead, TTP was energized after the Taliban takeover in Afghanistan.[188] Taliban released many TTP prisoners imprisoned by the former Afghan government and also provided political asylum to the top leadership of TTP. Since the Taliban's return to power, TTP has conducted 125-plus terrorist attacks in Pakistan, including suicide attacks, from their bases in Afghanistan.[189]

Likewise, after the Taliban takeover, AQ is also highly likely to gain vigour. The UN Security Council's Analytical and Sanctions Monitoring Team's June 2021 report mentioned that 'Taliban and Al-Qaeda remain closely aligned and show no indication of breaking ties. No material changes to this relationship, which has grown deeper as a consequence of personal bonds of marriage and shared partnership in struggle, now cemented through second generational ties.'[190] Further, the report said, 'Member states reported that a significant part of Al Qaeda leadership remains based in the border region of Afghanistan and Pakistan, where the core is joined by and works closely with Al Qaeda in the Indian Subcontinent. Large numbers of Al Qaeda fighters and other foreign extremist elements aligned with the Taliban are located in various parts of Afghanistan … there is regular communication between the Taliban and Al Qaeda on issues related to the peace process [in Afghanistan].'[191] AQIS, consisting mainly of Afghan and Pakistani nationals, 'operates under the Taliban umbrella' from Kandahar, Helmand and Nimruz provinces.[192] Further, the report says that AQIS is an organic part of the Taliban-led insurgency. Former AQIS chief Asim Umar's widow was among the 5,000 prisoners released in 2020 as a part of the deal with the US. Also, the Haqqanis act as a central liaison between the Taliban and AQ. Likewise, AQ has also maintained operational and ideological links with other Sunni extremist Deobandi groups, like LeJ and SSP, which also share the same Deobandi umbilical cord with JeM and the Taliban.

Having mentioned in detail the links between various terror groups operating in the Af-Pak region, and particularly between JeM and TTGs, it merits mention that the Pakistan state—represented by ISI and the army—acts as a common denominator to all the aforementioned outfits. The ISI in particular is the shared background against which all these groups operate. Though there are limitations to its influence, it regulates, manages, manipulates and controls the intra- and inter-group dynamics, logistics, finance, training, and the larger strategic and tactical matters. These groups function as the force multiplier for the Pakistani state. In the Afghan security forces' raid in the Nangarhar province, a JeM militant, Zarar, was caught alive.[193] He told his interrogators that the Pakistan army and intelligence were training them. Most of the militants escaped the raid with the help of the cover fire provided by Pakistani Army soldiers. However, having created these groups, it is not always possible to keep them on a tights leash. Religious extremist ideologies drive these groups; they exist in an informal, clandestine, hazy and covert space. Hence, there will always be rogue elements betraying the master, and forming new allegiances with external terrorist groups through defections and with intelligence agencies through covert double dealings. However, the ISI has successfully managed to counter and contain one group by raising new ones, and it has maintained the façade of deniability by fabricating the narrative of TTGs working beyond its control.

4

JeM's Organizational Evolution and India Operations

JEM, IN ITS TERRORIST AVATAR, HAS BEEN MOST ACTIVE and operational in Jammu and Kashmir, and only occasionally in other parts of India too. As an organization, its journey in Kashmir has shaped and defined its objectives, character, strategy and tactics. Hence, investigating JeM's journey in Kashmir forms the most crucial component of this exercise of exploring and understanding it.

JeM's Entry with 'Spectacular' Fidayeen Missions

Masood Azhar's 4 February 2000 announcement of forming Jaish-e-Mohammed made some astute observers in the Jammu and Kashmir police and India's intelligence operatives highly uncomfortable. Having been exposed to Kashmir's terrorist ecosystem, they knew the importance of Masood to Pakistan and the reason why the ISI tried so hard to get him released. They were apprehensive of Islamabad staging something spectacular in the Kashmir theatre. For Masood, since ISI orchestrated his release, he had to deliver results to his masters and benefactors, as they had invested massively in his liberation and raising JeM out of thin air, while navigating resistance from its powerful predecessors like HuM and a section of Deobandi extremists led by Fazlur Rehman Khalil.

As expected, Masood staged something spectacular and extraordinary, hitherto unseen in Kashmir—the phenomenon of suicide bombing, or fidayeen attacks. On 20 April 2000, Afaq Ahmad Shah, a JeM suicide bomber, rammed an explosives-laden car into the Valley's main army unit, Chinar Corps headquarters at Badami Bagh, Srinagar, killing four soldiers.[1] In October 2001, JeM fidayeen Muhammad Bilal, a British national, rammed an explosives-laden car into the J&K legislative assembly in Srinagar, leading to thirty-eight casualties.[2] Finally, on 13 December 2001, JeM gained international attention after five fidayeen cadres attacked the Indian Parliament building in the national capital city of Delhi, killing nine security personnel, and injuring eighteen individuals. Though the number of casualties was not very high, the Indian government perceived it as an attack on its 'democracy', in which the Prime Minister of India could have died. Left with no option, the PM ordered the largest mobilization of troops to the Pakistan border and war games under Operation Parakram, to which Pakistan responded with its own mobilization and war games. India demanded Pakistan sever all ties with JeM and hand over its leaders.

Indian authorities soon discovered that the attackers were Pakistani citizens and were members of Jaish-e-Mohammed. Notably, at that time, Pakistan said that it was a put-up job by India; however, later, former ISI chief Javed Ashraf Qazi admitted that JeM was behind the attack.[3] Bruce Reidel, a CIA veteran and South Asia expert, has expressed reservations about the direct role of ISI in planning that attack. He argues that AQ might have designed the attack because it was the immediate beneficiary, as discussed previously. A crucial event lending credence to Reidel's argument is the arrest of an AQ member, Mohammad Afroz,[4] an AQ suspect, trained as a pilot in the US, UK and Australia, around 6–7 December 2001, allegedly for plotting to attack the Indian Parliament with planes, on the lines of 9/11. It happened just a week before the actual attack on the Indian Parliament. Also, given the history of AQ's involvement in planning the IC-814 hijack and its robust ties with Masood Azhar, it is likely that Masood decided to return the favour to bin Laden.

However, we cannot absolve Pakistan and ISI of any role in the Parliament attack. The most palpable evidence of ISI's intent and efforts to help the Taliban and Al Qaeda is in the Kunduz airlift.[5] Popularly known as the 'airlift of evil', reportedly, Pakistan covertly airlifted hundreds of Taliban fighters, AQ militants, ISI operatives, Pakistan army officers and volunteers from Kunduz[6] in November 2001 before its capture by the US and the Northern Alliance.[7] The earliest reports appeared in the Indian press. National Security Advisor Brijesh Mishra said that 5,000 Pakistanis, including Taliban fighters, had been rescued by the state.[8] Though, officially, the US and Pakistan denied any such evacuation, according to a CIA analyst, the evacuation was sanctioned by the US to help Pervez Musharraf, who had apparently told Americans that body bags returning from Afghanistan would imperil his political position in Pakistan. Given the country's clandestine links with AQ and the Taliban, the ISI emerges as a prime suspect in planning the Parliament attack to bail out AQ cadres stuck in Tora Bora unless proven otherwise. Also, questions like whether Musharraf knew about it or if some rogue jihadist elements in the ISI planned it without informing him remain unanswered.

Former R&AW chief and advisor to PM Vajpayee, A.S. Dulat, has suggested that the Parliament attack must be seen in the context of the IC-814 hijacking.[9] Pakistan got Masood Azhar released, lionized and paraded him as a celebrity, and supported him with men, money, training and weapons to raise JeM. They expected him to deliver the results, which they desperately needed, as, by 1995–96, militancy had become stagnant and Kashmiri militant groups were not delivering results as expected. Besides, terrorist groups' internal feuds were disturbing Pakistan. In this scenario, the state allegedly asked all the groups to prove their loyalties.[10] LeT had already established it; it was JeM's turn now. Also, having placed the Taliban in power, having acquired nuclear weapons and successfully humiliated India in the IC-814 hijack, Pakistan was emboldened enough to order big-ticket and risky attacks—it thought that the Indians would not escalate beyond a point. This resulted in a series of spectacular fidayeen attacks in Kashmir, as discussed above. The Parliament attack was just one in that series. Pakistan did not stop even after India ordered the largest mobilization of troops after the Parliament attack. Though under US pressure, Musharraf made a promise on 12 June 2002 to sever Pakistan's ties with terrorist groups;[11] however, Islamabad had no intention of making good on those promises, as, on 14 May 2002, LeT attacked a tourist bus and an army camp at Kaluchak, near Jammu, killing thirty-four people.[12] And, all this while, Musharraf kept threatening India with Pakistan's nukes, which makes it amply clear that the Parliament attack was just one of the many attacks that occurred following the country's acquisition of nuclear weapons, which encouraged it to undertake risky terror missions without fear of Indian retaliation. Further, the US dependence on them for the Afghan war made them even more confident that America would ensure India would never counterattack. Additionally, for a terrorist leader who had just been released from an Indian jail, bereft of men and money, it was impossible to raise JeM, and execute sensitive attacks and big-ticket fidayeen missions like the Parliament attack without powerful backing.

In an interview with me, former R&AW chief C.D. Sahay discussed at length how ISI supported Masood Azhar in the early days of creating JeM. According to him, Masood was flush with ISI money and was buying out cadres and commanders from HuM. In an interview with a JeM OGW, active in 2000–04, I learned that the cadres from HM and LeT were upset with ISI pumping in large amounts of money into JeM. His information was also confirmed by retired Indian intelligence operatives whose assets in HM complained that this new organization would take away all the money and cadres. Fidayeen attacks—like the one executed at the Indian Parliament—could not be planned in a day as there are complex intelligence and costly logistics involved. They are a result of long and arduous planning with the deep state's strong logistical and intelligence support. Given ISI's support, interests and stakes—and the fact that the organization was still in the infancy stage—it is doubtful that JeM could have pulled off such a spectacular attack loaded with international ramifications without the ISI's nod and support.

In the 1990s, when AQ sought refuge in Afghanistan, it was granted on the condition that the organization didn't indulge in any political activity. However, after the Taliban came to power (1996), AQ was now under a favourable and patronizing regime, and was encouraged to carry out its political activities. Under bin Laden's leadership, it soon established training camps like Khost 1, Khost 2, Khalid bin Waleed and Muawiya. Pakistan, with its deep state's involvement in Afghanistan through an array of proxy actors since the 1980s, facilitated and supported the entrenchment of AQ in Afghanistan. Reportedly, the ISI tipped off AQ about the US attacks, raid plans and movements after the US invasion in October 2001.[13] ISI allegedly gave only 'crumbs to the US and passed on the information to Osama'.[14] As a result, AQ escaped any major damages in the US raids.

Hence, the Pakistani commitment to the US GWoT against AQ and the Taliban lacked sincerity and needs to be read with scepticism. After the Parliament attack, JeM and Pakistan were the primary beneficiaries. It established the outfit as a leading international terrorist group and a trusted asset of ISI. Pakistan wanted to protect and shelter AQ; however, it could not do so in the face of US pressure without a legitimate reason. The Parliament attack ensured that Pakistan had a legitimate reason to divert troops from Afghanistan. As a result, hundreds of Taliban and AQ fighters entered Pakistan unscathed. Meanwhile, the Americans wanted to prevent a full-scale war between India and Pakistan at any cost, for it had the potential to derail its anti-Taliban operations. Hence, Deputy Secretary of State Richard L. Armitage met Musharraf and read him the riot act, categorically asking him to stop funding and arming cross-border terrorism.[15] After that, he arrived in Delhi on 7 June 2002 and assured the Indian leadership of Musharraf's promises. He also asked the Indians to de-escalate and withdraw their troops. For India, withdrawal had become a challenge as, after such a massive mobilization, withdrawal without any punitive action would be an embarrassment with heavy political costs for the ruling party. However, after the successful provincial election in J&K, India got a reason to withdraw its troops.

Facing the Heat

Alarmed by the JeM fidayeen attack on the J&K assembly that killed thirty-eight civilians, the Indian government made intense diplomatic efforts, which finally resulted in the UN listing JeM as an international terrorist organization under paragraph 8(c) of resolution 1333 of the UNSC (2001). After the Parliament attack, India's Operation Parakram, combined with a diplomatic offensive,[16] led the US to designate JeM as a foreign terrorist organization,[17] along with LeT, on 26 December 2001. The US was also unrelenting in its demand on Musharraf to ban JeM to prevent an escalation between India and Pakistan. Finally, under intense global pressure, and to prove its credibility and commitment against terrorism to the world community, Pakistan banned JeM in January 2002.[18] However, Pakistan did so reluctantly and it wanted to protect JeM, as, by then, it had proven its utility by orchestrating a series of fidayeen attacks in India. So, the deep state allowed JeM to function under a different name—Khuddam-ul-Islam.[19] Some top-level commanders, such as Abdul Jabbar, Umar Farooq and Abdullah Shah Manzar, left JeM due to differences with Masood Azhar over ideology, power and leadership and formed Jamaat-ul-Furqan in late 2002.[20] This faction was adamantly against Musharraf's betrayal of the jihadist cause and demanded his resignation.[21] In protest, their cadres returning after the fall of the Taliban also executed several suicide attacks on Christian centres, Shia mosques and diplomatic missions in various cities, including Islamabad, Murree, Taxila and Bahawalpur.[22] The government asked Masood to control the rebellious factions, but he complained that he could not. However, he did have absolute power in the Khuddam-ul-Islam faction.[23]

Khuddam-ul-Islam was banned by the US in 2002, which intensified the pressure on Pakistan to impose the ban, but Islamabad was reluctant. Finally, in November 2003, enraged with devastating JeM-linked suicide bombings in the country,

Pakistan banned both Khuddam-ul-Islam and Jamaat-ul-Furqan. Following the ban, JeM was reincarnated as Al-Rahmat Trust.[24]

Incensed with Musharraf's betrayal of the jihadist cause and the ban, JeM's rebellious factions orchestrated two assassination[25] attempts on Musharraf in December 2003—on 14 and 25 December. In the first attack, no one died, but in the second attack, fourteen people died, including the two suicide bombers. Before the December attacks, Musharraf was also targeted on 26 April 2003, when militants tried to blow up a car parked on Shahara-e-Faisal Road in Karachi while his convoy passed by.[26] The fourth and last attempt to kill Musharraf took place in February 2004, when R&AW's timely intelligence saved his life.[27]

Reportedly, the first suspect was AQ because Musharraf's decision to support US's GWoT led to an existential threat to AQ, damaging its safe havens in Afghanistan. The March 2004 audio tape of AQ's deputy chief, Zawahiri, threatening Musharraf and calling him a traitor also lends credibility to the conjecture of AQ being the first suspect. The Al Jazeera channel had played the video and the voice was attributed to Zawahiri; however, there was no independent verification. Inciting the people and clerics against Musharraf, he had said:[28]

> All Muslims in Pakistan should attempt to get rid of this traitor government, which has surrendered to the Americans, leading to the destruction of Pakistan so the Indians can be in control ... I call on the Pakistani Army, the poor army that was put in a miserable state by Musharraf, the Indians are in front of you and behind you in Afghanistan ... Musharraf has disposed of your nuclear arms. Are you going to remain silent until the partition of Pakistan once again?

Primary investigations revealed AQ operatives' involvement in collusion with the local militants. The Pakistani intelligence suggested that the attacks were the follow-up of the threats given by Osama's deputy, Ayman-al-Zawahiri, in September 2003, to Musharraf for betraying Islam, communicated by Al Jazeera and Al Arabiya.[29] The FBI-wanted Arab AQ operative, Hadi-al-Iraqi, based in Waziristan, was suspected of having travelled to Karachi and other cities, and planned the attack with Amjad Farooqi, involved in the murder of Daniel Pearl.[30] Further investigations unearthed the role of Brigade 313, a loose alliance of five terrorist groups—JeM, HuJI, LeT, LeJ and HuMA. The group was formed shortly after the US started bombing Afghanistan in October 2001. Reportedly, its leaders pledged to eliminate Pakistani leaders collaborating with the Americans to advance their agenda, thus betraying the cause of jihad. The two suicide bombers of the 25 December attack, Muhammad Jamil and Hazir Sultan, belonged to JeM and HuJI, respectively. Jamil was from Pakistan-administered Kashmir, while Hazir was from Afghanistan.[31] Thus, it can be said that Brigade 313 was a kind of nexus of militants from Kashmir to Afghanistan. Harkat groups, believing in the hardcore Deobandi ideology, along with their robust ties with AQ and the Taliban, were further aggravated in their hatred for Musharraf and his pro-American policies. Later, the investigation led to the arrest of Akram Lahori, a LeJ leader, who said that 100 HuJI leaders had pledged on the Quran to kill Musharraf and other senior members of his government in May 2002.[32]

After the 25 December attack, security agencies arrested Mufti Rauf Azgar, Masood's brother and deputy chief of banned JeM, from Rawalpindi. Allegedly, Masood could not be detained as he had gone into hiding after the ban on his organization. Abdul Jabbar and his colleagues were also interrogated about their links with AQ. The police also began the manhunt for other JeM and Furqan suicide bombers involved in the Muree, Taxila and Islamabad suicide missions. Besides the individuals mentioned above, some rogue elements from the Pakistan Army and intelligence, including a high-ranking major general,[33] were apprehended for supporting JeM's rebellious factions in plotting to kill Musharraf.[34] Many of them were sentenced to death and others were given long imprisonment.

Interestingly, JeM and LeT constitute the core Pakistan-sponsored terrorist ecosystem in Kashmir—however, LeT did not revolt against the state, but JeM did. Popovic, a security expert from Budapest-based Central European University, says that despite the 'similar strength, ethnic ties to the regime and the presence of alternate supporters', only JeM revolted because, compared to LeT, it has been more decentralized and faction-ridden. Its 'weak command and control system' and 'dispersed decision-making' made it difficult for the group's leaders to abide by the commitments made to the sponsors. On the other hand, sponsors found it challenging to control a faction-ridden organization like JeM. Popovic's arguments offer an exciting insight; however, there are some caveats. In the domain of strength, it needs to be noted that JeM has a far more robust historical presence in Pakistan's social, cultural, religious and political space as compared to LeT. JeM's dispersed Deobandi ecosystem might decentralize it; however, this ecosystem also empowers it with more ground strength and less dependence on the ISI.

As regards the question of Masood Azhar's direct involvement in the assassination plot, the discussion can begin with his house arrest in Bahawalpur during US President Bill Clinton's Pakistan visit in April 2000.[35] The visit happened in a very tense setting as the US was upset with Musharraf's coup and the suspension of democracy, and was pressuring Pakistan to act against terrorist groups. The US asked Pakistan to proscribe HuM, a group that the US accused of terrorism. Reluctant, Pakistan did not initiate any serious action except putting Masood Azhar, formerly one of the key leaders of HuM, under house arrest. Referring to this incident, a former chief of R&AW told me, on condition of anonymity, that the incident deeply disappointed and angered Masood, and shattered his faith in the ISI. He realized that for the Pakistani Army, Kashmir was more of a strategic issue than a religious one—Pakistan could always give in under US pressure. Hence, he could not rely on the ISI for his pan-Islamist ambitions. Also, he understood that for his projects, he would have to build ties with global Islamist entities like AQ. This showed that he could dare to cross ISI. According to Popovic, after Musharraf declared his support to the US, Masood Azhar, too, had called publicly for his assassination. After the Pulwama attack, Musharraf, in his interview with the Indian media house *India Today*, admitted that 'Masood Azhar is a terrorist' and 'he tried to kill me'.[36]

However, Dr Raj Verma, a visiting fellow at the Manohar Parrikar Institute for Defence Studies and Analyses (IDSA),[37] suggests that, enraged with Musharraf's betrayal, several factions of JeM were involved in Musharraf assassination plots; however, Masood Azhar and his coterie—primarily his family—remained loyal to the Pakistani state. An objective study of the situation begs the question why Masood would go against the Pakistani state when he owed everything—his release, finances and logistical support to raise JeM—to the ISI? Were ideological differences the most critical reason for him to betray his paymasters? Finding precise answers to such questions seems eternally challenging because of the lack of clinching evidence in the open sources. If the intelligence agencies have more detailed information, they are least likely to share it. Dr Raj Verma has also not provided substantial evidence to support his claim. However, in an interview with me, the former chiefs of R&AW, C.D. Sahay and A.S. Dulat, said that after the ban on JeM, ISI leadership told their Indian counterparts that they were searching for Masood to arrest him, but he was hiding.

In February 2004, India shared intercepts of JeM communications about assassinating Musharraf with the then director general of ISI, General Ehsan ul Haq, which saved Musharraf's life.[38] Sahay is of the opinion that after his release, Masood Azhar catapulted from a rhetorician, a rabble-rousing motivator, to an international terrorist. The Taliban recognized him and he soon figured in the league of global stalwarts like Osama bin Laden. This popularity, wealth and cadre strength blinded him with power and made him highly arrogant. Even during his Kot Bhalwal jail days, he allegedly displayed narcissistic tendencies and self-praise.[39] His attitude towards his former colleagues of HuM and other terrorist groups had changed a lot. It wasn't very respectful in many ways. Other groups like HM, HuM and LeT felt let down by ISI's move of showering him with money and cadres. Masood's friends and masters in the deep state also grew disturbed by his growing arrogance, influence and power. They did not want LeT to be ousted from Kashmir's jihadist scene and, to that effect, they tried to halt and contain Masood's growing status. Hence, it is likely that—blinded by power—Masood dared to challenge the state. Besides the ideological factor—angst over Musharraf's U-turn—Masood's strong ties with bin Laden might have been a compelling motivation to rebel against the Pakistani state.

Another related question that arises is that if Masood was involved in the Musharraf assassination plot, why was he not punished—either with a life sentence or a death sentence?

About 100 people were apprehended and given harsh punishments, including execution. A senior major general was also given a death sentence. Why was Masood spared? Was he so indispensable as an asset that Musharraf had to buckle down under the pressure of other elements in the intelligence and military? Or was there no concrete evidence? Or was he cooperating in the investigation, sharing the details of the other suspects? Hence, from an academic point of view, the extent of Masood's involvement in the assassination plot needs more investigation, which is not possible without accessing the classified archives.

After 2004, despite pressure from colleagues and JeM cadres, Masood and his family remained loyal to the ISI, keeping it informed about the developments among the Deobandi extremists.[40] In return, his organization was allowed to grow slowly. The Jamaat-ul-Furqan–affiliated faction ultimately ended up with Tehreek-e-Taliban Pakistan after the Lal Masjid siege.

Ban in Pakistan and the Journey Downhill

As discussed in the previous section, under growing international pressure, Pakistan had to ban JeM in January 2002 after its name cropped up in the Parliament attack. After the ban, to escape the subsequent crackdown, JeM started shifting its offices to J&K, and its leader, Muhammad Abdullah, made lofty claims to infiltrate it despite the heavy Indian security.[41] Disturbed by the fact that Pakistan had buckled to international pressure, in February 2002, JeM said that it would confine its activities to J&K only and revive the suicide bombing trend to destroy vital security installations in the state.[42]

However, after JeM's involvement in the Musharraf assassination attempt, the organization faced a state-wide crackdown and its fortunes dwindled. The ISI's financial and organizational support to the outfit significantly declined. Though ISI wanted to keep its one-time favourite asset intact, it also wanted to discipline the organization and signal that crossing the ISI would impact its future. In January 2005, the police identified a network of nineteen people suspected of involvement in the 30 July 2004 suicide attack on Prime Minister Shaukat Aziz in Fateh Jang. They arrested three brothers belonging to the proscribed Jaish-e-Mohammed and Jamaat-ul-Furqan outfits.[43]

On 17 August 2006, Masood Azhar's father said that Rashid Rauf, the Briton who was allegedly involved in the aborted mission to bomb a transatlantic airliner, left JeM to join their 'rivals' AQ.[44] Given the past history of JeM–AQ bonhomie, the statement was doubtful. After his statement, the needle of suspicion fell on JeM and its offshoots like Jamaat-al-Furqan; Pakistani officials were quick to identify Rauf as an AQ member as well. On closer scrutiny of the facts, it appears that Pakistan did not want JeM's name cropping up in the bombing plot as it would have angered the Americans who were already suspicious of Islamabad's commitment to sever ties with terror groups. Interestingly, Rashid Rauf was married to Masood Azhar's family member.[45] In JeM, Masood Azhar's family members play a crucial role in running the various divisions of the organization. They are a close-knit family; hence, it is unlikely that they did not know about Rashid's involvement in the plot. Rashid's marriage into Masood's family made JeM's involvement and hence ISI's more obvious for the reasons explained above. Additionally, Masood's father said that Rashid joined their 'rivals' AQ, which was anti-US and Afghanistan-focused, whereas JeM's focus was Kashmir. Both claims cannot be accepted at face value because JeM and Masood Azhar had strong ties with AQ and Taliban; and secondly, Masood Azhar, through his statements after his release, made it amply clear that he was against the US. Also, JeM has always been interested in Afghanistan. In 2008, JeM shifted its focus from Kashmir and Pakistan to Afghanistan, and most recently, the organization fought with the Taliban against the coalition forces (2021). Hence, it is likely that Masood's father made such statements under the guidance of their friends and masters in the ISI to ease the pressure on Pakistan to prove its innocence by acting against JeM.

In Pakistan, the next crisis after the Musharraf assassination plot came in 2007 when the army had to battle Deobandi terrorists who had captured Lal Masjid in Islamabad. After that episode, terrorists were divided into the anti- and pro-state camps. Though JeM and LeT remained loyal, some of the former's operatives who were involved in the Lal Masjid siege defected to the anti-state TTP.[46] Though some leaders changed their minds later and rejoined JeM, many continued in TTP or joined AQ.[47] Due to its defections and anti-state behaviour, ISI mostly remained suspicious of JeM's intent and activities. It took harsh military measures against its cadres, which intensified after its association with the TTP. However, because of JeM's utility as a force multiplier, the ISI never dispensed with it.

On 25 March 2002, Masood was released from the Mianwali Jail (Lahore) and shifted to his Bahawalpur residence. In May 2003, the PoK government banned Masood's entry into the region. But he defied the ban and arrived in Kotli. JeM had built a strong base in PoK. It was a lifeline to his Kashmir operations; hence, Masood could not afford to lose it, sever ties and lose credibility among his supporters in PoK.

The restrictions and state action became harsher after his name figured in the Musharraf assassination plot. Even though he remained loyal to the state, throughout the 2000s, all the way until 2014, he was kept under house arrest at his Kausar colony residence in Bahawalpur.[48] Occasionally, he was arrested, jailed, and subjected to judicial remands and bail. Other JeM leaders, like Abdul Jabbar, were also arrested, imprisoned and released on bail a few times. In several encounters, the police killed many JeM cadres.[49]

Pakistan's Tacit Support to JeM and the Futility of the Ban

Was the state crackdown against the group meaningful or just an eyewash to protect its image before the world community? A closer examination of JeM-related developments following the ban suggests that Pakistan was not serious in acting against the organization and that it continued to receive the ISI's blessings and protection.

To begin with, Pakistan's non-cooperative attitude and consistent refusal to the multiple US requests to extradite Omar Saed Sheikh,[50]—arrested for luring Daniel Pearl, South Asia bureau chief of *The Wall Street Journal*, to visit Pakistan, and then abducting him and being involved in his murder—reveals ISI's covert ties and tacit support to the terror group. Additionally, he was also accused of transferring USD 100,000 to AQ operative Khalid Sheikh Muhammad, who planned the 9/11 attacks. B. Raman, one of the finest intelligence minds of India with expertise in Pakistan, offers valuable insights into the suspicious role of Pakistan state and ISI in the Daniel Pearl episode. After Omar Saed's release (with Masood in the IC-814 hijack), he helped form JeM.[51] Omar Saed opened an office in Lahore and started helping bin Laden's International Islamic Front (IIF)—formed in February 1998, to fight against Jews and Christians—in fundraising. HuM was one of the founding members of IIF. However, around this time, Omar Saed drifted more towards the ISI. Reportedly, he was recruited by them and was in touch with senior ISI generals. He was sent by the ISI to Afghanistan on missions, where he frequently met with the AQ leadership.[52] Shortly after Pearl's abduction and before his murder, when US pressure had mounted and when Pakistan's police were searching for him, he surrendered to his close confidante and allegedly his handler, Brigadier Ijaz Ahmed Shah—a former ISI official and Musharraf confidante—at Lahore, who was then posted as home secretary of the Punjab government. Later, Musharraf appointed Ijaz Ahmed Shah as the chief of the IB from 2004–08. After keeping Omar Saed in custody for a few days,[53] without any public announcement of his surrender, the ISI transferred him to the Lahore police, who eventually handed him over to the Karachi police. In their interrogation, he admitted to his role in Pearl's abduction, the J&K legislative assembly attack in October 2001 and the Indian Parliament attack. He also mentioned his meeting with Osama bin Laden before 9/11 in which he came to know about the attack, which he duly conveyed to the ISI chief, Ehsan ul Haq, upon his return. Between Pearl's abduction and the recovery of his body, General Musharraf was on his maiden visit to the US after the military coup. While there, he was kept informed about developments in the case; however, he concealed the truth from US authorities and feigned to them that Pearl was alive, lest his US trip got spoiled. Shortly after his return, the ISI announced that Pearl's mutilated body had been found.

Though the ISI was reluctant, they were forced to establish Omar Saed's involvement in Pearl's murder after FBI cyber expert, Ronald Joseph, proved that Omar Saed had sent emails claiming responsibility for Pearl's murder. Omar Saed's accomplices were given long jail sentences and he was handed a death sentence. Both sides—the state and Omar Saed Sheikh—filed appeals against the decision. Interestingly, the Nawaz Sharif government and Musharraf were both cautious and made sure that in terrorism cases, convicts were not able to delay their execution of the punishment by filing regular appeals. However, an exception to this practice was seen in Omar Saed Sheikh's case when his death sentence was delayed due to repeated adjournments after his appeal hearing. Also, he was actively carrying out his jihadist agenda from jail—communicating with the other jihadists in South Asia, the UK and Europe. In 2005, he managed to disseminate his observations in Pakistan and Afghanistan on the alleged desecration of the Quran by US guards in Guantanamo Bay. Reportedly, two perpetrators of the July 2005 London explosions met him in jail during their Pakistan visit.[54] After the Mumbai terror attacks of 2008, Omar Saed made hoax calls to Pakistan PM Asif Ali Zardari, Pakistan Army chief Ashfaq Parvez Kayani, and India's then foreign minister Pranab Mukherjee to intensify tensions between the two countries.[55] In 2011, a report prepared by a group of Georgetown University students working on the Pearl Project, with the International Consortium of Investigative Journalists, mentioned that Omar Saed and his accomplices were responsible for the abduction of Pearl, but not his murder.[56] Instead, he was allegedly killed by Khaled Sheikh Mohammad, an AQ operative who masterminded 9/11.

In April 2020, a Sindh court acquitted Omar Saed of the murder charge and commuted his death sentence to seven years in jail.[57] The court then declared his prison term as complete since he had already spent eighteen years imprisoned by then. After that, on 24 December 2020, the Sindh High Court instructed security agencies not to keep Omar Saed and his accomplices in detention.[58] According to *The Sunday Guardian*, an Indian media outlet,[59] the moves to get him released were being directed by Brigadier Ijaz Ahmed Shah, who was—until recently—an interior minister in Imran Khan's Cabinet. He gave directives to provide home-like facilities to Omar Saed in jail. However, this report has not been independently verified by other sources; hence, its claims need more investigation. Finally, in January 2021, Pakistan's Supreme Court acquitted Omar Saed Sheikh and his three accomplices, and ordered their release.[60] Reportedly, after his release, he has kept a low profile—however, he regularly interacts with Taliban leaders and Sajjad Gul, the PoK-based chief of TRF, a Kashmir-centric terrorist organization and reportedly a front of LeT.[61]

After 9/11, Musharraf was proactive in extraditing terrorists to the US. Reportedly, he handed over 300 terrorists, including some high-profile ones like Abu Zubaydah, Ramzi Binalshibh, Khaled Sheikh Mohammad, and Abu Faraj al-Libbi (the AQ terrorist who allegedly masterminded Musharraf's assassination attempt).[62] However, Musharraf refused, and never allowed, the extradition in two cases. The first was of Pakistan nuclear scientist Dr Abdul Qadeer Khan because it would have exposed General Zia's role in selling nuclear technology to Iran, and his own role in selling it to Libya and North Korea. And the second one was of Omar Sheikh Saed.[63] The mystery of why he refused to hand over Omar Saed Sheikh remains unresolved. However, former R&AW chief, C.D. Sahay, offers a crucial clue. One of the key members of the Indian team sent to negotiate with the Kandahar hijackers told me that Omar Saed Sheikh was a brilliant strategist, one of the finest and most trusted ISI assets, and, interestingly, a mole in Al Qaeda. He told me that when the three terrorists were released by the Indians, the ISI officers present at the exchange hugged and kissed Omar Saed Sheikh, not the other two, making it clear that ISI was behind Omar Saed's, not the hijackers.[64] Taliban leaders and the hijackers greeted Masood and Mushtaq 'Latram' Zargar. Therefore, the ISI could never betray him. In the future, given Omar Saed's deep ties with ISI, Pakistan is most unlikely to ever extradite Omar Saed to the US as it would uncover all its 'dirty' deals with terrorist operatives, and possibly the truth about Pearl's abduction and murder, and inconvenient truths about the ISI's role.

Even after the ban on JeM, Masood could move freely and organize congregations. The very fact that he could visit PoK (2003), despite the ban on his visit and his organization, suggests that he still had powerful friends in the Pakistani security establishment who wanted to help him protect and consolidate his base in PoK—the lifeline to his Kashmir operations. After JeM's name figured in the Musharraf assassination plot, the police arrested Masood's younger brother and JeM deputy chief Mufti Rauf Azgar. At first, Pakistani authorities maintained—and told India's R&AW, which had given them the intel saving Musharraf's life—that Masood was in hiding. However, he was subsequently arrested and placed in Bahawalpur Central Jail. Soon, he was shifted to Dera Ghazi Khan Jail because the administration allegedly feared that his supporters and followers would attack them. From there, his house in Bahawalpur was declared a sub-jail and he was kept under house arrest. Some of the OGWs of JeM interviewed by me said that the ban had soured the group's relations with the state and adversely impacted its finances; however, the narrative around the ban straining JeM's relations with Pakistan's deep state was more for public consumption. According to JeM OGWs, the recurring house arrests ordered by the ISI were to keep Masood safe, lest any covert action by India take place. The estrangement of JeM from the state has nuances. It was the Abdul Jabbar–led JuF faction that was involved in the Musharraf assassination plot. After 2004, JeM's Masood Azhar–led faction remained loyal and engaged with the establishment. The ISI allowed Masood to rebuild his organization because it believed that as long as the militant cadres were loyal to Masood Azhar, they would not join rebellious factions like JuF working against the state.[65] JuF never found state patronage. When its district chief was killed in Bahawalpur in 2009, the ISI and district administration turned a blind eye to his death.

Between 2003 and 2007, JeM operated openly in various parts of Pakistan and conducted many high-profile terror activities. In J&K, it was progressively establishing itself as a leading terror outfit. In 2006, JeM owned up to killing many Indian police officials in the Valley. Masood Azhar, who had been released, was openly moving around, recruiting cadres and preaching across the country. However, after JeM cadres were found involved in the Lal Masjid siege (2007), leading to a major rupture between the jihadists and the state, Masood went underground once again.

Regarding financial support, a report attributing an article in *Herald* provides substantial information about the ISI's continuing financial support to terror groups, including the JeM, despite its lofty claims of having denounced them.[66] The report mentioned that over 1,000 trained Kashmiri militants were 'currently stranded' in three camps of the HM in the Hazara region of NWFP. Of these, the Hisari and Batrasi camps were in the Mansehra district, while the third camp was in Boi in the Abbottabad district. Further, the report added that thousands of other terrorists were confined in camps run by about half a dozen smaller Kashmiri groups and Pakistani terrorist groups like the LeT, JeM and Al-Badr Mujahideen in the frontier and Pakistan-occupied Kashmir regions. The report claimed that until around 2005–06, small groups like the Tehreek-ul-Mujahideen, Al Umar Mujahideen, Jamiat-ul-Mujahideen, Al-Fatah, Al-Jihad, Al-Barq, Tehreek-e-Jihad and Islamic Front were receiving between PKR 4,00,000 and 7,00,000 a month. The more prominent organizations like HM, LeT, JeM and others received more money, ranging between PKR 2–3 million. Besides state support, the terrorist groups received generous donations from middle-class residents and trader-merchants of south Punjab and from Gulf-based donors, despite the ban.[67]

Reportedly, by 2007, JeM was reorganizing itself under its new commander, Mufti Rauf Azgar, the younger brother of Masood Azhar.[68] JeM had established a transit camp in Islamabad for its activists visiting from southern Punjab and traveling to Kohat, where they set up another camp.[69] Mufti Abdul Rauf was at the forefront of overhauling and revitalizing JeM. He became more prominent after Masood went underground after the attacks on Musharraf. JeM decided to use the Islamabad camp as the base for its propaganda drive and to distribute pamphlets in tribal areas. In 2011, Rauf travelled to Chile on a fake visa. He was reportedly arrested by the Chilean police, who discovered that he carried an INTERPOL notice for his involvement in the IC-814 hijack.[70] Given the global ban on JeM and the INTERPOL notice, Rauf's international travel was highly unlikely to occur without ISI support.

Contrary to official claims that Masood had not visited his Bahawalpur home for many years, he organized a grand book launch for his *Fatah-ul-Jawaad* on 28 April 2008, in Bahawalpur.[71] Moreover, JeM's armed militants guarded all 'entrances and exits to the city that day and there was no police force in sight'. Ayesha Siddiqa, in her field research, found that contrary to the general perception of JeM fighting against the state, the Taliban in the KPK region suspected the organization of having links with the state. Further, she came across Pakistani intelligence officials warding off local residents, and local and foreign journalists who tried to probe into the affairs of JeM. In some cases, the ISI even tarnished the image of the scholars and journalists investigating jihadist organizations and their ties with the ISI.

In December 2008, following India's extradition requests, Pakistani authorities imposed restrictions on Masood Azhar's movement.[72] India gave a list of three persons—Masood Azhar, Dawood Ibrahim and Tiger Memon—for their immediate extradition. The CBI had demanded Masood's extradition to prosecute him on the charge of orchestrating the Parliament attack. The ISI's refusal was not a new development. Next, India demanded that the UN declare Masood Azhar a global terrorist and blacklist him, but Pakistan blocked India's attempts thrice with the help of China. Masood remained dormant, keeping a low profile until February 2014, when he addressed a public gathering in Muzaffarabad (PoK),[73] where he claimed to have 313 suicide bombers ready to die, and, if needed, the number could go to 3,000.[74] He also threatened to kill Narendra Modi if he became India's Prime Minister.[75]

Further, by 2007, the peace process with India that began under the stewardship of Vajpayee and Musharraf had nearly met its sad end, incentivizing the revival of terror groups with renewed vigour. Also, in 2008, after General Parvez Kayani took over as army chief, he started reaching out to the estranged jihadis.[76] Seeing the opportunity, JeM began building bridges with Pakistan's security establishment. After meeting other leaders of Deobandi extremist groups, JeM decided to shift focus to Afghanistan from Kashmir and Pakistan. It decided to help the Taliban drive the foreign forces out of Afghanistan.[77] They started targeting the US and coalition forces. However, they continued their attacks in Kashmir, but kept them on a low burner.

This relationship between the state and JeM strengthened over the next few years. In return for the Pakistan military allowing the group to carry on its activities freely, it agreed to sanitize the organization and expel anti-Pakistan elements.[78] After the 26/11 Mumbai attacks, Masood was detained for a while, but was released shortly afterward.[79] The LeT was the target of global scrutiny for its role in the attacks, since many Westerners died in that; hence, the organization could not be used with the same intensity for the next few years. Given this fact, JeM was the best alternative. The result was a sudden upsurge in its activities and it was 'back in full force with offices in every neighbourhood'.[80] Ayesha Siddiqa, during her field research,[81] discovered that the JeM infrastructure in Bahawalpur was quite extensive, and the terror groups were quite 'ubiquitous' and 'overt'. Further, she noted that they openly recruited cadres despite the presence of the Pakistan Army's 31 corps, headquartered just a few miles from the JeM complex in Bahawalpur.[82] All this could not have happened without the tacit support of Pakistan's military and intelligence agencies.

Around this time, JeM started expanding its real estate holdings. It acquired a new site at Chowk Azam in Bahawalpur, allegedly used for training purposes.[83] It also commenced the construction of its headquarters. In September 2009, a 4.5-acre compound outside Bahawalpur was inaugurated as its headquarters.[84] The new police chief of the area tried to stop the construction work, but JeM continued appropriating more land. Senior authorities had ignored the construction despite reports that the compound might be a radical madrasa or training camp, with senior police officials claiming there is no militancy problem in southern Punjab. A US Department of Defense document from November 2008 mentions the presence of a newly constructed madrasa on the outskirts of Bahawalpur city, managed by Maulana Al-Hajii, a follower of Maulana Masood Azhar.[85] A 2009 investigative report by an Indian media outlet unearthed JeM's financial dealings.[86] According to the report, in 2009, a few months after the 26/11 Mumbai attacks, Rauf visited a small government office in Bahawalpur to register the purchase of nine acres and one kanal of farmland off the Bahawalpur–Karachi highway. With such a strategic location, JeM could block the national highway during any crisis. Ahmad Nayeem, a resident, sold the property to Rauf and his partner, Rashid Ahmed, on 23 March 2009 for PKR 1.5 million (INR 7.6 lakhs).

The property became an extensive JeM complex over the next few years, with space for 12,000 students, sports facilities and prayer areas. Reportedly, local police officials have claimed to witness tunnels being dug inside the campus and the regular visits of unknown trucks at odd hours of the night, carrying weapons.[87] One of my sources showed me pictures of the complex on the condition that his identity be kept confidential. It is a lavish property with a large swimming pool, a horse stable, a gymnasium, ornamental fountains and recreational slides for children. It is protected by guards armed with automatic rifles. The compound also has an impressive collection of Turkish horses, cheetahs, ducks and exotic animals like ostrich. Besides, the value of the military equipment, several SUVs and Range Rovers JeM owns is in the range of millions of dollars.

The gate at the seminary has a sign that reads, '*Delhi, Delhi ya hanood, Jaish-e-Mohammed sauf yauood* (To Delhi, O Hindus, the army of the Prophet will soon return).[88] Besides this, JeM has also developed a few more secret training facilities—Fort Maujgarh, 62 km from Bahawalpur and Fort Abbas, 72 km away from Fort Maujgarh.[89] The fidayeen militants of the Pathankot attack (2016) were reportedly trained at Fort Maujgarh.[90]

In 2009, Indian intelligence found that JeM was training its cadres at Fort Abbas. New Delhi was alarmed because the facility was at a short distance from Faqirwali, on the India–Pakistan border. It had an airstrip, making it likely that JeM was training its fleet to carry air-borne missions. After the Pulwama attack, Pakistan announced its taking over of Jamia Masjid Subhanallah and Sabir Seminary, both part of the JeM complex; however, a day later, the Bahawalpur administration stated that the JeM complex was an ordinary seminary with 600 students and no link to JeM.[91] A closer scrutiny of facts makes it almost impossible to cover up JeM's ownership of the property as the organization's publication *Al Qalam* mentioned Abdul Rauf, in whose name the property was registered, as 'General of the Jaish-e-Mohammed' in its 9 February 2017 issue.[92] Further, it noted that Rauf had addressed a gathering in the Gumtala village, saying that 'Islam is a world power and cannot be destroyed' and 'jihad is the most important obligation of our faith'.[93] Notably, Rauf was sanctioned in 2010 by the US Treasury Department for his involvement in 'deadly attacks against civilians in India, Pakistan, and Afghanistan'.[94]

In 2011, JeM's front organization, a charity—Al-Rahmat Trust—was busy raising funds for its parent body in KPK and Punjab.[95] The trust was collecting funds for building mosques and for relief work during natural calamities. A 2010 JeM-affiliated publication revealed that the trust, once run by Masood's father, Allah Baksh Sabir, was paying pensions to the 850 families of terrorists killed and imprisoned in India and other countries.[96] JeM publications like *Al Qalam* and *Muslim Ummah* were out in the market with renewed audit certificates issued by the Ministry of Information and Broadcasting, which permitted them to raise money through advertisements.[97] Video footage from 2016 showed volunteers in Karachi collecting jihad funds from congregants for the Al-Rahmat Trust, saying it was for 'the brave young men of the JeM who are fighting for the victory of the name of god and Islam'.⁹⁸ *Al Qalam*'s 2016–17 issues also mentioned large JeM gatherings in Karachi and Bahawalpur, unaffected by the India–Pakistan crisis of the time.

Interestingly, Al-Rahmat Trust was designated as a foreign terrorist organization by the US State Department in 2001 and 2008, and as a JeM front in 2010 by the US Treasury Department.⁹⁹ However, the Pakistan government's list of proscribed organizations released in November 2011 mentioned JeM and affiliates like TAF (Tehreek-al-Furqan) but did not mention the trust. Despite its global ban, Al-Rahmat Trust continues to be fully functional in Pakistan, collecting donations through legitimate and formal banking channels for building 313 mosques.¹⁰⁰ This combined with the fact that it is not listed in Pakistan's banned organizations, makes it amply evident that state authorities have paid no heed to the activities of JeM and JeM-affiliates.

By 2010, JeM's public activity had also increased. Meetings headed by the outfit were organized in Dera Ismail Khan and Muzaffarabad.¹⁰¹ In one such meeting (in January 2010) organized by the United Jihad Council (UJC)—an umbrella organization of Kashmir-centric terrorist groups, of which JeM is also a part—chaired by former ISI chief General Hamid Gul, invigorated jihad was called for until Kashmir was free of 'Indian occupation'.¹⁰² In January 2014, Masood Azhar addressed his followers in Muzaffarabad from an undisclosed location, calling for the resumption of jihad against India. Further, he claimed to have 313 suicide bombers ready and threatened to kill Narendra Modi if he became India's Prime Minister.¹⁰³

JeM's uninterrupted and big-ticket Kashmir operations, organizational activities, meetings, fundraising, rallies, recruitment, acquisition of property, online propaganda publications and printing, all with the required state permissions, despite the much-publicized ban, raises serious questions on the credibility and the impact of the ban. Further, it suggests that the ISI funding might have declined in the public eye, but never stopped through training, protection from law enforcement agencies, logistics and organizational work. JeM, on account of its proven hold in Kashmir, remains indispensable for the ISI. Hence, it can be argued that post-2004, JeM never faced severe state action, which could threaten its very existence. At the most, its position after 2004 was sustaining itself, and operating under controlled freedom and the space allowed by the deep state, but not a complete cessation of its activities.

Pakistan never really dismantled the terror infrastructure. It was not only JeM but the other anti-India terrorist groups were also kept intact and allowed to flourish. By 2005, Pakistan started reviving its anti-India terror infrastructure. Journalist and author of a book on LeT, Arif Jamal opines, 'The fact that the Pakistan Army kept the jihadist infrastructure intact shows that they wanted to revive jihad in Kashmir and Afghanistan at a later time. They slowly started reviving it as an instrument of the defence policy around 2005.'[104] He added that terrorist proxies have been the quintessential and the 'first element of Pakistan's foreign policy' since 1947 to compensate for its economic and military weakness.[105] General Pervez Musharraf did not wholly destroy the terrorist groups; instead, after imposing a superficial ban, he allowed them to rebrand themselves as charity groups and continue their work—JeM rebranded itself as Al-Rahmat Trust, HuJI as Ansar-ul-Ummah (headed by Fazlur Rehman Khalil)[106] and JuD/LeT continued its work through Falah-i-Insaniyat Foundation (FiF). The new avatar of charity groups with a welfare agenda allowed them to grow, and helped create a solid support base and allowed for fertile recruitment grounds. Ashfaq Parvez Kayani was the man behind the revival of terror infrastructure, and General Raheel Sharif continued to do so.[107]

The much-publicized National Action Plan against terrorism after the TTP attack on the Army Public School, Peshawar, of 2014 was always aimed at the anti-Pakistan terrorist groups like TTP, not the anti-India groups. Instead, the latter groups served as parking lots for rehabilitating anti-Pakistan terrorist cadres of TTP. How Pakistan allowed the anti-India groups to flourish is amply evident from the mass rallies and processions organized by HM, LeT/JuD, Jamaat-i-Islami and HuM members after the massive unrest and violence that engulfed Kashmir following the encounter death of Burhan Wani in August 2016. Globally designated terrorist of the banned LeT and the alleged mastermind of the Mumbai attack of 2008, Hafiz Saeed led the 'Azadi March' procession stretching over several kilometres in Lahore and Islamabad.[108] Hafiz Saeed, expressing his solidarity with Kashmiris, said, 'Where your blood will spill, ours will flow with you.'[109] In his speech, he targeted the civilian government but did not speak a word against the Pakistan Army—the alleged benefactor and paymaster of anti-India terrorist groups. Protestors shouted anti-India slogans like '*Bharat ki barbadi tak, Jung rahegi jari* (until India's destruction, the fight will continue).' In these rallies, terror groups and their affiliated charity organizations openly collected donations. It seems that Pakistan was waiting for the right opportunity to revive the anti-India terror groups, and the 2016 unrest in Indian-administered Kashmir and the need to rehabilitate TTP terrorists provided that opportunity.

JeM's Early Days in Kashmir: Insider Narratives

I interviewed Akram Bhai (name changed), a JeM OGW and a former cadre in Srinagar. Hailing from Pulwama district, a JeM stronghold in south Kashmir, he was an active terrorist from 2000–07; then he left active militancy and became an OGW. Since then, he has continued his association with the outfit. Akram Bhai revealed crucial insights about the organization in its early days in Kashmir.

After Masood announced its formation, he received enormous financial support from the ISI. His stature and image in jihadi circles had become very powerful, and he commanded massive organizational resources, leading to the mass shifting of cadres from HuM to JeM. Almost 75 per cent of JeM cadres came from HuM. During his jail days, Masood befriended Mushtaq Ahmad Zargar, alias Latram, a prison inmate.[110] Reportedly, Masood, in his interactions, realized the importance of Mushtaq 'Latram' Zargar for expanding and running a terrorist organization in J&K. The HuM hijackers demanded the release of Zargar along with Masood Azhar and Omar Saed Sheikh. After his release, Zargar helped Masood establish JeM in the Kashmir Valley, and managed finances and operations for the organization. However, he operated in the shadows and, hence, never came under the scanner of the intelligence agencies. The ISI turned to him again in 2017 after the death of some top-level LeT commanders like Abu Dujana.[111] Zargar had joined JKLF in 1988 and was trained in PoK. After returning to the Valley, he worked with JKLF but later formed his own outfit, Al Umar Mujahideen (AuM), in 1992 because of his differences with Yasin Malik, the new chief of JKLF.[112] As the chief of AuM, he was involved in the murder of many security officials and Kashmiri Pandits. He was arrested in 1993 and was released along with Masood in 1999.

In the early 2000s, the militancy was primarily centred in north Kashmir and the Pir Panjal districts of Doda, Kishtwar, Poonch, and Rajouri. JeM used the tried-and-tested infiltration routes of the north Kashmir and Poonch–Rajouri border. In the Kupwara district, they entered the Keran region from Jura and Dudhnial (Neelam Valley area), known launching pads[113] in PoK. The Keran group crossed the villages of Farkiyan top, TP, Kemal water nullah, Hachmarg, Hajreda, and Hignikoot. Militants crossed into India from the Tangdhar area (Kupwara district), via Beari village, which lies on both sides of the LoC. From Beari, they passed through Shamsabari, Encha, Baleyan and Thamthora villages to come to the Rajwar area. At TP and Encha, there are Jiyarats (religious shrines), which sometimes became resting points for them. From the Hignikoot and Rajwar areas, their coordinators and other OGWs received them, and escorted them to different parts of Kashmir.

Until 2003, JeM took the help of LeT, HM guides and OGWs in infiltrating the Valley. LeT and HM had been operational for almost a decade, and had a robust local network of OGWs. After 2003, JeM became independent with its own set of OGWs and guides. LeT and HM were also circumspect about sharing their best, high-quality and skilled OGWs as they feared that—with its vast financial resources—JeM would induce them to shift their allegiance, as it did with HuM cadres. Moreover, as JeM was a new entrant, there were trust issues between the groups. Hence, it is believed that LeT and HM shared their second-category OGWs, who only had a superficial knowledge of their activities.

Initially, Akram Bhai told me, JeM militants made hideouts[114] with LeT and HM cadres because of their knowledge of the local geography, the movement of security forces, and social and cultural conditions. After 2003, when JeM had built its own network of OGWs, it stopped sharing hideouts with other organizations. The OGWs were used by JeM mainly for logistics, and moving men, weapons and cash, and for arranging shelters. JeM was always a very secretive entity, more so in the beginning—hence, it preferred not to share its OGWs with other terrorist groups. Also, in those days, JeM cadres brought lots of money with them. Each cadre had about INR 2,00,000 to 2,50,000 in cash on him. The leader would carry around INR 15–20 lakh, and the total amount could go up depending on the operational requirements in the Valley.

Until 2008–09, the majority of the JeM cadres were Pakistanis. By 2007, their hideouts in the jungles were being exposed by the local Gujjar population working as informants of the army, as they had a fair understanding of JeM tactics by then. As a result, several cadres were killed in encounters with SFs. To address this deficiency in the local base, JeM started recruiting local Kashmiris so that they could get more local support, sympathy and shelter in urban areas, where they could hide easily and minimize encounters. Initially, they recruited local Kashmiris from Sopore and Baramulla in north Kashmir, as these areas were the strongholds of Jamaat-i-Islami—a pro-Pakistan Islamist organization. Jamaat recommended trustworthy candidates to tanzeems.[115] JeM gave money to the poor and the needy in the Sopore–Baramulla area, and asked them to build houses using that money and keep one room for their cadres. The room had to be designed as an underground basement or another hidden area that could not be noticed easily. This arrangement was mostly for the winters as living in the jungle and garden hideouts in winter was almost impossible because of heavy snow. Shah Nawaz Khan, alias Ghazi Baba, JeM's famous commander who organized its early suicide missions, was hiding in a house in the Noor Bagh area of Srinagar when the Border Security Force (BSF) raided it and killed him in an encounter.

JeM cadres, said Akram Bhai, were highly cautious about their movement and security as they were the newest and youngest tanzeem in Kashmir. They were also apprehensive about trusting other tanzeems as the latter were uncomfortable with the special favour ISI showed JeM. Initially, the group hardly trusted the local population. Generally, they never shared the location of their night-shelter houses with anyone. The OGWs would bring dry fruits, shoes, trousers, jackets and other essentials to a specific home from where JeM cadres collected the materials, but they never stayed in that house. They stayed in other homes in the same village. To throw people off their scent, they would travel two or three kilometres outside the village, and then return at night to sleep in the village. In severe winters, the cadres mostly confined themselves to hideouts and protected themselves from the SFs. In snowy winters, the militants preferred urban shelters where two to four militants stayed in one urban shelter. In the summers, eight to ten militants stayed in 'jungle-garden' hideouts. With the house owners, JeM cadres were usually well-behaved. In the initial phase, when they were flush with money, they could offer their hosts much more money compared to other groups.

Females, particularly the girls of the houses, were attracted to JeM cadres because they were younger, well-mannered, soft-spoken, and wore better clothes and perfumes. Plus, the attraction to a gun-wielding mujahid quickly made the girls vulnerable. Sexual intimacy between the girls of the host's household and the JeM cadres allegedly became a common occurrence. Sometimes the families knew about it and approved. And if they did not like it, they could hardly raise a word against an armed jihadi. Also, it was considered a religious duty to offer all kinds of pleasure to jihadis, perceived as dying for Islam and Kashmir and fighting against the infidel forces. However, the senior commanders always discouraged love affairs and sexual intimacy for both religious and security reasons.

Compared to the JeM cadres, HM cadres, mostly locals according to Akram Bhai, were not well-behaved. They came in large groups, and exhibited carelessness and a lack of professionalism. They offered less money and often behaved badly with their hosts. They were locals and, after acquiring a gun and a membership in a terrorist organization, indulged in a crude display of power and authority. Allegedly, their unreasonable demands often irritated house owners.

JeM's Trajectory in Kashmir Post Ban

After the international ban and the ban in Pakistan, JeM operated in Kashmir as the Al Murabitoon brigade and collected money under that name. Indian SFs also intensified their intelligence-driven operations against JeM after its involvement in some of the lethal suicide attacks discussed earlier in this chapter. In August 2003, JeM's operational chief Ghazi Baba was killed. His successor, Sahrai Baba, alias Qari Asif, was originally from Karachi. He was killed in April 2004 at Kupwara. Enraged with the loss of its top commanders, in September 2003, a JeM spokesperson, in a telephonic interview with the Associated Press (AP), threatened to avenge Ghazi Baba's killing by targeting Indian leaders in suicide attacks that would be 'shocking for India'.[116] In 2004, in an intelligence-driven operation, Indian SFs placed a mole in the organization, who organized a meeting of top JeM commanders in Lolab Valley (a JeM stronghold in north Kashmir), which was raided by the SFs, leading to the top brass of the organization getting killed.[117] On 2 November 2005, a few hours before the swearing-in of the new chief minister (CM) of J&K, Ghulam Nabi Azad, a fidayeen terrorist, detonated a powerful car bomb in the Nowgam area of Srinagar, near the old residence of the outgoing CM, Mufti Mohammad

Sayeed, killing at least ten people and injuring eighteen others.[118] A JeM spokesperson, Abu Qadam, told the local media that a Mohammad Mubashir, a resident of Abbaspora in PoK, was the fidayeen who carried out the attack. On 8 August 2006, the Jammu police foiled a fidayeen plot in Jammu city set to take place on 15 August and killed two JeM cadres.

Next, on 26 April 2007, the police foiled another plot to assassinate Chief Minister Ghulam Nabi Azad in a suicide attack during a rally in Bandipora. A senior police officer said that a top LeT militant, Showkat Ahmed, was arrested from the capital, Srinagar, on 24 April. During interrogation, he apparently revealed that the LeT, JeM and HM had a joint conspiracy to kill Azad. The police raided a militant hideout on the outskirts of Srinagar, from where two associates of Showkat were arrested—this included one Pakistani national, Abu Sikander.

In 2007, SFs started intercepting the telephonic communications of militants. Unaware of this, militants continued calling up their girlfriends and OGWs. Communication intercepts enhanced the quality of the intelligence, leading to many successful encounters. Many top-level commanders like Tamim Iqbal, a Pakistani JeM cadre, and division commander, north Kashmir, from PoK, were killed in encounters due to such interception.

In August 2007, Saifullah Qari, the JeM commander who plotted the attack on the makeshift Ram temple at Ayodhya in Uttar Pradesh, was killed in an encounter near Janipur colony in Jammu.[119] With Ghazi Baba and Saifullah Qari's death, JeM's capabilities to mount attacks outside J&K were significantly hurt.

On 21 February 2008, SFs killed three JeM militants in the dense forests of Batnar Kooligam in Lolab Valley.[120] Another JeM commander was reportedly killed that day. On 19 April 2008, SFs, in a day-long encounter, killed four militants in the Rang

Forest area in the Kupwara district. Three of the slain militants, residents of Pakistan-occupied Kashmir (PoK), were identified as Amjad Bhai, Abu Saifullah and Irshad Ahmed. While Amjad Bhai was a top-level 'district commander' of JeM, who had been active in the Kupwara region for the last six years, Abu Saifullah and Arshad were LeT militants. In September 2008, SFs killed Barkatullah Ansari—alias Hyder—a top-level district commander of JeM and a resident of PoK, in an encounter in Baramulla. He was the key coordinator between various militant groups and planned many terror incidents in the Sopore–Baramulla region. His death was also a shattering loss to JeM. In January 2010, Abdullah Sani, alias Dawood Khan, a Pakistani national and the division commander of JeM in Poonch district, was killed. Dawood was also coordinating with other militant outfits, and was brainwashing and luring youths into militancy. In fact, in 2009–10, the most wanted JeM commanders in the Poonch region—Omar Khitab, Dawood and Parbat Shikari—all three Pakistani nationals, were killed. In October 2010, some JeM fidayeens, trying to attack the 15 Corps headquarters in Srinagar, were killed.

After suffering major setbacks in 2009–10, JeM struggled to make a comeback; however, SFs continued to foil its attacks due to the high quality of human intelligence (HUMINT) provided by its robust network. In 2011, JeM suffered another major blow with the encounter death of its Kashmir operations chief, Sajjad Afghani,[121] and his associate Omar Bilal at Foreshore Road on the banks of Dal Lake.[122] A cache of arms and ammunition was recovered from the slain militants, including one AK-47 rifle, eight grenades, one Under Barrel Grenade Launcher (UBGL) and some magazines. Sajjad Afghani hailed from Balochistan in Pakistan.[123] He was behind a spate of attacks in 2010—the Maloora attack in October 2010, the Qamarwari militant attack in Srinagar on 29 November 2010, in which three JeM militants were killed, the Pattan attack in Baramulla and the attack on the superintendent of police in Sopore in December 2010. Besides, he was vigorously pursuing the regrouping of JeM militants in the Tarzoo area, and was active in the Sopore, Rafiabad and Zainageer areas of Baramulla district. He had shifted to Srinagar and planned to conduct operations in the city.

A few months later, a mole inside JeM orchestrated a meeting between LeT and JeM commanders, which led to the top leadership of both organizations getting killed. Afghani's successor, Qari Yasir, a Pakistani militant from Swat Valley, was killed in July 2013 in Lolab.[124] His successor, Adil Pathan, was killed in 2015, along with his associate Abdul Rahman alias Chota Burmee, a Burmese citizen, at Tral. Adil Pathan was the brother of Mufti Asghar, Pakistan-based operations chief. Adil Pathan was active in Kashmir during Ghazi Baba's tenure; however, he returned to Pakistan after Baba's encounter death in August 2003, only to return in 2012. The return of Adil Pathan to Kashmir signalled Pakistan's intent to revive the dwindling presence of JeM in Kashmir. After stalwarts like Sajjad Afghani and Qari Yasir were killed, JeM needed an experienced strategist like Adil Pathan to take over operations in the Valley. In the meantime, JeM had also created a group in Kashmir headed by Altaf Baba, a local. Altaf Baba, trained by Sajjad Afghani, was killed in July 2013 after a fierce nineteen-hour-long encounter in Pulwama.[125] With the elimination of its top-level commanders, particularly Adil Pathan and Chota Burmee, JeM's foundations in Kashmir were shattered, bringing its typical big-ticket fidayeen operations—which had been its hallmark—to a grinding halt. In November 2015, JeM claimed responsibility for the attack on the Tangdhar brigade headquarters near LoC, in which three militants were killed.[126] The militants fired grenades at the oil depot, starting a fire that destroyed some vehicles and barracks. Though, according to the police, the militants carried bags inscribed with the words 'Afzal Guru Squad', SFs denied the group's role in that attack.[127] JeM's claim could have well been a psychological operation (psyop) to keep its image and relevance intact during those testing times when it had lost most of its leadership.

The main reason for the success of the SFs was its intelligence-driven operations. The HUMINT network had become so strong, precise and deep that JeM came to be regarded as the most penetrated organization. The SFs' success in the Pir Panjal region in rooting out the top leadership of JeM, LeT, HuM and HM can also be attributed to 'surgical strikes'.[128] Here, the forces used two types of planning—'track and target' and 'scout, seek and kill'. Under the strategy, many special operation groups (SOGs) generated critical real-time information and conducted meticulous operations in high-altitude areas. Small teams of five to six men were deployed instead of big teams of twenty to thirty members. As a part of their strategy, the police targeted militant sympathizers, including women.

Moreover, in 2008, Darul Uloom issued a fatwa against suicide bombings, which was JeM's forte.[129] Post fatwa, JeM stopped its fidayeen missions for a while. This made it less noticeable and less attractive to potential jihadis. In the early 2000s, the group could infiltrate about 2,000 cadres in the Valley. By 2010, 1,500 cadres were killed.[130] With barbed-wire fencing introduced (2005 onwards) along the LoC, infiltration became an increasingly strenuous exercise for all the groups. Many JeM guides and cadres were killed during such attempts. By 2010, JeM infiltration had significantly declined—only about fifty cadres in a year. Moreover, the group's base—the Rajwar–Lolab area of north Kashmir—became a hotbed of SF spies. Because of the enhanced intelligence, JeM OGW networks were busted, leading to the arrest of their key members. All this helped SFs get precise and actionable intelligence, resulting in successful encounters.

Due to the pervasive presence of intelligence agencies, the local populace was reluctant to shelter JeM cadres. Besides, it was also losing local support in the Kupwara–Handwara–Lolab–Rajwar–Sopore belt because JeM began a major crackdown, killing locals and their supporters on the suspicion of spying for the SFs. In May 2003, JeM militants beheaded four women and two children in Rajouri.[131] On 18 June 2004, the group abducted and beheaded a civilian and his son in Tral on the suspicion of being informants. In another such attempt, a JeM commander and another militant entered the house of a local tribal Muslim family in Rajouri to kill two brothers. However, in the scuffle that ensued, the children of the house killed the commander on the spot, while the other militant escaped. Such brutalities made them unpopular and motivated locals to work for state agencies, who were offering lucrative monetary incentives. Besides, in its initial phase in the early 2000s, JeM, being a hard-line Deobandi extremist organization, tried to impose its extreme version of Shariah laws regarding burqas, beards and other Islamic symbols, mainly in the Doda–Kishtwar and Poonch–Rajouri region. It led to strong local resentment as the local Gujjar Muslim population did not want to follow such rigid Shariah doctrines. They followed many Hindu traditions and cultural practices, and had a liberal religious outlook. Realizing the growing intensity of local resentment, in 2003, JeM withdrew such directives issued in the name of its Central Jihad Council.

On 21 August 2011, Lt Gen. Syed Ata Hasnain of Chinar Corps said, 'Security forces are targeting the leadership of JeM and LeT, and our intelligence this year has been extremely good. Because of this, they achieved major successes this year, and their desperation to infiltrate has increased.'[132] However, that JeM was on the wane was not merely a perception popular among SFs. It was a fact evident in the jihadist circles as well, and duly realized by them. Many intragroup communications intercepted by intelligence agencies and interrogation reports of arrested terrorists reflected this thinking. In an intercepted communication of an HM terrorist with his PoK-based commanders and handlers, he reported that successful counterinsurgency operations in 2009–10 by SFs had led to the near total elimination of the top JeM commanders.

In one such interrogation report,[133] an HM militant-cum-trainer, Mohammad Ashraf, said that thousands of misguided Kashmiri youth were receiving training in camps in PoK. Disclosing more details, he said that LeT and HM were the only two dominant outfits to which most militants were affiliated. At the same time, JeM, once a force to reckon with in Pakistan, had almost become non-existent and irrelevant, with very few cadres remaining. Only a few JeM training camps were now active in PoK. In another interrogation in October 2010, Abdul Waris alias Tauseef, from Kishtwar, and Musarat Hussain Zargar alias Firdous, a resident of Doda—close associates of HM chief Syed Salahuddin—said that 1,400 militants from various parts of J&K, with a majority of them hailing from the Kashmir Valley, were still camping in the training camps of multiple outfits in Pakistan and PoK. The ISI allegedly planned to push many of them into the Indian side via the LoC and International Border (IB).

Further, they said that out of the 1,400, the majority had joined LeT and HM, while JeM's cadre strength had significantly declined as a large number of them had shifted to LeT. A US government report of August 2011, providing an outsider perspective, categorized LeT as the most lethal, extensive and organized Kashmir-centric Pakistani terrorist group, with thousands of members. JeM was far behind on the list—third, in fact—with merely a few hundred fighters.[134]

Since it had become challenging to infiltrate from the northern Kashmir region and many of its cadres died while moving cash in encounters with SFs, JeM changed its strategy for moving money. They tapped into the cross-border trade along the LoC to send money and weapons into the Indian side of Kashmir.[135] All the groups using this method befriended local traders and truck drivers, and bribed them to smuggle cash and weapons. India banned LoC trade after the Pulwama attack of April 2019.[136]

In its early days, between 2000 and 2002, almost all JeM encounters with SFs were in the north Kashmir regions of Kupwara–Handwara, Lolab region, and the Pir Panjal districts of Poonch, Rajouri, Doda and Kishtwar.[137] The Central Kashmir areas of Budgam, Srinagar, Bandipore and Udhampur (in the Jammu region) followed these zones. After a series of intelligence-based operations in the Kupwara–Lolab region, the group started expanding in south Kashmir townships of Anantnag, Pulwama, Awantipora, Bijbehara, Kulgam, etc. By 2005, JeM had found its foothold in south Kashmir, although the area was not entirely new to them. Notably, Masood, during his HuM days, had held meetings with HuM cadres in south Kashmir and was arrested in Anantnag. After 2003, Pulwama, Tral, Anantnag, Shopian, Kokernag, etc., increasingly figured as the principal encounter sites between SFs and JeM. They developed strong ties with local truck drivers and found a support base in the local population. In south Kashmir, JeM was recruiting locals by 2012–13.

Simultaneously, after the deaths of many JeM cadres during infiltration through the north Kashmir routes, new routes were discovered in the Pir Panjal region—notably, the Rajouri–Poonch districts. When SFs tightened their grip on this border, JeM started infiltrating from the Jammu–Punjab border area—Samba, Kathua, RS Pura, Akhnoor and Pathankot. Notably, JeM organized a major fidayeen attack at the Pathankot airbase in 2016. From the townships mentioned above, the IB, manned by the BSF, is hardly a few kilometres from the national highway. Local truck drivers befriended in south Kashmir helped JeM in ferrying militants and weapons in their trucks from Jammu to Srinagar along the national highway. JeM had been using these infiltration routes from 2015; however, it caught the attention of the SFs and the media only after the Pulwama fidayeen attack, as the perpetrators had crossed the border from the Jammu region. After this attack, the SFs tightened their vigil on the Jammu border region, which once again made infiltration very difficult for all the groups. JeM had hoped for a full-fledged war between India and Pakistan after the Pulwama episode in a bid to dismantle the anti-infiltration grid and infiltrate hundreds of its cadres in Kashmir.[138] The terrorist groups, despite the odds, are sending foreign cadres into Indian Kashmir; however, the number has significantly gone down since the early 2000s. Currently, LeT is still sending the maximum number of cadres, followed by JeM.

Revival of JeM in 2016–17: Pathankot to Pulwama

With the deaths of its top commanders like Adil Pathan, Chota Burmee and Altaf Baba, JeM's moderate revival attempts, which began in 2008 and picked up pace in 2010, almost came to a halt. The organization faced a serious leadership crisis, with all its top commanders dead. In such a situation, Noor Muhammad Tantrey, also known as 'four-foot', succeeded Altaf Baba and took over the leadership in Kashmir. In the Valley's jihadist and security circles, Noor Muhammad Tantrey is credited with the single-handed revival of JeM. On the Pakistani side, in 2013, the Pakistan Taliban split into the Punjabi and Afghan factions, and the Punjabis joined JeM.[139] Afzal Guru's hanging offered the organization a new lease on life and, without any delay, JeM announced the formation of Afzal Guru Squads.[140] Afzal Guru was a JeM militant who received the death sentence in the Parliament attack case. He was hanged in 2013. The next year, in 2014, Masood Azhar made a grand comeback after a decade of hibernation, with a public appearance in Muzaffarabad (PoK) to release *Aaina*, the book written by Afzal Guru in his Tihar Jail days.[141] In an event that strictly barred any media presence, Masood, in his speech, threatened India with suicide attacks and vowed revenge for the execution of Afzal Guru.[142] Pakistan's eminent newspaper, *Dawn*, in its report, criticized the state's tacit revival of terrorist organizations like JeM and leaders like Masood, Fazlur Rehman Khalil—who frequently appeared on television debates and helped Pakistan in backchannel talks with the Taliban—and Hafiz Saeed, who was being mainstreamed into national politics. The report called them a threat to Pakistan's national security.[143] On India's objection, Pakistan replied that Masood escaped vigilance and called it a 'one-time event' that should not worry India much.[144] Masood's resurfacing on the politico-jihadist landscape alerted security analysts in the subcontinent of the impending revival of JeM.

Most security analysts tracking Kashmir militancy from distant quarters found the attacks on the brigade headquarters at Tangdhar in July 2015 and the Pathankot airbase attack of 2016 as a sign of JeM's revival because of their very nature. However, contrary to popular perception, JeM never ceased its operations in Kashmir altogether, even after the so-called ban in Pakistan. Between 2000 and 2015, the period before its perceived revival in 2016, JeM continued to send highly trained militants from Pakistan into the Valley, and planned several terror attacks in J&K and other parts of India. However, the lull came after the 2013 encounter deaths of Adil Pathan, Chota Burmee and Altaf Baba. A serious attempt to arrange JeM's revival in a chronological framework has to go back to 2007–08, when the outfit started reorganizing itself—which I have discussed in detail earlier in this chapter. However, between 2007–13, JeM's attempts to revive were met with robust intelligence-driven counterterror operations in J&K, resulting in the elimination of its leadership in Kashmir. These low-key and not-so-successful attacks become reasonable grounds to argue that JeM was dormant and stayed in revival mode. However, they did not get international traction, which finally came with Masood Azhar resurfacing in 2014 at the launch of the Afzal Guru Squad. This was followed by the high-profile attacks in Tangdhar and Pathankot.

Before exploring the details of JeM's second phase, an investigation into the reasons for its revival deserves some focus. Former CIA officer and South Asia expert Bruce Riedel argued that the Pathankot attack was to sabotage the peace process with India, which was supposed to begin a few weeks after PM Modi's surprise visit to Pakistan in December 2015 to attend PM Nawaz Sharif's family event.[145] The attack happened a week after his visit. Reidel suggested that the Pakistan Army and the deep state have always been wary of Nawaz Sharif as he had tried to improve ties with India in the past as well. In 1999, before the Kargil war, Nawaz Sharif responded positively to Vajpayee's peace initiatives; however, the attempt met a sad end with the Kargil invasion and Sharif was sent to a ten-year exile in Saudi Arabia after Musharraf's coup. The Pakistan Army and ISI justify their colossal share of the annual Budget in the name of the 'India threat'; hence, a fall in tensions is likely to raise questions on the Pakistan Army's control of the state's security policy vis-à-vis India. It can dilute its narrative of the enormous security risk posed by India. As a result, the Pakistan Army always tries to sabotage such peace-building measures.

Riedel's arguments are rooted in the geopolitical developments of the region in the last seven decades. Pakistan's Kashmir obsession goes back to 1947. After that, the country, being an artificial creation, faced many separatist movements like Bengali separatism, which led to the creation of Bangladesh and a few others in Sind, Balochistan, KPK and the Saraiki region. What kept its territorial integrity intact was the army, not democracy. Secondly, religion became the uniting factor, leading to the rapid destruction of Sufi practices and local cultural identities, and the spread of an extremist version of Islam. Thirdly, the perceived threat of India could keep the army's control over the state intact. Hence, nurturing proxy terrorist groups in Kashmir as a force multiplier became a compulsion to such a degree that when Pakistan itself faced the terrorism menace, instead of abandoning these groups, Islamabad differentiated between supposedly 'good' and 'bad' terrorists. Kashmir-centric groups like LeT, JeM, HM and Al Badr are 'good terrorists,' while TTP, which targeted the Pakistani state, became 'bad terrorists.'

Christine Fair disagrees with Riedel's assessments, saying that the Pathankot attack was not a spontaneous reaction to disturb the peace process that was supposed to begin with Modi's 2015 visit to Lahore.[146] She explains that there can be no eternal peace between the neighbours as long as Pakistan presses its illogical claim on Kashmir, which is based on ideological reasons rather than security.[147] The Pakistan Army knows well that no peace can be achieved between India and Pakistan until some fundamental issues are resolved, and that includes its claim over Kashmir. Also, the meeting between Nawaz Sharif and Narendra Modi could not have led to any substantial development towards peace as the army calls the shots and the civilian government is subservient to the military. Nawaz Sharif's party's track record of funding JuD and LeT in Punjab reveals his deep-rooted ties with these groups, and also his duplicitous approach towards pursuing peace with India.[148] Delving deeper into Pakistan's true intent, Fair says that Pakistan's reinvigoration of JeM was part of its broader geopolitical strategy in South Asia,[149] where it uses proxy terrorist groups in the pursuance of its ultimate revisionist agenda vis-à-vis Kashmir and Afghanistan.[150] However, JeM's revival, in addition to being a core of Pakistan's proxy war strategy against India, was also a critical component of Islamabad's domestic security strategy. According to Fair, since 2011—if not earlier—Pakistan's core strategy behind reactivating JeM under Masood's command was to rehabilitate those cadres who had defected to the Pakistani Taliban.[151] Before unleashing the Zarb-e-Azaab military offensive in 2014, Pakistan gave TTP's rank and file the option of either joining the Afghan Taliban or Kashmir-centric groups like JeM and LeT. TTP cadres always preferred JeM over LeT because of the common allegiance to the Deobandi school of thought. Moreover, my interviews with JeM OGWs and Kashmir-based Indian intelligence operatives also confirmed that militants of the group had been assembled at the launch pads in PoK for over a year to infiltrate the Valley. Hence, they were expected to infiltrate before PM Modi's Lahore visit. That said, what surprised the JeM militants was the timing of the attack, as they expected them to enter earlier—before the PM visit—and attack the airbase.

According to C.D. Sahay, after the 2008 Mumbai attack, LeT and other Kashmir-centric terrorist groups like HM came under the scanner of global terrorism watchdogs. Many Westerners had died in the Mumbai attack, which raised alarm bells in Western intelligence communities and think-tank circles. They began to perceive LeT as a threat to Western assets. As a result, think-tanks started publishing reports and counterterrorism experts wrote well-researched books on LeT. The UN included Hafiz Saeed in its list of global terrorists under UN Security Council Resolution 1267 (United Nations Security Council 2009).[152] The US also designated Saeed as a global terrorist and has announced a reward of US $10 million for information leading to his arrest and conviction.[153] Likewise, the US listed Mohammad Yusuf Shah, alias Syed Salahuddin of HM, as a specially designated global terrorist (SDGT). The US also designated HM as a foreign terrorist organization in August 2017. Given the overexposure of LeT and HM, and its links with the Pakistani state, JeM, which had not attracted significant international attention after the 2001 Parliament attack—though it continued its low-key terror attacks in the Valley—was Pakistan's natural choice to sustain militancy in Kashmir.

Further, in 2016–17, particularly after Burhan Wani's encounter and the state-wide agitations, SFs launched a massive counterinsurgency drive popularly known as 'Mission All-out'. The state's onslaught led to a large-scale elimination of terrorist cadres. In 2017, the J&K police clarified that of the 190 terrorists killed, eighty were locals and 110 were of foreign descent.[154] Amongst the 110 foreign terrorists, sixty-six were killed near the LoC while trying to infiltrate into India. In a press conference on 19 November 2017, the GOC (general officer commanding) of Chinar Corps said through the counterinsurgency drive, SFs had killed the entire leadership of LeT, along with many others.[155]

In 2017, twelve commanders of LeT, and fourteen prominent militants and commanders of HM were killed by the security forces. In a parallel development, the NIA's crackdown on separatist Hurriyat leaders, OGWs and terror-funding networks had also gained momentum. In this drive also, LeT and HM suffered major reverses. This adversely impacted the overall separatist and jihadist ecosystem in J&K. To inject a fresh lease of life into the movement, once again, JeM was the preferred choice.

Last but not the least, after the encounter death of Burhan Wani in 2016, massive riots and protests erupted across the Kashmir Valley. In many areas of south Kashmir, police stations were burnt. Veteran journalist Praveen Swami described the situation in the following words:[156]

> In 2016, following the killing of jihadi icon Burhan Wani, massive Islamist-led protests had led to the eviction of the Indian state from large swathes of southern Kashmir. For all practical purposes, jihadist groups ruled the region, even hoisting their flags and holding military parades. In villages where they operated, the Jaish-e-Mohammed's Pakistani cadre had become heroes, drawing crowds of frenzied young followers.

In the vacuum created by the failure of law and order, the lack of governance and massive protests, terrorist organizations got the opportunity to consolidate and firmly establish themselves, dominating the region psychologically, culturally and militarily. They established and consolidated links with the local youth and built a strong OGW network, which helped recruit local boys, arrange logistics and provide timely intelligence on the movement of SFs. JeM's revival coincided with this unrest, resulting in its commanders getting the golden opportunity to rebuild the organization. Moreover, JeM got some highly talented local commanders and OGWs like Noor Muhammad Tantrey, who played an instrumental role in recruiting the best local talent and infiltrating a highly skilled, radicalized and trained lot of Pakistani militants who spearheaded JeM till Pulwama, and even after that.

This situation can be understood within the theoretical framework of the relationship between failed states and the growth of terrorist organizations.[157] It can be compared with places like Somalia, Sudan and the Af-Pak region, where the failure of state institutions and governance constituted one of the crucial reasons for the consolidation of terrorist organizations.

Thus, by 2015, JeM, more or less written off by the intelligence community, emerged as the single-largest jihadi organization in Pakistan. Desperately needed as a counterweight to jihadis fighting against the Pakistani state and valued for its old ties with the Taliban, which more or less looked poised to take over Afghanistan after the US withdrawal, the Pakistani security establishment facilitated the resurgence of JeM by rehabilitating a large chunk of anti-Pakistan terrorists, and allowing it to raise money and continue its propaganda work through magazines, journals, schools and congregations. In his February 2014 speech, Masood claimed to have 313 suicide bombers; by 2015, the Indian intelligence sources' assessments indicated that JeM had 500 trained jihadis and was training hundreds of others in its camps stretching from PoK to Afghanistan.

Beginning with the 2013 attack on a police station and an army camp in Samba district, the Afzal Guru Squad conducted ten major attacks—including the 2016 Pathankot air base attack.[158] In this instance, the attackers left a note in SP Salwinder Singh's car, which read, '*Jaish-e-Mohammed Zindabad—Tangdhar se le kar Samba Kathua, Rajbagh aur Delhi tak, Afzal Guru shaheed kay jaanisar tum ko miltay rahega inshallah A G S 25-12-15'* (Long live Jaish-e-Mohammed—from Tangdhar to Sambha, Kathua, Rajbagh and Delhi, you will keep meeting with Afzal Guru's loyalists who are ready to lay down their lives for him).[159] No sooner than the Pathankot mission ended, JeM attacked the Indian mission in Afghanistan's Mazar-i-Sharif on 3 January 2016.[160] The attackers left a note here too—written in blood on the mission walls that they had attacked to avenge Afzal Guru's hanging; 'one martyr, a thousand fidayeen'.[161]

Indian intelligence agencies believed that these attacks were to avenge the execution of Afzal Guru. However, the Pathankot attack, Mazar-i-Sharif attack and the July 2015 Gurdaspur attack (at Dinanagar Police Station, by LeT) can be analysed in the broader context of Pakistan's proxy war and objective of testing India's tolerance threshold. The 2014 victory of the Narendra Modi–led Hindu nationalist BJP in the national elections generated a sense of curiosity, concern and scepticism in the Pakistani security establishment about India's future policy vis-à-vis Pakistan. It is so because the BJP, particularly PM Modi, had a track record of a zero-tolerance approach against terrorism. Following his election victory, India's elite forces, 21 Para, conducted a surgical strike in June 2015 inside Myanmar's territory. They killed Naga insurgents of the separatist National Socialist Council of Nagaland, Khaplang (NSCN-K).[162] After the surgical strike, many Indian politicians of the ruling party made boastful statements warning Indian neighbours that those who sheltered terrorists would be dealt with surgical strikes, wherever needed, including Pakistan. Hence, with the attacks mentioned above, particularly the Gurdaspur attack, Pakistan wanted to signal that it is not Myanmar and to call out India's statements of conducting surgical strikes, exposing them as hollow rhetoric.

Also, Pakistan wanted to test the Modi government's response in the event of high-profile fidayeen attacks to get a clearer picture of the government's mindset, which would help it determine the degree of escalation in the terrorist attacks against India.

Interestingly, the attacks happened with a complete disregard for the peace initiatives between the two countries. The Gurdaspur attack occurred on 27 July 2015, seventeen days after the Modi–Sharif meeting at Ufa (Russia) on the sidelines of the Shanghai Cooperation Organization's summit, where both the leaders unequivocally condemned terrorism, and agreed to work for peace and development.[163] The Pathankot and Mazar-i-Sharif attacks happened barely a week after Modi's Lahore visit. The timing of the attacks provides substantial reasons to argue that Pakistan's security establishment had no interest in pursuing peace initiatives with India. Instead, it explored and understood the Modi government's mindset to sustain and further its proxy war in the new political setting.

Parallel to the JeM attacks in India in 2016–17, the group's activities in Pakistan were also on the rise. Al Murabitoon organized training conclaves branded as an 'Islamic and Training Convention' at Balakot from 28–30 July 2017. Masood's close relative, Talha Al-Saif, addressed the convention.[164] Also, JeM enhanced its recruitment activities. It inducted a batch of about thirteen students at Markaz Usman-O-Ali, Bahawalpur, from 10–21 July 2017, and about seventy students from Peshawar, Mansehra and Balakot joined. JeM's Karachi centre also conducted a training session in that period.[165] It was imparting advanced cyber communications and weapons training to Kashmiri students visiting Pakistan on visas. I came across this practice during my fieldwork for my book on Kashmir's terror financing.

On the financial front, the Al-Rahmat Trust had intensified its fund collection in the form of cash and animal hides to meet the expenses incurred on jihad, education and the welfare of the families of the militants killed in terrorist attacks. In JeM's Naafil Qurbani fundraising campaign, Talha Al-Saif stressed on the urgency to raise funds as the number of dependents of the militants killed in the encounters had increased. Parallel to these developments, Pakistan's outreach to China to block India's attempts in the UN to get Masood Azhar declared a global terrorist also speaks volumes about its intent to resurrect the organization with robust backing in terms of arms and finance.

Pakistan's Response after the Pathankot Air Base Attack

After the Pathankot attack, Pakistan's PM Nawaz Sharif said that the country would examine the evidence furnished by India proving JeM's involvement and act accordingly. Indian leadership and global counterterrorism watchdogs mounted pressure on Pakistan to act against Masood. However, a reluctant Islamabad merely paid lip service by putting him under 'protective custody'. Punjab's law minister, Rana Sanaullah, said there was no law under which Masood could be arrested. However, Pakistan could have detained him under section 11(F) of its 1997 Anti-terrorism Act (membership, support and meetings of a terrorist organization) for a minimum period of six months to a maximum of five years.[166]

Since 1999, Pakistan has refused Indian requests to extradite Masood on the pretext of the government having no clue of his whereabouts. However, after the Pathankot attack, with global pressure mounting, Pakistan could not have afforded to be seen as favouring JeM. One can discern that there were actors invisible to the rest of the world who were trying to protect Masood Azhar.

After the Pathankot attack, Masood Azhar warned the Pakistani government in JeM's publication, *Al Qalam*, writing under his pen name Saadi, that any crackdown against JeM could be 'very dangerous'.[167] In a critical message to Pakistan, he wrote:[168]

> ... There is a lot of noise coming from India regarding us—arrest, kill, arrest, kill—and here our rulers are in anguish because, perhaps, we have disturbed their intimacy and friendship [because] they want that on the day of judgment, they should stand as friends of Modi and Vajpayee.

Threatening a violent jihad, he wrote:[169]

> ... With my killing, neither will my friends miss me, nor will my enemies ... An army which loves death has been prepared ... Allah willing, this army would not let [our] enemies celebrate for too long. It [the army] would not let my absence be felt at all. Thanks to Allah, I do not have any desire that will remain unfulfilled at my death ... As for my family and children, they are taken care of by Almighty Allah, and Almighty Allah will take care of them tomorrow as well.

Demonstrating his loyalties to Pakistan, he said:[170]

> Our thinking regarding Pakistan has always been based on wishing it well and peace ... There is not a single case registered against me in any police station across Pakistan ... [This is] not to save our life and skin but for the interests of Muslim Ummah and in the interest of jihad. I am sorry that the rulers here have no respect for that. They [have] continued to be guided by those who are not our own—and

they continue to turn their own country into a heap of explosives and fire. Each one of them comes and puts their own country on fire and then they flee.

In this message, Masood balanced his threatening posture by showing JeM's utility to Pakistan. Also, he has targeted the civilian government for its peace initiatives with India. Having explained earlier that the revival of JeM was a deliberate strategy, it appears that the Pakistan Army and deep state encouraged Masood to write this warning letter to discourage the civilian government from pursuing any peace-building measures. Also, the letter served the purpose of showing Pakistan in a positive light—a nation willing to cooperate in the face of such terrorist threats, thus absolving itself of any involvement or ties with JeM.

2017

In June 2017, JeM carried out five attacks in a span of a few hours across the Kashmir region; however, no one was killed in them.[171] Then, on 3 October 2017, JeM attacked a paramilitary camp in Srinagar, in which three terrorists and a soldier died. Less than a week later, a top-level JeM commander, Khalid, the mastermind of the Srinagar paramilitary camp attack and an attack on the police lines in south Kashmir, was killed in north Kashmir. He was one of the longest surviving militants in the Valley who had been entrusted with the task of attacking critical security installations. His death was a temporary set-back to the outfit.

Interestingly, JeM's revival coincided with the revival of Mushtaq Ahmad Zargar and his Al Umar Mujahideen (AuM) in Kashmir. As per intelligence sources, the ISI has sent him to J&K and pushed his organization back into action to help Masood.

According to some media reports, he was in Doda (Jammu) talking to some journalists from a satellite phone.[172]

In the second phase of JeM's revival, Noor Muhammad Tantrey—also known as Noor Trali, for he was from Tral—played the most crucial role.[173] Previously, he served as Ghazi Baba's OGW and was arrested in Delhi. In 2011, he was given life imprisonment by the Prevention of Terrorism Act (POTA) court. After some time in Tihar Jail, he was shifted to Srinagar, where he was released on parole in 2015. Following that, he jumped his parole and devoted himself to reviving JeM. His long-time associates Feroz Ahmad Bhat and Parvez Mir assisted him in resurrecting the organization from jail. After the encounter killing of Parvez Mir, Tantrey joined JeM as an active militant under the leadership of Mufti Waqas, alias Abdul Mateen, and became JeM's divisional commander of south Kashmir. He was the man behind the infiltrations of some key JeM militants in 2016–17 and the arranging of logistics for some high-profile terror attacks. A forty-seven-year-old man standing at just four feet in height, Tantrey shocked everyone with his keen sense of strategy allowing for the revival of the organization. In 2017 alone, he was the mastermind of three attacks.

The earliest reports about the activities of Tantrey and the foreign terrorists (FTs) who had infiltrated the Valley were received by the J&K police in April 2017 from its HUMINT sources. After the Pulwama district police lines and the BSF camp attack, JeM terrorist Aarzoo Bashir, an accomplice of Feroz Ahmad Bhat, was arrested. In his interrogation, he spoke about the presence of thirty to forty JeM FTs in the region and its plans to organize a vehicle-borne IED (VBIED) attack at Lethpura CRPF camp on 31 December 2017 with local Kashmiris, Fardeen Ahmed Khandey and Manzoor Ahmed Baba. Abdul

Shakoor, the third fidayeen in this attack, was from PoK.[174] With the help of inputs shared by him, the police launched a targeted drive against the terrorists, as a result of which the following JeM militants were killed:

1) Waseem Ghanai, Talha Rashid (Masood Azhar's nephew) and Mahmood Bhai, in Pulwama on 6 November 2017.
2) Rashid Billa and three other accomplices, in Budgam on 30 November 2017.
3) Abu Ummer, in Tral on 16 December 2017.
4) Tanveer Ahmed Bhat alias Nauman and Ali Bhai alias Qari, in Shopian on 18 December 2017. The duo was involved in an attack on a J&K bank cash-carrying van, which resulted in the killing of its two guards.
5) Noor Muhammad Tantrey, in Pulwama on 26 December 2017.

In 2017, twenty-three JeM terrorists were killed, out of which fifteen were foreign terrorists. The successful encounters were the result of robust technical intelligence generated from the close surveillance of twenty-nine hardcore JeM OGWs of south Kashmir.

2018

With JeM activities rising, SFs turned their attention to Manzoor Reshi and Mudasir Khan from Tral, key OGWs of JeM chief Mufti Waqas. These individuals were employed at a Vodafone centre and associated with the networking team. On 17 January 2018, they visited the Babadam area of Srinagar, a scrap and vehicle-accessories market, to buy a remote used in remote-controlled IEDs (RCIED). Based on these inputs, the police tried to arrest them, but only Reshi was captured. Mudasir Khan escaped and reported to Mufti Waqas, who recruited him as an active cadre within a week. On 6–7 February 2018, technical intelligence inputs verified the location of Mudasir in the forests of Verinag and Kokarnag in south Kashmir. It was suspected that they would conduct a suicide attack either in the Qazigund region of Kulgam district or in Anantnag; however, the attack happened in the far south, in the Jammu region, at Sunjwan army camp on 9 February 2018. Due to highly sophisticated and complex mobile usage patterns, Mufti Waqas successfully eluded various cordon and search operations (CASOs) by security forces. However, detailed profiling of his OGW network led to his death on 5 March 2018 at a village, Hatiwara, by a small team comprising officers from Jammu and Kashmir police and 50 Rashtriya Rifles. Based on precise technical intelligence (TECHINT), which included details of the kind of weapons Mufti Waqas carried, the operation concluded in just forty-five minutes. Mufti Waqas had masterminded the Sunjwan army base suicide attack and also radicalized Fardeen Khandey and Ishaq Khan (both locals), who led the suicide attack at Lethpura on 31 December 2017.[175] The killing of Mufti Waqas was celebrated in the intelligence community as he was planning some large-scale suicide attacks outside Kashmir. Also, catching hold of his OGW networks revealed significant information about JeM's activities in Pakistan. On 24 April 2018, the JeM commander of the Tral region, Ishfaq Khan, was killed with his four associates.

After a series of successful encounters in which they lost top leadership, JeM terrorists changed their strategy and resorted to sniper attacks in September 2018. These attacks were concentrated in the south Kashmir region and the most famous one was the attack at the Wagoora power grid in Srinagar. Notably, a Pakistani JeM terrorist, Usman Haider, planned and coordinated these attacks. Using various technical inputs and intelligence from human assets, SFs were able to kill Usman Haider on 31 October 2018 at Mandoora, in Tral, along with JeM operative Showkat Ahmed Khan (cousin of Ishfaq Khan) of Handoora, Tral. In 2018, along with Mufti Waqas, forty-nine JeM terrorists were killed in the Kashmir zone. Of this, thirty-four were foreigners and fifteen were identified as locals.

2019

In January 2019, three top commanders of JeM—Zubair, Maulvi Asadullah, and Shahid Baba were killed in south Kashmir.[176] On 27 July, Munna Bihari, who masterminded the Banihal IED blast, was killed in an encounter at Bonpora in Shopian. Out of the forty-one JeM terrorists killed in 2019, fifteen were foreign terrorists.

The most impactful terrorist attack of 2019, which set some new redlines in South Asian geopolitics, was the infamous Pulwama fidayeen attack of 14 February 2019. An explosives-laden car driven by a local Kashmiri suicide bomber, Adil Dar, rammed into a CISF vehicle on the national highway, killing over forty Indian paramilitary soldiers and the bomber. This resulted in Indian airstrikes at the Balakot camp of JeM on 26 February 2019, following which, on 27 February, Pakistan violated Indian air space in the Nowshera sector of Rajouri district and dropped bombs near the Indian army base.[177] In the retaliatory action, India downed one of Pakistan's F-16s three kilometres inside Pakistani territory. Islamabad claimed that two Indian jets were shot down and one Indian pilot was captured, leading to high-pitch diplomatic drama. JeM once again brought the two nuclear adversaries on the verge of war.

However, Pakistan's response again reflected a deep schism between the military establishment and the civilian government, and the former's reluctance to punish JeM. Pakistan's then foreign minister, Shah Mahmood Qureshi, admitted in an interview with CNN that Masood Azhar was present in Pakistan.[178] However, Major General Asif Ghafoor, DG ISPR (Inter-Services Public Relations), denied JeM's presence in Pakistan altogether.[179] In an attempt to shield ISI's covert ties and protect Masood, he said in his interview with CNN, 'Jaish-e-Mohammed does not exist in Pakistan. It has been proscribed by the United Nations and Pakistan also. Secondly, we are not doing anything under anybody's pressure.'[180] Ghafoor also said that JeM's claim of conducting the Pulwama attack was not made from inside Pakistan. However, his statements contradicted the developments on the ground after forty-four 'members of proscribed organizations' were put in 'preventive detention'[181] for investigation, including two family members of Masood Azhar. Qureshi's interview referred to Masood Azhar as the JeM chief and proved that the state authorities were in touch with him as he mentioned details about the latter's health. Also, my interlocutors said that Masood Azhar had been ill for a long time—he was suffering from renal failure, was being treated in different army hospitals in Pakistan and was being moved around very discreetly. Likewise, as mentioned earlier, the Bahawalpur administration also, after some perfunctory action of taking over Madressatul Sabir (Sabir Seminary) and Jamia Masjid Subhanallah (both part of the JeM's Bahawalpur complex), claimed that the complex was an ordinary madrasa with the capacity for 650 students and seventy faculty members, and had no connection to JeM or any proscribed organization.[182] The information and broadcasting minister, Fawad Chaudhry, also echoed the Bahawalpur administration. He said, 'This is a seminary, and India is doing propaganda that it is the JeM headquarters.'[183]

2020–2021

After the abrogation of Article 370, the erstwhile state of Jammu and Kashmir was subjected to severe security and a communication lockdown. The intelligence agencies had received inputs of large-scale IED attacks and violent protests in reaction to the abrogation of Article 370. However, the strict implementation of the lockdown made encrypted communications between militants extremely difficult. Jamaat-i-Islami was already banned and key OGWs were arrested. In addition to the ban on LoC trade, NIA's decisive action—involving the arrests of main coordinators, OGWs and hawala operators—dealt a severe blow to terror funding. SFs intensified their operations against JeM and it led to the deaths of thirty-two cadres, nine of whom were foreign terrorists.[184] Two leaders in particular, Abu Saifullah and Samir Ahmed Dar, were considered particularly dangerous. Trained with the Taliban in IEDs, Saifullah was a close associate of JeM's top leaders.[185] Moreover, he was involved in the Pulwama fidayeen attack. After Pulwama, JeM became the prime target of SFs and had to lie low. Saifullah was tasked with the responsibility of re-establishing and strengthening the organization, using south Kashmir to find recruits, train them in IEDs and send them to the other parts of the Valley. Samir Ahmed Dar, a local, was a conspirator in the Pulwama attack and the last one to be killed among the masterminds of the terror operations.[186]

According to a confidential state police intelligence dossier, JeM found itself especially under the scanner and it started operating under different names—Majlis Wurasa-e-Shuhada Jammuwa Kashmir, Lashkar-i-Mustapha, Kashmir Tigers, Kashmir Frontiers and People's Anti-Fascist League (PAFL)—to collect funds, and enable movement and logistical support. In north Kashmir, JeM has not been able to add locals to its cadre strength. It is mainly dominated by FTs, especially in Kupwara, Handwara, and Sopore, especially in areas adjoining Handwara. Amir Siraj Bhat, a prominent local terrorist of JeM from Sopore, acted as a guide by recruiting locals in its OGW cadre strength. The SFs killed him in December 2020. One JeM group under the command of Abu Sufyan, a foreign terrorist, infiltrated the Valley after the abrogation of Article 370 and they were active in northern Kashmir before SFs killed them.

In central Kashmir, Budgam has emerged as a JeM hotbed. In the past, Ganderbal, Safapora and Kangan areas have remained a stronghold for JeM. Still, in recent times, there is a possibility that the active recruits of the organization may activate dormant OGWs in these areas. In south Kashmir, the outfit has been successful in recruiting locals into its terror fold. The majority of JeM terrorists in south Kashmir, mainly locals, are from the Police District (PD) of Awantipora region. PD Awantipora has remained the central hub of JeM terror activities as most of the top local commanders of JeM —Noor Mohammad Tantrey, Fayaz Thoker and Mudasir Khan (all killed)—were all from here. These commanders had strengthened their OGW network base in the region and cultivated a fertile ground for local recruitments. Other JeM hubs in south Kashmir are Pulwama, Shopian, Anantnag and Kulgam. After June 2021, intelligence agencies recorded a rise in JeM activities. In October 2021, some Afghan-trained JeM militants also infiltrated the Valley and most of them are present in south Kashmir.[187]

Outside of India, JeM was also occupied in this time with supporting Taliban forces against the Americans in Afghanistan. However, that may not be the sole reason for the decline in its infiltration and terror attacks in Kashmir. Pakistan's security establishment tried to rein in JeM primarily because of the fear of FATF sanctions and the pressure of Saudi Arabia.[188] A large number of JeM fighters were shifted to Afghanistan after India's Balakot airstrikes. The Saudis unequivocally told Pakistan that they are not keen on the idea of supporting terrorist groups in India.[189] For Pakistan, it was difficult to ignore these directions as Saudi Arabia has been a prominent economic partner, development aid and grants donor—more so, given Islamabad's precarious financial condition. Lately, due to the strengthening ties between India and Saudi Arabia, it has become increasingly difficult for Pakistan to carry on its anti-India proxy war and be in the good books of the Saudis at the same time. This is also evident from a series of articles published by JeM in its media and digital platforms asking the Imran Khan-led government to lift restrictions on terrorist groups in Kashmir and support their activities across the Valley.

Al Qalam's editorial in the 12 August 2020 issue said,[190] 'Kashmir's people had hoped there would be help for their struggle from across the border … but what they got instead is their names on highways, banners and billboards, and a few minutes of silence for fallen martyrs.' A poem in the 4 September 2020 issue urges the Pakistani government to 'talk to the preachers of power in the language of power … do not even mistakenly talk to the enemy with softness.'[191] An article citing Musharraf's failure to control jihadist organizations sermonized the Imran Khan government to learn from the past. It said,[192] 'General Pervez Musharraf tried to impose restrictions on the Kashmir struggle, but he failed and got mud on his face … the movement emerged even more powerful in both military and non-military terms.' To motivate followers and jihadist cadres, the article further observed,[193] 'These people also want to kill the movement … they also want to wear a medal of peace; but don't worry, things will change, they will fail. The morning will dawn when Jihad will become prominent again.'

After the abrogation of Article 370, terrorist groups changed their strategy. Due to FATF pressure, and the overexposure of Pakistan's links to LeT and JeM, ISI masterminds devised the strategy of creating proxy terrorist groups. For example, TRF emerged as a proxy of LeT, and the Kashmir Tigers, Lashkar-i-Mustapha and the People's Anti-Fascist Front (PAFF) emerged as JeM fronts. The main objective behind creating these fronts was to project Kashmir militancy as local and secular. Wasim from Dagerpora, in south Kashmir, and Mufti Altaf, from Anantnag, started Kashmir Tigers.[194] Mufti Altaf was formerly a member of JeM.[195] Kashmir Tigers claimed responsibility for the attack on the bus carrying police personnel on 13 December 2021—the twentieth anniversary of the Parliament attack. Two policemen were killed and twelve were injured.[196] It was the biggest attack after the abrogation of Article 370. To project itself as a secular entity, the group dedicated the attack to 'all the martyrs of the Kashmir resistance'. Further, it said, 'The strike is an answer to the occupational regime and their stooges for the atrocities they were carrying [out] against innocent civilians.'[197]

Lashkar-i-Mustapha emerged as another JeM front with Maulvi Hidaytullah, from Shopian, as its chief. Arrested in Jammu's Kunjwani area with a grenade and pistol,[198] he had conducted a recce of national security advisor (NSA) Ajit Doval's office and his security detail, along with other high-value targets in Delhi.[199] The police recovered the video of the recce of NSA Ajit Doval's office, which he had sent to his handler in Pakistan.[200] Some associates of Lashkar-i-Mustapha were apprehended in Bihar too, as mentioned earlier.

Though these groups were identified as proxies of a specific terror outfit by agencies, it was based on inputs derived from their assets, which did not have precise and detailed information. These groups have fluid memberships; for example, TRF has members from HM, LeT and JeM. In many cases, the parent outfit could never be identified. Mostly, these groups have an online presence—however, the practice of cadres announcing on social media about their joining a particular outfit has been done away with. Hence, it is incredibly challenging to know accurately the militant cadre and organization to which he is associated. More recently, terror groups have started operating through hybrid or part-time militants.[201] This phenomenon makes it almost impossible to identify the terrorist organization involved in the act. Senior intelligence officers told me on the condition of anonymity that after the abrogation of Kashmir's special status, Pakistan put intense pressure on the United Jihad Council (UJC) to prove their importance by organizing multiple terror attacks; it asked them to stop their infighting and synergize their efforts.

Lastly, in the more recent encounters of 2021–22, it can be seen that as compared to other terrorist groups, JeM has a much better weapons' profile.[202] From some encounter sites, MP4, high-quality night vision devices (NVDs) and Pika guns were recovered. According to Brigadier Pandey (name changed to maintain anonymity), a sector commander in Kashmir, in 80 per cent of JeM encounters, the militants had AK-47s. In 50 per cent, the militants had an additional weapon, a Glock pistol.[203] Also, after the India–Pakistan ceasefire in February 2021, infiltration along the LoC declined; however, along the IB in the Jammu region, it increased. LeT's infiltration is mainly from the LoC side, while JeM's is from the IB. It is highly likely that, unlike LeT, JeM is not in complete compliance with the Pakistan Army's state agenda of decreasing infiltration after the ceasefire. Let's suppose this trend is seen in the context of JeM's intention to spark a full-fledged India–Pakistan war (discussed earlier) to facilitate the large-scale infiltration of its cadres. In that case, it can be reasoned that the outfit is gradually increasing its numbers in J&K for actions in the future. Also, with a better weapons' profile, it has emerged as the most attractive terror outfit for radicalized youth.[204]

Review of the Statistical Figures[205]

JeM's Yearly Terrorist Incidents and Fatalities[206]

Year	Incidents of Killing	Civilians	Security Forces	Terrorists	Not Specified	Total
2000	33	7	8	63	0	78
2001	107	38	28	207	0	273
2002	88	16	11	137	1	165
2003	94	13	11	153	1	178
2004	37	2	5	58	0	65
2005	48	8	9	68	0	85
2006	29	0	13	38	0	51
2007	18	0	2	21	0	23
2008	12	0	1	22	0	23
2009	14	0	6	15	0	21
2010	6	0	0	10	0	10
2011	5	0	0	9	0	9
2012	1	0	0	1	0	1
2013	5	0	0	5	0	5
2014	6	0	0	10	0	10
2015	4	1	0	7	0	8
2016	5	0	24	9	0	33

Year	Incidents of Killing	Civilians	Security Forces	Terrorists	Not Specified	Total
2017	16	0	18	24	0	42
2018	22	9	12	34	0	55
2019	32	2	49	51	0	102
2020	13	0	2	26	0	28
2021	13	2	1	22	0	25
2022	14	0	3	26	0	29
Total	622	98	203	1016	2	1319

Analysis

The total number of incidents involving JeM from 2000 to 2022 is 622, out of which 407 deaths occurred between 2000 and 2005 alone. From 2000 to 2003, incidents were on the rise. The year 2001 tops the chart with 107 incidents. After that, till 2005, JeM maintained a robust activity level; however, its terror activities registered a significant decline after 2005 due to its ban in Pakistan. The years 2010 to 2015–16 is the leanest phase of its activities. In 2017, there was a sudden rise in incidents, which peaked in 2019 with thirty-two, following which JeM kept a moderate level of activities of thirteen–fourteen incidents every year till July 2022.

The total number of JeM terrorists killed in Kashmir is 1,016, out of which 724 terrorists were killed between 2000 and 2006 alone. The year 2001 tops the chart with 207 casualties. Between 2000 and 2006, SFs were most successful in killing the largest number of JeM terrorists. From 2007 onwards, a sharp decline in casualties continued till 2016. In 2012, there was one JeM militant killed. From 2017 onwards, JeM saw a resurgence in

Kashmir, with the highest fifty-one losses in 2019. Between 2019 and 2020, JeM casualties have ranged between twenty to twenty-six every year. Though JeM entered its second phase in 2016–17, the casualties and incidents here are much lesser than in the first phase—most likely due to a general decline in infiltration with the introduction of concertina wire fencing along the LoC. Additionally, it seems that JeM's strategy evolved in the second phase. Here, it appears to be focusing on pointed and optics-generating high-profile suicide attacks instead of frittering away its resources on small-scale terror incidents. Also, thanks to a large number of casualties in the first phase due to penetration by Indian intelligence agencies, JeM is possibly following a high level of caution and secrecy in the second phase. Additionally, from 2016 onwards, SFs in J&K have relied heavily on TECHINT rather than HUMINT. The latter has suffered a decline in quality, due to which the older techniques of infiltrating and exfiltrating human assets into the terrorist group fell into disuse.

Jaish-e-Mohammed: Major Yearly Incidents[207]

Year	Total Number of Incidents
2000	12
2001	35
2002	26
2003	18
2004	5
2005	9
2006	4
2008	3
2009	4
2014	2

Year	Total Number of Incidents
2015	1
2016	3
2017	6
2018	8
2019	8
2020	5
2021	4
2022	5
Total	158

Analysis

The total number of major JeM terrorist incidents is 158, out of which ninety-one alone are between 2000–03. Between 2009 and 2014, it did not conduct any significant terrorist incidents; however, the trend began to reverse after that. From 2016 onwards, JeM incidents registered a major spike, which peaked in 2019. After that, the outfit has continued moderate levels of terrorist activity. It is highly likely that after the abrogation of Article 370, JeM cadres are orchestrating terrorist activities through proxy groups like Lashkar-i-Mustapha, Kashmir Tigers, People's Anti-Fascist Front, etc., as a result of which the number of terror incidents directly attributed to JeM have declined.

Jaish-e-Mohammed: Arms Recovery[208]

Year	Total Number of Incidents
2000	1
2001	15

Year	Total Number of Incidents
2002	33
2003	48
2004	22
2005	22
2006	19
2007	12
2008	13
2009	7
2010	3
2011	2
2012	1
2013	3
2014	2
2016	4
2017	10
2018	9
2019	17
2020	23
2021	16
2022	9
Total	291

Analysis

The total number of arms recovery incidents between 2000 and 2022 is 291, of which 160 were between 2000 and 2006. After 2006, there was a major decline, which continued till 2016. From 2016 onwards, there was a sudden rise in arms recovery incidents, suggesting JeM's revival in J&K. The year

2020 recorded the highest number of arms recovery incidents—twenty-three.

Jaish-e-Mohammed: Yearly Explosions[209]

Year	Total Number of Incidents
2000	4
2001	2
2002	2
2005	3
2006	9
2016	1
2017	3
2018	2
2019	9
2022	1
Total	36

JeM's Penetration in the Indian Hinterland

Masood Azhar, after forming JeM, categorically declared in his public speeches that his aim was not only to liberate Kashmir but also to take control of Ayodhya's Babri mosque, Amritsar and Delhi. JeM regards Kashmir as a 'gateway' to all of India, whose Muslims are desperately in need of liberation.[210] After securing Kashmir's accession to Pakistan, the organization allegedly aims to continue its jihad in other parts of India, with the intention of evicting Hindus and other non-Muslims from the Indian subcontinent.[211]

While launching JeM in Karachi, Masood said, 'I have come here [to Karachi] because it is my duty to tell you that the Muslims should not rest in peace until they destroy India and the US.'[212] These statements indicate JeM's global ambitions with Pakistan as its centre. An Indian intelligence report from 2010 makes the following observations about JeM's pan-India ambitions, 'Maulana Masood Azhar was already an extremist, and his incarceration in [an] Indian prison left a deep mark on his mind and created intense abhorrence towards India.'[213] Further, it mentions that JeM projects Jammu and Kashmir as the gateway to India and retains its ambition to liberate Muslims in other parts of India after Kashmir. In the subsequent phases of its jihad, JeM believes in broadening the struggle by taking the battle to the people of India, and endorses the idea of expelling Hindus from the Indian subcontinent in order to establish an Islamic caliphate in South Asia followed by a global caliphate. JeM's strategy also envisions carrying out attacks deep inside India rather than focusing only on Kashmir.

Besides, Masood also has some purely tactical and strategic reasons for launching attacks beyond Kashmir. In one of his motivational and indoctrinating speeches, he said that if a Kashmiri dies, it does not hurt India, it hurts Kashmiris; however, if they attack other parts of the country, India would be shattered. He also claimed that Vajpayee begged Musharraf for peace talks after JeM sent mujahideens into places like Delhi and Lucknow.[214]

The first attack JeM carried out outside of Kashmir was the Parliament attack. After its ban (global and domestic), JeM felt the pressure and announced that it would confine its activities to J&K.[215] However, it continued to expand its network in India. In those early days, the organization's enthusiasm for pan-India operations was high and it made serious attempts to build sleeper cells in the Indian heartland.[216] In August 2003, Noor Muhammad Tantrey was arrested in Delhi with his associates, Parvez Mir and Feroz Ahmad Bhat, at Millennium Park in New Delhi.[217] The two other terrorists with them, Zahoor Ahmed and Habibullah, were killed. In a connected development, the police arrested two Pakistan-trained militants, Atiq and Raees, from Sikandrabad in UP. In the police interrogation, the arrested militants revealed that they were JeM cadres who were delivering a weapons consignment to Atiq and Raees in Sikandrabad. The slain militants were entrusted with the responsibility of providing weapons. Reportedly, they created a base in Sikandrabad to conduct a major strike in Delhi. The interrogation also revealed that the organization was planning to attack the Mumbai stock exchange.

After the Gujarat riots of 2002, JeM planned to organize large-scale terror attacks across the country to avenge the killing of Muslims in the unrest. It developed many underground sleeper cells in various parts of India. These cells worked covertly, kept a low profile, and helped arrange logistics, recruits and shelters. JeM and LeT were recruiting dozens of young boys to execute terror attacks. Several such cells existed across the country; however, the murder of the former home minister of Gujarat, Haren Pandya, helped the Gujarat police identify and eliminate one such cell—the Sufiyan cell—operating in Gujarat. Investigations unearthed the role of Maulana Sufiyan Patangia, a Tablighi Jamaat preacher and the head of Waliullah Seminary in Ahmedabad. Reportedly, Patangia ran a JeM-linked Sufiyan network, the largest terrorist cell in the Gujarat region.[218] Patangia had two channels of support—Farhatullah Ghauri and Abdul Rehman, Saudi-based JeM fundraisers of Hyderabadi origin.[219] They were raising funds for the victims of the Gujarat riots in public meetings held by South Asian expatriates.

Salim Sheikh and Rashid Ajmeri, originally from Ahmedabad and living in Saudi, introduced Patangia to the fundraisers. They allegedly discussed the details of organizing large-scale attacks to avenge the Gujarat riots. According to the Indian investigators,

INR 5 lakh was sent through hawala channels to fund Pandya's assassination. Patangia received the funds some six months before the assassination itself, around October 2002. He also developed contacts with Rasool 'party', a local gangster group of Ahmedabad which worked with the city's local mafia don, Abdul Latif Sheikh. Abdul Latif Sheikh was close to Karachi-based Dawood Ibrahim, who had masterminded the Mumbai serial blasts of 1993. After Latif died in a police encounter during his alleged escape, Rasool 'party' contacted Dawood Ibrahim. In this entire nexus, Karachi-based JeM commanders emerged as a crucial node as they planned terror attacks, and local individuals like Patangia and Rasool 'party' were expected to arrange logistics and cadres. Abdullah Shah Mazhar, a JeM commander estranged from the Masood Azhar faction, wanted to prove his worth by organizing a spectacular strike. On his directions, Patangia first organized five low-intensity bomb blasts in public transport buses in Ahmedabad on 29 May 2002, injuring twenty-six people.[220] Then, he arranged ten recruits, who travelled to Pakistan via Bangladesh, where JeM assured them that their training would be arranged.

In November 2005, an alleged JeM conduit shuttling between India and Bangladesh was arrested by the special cell of the Delhi police at the Old Delhi railway station.[221] He had ferried the terrorists who perpetrated the 5 July Ayodhya attack. Initially, the UP and J&K police were investigating the role of LeT in the Ayodhya attack, but soon, the arrests proved that JeM was behind it. Muhammad Qari, the mastermind, was a local commander of JeM.[222] The five militants who died in the failed attack had visited Deoband. The conspiracy was hatched at a clinic in Delhi belonging to Irfan, a member of the local Jaish sleeper cell.[223] Irfan was arrested in the case and was handed a life imprisonment term later. He arranged cell phones, travel and accommodation for the militants. JeM's modus operandi demonstrated that it had kept smart and efficient sleeper cells in Delhi intact even after the 2001 Parliament attack and the international crisis that followed. Its sleeper cells could provide surveillance and recce services, and arrange all the logistics for a low-key or high-profile attack. Notably, they could evade the radar of Indian intelligence services and plan a sensitive attack like the one in Ayodhya—though it failed—clearly showing their penetration and network in the national capital. The arrested individuals said in the police interrogation that it was Masood Azhar's unfulfilled dream to attack the sanctum sanctorum of Ayodhya temple.[224]

In August 2006, Mumbai police's Anti-Terrorism Squad (ATS) said that two Pakistani militants, one of whom was arrested and one of whom was killed in an encounter on 21 August, had links to JeM.[225] Muhammad Riaz Nawabuddin, who was arrested, said in the police interrogation that the duo was trained at a JeM camp in Pakistan. They planned to attack five places in Mumbai, including Bhabha Atomic Research Centre at Anushakti Nagar and the Siddhivinayak Temple. In November 2006, two Jaish-e-Mohammed militants were apprehended by the police at the Old Delhi railway station. The arrests followed a tip-off that the duo was aboard the Kalka–Delhi Mail. The police recovered two kilograms of RDX and INR 5 lakh from them.

In December 2006, the Union Ministry of Home Affairs came up with a paper that detailed Lashkar-e-Taiba and Jaish-e-Mohammed activities where they used territory and elements in Bangladesh and Nepal to move terrorists and finances.[226] These groups recruited Indian youth and then, with the help of HuJI in Bangladesh, sent them for training to Pakistan via Bangladesh and Nepal then ferried them back to India via Bangladesh and Nepal. Further, the paper mentioned that the group maintained a regular flow of finances to sustain its terrorist network, stoke communal tensions, target economic infrastructure and vital installations, radicalize, recruit and train local modules, and attack soft targets like marketplaces, public transport systems, places of worship and congregations. The paper's assessments aligned with the facts on the ground, such as the attackers in the Varanasi serial blasts (2006), Mumbai blasts (July 2006), and the Indian Institute of Science attack (December 2005) infiltrated via the India–Bangladesh border.[227]

In January 2007, the intelligence reports indicated that JeM, LeT and Students Islamic Movement of India (SIMI) cadres were planning a terrorist attack during the India–West Indies one-day international cricket match in Cuttack, at the Barabati Stadium on 24 January 2007.[228] In addition, the terrorists also planned to carry out attacks in Kochi (Kerala), Bhubaneswar (Odisha), Guwahati (Assam) and Bengaluru (Karnataka) before Republic Day on 26 January.

In February 2007, four suspected JeM militants, including a Pakistani national, were detained after an encounter with the Delhi police near Connaught Place (CP).[229] The police recovered three kilograms of RDX, four detonators, a timer, six hand grenades, a .30-bore firearm, USD 10,000 and INR 50,000 from them.[230] The encounter resulted from an intelligence input that some JeM members were in the capital to carry out a major operation and that they would meet near a flyover. The joint commissioner of police (special cell) Karnal Singh said that the militants identified themselves as Shahid Gafur from Sialkot in Pakistan, and Bashir Ahmed, Fayaz Lone and Abdul Majid from Jammu and Kashmir. The three Kashmiris disclosed that they arrived via Malwa Express earlier.

In November 2007, three JeM militants, arrested in Lucknow with arms and ammunition, planned to kidnap the Congress leader Rahul Gandhi to use him as a bargaining chip to get forty-two prisoners released.[231]

As the aforementioned home ministry paper highlighted, by 2007, JeM and LeT had built robust links with HuJI Bangladesh. The report mentioned:[232]

> The hand of Pakistan-based terrorist organizations—LeT and JeM—and, increasingly of the Bangladesh-based HuJI, known to have close links with ISI, has been observed in most of these cases. The incidents showed these groups have been using sleeper cells in the country to carry out such activities and have also been using the territory of other neighbouring countries such as Bangladesh and Nepal.

These links were instrumental in expanding the terror network across India. In December 2007, the director general of the BSF, A.K. Mitra, said in a media briefing that the 'western frontier of India was relatively tough for Pakistani militants. Still, the eastern border with Bangladesh had become more useful for them. Foreign militants were utilizing the south Bengal border for anti-Indian activities.'[233] He also mentioned that fourteen militants of LeT and JeM were arrested on the south Bengal border, trying to sneak into India from Bangladesh in the past six months. In February 2008, five militants of JeM were arrested in Dhaka (Bangladesh), following which another JeM terrorist, Nannu Mia alias Belal Mandal alias Billal, was arrested by the Rapid Action Battalion (RAB) in Dhaka on 28 February. He admitted to having ensured safe passages for several terrorists from Bangladesh to India. Some of them facilitated the IC-814 hijacking from Bangladesh. In March 2010, JeM's main coordinator in Bangladesh, Rizwan Ahmed, revealed the 'identities' and 'whereabouts' of three other Pakistani terrorists who were his accomplices.[234] As per his inputs, Sohel, Ali and

Zawad had come to Bangladesh with him in August 2009 to cross over to India for terrorist activities. However, due to logistical issues, they could not cross into the Indian territory, and thus Sohel and Ali returned to Pakistan, while Zawad left for Singapore after over two months' stay in Bangladesh. The Bangladeshi state agencies, alarmed by the increasing activities and networks of the Pakistani terrorist groups, launched a drive that led to several arrests. The detained militants and coordinators confirmed in their interrogation that LeT and JeM were using Bangladesh for shelter and as a transit point, and the ISI was helping them with funds and training.

The Pakistani terror groups and HuJI were also trying to build contacts with the insurgent groups of northeastern India, with the idea of sabotaging India's national security in the Northeast.[235] HuJI was formed in 1992, but became active after 2000. With the help of the ISI and Bangladesh Directorate General of Forces Intelligence, it established links with Kashmiri terrorist groups like HuM, JeM, LeT, United Liberation Front of India (ULFA) and National Democratic Front of Bodoland (NDFB). In July 2010, Paresh Barua, chief of ULFA, met JeM, HuJI and LeT leaders.[236] According to Indian intelligence sources, HuJI's long-term goal is 'Islamic revolution in India's North-East'.[237] It has links with AQ. The terror group had sent funds to Bangladesh through the 1990s, channelling them through the Al-Haramain Foundation of Saudi Arabia and the Servants of Suffering and Humanity International Charity in Dhaka.[238] HuJI Bangladesh established contacts with AQ through the Taliban. Between 1996 and 2001, several HuJI (B) activists were trained at AQ camps in Afghanistan. Sheikh Abdul Rahman, a leader of the 'Jihad Movement of Bangladesh', to which HuJI belongs, was the signatory to the 1998 'Khost Fatwa against Jews and Crusaders'. AQ ties with HuJI developed in 2002. That year, Zawahiri was in Bangladesh to explore the possibility of expanding AQ networks in Bangladesh. Indian intelligence found that a fishing vessel, *MV Mecca*, was smuggling AQ operatives and weapons into Bangladesh, and illegal madrasas funded by Al-Haramain were providing training and weapons to Arab and north African militants from Algeria, Yemen, Sudan and Libya.[239] Given HuJI's motives, its network in Bangladesh, and its robust links with JeM, LeT and AQ, it can play a crucial role in nurturing sleeper cells in the northeastern states of India—such as Assam and West Bengal—which are already facing a severe migration onslaught from Bangladesh and sweeping jihadi radicalization.

In December 2011, a JeM module operating in Bihar was busted.[240] Mohammed Qateel Siddiqui and Gauhar Aziz Khomani, both from Darbhanga in Bihar, were arrested in Delhi on 23 November 2011, and Gayur Ahmad Jamali, from Madhubani, Bihar, was detained in Darbhanga on 24 November. In connection with this module, Mohammad Adil alias Ajmal from Karachi, trained by JeM as a shooter and sent by the Bhatkal brothers of IM first to Nepal and then to India to recruit local Muslims for terror attacks, was held from Madhubani on 25 November. Allegedly, Mohammad Adil was in India to create sleeper cells for JeM, which could work in close cooperation with Indian Mujahideen (IM).[241] Delhi police's special cell said that Adil was involved in the attack at Delhi's historic Jama Masjid in September 2011, the serial bombs outside Bangalore's M. Chinnaswamy Stadium in April, and the bombing of German Bakery in Pune in February.[242] Two more men from Bihar were apprehended in Chennai on 27 November—Abdur Rehman and Mohammad Irshad Khan. All of this shows that the ISI wanted its trusted terror groups like JeM and LeT to work closely with IM in the Indian hinterland.

In 2016, JeM made a grand comeback with a suicide attack at the Pathankot airbase in Punjab. In April 2019, it threatened to bomb railway stations in Rajasthan, Gujarat, Punjab and Uttarakhand.[243] More recently, it has planned to target north India's electricity power grid and its supply lines in Kashmir.[244] Given its interest in the Indian hinterland and target preferences, it will likely target critical economic infrastructure, military installations, and power infrastructure.

In November 2018, JeM released a video threatening widespread attacks if the Ram temple was built at the disputed site in Ayodhya.[245] In the video, Saifullah, JeM spokesperson, was reading a script dictated by Masood Azhar. It read:[246]

> Babri Masjid was taken away from us because of our cowardice and our sins. A mandir was created in that place. These days, non-Muslims are assembled over there for the issue. They are demanding to build Ram Mandir. They have swords and spears in their hand, while the Muslims are scared. The call for Babri Masjid is a test for the Muslims; it's a dangerous time, and we are ready to sacrifice our lives. I pray to you to give us back the Babri Masjid, give us back the honour of the Muslim Community. Forgive us, as we have sinned.

Sounding a war cry, he added,

> Just stop the construction of Ram Mandir, and show your warriors a path. They are desperate to show you their love and loyalty. The slogans crying 'Allahu Akbar' will be raised on the dome of Babri Masjid ... The bloodshed, injuries, the bodies imbibed with the perfume of love, the parts of the body. The victory of religion, oh lord, not just one or two, thousands of men are ready in your service, they are emotional, trembling that the Babri Masjid should be

brought back. We have to protect our mothers' dignity. We won't let an idol be built in the place where we prostrate.

Targeting Indian politicians from the Hindu right, he said:

Oh Lord who enlightens the darkness, just show us a path, if Allah wills this yellow terror will turn into a red storm. Then [Bal] Thackeray will be on his knees, Modi will crumble like a cobweb. Those who are too fond of being a Muslim Leader, they should be responsible enough and tell India that Ram Mandir instead of Babri Masjid will not be tolerated.

From the tape, it can be discerned that there is a distinct religious tone to the threat. It also clarifies that JeM continues to nurture pan-India ambitions. Its fight is not confined to Kashmir. Secondly, the videos suggest that JeM intends to instigate communal riots, and foster communal frenzy and violence in India over issues like the demolition of the Babri mosque, which has nothing to do with pan-Islamist issues. Fomenting large-scale communal riots is likely to prepare a fertile ground for the recruitment of Muslim cadres from the Indian hinterland. So far, Indian Muslims have been mostly reluctant to join global Islamist movements; however, by linking purely local issues with the international Islamist agenda, JeM is provoking and radicalizing ordinary Indian Muslims. This trend has already picked up pace in the last two decades. In the future, the rising Hindu–Muslim friction over local issues such as the ownership of religious places—for example, the Gyanvapi case in Varanasi and the Shahi Idgah case in Mathura—will provide a fertile ground for organizations like JeM and AQ to find more support in India's Muslim cultural, social and religious spaces. JeM is expected to enhance its involvement in local issues and radicalize Indian

Muslims. In the domain of terrorism, it is likely to increase its attacks on Hindu religious places, Hindu religious and political figures of India's saffron parties and other affiliated organizations, buildings and political offices of these political parties and other related organizations. Lastly, it can be said that JeM has remained more or less consistent over the last two decades in its efforts to pursue pan-India ambitions; however, the response has been poor and its success in comparison to its Kashmir operations is still low.

ISI's Strategy of Using LeT, JeM and HM in a Phased Manner

JeM's rise and fall also needs to be understood in the backdrop of ISI's overall strategy to promote and project a particular group in one phase, while keeping the others on a low burner.

In Kashmir, one comes across the phenomenon of one specific group being dominant in one phase and the other in the next. Jagmeet Singh (name changed to protect anonymity)—a police officer from J&K, who served in various capacities throughout his police career in the Valley, including in south Kashmir, and helped build intelligence networks—told me that the ISI strengthens a particular terror group at a time, and after it gets too exposed or tired, it turns its attention to the next group, while the former lies low. Such decisions depend on other strategic and tactical considerations like finances, equations with ISI handlers, etc. For instance, after JeM's involvement in the Musharraf assassination plot, ISI decided to put a check on its activities and withdrew its support. In its place, LeT was revived, strengthened and projected as the leading terror outfit in Kashmir. As discussed in the previous chapters, when militancy reached stagnation (1995), local groups like HM showed signs of going against the ISI, and the ISI preferred foreign groups like

HuM, JeM and LeT. From 2010 to 2015, LeT was more active on the militancy front under the leadership of Abu Qasim alias Abdur Rahman (killed in 2015) in south Kashmir and Abdullah Yumi in the north. After 2014, JeM intensified its activities and conducted many strikes jointly with HM. It also strengthened its hold in Pulwama, Shopian and Tral. In those days, JeM was mixing generously with the local population, and recruiting and preparing local boys for fidayeen attacks. As seen from its more recent attacks, it had created a successful fidayeen base.

Jagmeet Singh's thoughts about the ISI pushing one group and keeping others on the low burner on strategic grounds also get confirmed by the militancy scenario after the abrogation of Article 370. Due to FATF pressure, Pakistan kept leading groups like HM, LeT and JeM on the low. It projected their front organizations with secular-sounding names like The Resistance Force, Pir Panjal Peace Forum, Kashmir Tigers and Lashkar-i-Mustapha.[247] Also, ISI masterminds keep changing the militancy-focus areas in phases. When north Kashmir is active, they keep south and central Kashmir quiet, and vice-versa so that militants can find safe havens in the quieter areas. From 2016 onwards, south Kashmir became a hotbed of militancy, which peaked with the Pulwama fidayeen attack.[248] After Pulwama, due to intense action by SFs in south Kashmir, the focus shifted to Budgam (central Kashmir), Poonch–Rajouri and Srinagar (north Kashmir). After 2020, over the last one and a half years, both the areas have emerged as hotbeds of militancy.

Hence, despite the elimination of hundreds of JeM militants so far, Masood Azhar's death cult continues to exist, flourish and grow. Once, in the past, it was written off by intelligence agencies; however, it rose again like a phoenix. And it cannot be written off again.

5

JeM and Its Fidayeen Missions: Training and Tactics

IN ANY RANDOM CONVERSATION WITH A TERRORISM and counterterrorism enthusiast in Jammu and Kashmir—be it security personnel, an OGW, a teenage stone-pelter, an aspiring militant, or an active or surrendered militant—LeT figures as the most attractive, robust and 'cool' organization. For radicalized youngsters, its militants, with their high-tech gadgets, weaponry and Islamic beards and appearances, are inspirational role models with an appeal comparable to film stars. Its Saudi connections and Ahl-i-Hadith affiliations make it look even more trendy and Al-Qaeda–like, a sought-after launching platform for an ideal jihadist career. On the other hand, JeM carries an image of a low-profile, poor, dull, vague and fluid terror group, with fledgling cadre strength and it looks like it's always on the verge of extinction. There is no shortage of experts writing obituaries of JeM. It is perceived as estranged from ISI, with feeble support from them, often a headache for Pakistan and highly penetrated by Indian spies. Its militants, with their ordinary and un-Islamic looks and appearances, hardly carry any glamour quotient. However, whenever JeM is perceived as being on the verge of extinction, it makes a comeback with its signature—a spectacular suicide bombing—attack claiming several lives, creating a war-like crisis between India and Pakistan, disturbing Western capitals, and leaving a lasting impact on the geopolitics of South Asia.

A senior intelligence officer from R&AW told me that JeM is the single most significant security challenge after LeT; however, the world has its eyes trained on LeT, whereas JeM remains undetected and unwatched. After every major attack, it manages to inject collective amnesia into the minds of intelligence agencies and security watchers after a series of editorials. This lethality, its ability to keep a low profile, and excellence in the art of deception and secrecy raises questions about JeM's 'mind', which I will attempt to understand and uncover in this chapter.

Organizational Structure, Networks, Leadership and Culture

The central office of JeM is in Haripur in KPK, with regional offices at Daska, Bahawalpur (both in Punjab, Pakistan) Karachi and Quetta, in Sindh and Balochistan, respectively.[1] Its cadre strength as of 2019 is estimated to be several hundred, reaching up to 1,000 at times, in addition to the thousands of students and recruits in madrasas.[2] Reportedly, JeM maintains a cadre strength of 200 in Afghanistan at any point in time.[3] Its structure is divided into various departments.[4] Each department is responsible for specific areas and duties. Some of these are:

1) Department of Dawat and Irshad: Responsible for publicity and religious preaching
2) Military Department: Responsible for the recruitment and training of mujahideen in Pakistan and Afghanistan,

launching them in Kashmir, and conducting terrorist operations
3) Martyrs' Department: Maintains records of fighters killed in the group's operations
4) Matrimonial Department: Arranges marriages for cadres
5) Broadcasting and Publication Department
6) Grievance Redressal System

Early Days (2000–04)

In the early days, Maulana Asmatullah Muawiya, a former militant of Sipah-e-Sahaba, was the emir of JeM's Kashmir wing.[5] Maulana Sajid Usman was the chief of the finance branch and used to be the deputy chief of HuJI. Maulana Qari Mansoor Ahmed headed JeM's propaganda wing, while Maulana Abdul Jabbar was the nazim (head) of military affairs.[6] Before that, he led military affairs in HuM. Mufti Rauf Azgar was the launching commander.[7] In Kashmir, Sajjad Afghani was the first commander of HuM. He established a strong base for the organization. JeM emerged as its successor after its formation in 2000, with 75 per cent of HuM cadres shifting to JeM. Sajjad Afghani was killed by the jail guards during a jailbreak in 1999 in Kot Bhalwal Jail in Jammu. Ghazi Baba was the first commander of JeM in the Kashmir Valley, who masterminded and executed its major attacks, such as the J&K assembly fidayeen attack and the Parliament attack. Masood Azhar's leadership is nominal, mainly limited to more significant strategic matters. From 2008 onwards, Masood's brother, Mufti Rauf Azgar, emerged as the de facto chief of the organization, who manages most of the operational, tactical and organizational matters.[8] Soft-spoken Mufti Rauf, known in the JeM rank and file by his code name,

MARA, is a typical maulvi and has strong bonds with Masood.[9] He plans the suicide missions, selects the fidayeen and manages their infiltration.[10] MARA does not believe in ostentatious living. It is said he uses a simple Nokia 1100 mobile and moves in non-AC cars.[11]

JeM: A 'Family Enterprise'

During the early days of JeM, Masood had mighty influence on the organization; however, its deputy commanders too were strongmen,[12] and it was not a typical family enterprise (as mentioned in the earlier chapters). However, by 2008, when Mufti Rauf had become a de facto operational chief, JeM became a 'family enterprise'. The Pakistani intelligence agencies likely devised the strategy of keeping Masood and his family in power as he was loyal to them. His loyalty had to be ensured because of the history of JeM leaders partaking in anti-state revolts and their involvement in terrorist violence against the state. After the Lal Masjid siege of 2007 and the formation of TTP, the Pakistani Army and intelligence apparatus understood the perils of uncontrolled Deobandi terrorist groups. They faced twin challenges—using them as geopolitical assets and, at the same time, ensuring that they did not slip out of their control as they had in 2001 after Pakistan joined the US-led GWoT. Besides, by 2008, political talks with India had more or less reached a point of disutility. Hence, the new chief, Ashfaq Parvez Kayani, started reviving the terror infrastructure, including Pakistan's tried-and-tested assets like JeM. However, given its rebellious past, confining the power to the loyal Masood family and sustaining it as a single point of contact might have seemed prudent.

Maulana Masood Azhar remains the emir, i.e., the organization's chief, while other members of his family have taken up powerful positions in the organization. In jihadist circles, JeM is sarcastically referred to as Masood Azhar's 'family enterprise',[13] when compared to LeT, which is a 'corporate empire' with an array of investments in legitimate business ventures,[14] such as the shoe industry, dairy sector, profitable school chains, criminal theft rings, etc. The Azhar family is a close-knit family with immense warmth and bonhomie amongst its members. The second-generation members often go for family vacations together in Pakistan-occupied Kashmir. In my interviews with senior NIA officers, I accessed pictures of the family, which clearly showed how tight-knit they are; however, they cannot be represented here due to official restrictions.

A recent intelligence dossier[15] also categorizes JeM as a 'family enterprise' and details Masood's sixteen relatives, both close and distant, controlling various organization wings. After Masood, Mufti Rauf is the most powerful man managing all the operational, organizational and financial aspects of JeM. His other brother, Ibrahim Athar, handles the Afghanistan operations and drug trade networks with the Taliban. Mufti Rauf Azgar makes vital decisions about fidayeen attacks, recruitments, training and infiltration with the help of his brother Ibrahim Athar and his brother-in-law Yusuf Azhar. The trio was also involved in the planning of the IC-814 hijacking. The dossier further mentions that 'the second generation of Masood's family also joined the rank and file of JeM in its operational and administrative hierarchy, which includes its massive properties in Pakistan and Pakistan-occupied Kashmir, comprising of Markaz Subhanallah and a madrasa, training infrastructure and financial corps collected through its Al-Rahmat Trust'.

1) Mohammad Tahir (Masood's elder brother) heads Bahawalpur's Markaz Usman-o-Ali Establishment (MUAE)

2) Abdul Rashid (brother-in-law) is in charge of administration and training at MUAE
3) Muhammad Anas (brother-in-law) is the stores in-charge at MUAE
4) Mansoor Ahmed (brother-in-law) is in charge of JeM's defense wing
5) Hafiz Jameel (brother-in-law) is an administrator at Markaz Subhanallah
6) Talha Saif (brother) is the chief editor of the publications wing and head of JeM's student wing Al Murabitoon
7) Mohiuddin Aurangzeb Alamgir alias Ammar (brother) is the supervisor of *Al Qalam Weekly*

Second-Generation Members of the Azhar Family

1) Abdullah (son) works in operations in Kashmir and Afghanistan
2) Walliullah (son) is undergoing jihadi training
3) Huzaifa (nephew) finished jihadi training at MUAE
4) Osama (nephew) looks after the affairs of MUAE and Afghan operations
5) Ataullah Kashif (nephew) is a preacher and motivator for the organization
6) Nephews killed in India include Kamran, Muhammad Umar Farooq, Saifullah alias 'Lamboo', Usman Haidar and Talha Rashid

Masood continues to be the chief; however, with his deteriorating health, his involvement in operational and organizational matters is minimal. He engages himself in writing jihadist literature, giving indoctrinating sermons, and conducting strategic outreach and messaging with Taliban leadership, senior Deobandi clerics, and allegedly with the paymasters in the ISI.

Local Leadership in Kashmir (2021–22)[16]

1) District commander of Pulwama: Gowhar Manzoor Wani (twenty-one years) B. Tech, resident of Hardumir, Tral
2) District commander of Baramulla: Ali Bhai, resident of Pakistan
3) Commander: Arsalan Bhai aka Shahid, Khalid and Bilal, resident of Pakistan-occupied Kashmir

JeM Launching Pads for Infiltration across LoC

Launch pads are temporary posts near the LoC and IB, where terrorists are sheltered to wait before infiltration into the Indian territory.[17]

1) Munawaar Hussain Kazmi's house in Manwa village, Rawlakote District (PoK). Its location is opposite the KG Sector (Mendhar, J&K) of the Indian side.
2) A building located near the Pakistan army base in Village Battal (Rawlakote). It is opposite KG Sector, Mendhar.
3) Sherazi camp of the Pakistan Army, opposite India's Kathua region (Jammu). Code name Yaseen is in charge of the launch pad.

While saying that JeM is a 'family enterprise', it is pertinent to mention that the family factor also strengthens its legitimacy and credibility as an apolitical and strictly jihadist organization in the sociopolitical set-up and the larger jihadist landscape. Many of JeM family members, like Usman, Saifullah and Muhammad Umar Farooq (Masood's nephews), led JeM in

Kashmir as terrorist commanders and died in encounters by the SFs. These deaths are leveraged by JeM ideologues as supreme sacrifices for Islam. The emotional element in these so-called sacrifices get further strengthened by the family connections. JeM recruiters use them to evoke public sentiment and motivate radicalized youth to join its jihadist missions. Besides Masood's family, Deobandi religious leaders, scholars and clerics also have a significant say in JeM. Among the historical figures, Deobandi groups, including JeM, greatly respect Shamil,[18] a Naqshbandi sufi of Dagestan in Chechnya. Mufti Nizamuddin Shamzai of the Binoria mosque of Karachi, well-known for his pro-Taliban stand, and Maulana Yousuf Ludhianvi, former commander of the Sipah-e-Sahaba Pakistan, were the major supporters of JeM. These two scholars emerged as the chief ideologue and the chief commander of the JeM, respectively. Maulana Dawood Kashmiri, a Deobandi leader running a madrasa near Islamabad, is also highly respected and is regularly consulted by Masood, Rauf and other Deobandi terrorist leaders.[19] In the political ambit, JeM, like the other Deobandi groups, has close ties with Jamiat Ulema-e-Islam, a pro-Taliban political party in Pakistan.[20] Another Deobandi leader respected in the JeM hierarchy and the Deobandi extremist ecosystem is Maulana Sami-ul-Haq,[21] the former head of Deoband seminary Darul Uloom Haqqania at Akora Khattak in Khyber Pakhtunkhwa.[22] The late Sami-ul-Haq, also known as the 'father of Taliban', is a well-known name in Afghan jihad and was elected to the Pakistan's senate twice and even headed a political party, Jamiat Ulema-e-Islam, Sami (JuI-S).[23] He tutored eminent Deobandi leaders like Maulana Fazlur Rehman Khalil and Mullah Omar.[24] Sirajuddin Haqqani, AQ leader Asim Umar, and former Taliban chief Mullah Akhtar Mansoor also graduated from the Akora Khattak seminary.[25]

Senior Deobandi leaders and clerics command much respect in JeM and are treated as masters. Their social, cultural and religious stature also strengthens JeM's foundations and credibility within Pakistan's Deobandi ecosystem, which, in turn, makes it even more useful for the country's security establishment. Respecting elders is deeply embedded in JeM's organizational culture. Close observation of the personality of JeM leaders, its ties with other Deobandi terror groups, and its evolution brings forth not only its rootedness in the history of the Deobandi movement in Pakistan and the Indian subcontinent but also an element of strong reverence for its past and the history of jihadism in South Asia. This was also evident in my findings from interviews of senior NIA officials who investigated the Pulwama fidayeen case. A senior NIA officer told me on the condition of anonymity that JeM respects its elders and follows their orders. He said, '*Ye apne buzurgo ki baat maante the* (They obey the orders of their senior clerics and leaders).'

Further, he added that JeM operatives in J&K wanted to conduct another major strike after the Pulwama attack, with the ultimate goal of escalating things to a war-like situation between India and Pakistan so that they could infiltrate 400–500 cadres in the Valley. However, when their field commanders in Kashmir proposed this idea to their superiors in Bahawalpur, they refused to give them a green signal. The local commanders obeyed this order. In a WhatsApp voice note, Pulwama mastermind Muhammad Umar Farooq said, 'We could have done a much bigger strike, but our elders didn't allow us.'[26] When he proposed the idea of a large-scale IED attack after Pulwama to his cousin and colleague, Saifullah, also a Pulwama conspirator and a member of the Azhar family, the latter firmly said that they needed permission from the elders first.[27] However, these permissions are required only for major attacks. Local commanders can conduct small-scale attacks, grenade explosions and assassinate informers without any sanction from their Pakistan-based elders.[28]

Senior Deobandi leaders and religious figures were least involved in operational, organizational and tactical matters. These senior leaders had a symbolic presence that was more political than anything else. Also, in the early days, top-level Taliban and AQ leadership exercised tremendous influence in JeM, as they had supported the formation of the organization and had rendered financial support, shelter, training camps and other organizational needs. In JeM, it has also been seen that terrorist leaders and commanders without any formal designation also wield influence. For example, Omar Saeed Sheikh played an important role in the organization during its formation and early days. Likewise, Mushtaq 'Latram' Zargar, the chief of Al Umar Mujahideen, who was from Indian Kashmir and was released with Masood Azhar, was a great friend of Masood's and helped immensely by guiding JeM in its Kashmir operations, setting up financial networks, etc. He was an influential man in JeM and, as per some intelligence reports, he continues to be a close advisor to Masood Azhar. However, he never had any formal position in JeM, to the best of the knowledge of intelligence agencies. Another veteran Deobandi terrorist leader who continued to have a strong say in the organization even after its splintering from HuM is Maulana Fazlur Rehman Khalil. Security analysts maintain that the rift between Masood and Khalil led to the creation of JeM and that the split persisted after that. However, Farzan, my interlocutor, told me that Khalil is a highly respected figure in the Deobandi ecosystem. In the late 1980s and 1990s, he was the mighty commander of HuM, and allegedly was a friend of the CIA as well.[29] After JeM emerged as a separate outfit, Khalil was officially never a part of it, but Masood and his brother Rauf still respected him greatly, according to Farzan. The ISI also allegedly finds Khalil helpful in maintaining control over the organization for its leaders would listen to a stalwart like Khalil. Reportedly, Khalil mediated between the state and Masood Azhar after the latter's name emerged as a key conspirator in the Musharraf assassination plot. Ilyas Kashmiri, leader of Brigade 313, which planned Musharraf's assassination, also held Khalil in great esteem; however, according to Farzan, he had to abandon him after his involvement in the assassination plot.[30] The Pakistan Army was apparently entirely unwilling to tolerate Ilyas Kashmiri. Later, in 2011, the Pakistanis allegedly tipped off the Americans about Ilyas Kashmiri's location and he was killed in a US drone strike in south Waziristan. Khalil also mediated between the Haqqanis and the Pakistani government. The Haqqanis were disappointed with Pakistan for giving ground space and logistical help to the US forces in its Afghanistan operations in the early 2000s; however, Khalil, a close friend of former army chief of Pakistan Ashfaq Parvez Kayani, mediated peace between the two.

Hizb-ut-Tahrir, a pan-Islamist organization, has maintained ideological affinity and links with JeM and the larger Deobandi pan-Islamist vision.[31] Allegedly, Omar Sheikh Saed was working for Hizb-ut-Tahrir.[32] In Pakistan, it is seen as a political movement, comprising intellectual and economic elites like doctors and academics. They started entering Pakistani state institutions after Musharraf's assassination plot to sanitize the state of irreligious elements. However, it made the Pakistan Army sceptical as it suspected the group of usurping and hijacking state institutions.

JeM is one constituent in the larger Deobandi ecosystem of Pakistan. There exists a strong interconnectedness and overlapping memberships with other terrorist groups of the ecosystem, making it a potent force to reckon with. JeM's internal culture and the lifestyles of its militants and senior leaders are simple and low profile—quite similar to other Deobandi groups like the Taliban, SSP and LeJ. Unlike LeT leaders, who live a glamorous and flashy lifestyle with fancy cars and costly SUVs, JeM believes in simplicity and frugality. Also, unlike LeT and HM, JeM does not believe in propaganda through social media and photo-ops. It believes that its attacks speak for the organization. And once again, unlike LeT, JeM is entirely apolitical. LeT has a range of NGOs engaged in social work and affiliated political groups like JuD and Milli Muslim League. JeM is an entirely religious project with no political groups attached.

Pakistan's Deep State and Its Ties with JeM and LeT

JeM has its own standing, a constituency and robust Deobandi support system that originated and evolved much before the birth of the Pakistani state, and it goes beyond the ambit of the patronizing and protective umbrella of the security establishment. Its independent standing rooted in the nation's history, society and culture lends it unique leverage and influence, which it often uses to negotiate with the state. Generally, it does not go against the state; however, it does not hesitate to threaten to go against the state whenever required, particularly in the pursuit of its Pan-Islamist vision. On account of its grassroots base, and robust socio-political and religious standing, it has a strong influence on a significant segment of the Pakistani Army and the deep state. Deobandi sympathizers and followers in the Pakistan Army nurture strong sympathy, linkages and informal affiliations with Deobandi extremist groups. Such rogue elements in the army have often conspired against the state; for example, as discussed previously, investigations into the Benazir Bhutto (1995) and Musharraf (2004) assassination plots unearthed the role played by senior army officers, including two-star generals. Also, after Musharraf supported the US against Taliban in the GWoT, allegedly, many state agents working in the army and the ISI went rogue, and assisted the rebel factions of Badri 313 and Jamaat-ul-Furqan in orchestrating terrorist attacks against the state.[33] Because of this delicately balanced relationship, at times skewed in favour of rebellious Deobandi groups, it is often argued that Pakistan's control over JeM is much weaker as compared to its hold over LeT. Generally, JeM takes approval from ISI; however, in some cases, if the ISI does not give it permission, Masood Azhar decides on his own.[34] However, despite the friction between JeM and ISI, the organization and Masood Azhar remain quintessential assets of the state, which, in turn, has never ceased to patronize, protect and promote it. ISI places strong faith in JeM; it does not micromanage its activities. One of my sources, who wished to remain anonymous, told me that generally ISI gives JeM the outline of a plan, but never the details.[35] The local unit base then fills in the contours of the plan. Whereas, in the case of LeT, it is believed they get detailed instructions on planning a terrorist attack because its relationship with the state is very different—it also ensures better interaction and coordination between the group and ISI.

JeM's unbeatable expertise in high-profile suicide bombings renders it indispensable to the state. Also, for ISI, Masood's ties with Taliban, and his stature and clout in the Deobandi ecosystem are immensely helpful in staying informed about the system's internal developments, along with its controlling and monitoring. Praveen Swami, eminent journalist and author, told me in an interview that the relationship between the army and JeM is a 'kind of mystery'.[36] The Pakistan Army has a segment that believes in Musharraf's idea that nurturing terrorist proxies has not yielded any positive dividends; however, there is another section that strongly adheres to extremist religious views and is supportive of terrorist groups. The pro-jihadist faction of the army has a history going back to the 1970s and 1980s, when proxy war veterans like General Hamid Gul, General Javed Nasir,

General Akhtar Abdul Rahman, Colonel Imam, and Colonel Khwaja created, trained and nourished the Deobandi terrorist ecosystem, including the Taliban, and even fought alongside them in the Afghan jihad. Hence, despite occasionally rubbing each other the wrong way, the ties between the Pakistan Army and Deobandi terrorist groups are organic, old and inherently robust. However, the segment that believes that these groups have not helped the state, which includes the new generation of army officers (2000 onwards), has seen terror groups like TTP unleashing destruction within Pakistan, such as the horror of the Peshawar army school attack of 2014. Therefore, their faith in terrorist proxies is weak; but Pakistan's engagement and support of terror groups continues without compunctions, even after seeing the violence these groups can unleash in its own territory.

It is difficult to measure precisely the degree of influence each group wields, but it can be said the Pakistan Army trusts JeM more than the others at some fundamental level.[37] The foundations of the relationship are firm and robust. Amongst Indian security forces and their senior commanders, the general perception is that LeT and HM control routine militancy; however, ISI uses JeM for lethal and morale-shattering fidayeen attacks, loaded with psychological motives. It uses JeM only when it sees Indian SFs becoming dominant and trying to weaken the militancy ecosystem by inflicting severe damage on its terror proxies.

LeT adheres to the Ahl-i-Hadith ideology, which does not have a support system as strong as that enjoyed by Deobandi groups. Hence, its relationship with the state is strongly tilted in the latter's favour. Moreover, LeT has serious disputes with the Ahl-i-Hadith leadership in Pakistan, which makes it even more dependent on the state. This strong bonding is visible in LeT's activities and policies. Unlike Deobandi groups, LeT advocates for peace within Pakistan and abjures violence against Shias within the state.[38] LeT pursues the state agenda very loyally and can be called a Pakistani version of Wagner and Black Waters, deployed and used in national strategic interests when and where required.[39] Farzan, who has close connections with the Pakistan Army's top brass, Jamaat-i-Islami and other terrorist groups, said that in unofficial conversations in Pakistan, LeT is referred to as 'Pakistan Army soldiers without uniforms'. He told me that Pakistan Army regulars work in close coordination with LeT and, on many occasions, they have worked from within LeT too.

Further, Farzan told me that while discussing the Pakistani jihadi ecosystem, Indian and Western analysts tend to see the army, ISI and terrorist groups as separate entities. The ISI, or the de facto Pakistani state, is seen as a modern and formal entity governed by acceptable, objective and non-religious rules of engagement and operations, while terrorist groups are seen as non-state, primitive and as religious extremist organizations guided by jihadist doctrines. The relation between the two is viewed as that of a typical state intelligence agency, inherently secular and modern, nurturing terrorist groups as its geostrategic assets and force multipliers. As compared to Western analysts, Indians have a slightly better understanding of the ISI and its relations with terrorist groups. But this approach is primarily flawed, says Farzan.

According to him, the ISI and terror groups in Pakistan are tethered by the doctrine of jihad. The Pakistan Army and the ISI come from the same social, cultural and religious milieu as the terrorist groups. The Pakistan state itself is based on the two-nation theory—the doctrine of Hindus and Muslims constituting two different nations. Hence, it was destined to be an Islamic state or where Islam would reign supreme in the functioning of state and society. Thus, at a subconscious and very fundamental level, the Pakistan Army, and the ISI's vision is influenced by the doctrine of jihad. It is believed that a majority of people who make up its army nurture the same commitment toward pan-Islamism and jihad that the terrorist groups do. The terrorist groups are like an unofficial extension of the Pakistan Army and ISI. For Indian intelligence agencies, Kashmir operations may be a nine-to-five job, but for Pakistan, it is jihad—a religious duty. Hence, for any terrorist group, including JeM, a superficial organizational structure may include some clerics, motivators, operational commanders and financiers; but the hidden backbone is always the ISI and the Pakistan Army.

In the ambit of this patron–client relationship, the ISI has nurtured and protected Jaish-e-Mohammed against all odds. However, after the Afghan experience, the Pakistani state has had deep insecurities about terrorist proxies slipping out of its control. Though it created, trained and nurtured the Taliban, it showed rebellious and autonomous instincts when it acquired power in 1996 and then again in 2021. Hence, Islamabad's strategic masterminds have devised a range of mechanisms to keep the armed jihadists under control. One of ISI's most effective ways to maintain a firm grip on JeM is keeping the outfit's leadership in the control of one family. For the ISI, it is always easier to deal with one family instead of multiple terrorist commanders warring over power and the control of resources. Secondly, keeping it confined within the family of one towering figure who commands loyalty and reverence, and is seen as a spiritual leader, minimizes the chances of revolt. Thirdly, family control ensures better trust, and smooth and efficient functioning without bureaucratic delays; it also ensures the optimum utilization of money given to the organization. The Pakistani establishment has also used other methods to control terrorist groups. For example, JeM was allegedly created as a check on LeT; HM was unleashed to eliminate JKLF. In the case of JeM, after the Musharraf assassination plot, when Jamaat-ul-Furqan emerged as a splinter against Masood Azhar's leadership and Musharraf's decision to support the US in the GWoT against the Taliban and AQ, the ISI continued to protect and nurture the loyalist Masood faction to keep the Deobandi extremists divided, and get all the intelligence on the activities in the rebellious segments of the Deobandi extremists.

JeM's Relations with Kashmir's Other Extremist Groups and Deobandi Institutions

With other separatist and extremist groups, one comes across several disagreements, along with cooperation and synergy in tactical matters and broader strategic objectives. Masood Azhar was critical of the separatist Hurriyat Conference[40] because of the alleged cases of financial embezzlement[41] by members. JeM OGW Akram Bhai told me that Masood Azhar knew that the Hurriyat was swindling funds earmarked for the families of dead militants and those languishing in jails, which soured his personal opinion of the group.[42] However, the critical attitude was not reflected in any outward display of disagreement or conflict with the Hurriyat Conference. Also, JeM leaders have occasional interactions with political separatists.[43] Likewise, LeT also had disputes with HM and Hurriyat Conference; however, they were resolved with the intervention of Syed Salahuddin, PoK-based chief of HM, and the United Jihad Council.[44] One comes across many incidents of cooperation and JeM's joint operations with other terror outfits like LeT, HuM and HM.

JeM and LeT jointly executed the Parliament attack. Following that, there were many terror attacks jointly conducted by JeM and other groups. On 16 March 2010, the joint brigade of LeT, JeM and HM, called the Save Kashmir

Movement, claimed the 14 March grenade attack in Srinagar.[45] Also, coordination exists between the different groups in other operational and tactical matters like sharing OGWs and guides, infiltration through the Kashmir region, sharing details of shelters and hideouts, and building infiltration routes and bases in Bangladesh and Nepal.[46] On 21 April 2010, a conference was planned which would be jointly addressed by Syed Salahuddin, Masood Azhar and Hafiz Saeed. More interestingly, JeM's activities in the Indian hinterland have mostly been in close coordination and cooperation with LeT and Indian Mujahideen. Also, JeM worked closely with HuJI in the India–Bangladesh border region.[47]

This behaviour might puzzle a lay observer because JeM—known for its highly clandestine modus operandi—is expected to be reluctant and sceptical about working with others, least of all with ideologically different groups like LeT and HM. JeM believes in the Deobandi ideology, LeT in Ahl-i-Hadith and HM in Maulana Maududi's political Islam. However, this should not come as a surprise. JeM has experience working with other terrorist groups that were part of the Deobandi cohort, such as SSP, LeJ, Taliban, HuM, HuJI and Al Qaeda. As mentioned earlier, Brigade 313 was a conglomerate of five terrorist groups, including JeM. Hence, JeM has experience working with other outfits on operational and ideological matters. In Kashmir, terrorist groups operate under the strict monitoring and guidance of ISI in strategic and tactical issues. Following its directives, they keep ideological disputes on the backburner—lest it empower their adversaries and weaken the groups by enhancing the scope of espionage by opponents and dissidents, and expose their sectarianism and religious extremism.

Interestingly, hardcore Sunni extremist organizations like LeT, JeM and HM deliberately overlook the Shia–Sunni differences.

Overtly, they do not even spew venom against the Hindu-minority Kashmiri Pandits in the Valley, as it would expose that their struggle is driven by religious extremism. Hence, the groups are not interested in conflicts over ideological issues. Sometimes, differences emerge over purely logistical and operational matters like using OGWs and infiltration routes. Such disputes have not led to any significant armed conflict between the groups.

Further, after its ban in Pakistan, JeM's fortunes dwindled. In India, from 2004 onwards, JeM faced a progressive decline and weakening due to successful encounters eliminating its top leadership. Hence, the fall in its cadre strength, monetary resources and existential crises might have motivated it to plan joint attacks with other terrorist groups. Secondly, in many encounters with SFs, it was discovered that JeM and LeT cadres and commanders were sharing a common hideout or would meet with other commanders to discuss operational and other relevant matters. Hence, it is difficult to identify the precise nature of the joint planning of such operations, barring a few cases where it is known that two or more terror groups participated. So far, JeM has conducted minor terror incidents with other groups like HuM, LeT and HM, except for the Parliament attack. In such dealings with other groups over logistical and operational matters, JeM prioritizes guarding its secrecy; hence, it never shares its contact details with OGWs and militants of other groups. Generally, JeM prefers HuM, Al Badr and HM over LeT, with whom they have ideological differences.[48] With HuM, JeM has the best camaraderie because of a common religious ideology and origin.[49] Their cadres mostly lived together as well. HuM was active in Kashmir until 2010, after which it is near totally absent.

JeM has ideological differences with other groups; however, in the case of LeT, it is more than mere ideological differences.

JeM's comfort level and coordination with LeT is generally poor, and many reasons exist for this—ranging from ego issues to state patronage.[50] However, as mentioned earlier, when JeM took part in joint operations with LeT, they were usually minor ones. In high-profile suicide missions, JeM handles the planning and execution independently, and with utmost secrecy.[51]

JeM has a cordial functional relationship with the now-banned extremist Jamaat-i-Islami (JI) through HM, its terrorist arm.[52] Reportedly, the organization uses these ties to conceal its identity—for example, there have been cases when a JeM OGW or militant acclaimed to be a JI worker and evaded suspicion.[53] In case of detention or arrest for suspicious activities, they were booked as Jamaat workers and their real identities remained hidden. In another such case, a JeM operative ran a school in Kreeri-Pattan (Baramulla). The billboard outside the school read 'Maktab Ahl-e-Jamaat'. It was easy to use the JI school identity because the organization runs many schools in Kashmir through its Falah-i-Aam Trust (FAT).[54] When the owner's identity was revealed, he escaped to Pakistan. As discussed previously, in some of its strongholds like Tral, Pulwama, Shopian, Kulgam, Awantipora (all south Kashmir) and Bandipora (north Kashmir), JeM—mainly after 2004-05—mixed with locals and created a robust base, which, in turn, created a smooth bridge at the grassroots level with HM, a local terrorist organization, comprising mainly of Kashmiris. J&K police officers maintain that JeM cadres share an affinity with local Kashmiris, so they have better coordination and a working relationship with HM.[55] Some of the top commanders, like Ghazi Baba, married Kashmiri women, and many other top-level JeM commanders allegedly had affairs with Kashmiri women.[56] Such relationships also resulted in successful encounters as their girlfriends tipped off the police, or, in some cases, their telephonic communications were intercepted. The interaction between JeM foreign terrorist Waleed Bhai and the local HM commander Farukh Nalli in Kulgam shows us the impressive level of understanding between the two groups.[57] Waleed had allegedly infiltrated into India in 2016 and was operating in many districts. Three months before his encounter death in 2020, he came to Kulgam and met Farukh. He asked the latter to hand over the DH Pura area (Dhamal–Hanjipura) of Kulgam from HM control to JeM. Farukh allegedly agreed and allowed JeM to operate as the leading group in the area.

After the abrogation of Article 370, in some encounters, JeM militants were killed along with those from HM and Al Badr, most likely because the group has not been able to get a sufficient number of cadres from Pakistan into India over the last two or three years because of the security and communication lockdown, and the enhanced vigil and India–Pakistan ceasefire of February 2021.[58] However, JeM's robust links with HM, facilitating smooth coordination in operational matters, continued as long as Mohammad Abbas Sheikh was in HM.[59] The best example comes from the Pulwama fidayeen attack. Mudasir Khan, one of the key conspirators of the attack, was initially working as an OGW for Mohammad Abbas Sheikh during his HM days. Later, Mohammad Abbas Sheikh got him inducted into JeM through his close friend, Noor Muhammad Tantrey. Reportedly, the best phase of JeM–HM bonding was between 2017 and 2019, which ended after Abbas shifted to TRF in 2020.[60] Also, after celebrity militant and Ansar Ghazwat-ul Hind chief Zakir Musa's encounter death in May 2019, JeM was hesitant to work with HM as its commanders suspected that the latter had leaked information about Musa to SFs.[61]

Also, it is believed that other terrorist groups feel somewhat uncomfortable with JeM at times, because of its aggressive and intense activity. HM and LeT militants in a particular area tend to get into a comfort zone. They hide in safe shelters, live in a specific area and strive to prolong their survival. However, JeM militants, it is said, are not content with a passive status quo. They indulge in activities and move around openly among civilians, though they maintain the highest levels of tradecraft in keeping their plans a secret. Open movements with civilians challenge the domination of SFs in that area; hence, they are compelled to act. In the words of a senior police officer in south Kashmir, Farhad Hussain:[62]

> If the Jaish group comes into our area, it becomes known in twenty days because they meet with people and openly move around with civilians. Once it gets known that the group has arrived, it becomes the top-most priority of the district police. Also, there are occasions when one encounters a subtle competition between various terrorist groups. When JeM conducts a big-ticket fidayeen attack with double-digit casualties, LeT comes under pressure and tries to orchestrate an attack on a similar scale. The other groups, like HM and Al Badr, also act to maintain their relevance. Continuous terrorist activity by a group also guarantees a regular supply of recruits.

Some cooperation and coordination between JeM and LeT has occurred in Pakistan. On 26 June 2012, Mohammad Adil alias Ajmal, a Pakistani national, told the police that in 2009, Jundal, an LeT cadre, trained ninety recruits at the Bahawalpur camp in Pakistan. Later, many of them joined the Indian Mujahideen (IM) in India. In his statement, which is now part of judicial records, Adil mentioned that he met Jundal at the Bahawalpur camp along with another LeT leader, Zaki-ur-

Rehman Lakhvi, and JeM commander Abdul Rauf, brother of Masood Azhar.[63] However, JeM is not involved in executing joint operations with LeT, and the cooperation may be limited to sharing training compounds, trainers, and other organizational/logistical and non-combat domains. Recently, as mentioned in the previous chapter, LeT and JeM cadres fought alongside Taliban to drive out foreign forces in Afghanistan. Hence, more than ideology, the ISI directives matter, and these outfits work as Pakistan's irregular army, deployed wherever and whenever needed, under the ISI's command and direction. However, they do maintain a façade of ideological differences and separate existences, and this may be, to some extent, a deliberate tactic, as it successfully creates an illusion that not only absolves Pakistan in the eyes of the world as the main force behind these groups but also projects the state as a victim of terror itself. However, ISI's control over some groups, like LeT and HM, is more robust than others, like JeM, SSP, LeJ, IS-K, Taliban and TTP.

In Kashmir, cadres do not join a terror organization based on its ideology. The more powerful determinants are its network, and the influencers and peer group in the organization. A tanzeem like LeT or JeM can have cadres following the Maududi doctrine and Barelwi thoughts. A terror group's most essential criterion is loyalty. However, the craze for joining LeT outpaces that of JeM and HM. Amongst all the groups, LeT is seen as the most radical and hardcore because it believes in Ahl-i-Hadith, also known as Wahhabism, and is seen as the most extreme and orthodox school of thought. LeT cadres are very particular about Islamic appearances in their dressing and beards, as opposed to JeM, which is relatively more lax. LeT is a bigger organization with much stronger support from the ISI as well. Technologically, it is more advanced in using modern gadgets and encryption devices. It has its own intelligence unit. Joining LeT has glamour attached and is seen as fashionable. JeM, on the other hand, keeps a low profile and is very professional in its approach.

As regards JeM's ties with Deobandi seminaries—Darul Uloom and Tablighi Jamaat—it needs to be noted that JeM, in Kashmir as well as the Indian hinterland, is ideologically linked to Deobandi and Deoband-affiliated institutions at a very fundamental level. Despite the differences between the Indian Deoband groups and Pakistani Deoband groups on the issue of terrorism, there is a shared history, legacy, and broad similarities in the fundamental religious and ritualistic beliefs. AQ has used TJ as a cover to secure travel papers and send its cadres to India and Pakistan.[64] In Kashmir, many terrorists across the spectrum have TJ backgrounds; however, it is difficult to pinpoint the exact nature of this as most of the interrogation reports are classified. During TJ's religious dauras (tours of religious preaching) of forty days, young Muslim followers get exposed to an austere, exclusivist and fundamentalist version of Islam, which indirectly prepares the ground for extremist indoctrination.[65] The global intelligence firm Stratfor's report on TJ's links with terrorist groups says, 'The TJ organization also serves as a de facto conduit for Islamist extremists and for groups such as al Qaeda to recruit new members. Significantly, the Tablighi recruits do intersect with the world of radical Islamism when they travel to Pakistan to receive their initial training.'[66] In Pakistan, terrorist outfits such as the Taliban, Al Qaeda and HuM try to woo TJ members to join them.

Further, the report says: [67]

> Because of the piety and strict belief system of the Tablighis and their focus on calling wayward Muslims back to an austere and orthodox Muslim faith, the movement has offered a place where jihadist spotters can look for potential recruits ... Although the TJ promotes a benign message,

the same conservative Islamic values espoused by the Tablighis also are part of jihadist ideology, and so some Muslims attracted to the Tablighi movement are enticed into becoming involved with jihadists.

Also, in Kashmir, TJ helps move terror money, particularly when there is enhanced vigilance on hawala operators and formal channels.[68] In agreement with the Stratfor report, it can be observed that JeM uses Deobandi jihad doctrines as reference points during its recruitment drives in madrasas.[69] Interestingly, Masood Azhar's journey in Kashmir begins with meeting HuM commander Sajjad Afghani at Darul Uloom Qasimiya at Lal Bazaar in Srinagar.[70] Qasimiya Darul Uloom is a prestigious Deobandi seminary in Srinagar affiliated with Darul Uloom.[71] My interview with Mahboob Gilani (name changed), a J&K police officer, also confirmed JeM's links with Deobandi religious clerics and institutions. He said that JeM commanders in the early days—2000 to 2006—had frequent interactions with Deobandi clerics and often visited Deobandi seminaries. During his tenure as police chief, Gilani set up many ambush operations outside Darul Uloom Rahimiya (Bandipora) because there were credible inputs about JeM commanders visiting it. In 2006, militants killed a police officer outside Darul Uloom Rahimiya and injured a civilian. After 2006, surveillance increased and the J&K police emerged as the leading counterterrorism force. It had much better ground-level intelligence on relations between the Darul Uloom maulvis, the administration and JeM; hence, due to enhanced surveillance and rigorous follow-up interrogations, Darul Uloom leaders started maintaining distance from JeM. In 2016, Deobandis were more active than Jamaat-i-Islami in the mobilization of crowds and stone-pelting in south Kashmir.[72] Most recently, in June 2022, NIA raided the compounds of Siraj-ul-Uloom, a Deoband seminary in Srinagar, and arrested its chief in a case of online dissemination of ISIS radicalization material through its India-centric magazine, *Voice of India*.[73]

Bashir Assad, a Srinagar-based journalist, suggested that Deobandis have also developed links with JeM across the border.[74] Further, he adds that in Kashmir, a kind of competition has emerged between various fundamentalist and extremist groups like Deobandis, JI and the Wahhabis. Each one intends to outsmart the other in projecting a radical and extremist religious discourse. Taking a cue from JI and the Wahhabis, the Deobandis—generally thought of as minor players with remote connections to militancy and extremism—have also started educational charities to spread radical and extremist versions of Islam.[75] Deobandi institutions also run orphanages and seminaries where children from a very young age are radicalized, and brought up with a very conservative and narrow worldview. JeM's Deobandi links emerged more prominently in the Pulwama attack. Sajad Mujtaba, who arranged logistics for the attack, was a student of a Siraj-ul-Uloom madrasa in the Shopian district.[76] The teachers apparently narrated exaggerated stories of the bravery shown by mujahideens to students, projecting them as role models.[77] Marhama village in Anantnag, where the Pulwama conspiracy was hatched, is the largest-populated village of that district with five madrasas of all the five sects present in Kashmir—Barelwi, Deobandi, Wahhabi, Tablighi Jamaat and Jamaat-i-Islami.[78] Marhama, thus, has emerged as an epicentre of JeM. Tral, another JeM stronghold in Pulwama district, has Madrasa-i-Noor, established by Maulvi Noor Ahmed.[79] As per J&K police, 70 per cent of the youth who joined militancy in Tral were former students of this madrasa.[80] In the Shopian district, Imam Sahib, Hermain and Zainapora have strong JeM concentrations; one of the biggest Deobandi madrasas is located in this belt.

However, JeM places the highest premium on secrecy, so it is most unlikely to maintain overt links with Deobandi institutions and TJ, as they will be the usual suspects for SFs. Likewise, the local Deobandi centres and clerics, despite their sympathy for JeM, are unlikely to get directly involved in order to avoid police harassment and interrogations. As compared to JI, the Deobandis and Ahl-i-Hadith discourage overt links with terror outfits and direct support for separatism.

Tactics, Traits and Training

Different terrorist groups operating in Kashmir tend to give a picture of uniformity regarding their tactics, strategy, ideology, training, objectives and militant profiles; however, closer scrutiny reveals that each group has unique characteristics, styles and traits. A holistic look at JeM reveals it to be professional, focused, highly secretive, old-fashioned and traditional in its tradecraft, style and strategy.

The most unique feature of Jaish-e-Mohammed is its expertise in fidayeen attacks. In this category, JeM is the only one to make the most lethal use of VBIEDs. The Badami Bagh cantonment attack (2001), the J&K assembly attack (2001) and the Pulwama attack (2019) were all VBIED attacks. From 2000 to 2019, J&K witnessed a total of eighty-seven suicide attacks, in which 130 civilians, 239 SF personnel and 143 terrorists died.[81] Out of these eighty-seven attacks, JeM conducted twelve suicide attacks, whereas LeT conducted twenty-eight suicide attacks (see tables on p. 227). A cursory reading of the statistics in the table contradicts the popular perception in the security establishment and lay watchers of terrorism that JeM has a monopoly over suicide attacks. LeT outpaces JeM by a huge margin if one studies it in terms of sheer numbers. However, a closer look reveals a different picture, which justifies the popular perception of JeM.

The phenomenon of suicide bombing/fidayeen became popular in Kashmir from the year 2000 onwards. Pakistan had already acquired nuclear weapons; therefore, it was in a position to undertake greater risks in Kashmir—executing suicide missions through its better-trained and radicalized foreign terrorist groups. Also, suicide attacks with greater casualty figures could help offset the damage done by the Kargil defeat to the morale of Pakistan's SFs and deep state. It can be seen that in the case of JeM, though the number of suicide attacks is less than that of LeT, the casualties are much higher. With twelve suicide attacks, JeM killed thirty-one civilians and ninety-nine soldiers, and lost only thirty militants. The LeT, with its twenty-eight suicide attacks, killed thirty-two civilians and sixty-one soldiers, and lost forty-eight militants. Next, JeM, as discussed earlier, faced state action after 2004; hence, it was deprived of the much-needed support and finances vis-à-vis LeT, whereas, during this period of 2005–16, LeT was the leading terrorist group getting the maximum support from its benefactors in the Pakistan Army. Despite this lean phase, JeM's performance in suicide attacks is more impressive than that of LeT. After 2002, LeT lost interest in suicide missions; however, it continued with its signature high-risk missions.

On the other hand, JeM, despite seeing rough patches, has been consistent in conducting suicide attacks and, after its revival in 2015–16, it vigorously conducted a series of such attacks. Also, with time, it evolved in its expertise. Its most significant achievement was its ability to recruit local Kashmiris like Fardeen Khandey and Ishaq Ahmed Khan in the Lethpura attack, and Adil Dar for the Pulwama mission, a feat which other terrorist groups like HM and LeT, with better resources and networks, could not accomplish. Kashmir is a relatively moderate society with strong Sufi influences, where Taliban-styled radicalization is not seen among the local militants; hence, indoctrinating a local Kashmiri to the extent that he volunteers for a suicide mission has always been a challenge for terror outfits. The very fact that JeM could do it raises many questions and alarm bells about its indoctrination techniques. Lastly, most JeM attacks are high on optics. Beyond rattling the Indian security establishment, they conveyed a strong political message by sabotaging the India–Pakistan peace talks in 2000, 2016 and 2019. Also, the sheer brutality, the element of surprise and the alarming number of casualties sent a strong psychological message, terrorizing Indian SFs and locals. Further, its fidayeen attacks have also sent geopolitical tremors across South Asia and in Western power centres by creating a war-like situation between nuclear-armed India and Pakistan.

Some of the intercepts of the conversations (given below) between JeM commanders, their handlers and seniors across the border suggest that the organization also keeps the information war and psyops front open with its fidayeen attacks. However, it cannot be argued with conviction that it is a general pattern because the data is scarce. One of many such intercepts, which I could access, gives a decent idea about JeM's information war. The intercept of a conversation of Mufti Waqas[82] during the Sunjwan army camp fidayeen attack in 2018 reveals that he tried to cover up the fact that Kashmiri Muslim soldiers of J&K Light Infantry were killed in the attack. He reported that Indians had killed Kashmiri soldiers later to bring bad publicity to JeM, which seems irrational as no army would kill its own soldiers and officers after a fidayeen attack. The Indian Army is making sincere efforts to woo Kashmiris to join the forces; hence, an act like this is most unlikely to happen on their part. Then, in the same conversation, Mufti Waqas said that more soldiers had been killed than reported; however, the fidayeens were in no position to calculate the exact number of Indian casualties.

JeM Operative Mufti Waqas's conversation in Urdu/Hindu with his seniors:[83]

a) *Asalamallkiumwarhematullahbarakatuh. Bhai jan apna 2 sathi yehi hai aur 1 inme nahi hai. Baaki sab theek hai khariyt aur baaki theek hain bhai jan. Yeh operation hafta subha se suru hoke, phir haftasham, etivaarsham,Somvaarsham ... mangal tak chalta raha hai. Aur abhi bhi media ko andar jaaane diya nahi jaa raha hai. Baki inka ... jo suru me sathi gaye the vo sedha office mess me gaye the aur officer ko unhone pakad ke giraftar kar liye the ... allamdullah ... uske baad unhe se malumaat ki hain ... saare camp ki to uske baad aage bade hain. Inhone jo Kashmiri dekhay hain aap khud andaza laga lo ki 3,000–4,000 banda waha mauzood tha unme se sirf Kashmiriyo ko hi goli lagne thi! Kashmiri baad me inhone yeh khud mare hain badnaami karne ke liye. Aur inka nuksaan asal yeh chup gaye hain ... inke officer mare gaye hain kaafi saare aur baarko me sathi pahunche hain ... 2 baje tak to inke commando to andar jaane ka moka hi nahi mila. Allamdullilah bhut hi kamyaab karvay hue.*

b) *Asalamallkiumwarhematullah .. bhai jan yeh faila do. Yeh such nahi hain yeh dokha hain yeh jang hain yeh failao kisi tarah - kahi harish ka naam estemaal karo. Kahi MD ka wo Midoora waala ka bas issi tarah khabre phailani chahiye ... phir dekho Hindustan ki media ko aur agency ko ... kaise pagal hote hain ... yeh phailna chaiye.*

JeM's Yearly Suicide Attacks[84]

Year	Total No. of Incidents	Civilians Killed	Killed			Injured			
			SFs	Militants	Total	SFs	Civilians	Militants	Total
2000	1	0	0	1	1	4	4	0	8
2001	1	24	11	4	39	0	67	0	67
2002	1	0	2	1	3	1	0	0	1
2005	2	6	3	5	14	1	18	0	19
2016	1	0	20	4	24	0	0	0	0
2017	4	0	17	11	28	13	0	0	13
2018	1	1	6	3	10	3	6	0	9
2019	1	0	40	1	41	24	0	0	24
Total	12	31	99	30	160	46	95	0	141

LeT's Yearly Suicide Attacks[85]

Year	Total No. of Incidents	Civilians Killed	Killed			Injured			
			SFs	Militants	Total	SFs	Civilians	Militants	Total
2000	5	0	13	9	22	2	6	0	8
2001	11	9	25	17	51	36	38	2	76
2002	6	12	12	10	34	14	48	0	62
2006	1	1	4	1	6	12	8	0	20
2007	1	0	0	2	2	3	0	0	3

Year	Total No. of Incidents	Civilians Killed	Killed			Injured			
			SFs	Militants	Total	SFs	Civilians	Militants	Total
2008	2	5	3	3	11	1	2	2	3
2014	1	5	3	4	12	0	0	0	0
2018	1	0	1	2	3	1	0	0	1
Total	28	32	61	48	141	69	102	2	173

Secrecy

JeM's hallmark is secrecy. Unpredictable and ambiguous, it prefers to operate on a small scale instead of running an army of militants and OGWs, and going for mass recruitment. Keeping a small number of cadres also helps minimize the use of electronic communication devices. JeM aims for one or two major suicide attacks in a year, which generates high optics. It is ready to shock when one least expects it. However, along with that, it also indulges in minor terrorist attacks to maintain its presence or for other reasons like killing informers, etc. JeM cadres keep a low profile. Compared to the cadres of other outfits, their presence on social media and use of modern technology is not impressive. They adhere to traditional methods of communication; JeM cadres prefer to go to the houses of their OGWs, from where they make calls mainly through encrypted applications. With OGWs, telephonic communication is minimal. They are given verbal instructions about meeting points, if any weapons or food items have to be collected, etc. The current perception in the intelligence circles in J&K is that infiltrating human assets in Jaish is fraught with huge risks. Human assets can be infiltrated in JeM only if there is a confirmation and verification of a trusted handler/authority in Pakistan.

In contrast, it is comparatively easier to infiltrate LeT and HM with the help of local networks and assets. Also, SFs and intelligence operatives find it easier to contact HM and LeT networks in PoK and Pakistan, but this is not the case with JeM. As a result, gathering HUMINT-based intelligence input about its activities in India and Pakistan is a highly challenging task. However, contrary to the current perception of JeM being almost impenetrable and highly secretive, in its first phase, it was perceived as the most infiltrated organization by the human assets working for security forces and intelligence agencies. This resulted in massive losses for the organization in the form of successful encounters eliminating its entire leadership. According to Srinagar's downtown-based anti-militancy activists Khubaib Mir and Rihan Mir, JeM militants were not overly secretive until 2007–08. They frequented mosques, instructing clerics to radicalize youth. They also read Khutba in the Jumma prayers. This callousness led to many successful encounters and massive cadre losses. It is pertinent to mention here an interesting strategy by JeM that can put a question mark on the successes of SFs in eliminating many terrorists.

Sources told this author that the organization leaks information to security forces itself to eliminate those cadres it considers problematic, such as womanizers or drug addicts.[86] Some of the successful encounters in the first phase might have resulted from this practice of JeM. In 2017, reportedly, JeM got some of its own militants killed by leaking information to SFs. However, verifying the exact numbers and details isn't easy. In the second phase of its existence, it seems that JeM learned from its mistakes, and prioritized being vigilant and secretive. Having said this, it also merits mention that SFs and intelligence agencies have undergone sweeping changes in their style of functioning as well. Post-2016, intelligence agencies mostly rely on TECHINT derived through hacking phone devices and communication intercepts. The HUMINT has reportedly declined in quality and quantity. Hence, it can also be argued that JeM was more susceptible to HUMINT due to its traditional approach. As mentioned above, it prefers to use electronic communication devices only when required, which makes it relatively immune to TECHINT-based operations.

JeM militants observe some of the standard safety measures employed by the cadres of most of the militant groups; however, as per the testimonies of OGWs, they tend to be more guarded and cautious. They sleep in shifts and do not sleep in one place for more than two to three days. They cook their own food. Even if a family member cooks food for them in their hideouts, they allegedly make them eat first to ensure it is not poisoned. Mostly, if they visit a house for dinner or lunch, they do not spend the night there. If JeM militants stay in a home for a few days, they do not open up to the household members as much as LeT and HM cadres supposedly do. The newer generation of JeM militants are a bit averse to staying perpetually in forest hideouts, it is believed. In several cases, they have rented apartments in urban areas, changing their houses every three months. During such urban stays, they do not go out and interact with the general public. For all their outside work and errands, they use OGWs. JeM commanders and militants prefer to stay away from the media.

Whereas commanders of groups like LeT and HM have occasionally given interviews, in the case of JeM's Kashmir commanders, there are hardly any recorded interviews—except that of Ghazi Baba, JeM's first commander in the Valley. He is remembered as an iconic commander in JeM circles. Many myths have grown around him, presenting him as some mysterious figure. Zee News reporter Nasir Ahmed interviewed Ghazi Baba; however, in the two-hour-long interview, Ghazi Baba's face was covered and the journalist could not see him. In 2003, when Ghazi Baba was killed by the BSF, initially, it was difficult to identify him because no one had seen him. He had married a local woman and had a daughter with her. After the encounter, she disappeared and resurfaced in Pakistan, where she posted on social media about Ghazi Baba, in which she addressed him as Shahbaz Khan because even she did not know his real name! Reportedly, he cooked his own food, never trusted locals and always had four to five Pakistani militants with him. He never took off his shoes and changed hideouts twice or thrice in a single night.

JeM militants prefer to hide in plain sight for movement and espionage. Their FTs tend to come from south Punjab, Karachi, Balochistan, etc., so they can smoothly pass off as north Indian workers from UP and Bihar in a crowd. During such routine movements, they carry a small pistol that can be easily hidden, unlike the cadres of other groups, who invariably prefer an AK-47. With informers, JeM is ruthless, showing no mercy. In several cases, they have killed the family members of the informers as well. JeM's ruthlessness is evident in a message sent by Mudasir, a JeM cadre involved in the Pulwama conspiracy, to his father, who had asked him to surrender at the behest of NIA's chief investigation officer in the case, Rakesh Balwal.[87] In his reply, Mudasir said that he would have surrendered if it were HM or LeT, but the JeM commanders were ruthless. He said his seniors in the organization would not let it happen, and would kill him and his family members if he surrendered.[88]

As regards the mortality rate of JeM militants in Kashmir, in the first phase particularly, FTs lived longer than LeT and HM cadres. Reportedly, JeM FTs survived for three to four years because they used OGWs or locals in most attacks. Secondly, as compared to other groups, they staged fewer attacks. However, the general perception about JeM terrorists is that compared to other outfits, they rarely get into survival mode—i.e., hiding, discreetly moving around and continuing their existence. They proactively plan their attacks. From 2016 onwards, the number of successful encounters has generally increased, impacting JeM cadres' mortality rates.

Encounters have become more successful because of the acquisition of advanced interception and cyber technologies by SFs, the government's policy of zero tolerance for terrorism and the continuous rule of one government at the Centre, due to which the separatists and Islamist ecosystem have not received the protection and patronization that they were allegedly blessed with during the rule of various state-level parties.

JeM does not entirely trust local Kashmiris because, in its first phase, it became a major victim of espionage by locals working for SFs. Besides, JeM does not find them sufficiently Islamic or passionate about jihad. The organization has a distinct obsession with jihad because of Masood Azhar's intense interest in the concept; hence, any deviation from the highest standards of motivation and indoctrination is treated with suspicion and looked down upon in the JeM rank and file. FTs heading JeM in Kashmir are vested with a lot of power by their higher-ups vis-à-vis commanders of HM and LeT. JeM chiefs play a crucial role in recruiting local cadres. Most of the senior JeM commanders in Kashmir have been FTs, except Noor Tantrey, who displayed exceptional talent in reviving the organization in 2016. However, despite this distrust, JeM has been able to win over the locals and inspire them with their spectacular fidayeens—as a result of which they have successfully recruited locals for suicide missions. Also, JeM has been more open to locals in its second phase because infiltration had become extremely difficult due to LoC fencing and high-tech surveillance. However, the distrust of locals remains firmly embedded in the minds of JeM commanders. Qari Yasir, a JeM commander, allegedly told Muhammad Umar Farooq, the Pulwama mastermind, that they were getting a large number of recruits because of the oppression and tyranny of the Indian state. He claimed that every individual was willing to take up arms and rise against the state, but, he added, that they needed to be cautious. Locals, he claimed, were immature, emotional and addicted to their mobiles. He said they were weak-hearted and extremely emotional for their girlfriends and mothers, and got lured by money easily.[89]

However, for secrecy, JeM, in general, keeps its cadre strength smaller and uses the locals for fidayeens and terror attacks, which also helps in protecting the foreign commander and prolonging his life. JeM's cadre strength in each district is much smaller than that of LeT and HM. Their focus is not on building widespread OGW networks and an organized cadre with commanders in each district. They prefer quality over quantity, and only the best are selected after rigorous scrutiny and background checks. Before recruitment, the background of the local militant is carefully verified to ensure that he does not have any police record. Post recruitment, they invest in their training, and transform them into highly indoctrinated and committed jihadist experts in their tradecraft. In the words of Rafiq (name changed), a guide who helps JeM in infiltration, '*Woh locals ko barood banate hai* (They transform the local recruits into explosives [i.e., highly radicalized and skilled terrorists]).' At the maximum, three or four militants, including one or two local militants of JeM, are active in a district. In LeT and HM's case, generally, there are eight to ten or even ten to twelve active militants in a district. Small cadre strength also makes JeM immune to penetration by SFs and intelligence agencies. Moreover, it is a highly focused organization. It does have the larger goal of Shariah-ruled India; however, its cadres and commanders in Kashmir are not interested in political and ideological debates. They concentrate on their immediate targets—i.e., fidayeen and terror attacks. They activate a minimal number of locals for fidayeen attacks instead of spreading thin and scattering cadres all over the Valley. In this objective of precise fidayeen attacks, they do not need a highly radicalized society at a mass level. They only need secrecy and the ability to spot one or two highly radicalized recruits who can be trained as fidayeen. Such a small number of indoctrinated individuals can be found with some effort in a society that is going through a pervasive terrorism and radicalization problem. This feature makes JeM more dangerous as, with this template, they can also recruit fidayeen from the Indian hinterland.

Once a local is recruited, they cannot visit their homes. JeM commanders place severe restrictions on the use of phones as well. After training, JeM commanders wait for instructions from Pakistan about an upcoming attack. The local recruits lie low. After the green signal from Pakistan, it takes about fifteen to twenty days to make the preparations which includes a recce, practice drills and assembling the explosives in a vehicle if it is a VBIED attack. During this period, the trusted OGWs feed high-quality intelligence about Road Opening Party (ROP) changes and security details at the target. Often for the target recce, JeM sends teams of two people (one FT and one local) in the early morning to the area. The whole day, they monitor the target and only return late at night. These recce teams are generally clean-shaven, dressed in ordinary-looking attire, and carry a small pistol and grenade for defence. The recce teams do not make an overt display of Islamic dressing and gestures in a bid to elude the gaze of SFs at various checkpoints.

In its missions, JeM sends a fixed number of attackers. In case of a VBIED, there is only one militant; in a camp attack, there are three militants, including two FTs and one local. Like other terror outfits, militants of JeM also carry a matrix sheet that has codes for relevant entities like camp, sentry, ammunition, etc. They use these sheets to communicate with their handlers, who are across the border. In LeT attacks, there are generally two to four militants.

Along with the matrix sheet, JeM militants also carry the jihadi handbook, which contains dos and don'ts for terrorists. When arrested, it lays down the standard operating procedure to evade and confuse interrogators, and even mislead them, to save the organization. Sometimes fidayeens are given drugs beforehand and morphine injections to bear the pain and prolong the operation for as long as they can.

The importance of deception and secrecy can also be seen in JeM's overall approach in Kashmir. JeM in Pakistan is staunchly against Shia Muslims, Sufis, Barelwis and Ahmadiyyas. However, in Kashmir, they rarely pay attention to these sectarian differences. In an encounter in Shopian (2002), a JeM militant's diary was found by SFs, which mentioned that the militant was earlier with Lashkar-e-Jhangvi, an anti-Shia Deobandi terrorist group of Pakistan. Further, the diary entries said that the slain militant had killed eleven Shia Muslims. JeM's high premium on secrecy is also evident because it has not yet left any major footprint in the terror-funding business. Terror-funding modules of both LeT and HM have been busted; however, JeM modules remain elusive. JeM, unlike other outfits, does not have visible and lavish office establishments in big cities like Islamabad and

Rawalpindi. Outfits like LeT, HM and Al Badr, on the other hand, do, which has allowed Indian assets in Pakistan to successfully infiltrate them. However, in the case of JeM, they have not been able to do so.[80] LeT and HM sent many Kashmiri boys on valid visas to Pakistan in 2017–18, where they received military training and returned to Kashmir. At times, such travellers were allegedly used by Indian agencies to penetrate the HM and LeT hierarchy. However, JeM, guided by its distrust towards locals, refrained from this practice, which has made infiltration by intelligence agencies difficult.[91]

Training

VISITED BY JEM OPERATIVES IN PAKISTAN AND AFGHANISTAN

S NO	GPS CO-ORDINATES	CAMP LOCATION DESCRIPTION	COUNTRY
1.	29.134155, 64.486610	DALBADIN CHAGAI BALOCHISTAN	PAKISTAN
2.	31.393471, 64.319459	NAWA-I-BARAKZAYI	AFGHANISTAN
3.	31.583650, 64.453329	LASHKARI BAZAR CAMP 1	AFGHANISTAN
4.	31.585191, 64.448433	LASHKARI BAZAR CAMP 2	AFGHANISTAN
5.	31.592666, 64.441492	LASHKARI BAZAR CAMP 3	AFGHANISTAN
6.	31.621483, 64.449270	GUZARE SUKH 1	AFGHANISTAN
7.	31.625181 64.444414	GUZARE SUKH 2	AFGHANISTAN
8.	31.633475, 64.424357	GUZARE SUKH 3	AFGHANISTAN
9.	31.668256, 64.576016	NAHRI SARAJ	AFGHANISTAN
10.	32.075499, 64.833994	SANGIN CAMP	AFGHANISTAN
11.	32.076461, 64.832747	MUSA QALA SANGIN	AFGHANISTAN

JeM training lasts from four to six months. The table above gives the names and GPS coordinates of the prominent JeM camps in Pakistan and Afghanistan.[92] JeM's predecessors—HuM, HuA and HuJI—have had a strong base in Afghanistan since 1979. Their cadres were trained in Afghan camps like Yavar, Sangin[93] and Rahmania (near Bagram). In the late 1990s, AQ had developed its Khost 1 and 2, Khalid bin Waleed and Al Farooq camps. According to Mr Dabwal (name changed), a senior NIA officer associated with the Pulwama fidayeen investigation, the first generation of JeM cadres was trained in Al Farooq camp, which was primarily an Al Qaeda camp. Likewise, they were also trained with Haqqanis and Taliban in their training camps, and followed the same training manual. Insiders like Farzan suggest that Bahawalpur is just a face for JeM, which has become famous; its real work happens in its bases in KPK. JeM's most important training centres were at Sayeed Ahmed Shaheed camp at Balakot and the Batrasi camp at Mansehra.[94] However, the Batrasi camp was abandoned after 2004. The Sayeed Ahmed Shaheed camp continued to function, becoming JeM's largest training facility directly under the supervision of Masood Azhar and Qari Shah Mansoor. According to an intelligence report from Indian sources, in 2014, 105 JeM cadres were trained at Balakot by five instructors. A small batch was given special training in planning and executing fidayeen attacks. It continued until February 2019 when India bombed the facility, allegedly killing 300 JeM cadres to avenge the Pulwama fidayeen attack.[95] In 2000, it had 7,000 students. Some of the other significant JeM bases are in Ilaqa-e-Gair (KPK), Al Hadid at Kotli (PoK), Masker camp (Chakoti, Bhimber Gali), Kuhat (KPK), Ragi Bazaar (Khurshidabad, PoK), Chuhi Nala (Muzaffarabad, PoK), Tabooq camp (Garhi-Habibullah forest, Manshera), Ambar (Muzaffarabad, PoK), Barfani Training camp at Makdha mountain (PoK), Dakhan (Muzaffarabad, PoK) Maskar Khaiba (Muzaffarabad, PoK), Daura-Bait-ul-Rizwan (Muridke, Pakistan), Karodi-Basa (PoK), Marsad camp (Muzaffarabad, PoK), Mardan, Deerkot, Deerbala and Abbottabad.[96] Most of these camps were operational between 2005 and 2015; however, it is difficult to get precise details about the nature and activities at these camps because of a lack of data.

Recent inputs indicate that the practice of formal and permanent camps is out of use due to FATF scrutiny. JeM has resorted to giving tough commando-type training to a few FTs, who can then train fifteen to twenty local recruits in Kashmir. Also, the new recruits are relatively educated, unlike the older ones, and the weapons are sophisticated now; hence, long training courses are not required. Mainly, after 2019, the training is short and smart, and done randomly in jungles and small villages to evade scrutiny. In the future, due to the adoption of drone technology, there will be even lesser reliance on long-duration physical training courses.

Additionally, ISI is also settling its human assets in India—Pakistani, Nepali and Bangladeshi nationals. These assets maintain a low profile and can be activated when required. Besides, they will also act as catalysts and coordinators in the event of some social unrest or protests against the government for its alleged pro-Hindu and anti-Muslim policies.

Abdul Rahman Mughal alias Raja/Shabir, a JeM terrorist (resident of Poonch in PoK) arrested in 2016, provided a detailed description of his training schedule:[97]

Name of the Training: Al Ra'd

Place: Balakot Camp (Manshera district, Khyber Pakhtunkhwa, Pakistan). It was 10 km south of Balakot city and 1.5 km away from the main road—national highway N15; Manshera–Naran–

Chilas road. The training camp was known by its code name, Madrasa Ayesha Sadiq. There were eighty trainees and twenty-five fidayeen trainees. Fidayeens were housed and trained separately. To become a fidayeen, one needed to file a separate application expressing commitment and desire.

Staff: Muhammad Ghori (commander), Ustad Sufiyan, Naved, Husaifa and Hanzala (all Punjabi-speaking instructors), Butt Sahab (cook) and Uzair (storekeeper).

Structure: The camp had two entry gates to the south. The main entry gate led to a field of 150–160 metres in length and 500 metres in width. There was a madrasa and a mosque to the left of the field. Next to it was Sheesh Mahal, which had the reception and the instructors' living rooms. For guests, there was Maskeen Mahal to the north. Between Sheesh Mahal and Maskeen Mahal were the fidayeen living rooms. The trainees' dormitory was east of Maskeen Mahal. It was a big hall where eighty trainees lived. The camp also had a canteen. The compound was fenced but had no boundary walls.

Training period: January–April/May 2014

Schedule:

3 a.m.–5 a.m.: Najil namaz/Tahajjud namaz/Tilawat (Quran recital)/Fajr namaz

5 a.m.–8 a.m.: Physical exercises—running, push-ups, chin-ups, sit-ups, crawling, high/long jump. Completing 100–120 push-ups in one set was considered a yardstick for ideal fitness.

8 a.m.–9 a.m.: Breakfast

9 a.m.–12.30 p.m.: Theory classes on weapons—AK47, Pika guns, hand grenades, pistols and UBGLs

12.30 p.m.–1.30 p.m.: Zuhr namaz

1.30 p.m.–3 p.m.: Lunch and leisure

3 p.m.–4.45 p.m.: Field craft, which included lessons on hiding, camouflage, ambush, escape, how to use wireless sets and matrix sheets

4.45 p.m.–5 p.m.: Maghrib namaz

5 p.m.–6.30 p.m.: Games, like football, and leisure

6.30 p.m.–8 p.m.: Maghrib Tilawat (Quran recital)

8 p.m.–9 p.m.: Dinner

9 p.m.–3 a.m.: Isha namaz followed by sleep

All JeM FTs are trained commandos and deft at martial arts. Since 2018, it has also been focusing on training cadre in sea-based jihad. In addition, cadres also get Kashmiri-language training and introductory cultural acclimatization courses on the Valley. According to Abdul Rahman Mughal, most of his colleagues found the training difficult. Twenty-two trainees left in the first week itself. The courses became more challenging over time and, finally, twelve of the most intelligent ones were chosen for IED and GPS training. During the last five days, the cadres were given practical training in weapons' handling with live ammunition. The firing range for the AK-47s was kept at 200–250 meters. The batch was taken to secluded and forested areas for firing practice. During training, the cadres were given PKR 200 per week. Once the trainees were ready to graduate, they were given ten rounds for their AK-47s, five rounds for their Pika gun, two grenades and seven rounds for their pistols, for the firing practice.

Mufti Abdul Rauf and Maulana Umar, both residents of Bahawalpur, visited the training camp, said Abdul Rahman Mughal. Mufti Rauf gave provocative and passionate speeches about global jihad, Afghanistan and the atrocities committed on Muslims in Kashmir. He allegedly said that the Muslim Ummah should not rest in peace till the enemies of Islam are crushed. However, Pakistan Army officials never visited the camp where Abdul Rahman finished his training.

Propaganda content in the training included:

1) Kandahar hijack videos and the ensuing celebrations showcasing JeM's success
2) A video of twenty-two Kashmiri Muslims being shot during namaz by Indian SFs
3) A video on the Gujarat riots titled '*Haan maine dekha hai Gujarat ka manzar* (Yes, I have seen the horrors of the Gujarat riots)'
4) Mob speeches to bring down Babri Masjid
5) A video of the Peshawar army school attack—JeM militants were told that it was done by Shia terrorist groups supported by Iran. Shias were categorized as the enemies of Islam and Pakistan.

Sajjad Afghani, the legendary HuM commander of J&K who was arrested with Masood Azhar in India, was trained in Afghanistan at Yavar camp. In 1988–89, he fought against the Soviets at the Liza and Bari camps in Afghanistan. It was decided by HuM at Bari camp to send fighters to Kashmir to train young mujahids rising in rebellion against India. This author managed to access the interrogation report of Afghani, which detailed the training he received.[98]

In the Yavar camp, Abu Usra from Palestine and Mufti Shahjahan from Bangladesh were the leading instructors. Afghani said there were twenty-five trainees (all Pakistanis). Weapons training included lectures as well as practical training on handling and using AK-47s, Pika guns, LMGs, pistols, rocket launchers, grenades and Russian/Chinese stick grenades. It was a month-long training with a tight schedule, demanding physical work, and lectures on the Quran and jihad. The recruits were highly motivated. They were also trained in using wireless sets. The cadres were given exposure to the following heavy weaponry:

1) SG-43 Goryunov: Heavy machine gun to shoot down choppers. It had a four-inch-long bullet, an ammunition belt of 250 rounds and a magazine of sixty-five rounds
2) Zoraki: Combat weapon with a three-inch bullet
3) DShK: Anti-aircraft gun with six-inch bullets
4) ZU-23-2: Anti-aircraft gun with a seven-inch bullet and the system of using an ammunition belt
5) RPGs
6) BM 21 launch vehicle: It destroys enemy camps. It has twelve barrels for missiles and every missile weighs 18 kg
7) 122-mm guns: Canon with a 1.5-metre-long barrel. It destroys installations, and its missile weighs 32 kg
8) Stinger missiles: To shoot down aircraft

Afghani told his interrogators that he and his team entered Indian Kashmir with AK-47s, LMGs, rocket launchers, hand grenades, pistols and daggers. Some other accounts also suggest that in the 1990s, Afghan-returned jihadis carried Afghan battle weapons, including RPGs (rocket-propelled grenades). From the training accounts given by Abdul Rahman Mughal and Sajjad Afghani, it can be concluded that HuM and JeM fighters of the early phase, due to their Afghan experience, had a much superior exposure to high-tech and lethal war weapons used in the Afghan jihad. Their training was rigorous and focused more on combat experience. After 2004, due to the ban on JeM and the ouster of Taliban from Afghanistan, JeM's links with its Afghan camps were majorly damaged. It also impacted the quality of training imparted to jihadis sent to Kashmir. Abdul Rahman Mughal, arrested in 2016, was part of the second phase of JeM and it can be seen that his training was comparatively more basic. The weaponry he was trained in was significantly less sophisticated. In the second phase, it can be said that jihadis were being trained to carry out shoot-and-run terror attacks, which was mostly the dominant phenomenon in Kashmir, besides the high-profile IED attacks and fidayeen missions. Let us suppose this trend is situated in the context of Taliban's return to power in Afghanistan. In that case, there is a strong possibility of JeM fighters once again receiving training and sharing camps with the Afghan Taliban and Al Qaeda.

Sajjad Afghani also provided details about HuM training camps in Kashmir in the early 1990s, which are as follows. He said that HuM-owned training camps in Pakistan and Afghanistan were at Kotli (PoK) and Yavar (Khost, Afghanistan). Training camps in Kashmir Valley included Dara Harwan (Srinagar), Kangan forests (Srinagar), Kapran (Anantnag), Chernar Breng, Pathribal (Anantnag), Malangam, Bandipora, Baramulla, Bhalesa and Mughal Maidan (Doda).

HuM militants communicated through very high frequency (VHF) wireless sets in the early 1990s. They used a different frequency each day. They used the following frequencies:

- General frequency one-hourly: 777, 555 and 786 (daily)
- Personal frequency: 015 (Friday), 030 (Saturday), 045 (Sunday), 060 (Monday), 075 (Tuesday), 090 (Wednesday), 105 (Thursday)

At the time of Sajjad Afghani's arrest, the HuA had 1,500 militants in Kashmir, 700 AK-47s, 25 LMGs, 100 pistols, eighty-eight rocket launchers, 1,000 grenades, two grenade guns, twenty-five mines, 100 daggers, six binoculars, fourteen wireless transmitter sets and 10,000 ammunition rounds.

Codes Employed by HuM Militants[99]

Place/Person	Code
Srinagar	Kandahar
Anantnag	Sri Lanka
Sopore	Gazni
Bandipore	Khost
Militants	Talib-e-Alim
Foreign Mercenaries	Ustad
Money	Books
Fresh Recruits	Fruit Boxes
Contact word of HuM	Al Toofan
Chief Sajjad Afghani Khan	01
District Commander, Anantnag	02
Dignibal Camp, Srinagar	03
Breng (Anantnag)	05
Pahalgam	06
Pathribal camp, Anantnag	04

That JeM's FTs receive high-quality training is evident in some of the encounters SFs have had with its militants. In January 2009, SFs started an operation targeting at least a dozen JeM commanders in the Bhati Dhar forests of Mendhar in Poonch district.[100] However, after ten days of heavy and intensive action, it came to an abrupt end. Despite the heavy deployment of SFs and the hostile terrain, all the militants successfully escaped. In an encounter in Kupwara in 2020, a group of four JeM militants were infiltrating into India. Four other militants, including the launch pad commander, came to escort them. Their local Kashmiri contact traded this intel with Indian SFs for INR 30 lakh. SFs laid a cordon with LMGs and fixed an IED at the point where the group was to emerge, as per the intel. It was a plain and grassy area, so the IED was expected to cause massive damage and the cordon was likely to succeed since the terrain lacked natural barriers like hills. In the IED blast that followed, only one person died on the spot and one got injured. The remaining militants successfully escaped. The fact that they could withstand and successfully escape from such a well-planned ambush speaks volumes about the combat effectiveness of JeM militants. In another such example, in the JeM fidayeen attack at Laizbal (Anantnag) CRPF camp in 2020, the suicide bomber, wearing a black Pathani suit, killed five CRPF soldiers and then waited on the other side of the road, for the vehicle, without any fear or nervousness. The moment it arrived, he lobbed a grenade at the fuel tank. Then, he killed a police officer and another CRPF soldier. The fidayeen could have easily escaped after the first attack; however, he chose to stay and unleash maximum damage before going down, which is also a fundamental lesson in fidayeen training.

Many SF personnel who had participated in encounters with JeM militants told me that the cadres are highly trained and courageous. They do not believe in wasting ammunition. They will fire one round in one hour but will make sure that they kill an SF personnel. They attempt to kill senior officers, which is considered a vital sign of successful operations in JeM circles. Sometimes, the encounter can last several hours, even with one highly trained JeM terrorist. Amongst FTs, the battle-hardened Afghan and KPK veterans act like lethal fighting machines. Sometimes, ten to fifteen bullets are found in their bodies after the encounters. In the second phase of JeM, its FT cadres use NATO weapons like MP4, MP5 and Pika guns. SFs have seized such weapons from many encounter sites. It has also been discovered that JeM militants now use armour-piercing bullets, which follow the pattern of three regular bullets followed by three steel bullets, in a magazine. These militants generally attack in a team of 2:1—two FTs and one local—or just two FTs.

JeM cadres also display much better discipline than those of other organizations. Continuously in touch with their superiors and handlers based across the border, JeM's FT commanders play the most powerful role in the organization's hierarchy. Ghazi Umar, a JeM FT commander with two tenures in Kashmir—first between 2005–09 and then in 2013–14—told his interrogators after his arrest in 2014 that the commanders are advised not to participate in the attacks and to keep themselves safe. They make crucial organizational and recruitment decisions, plan and execute the attack strategy, and select future fidayeens. They attack a target only after getting permission from the high command, whereas in the case of LeT, some mistakes have come to light where individuals carried out attacks and were killed without getting the green signal from their superiors.

Reportedly, JeM is training local Kashmiris in making IEDs, grenades and pipe bombs. They are also creating micro-IED modules in various districts that will work in silos, so that even if members of any one module are arrested, the others remain unaffected. Also, it is likely that in the future JeM will rely more on local men for carrying out IED attacks; however, JeM will not own the attacks. In its second phase, mainly from 2018 to 2019, JeM cadres have been asked to locate and send geospatial coordinates of intelligence, security, administrative and industrial installations. Mustapha (name changed), a former LeT terrorist, also informed me that he was invited to the Pakistan High Commission in late 2018 to meet some intelligence operatives after some initial meetings in an Old Delhi market. He was offered money for sending video recordings of geospatial coordinates of critical installations and highways. Notably, a few months after that meeting, the Pulwama IED attack happened. It seems probable that JeM will use this data in the future for drone-led attacks or IED attacks on key state installations. The organization may improvise in fidayeen attacks by developing remote-controlled IEDs and employing the methods of chemical and gas attacks. Also, given the degree of rapid radicalization of Muslim youth in Kashmir and in the Indian hinterland, it will not be difficult for JeM to spot and recruit fidayeen attackers. That said, it is also pertinent to mention here that JeM is trying to establish a foothold in Uttar Pradesh and Bihar, and, reportedly, JeM cadres are using the Nepal and Bangladesh borders to infiltrate and set up sleeper cells in these states. Besides, since 2017, JeM has also been planning to target airstrips in Kashmir, such as Malangpura (Awantipora) and Srinagar. In this context, it is pertinent to mention that given the rising border tensions between India and China in the Ladakh region, Beijing is likely to use terror groups like JeM through the Pakistani security establishment to target intelligence, military, aviation, civilian and transport infrastructure in J&K. China has objected to India's road and other infrastructure projects in the Ladakh region because they will be instrumental in speeding up the transportation of ammunition and military hardware, and will facilitate the rapid movement of troops in the event of a war-like scenario. China has also blocked attempts to designate Masood Azhar and, more recently, his brother Mufti Rauf, as a terrorist in the UN Security Council many times in the past;[101] hence, it seems logical that in return, Beijing may use JeM to further its strategic interests in J&K.

For JeM, the devil lies in the details. They take sufficient time in planning, and pay attention to finer details and organize things to the minutest level. Compared to JeM, LeT is a bit relaxed and casual in its approach. LeT militants are particular about their Islamic appearance, whereas JeM militants prefer blending in. Ghazi Baba, the first JeM commander, was a master of disguise. He roamed around clean-shaven and in suits across the Kashmir Valley.

The main codes used by JeM commanders are 'Sajjad Afghani', 'Aftab', 'Ghazi' and 'Usman'. One also comes across a frequent use of 'Muawiya' as a code name because it is despicable to Shias—as Muawiya opposed Ali, the Prophet's grandson, for the position of Caliph.

JeM has also followed the practice of killing select police officers. In 2006, the organization killed Vikram Singh, a head constable and the driver of the inspector general of police (Kashmir) S.M. Sahai, near the general bus stand at Batmaloo in Srinagar.[102] Terrorists also shot dead Constable Dilawar Ahmed at Telbal Morh near the Hazratbal Shrine on the outskirts of Srinagar. The trend of brutal cop killings by JeM began majorly after 2008 when the J&K police emerged as the leading counterterrorism force. In August 2018, JeM, in a joint operation with HM, killed four policemen in Shopian.[103] More recently, JeM foreign terrorists were allegedly planning to kill cops in the Kulgam district of south Kashmir.[104] On 27 June 2021, the organization killed Fayaz Ahmed, a special police officer (SPO), and his family in Awantipora.[105]

JeM is also known for occasionally conducting simultaneous attacks.[106] In 2015, it conducted an attack in the Nowshera area of Srinagar, killing two soldiers, which was followed by another attack thirty minutes later, in which two policemen were shot dead in Tangpura of Srinagar. The groups executing these simultaneous attacks were different, coordinated and controlled by different handlers, and had no clue about each other.

JeM Infiltration

JeM cadres infiltrate in their own groups.[107] JeM launch pad commanders choose their guides after rigorous scrutiny and verification. These guides are expert navigators who are familiar with the terrain and are in the business of leading infiltrator groups into Indian Kashmir. JeM does not share its infiltration route and the identities of its guides with anyone, even ISI. The guides are handsomely paid. Once selected, they have to live with the launch pad commander of JeM and are not allowed to use phones. The launch pad commanders reconnoitre the LoC two to three times with the guides, after which the guide takes the group of militants across the border. Only after they successfully cross into the Indian side does the organization share details of the guide with its handlers in Pakistan's intelligence setup because they make the payments to the guides. Also, they refrain from using the same guide twice over seven or eight months. Once they successfully infiltrate the LoC, the group does not make any contact with other terrorist groups in the area. In its first phase, when the LoC region in Lolab, Kupwara, etc., was the main infiltration route, JeM groups camped in shelters built at great heights in the mountains—so high that the army generally did not come that side.[108] Their OGWs collected rations from nearby villages and delivered them to the JeM infiltrators. From 2013 onwards, the organization started using Jammu's Samba–Kathua–Akhnoor–RS Pura border as an infiltration route; however, it emerged as its primary infiltration route only after 2016. For the Pathankot attack, it entered through Pathankot itself. For the Sunjwan and Pulwama attacks, it used the Samba–Kathua border. They prefer the Samba–Kathua–Pathankot–Sundarbani–Poonch region for infiltration because it is easier and involves less expenditure on guides as compared to the LoC region where the terrain is rugged and espionage is a serious challenge, as a result of which infiltrating parties need to change guides and OGWs in every district. As compared to LeT, JeM has fewer resources and funds; hence, the Samba–Kathua region is more attractive to it. Besides, JeM is also exploring new routes to infiltrate the Gurez sector in J&K, along with Rajasthan, Nepal, Bangladesh and Bhutan. Based on GPS coordinates sent by infiltrating terrorists, they are picked up by OGWs on the Indian side. From there, they travel to south Kashmir in trucks through the Jammu–Srinagar highway. Each cadre carries a lot of weight, which has shocked SFs who have arrested or killed them while infiltrating. Each militant carries two to four AK-47 rifles, ten or twelve grenades, eight to ten magazines, large quantities of food items and dry fruits. Sometimes, they also carry cooked chicken dishes that can last them for two to three days.

In the context of JeM's infiltration, we must briefly discuss its communication setup.[109] The main communication centre, Tuba, is located on a high mountain—about a one-day trek upwards from Dudhnial in PoK. Then, there are three relay stations situated in PoK across Poonch, Murree and Sialkot. However, in today's context, wireless communication has become outdated, but JeM has not shut down its wireless communication stations. It is a stand-by arrangement because mobile and landline networks will likely stop in case of hostility between India and Pakistan. This facility could have been used in the Pathankot attack as the fidayeens were carrying wireless handsets.

JeM's Infiltration Strategy after 2016

1) Abu Talha, alias Dr Talha, and his deputy, Wasim, are in charge of the launch pads in the Jammu region. They coordinate most of the JeM infiltrations from the Samba–Kathua international border.[110] It is suspected that four groups successfully infiltrated the border on these dates:
    a. 25 July 2017: Talha Rashid group
    b. 17 August 2017: Rashid Billa group
    c. 14 January 2018: Haider group
    d. 14 April 2018: Muhammad Umar Farooq group
2) Reportedly, Muhammad Umar Farooq helped and accompanied the other three groups in crossing the border before he infiltrated himself. Muhammad Umar Farooq was one of the key masterminds of the Pulwama fidayeen attack. All the infiltrations took place at the international border in the Hiranagar sector.
3) As observed, the possible points for infiltration are patches on the IB where the Indian portion seems to be surrounded on three sides by the Pakistan side. Infiltration generally occurs through tunnels; this way, the militants don't need to cut the fences along the border, which would immediately raise suspicion. Generally, JeM infiltrations take place in groups of five.

4) Usually, the infiltrations happen either in the late evening hours or the early morning hours.

5) Once they've crossed over to the Indian side, JeM operatives move into Kashmir Valley within a week—mainly through south Kashmir–based trucks or other modes of transport, either through the national highways or sometimes taking the route of Dhar Road and then joining the highway at Udhampur. The Kotli Jhajhar encounter of 13 September 2018, in Jammu, in which three JeM operatives were killed, points to these trends.

6) Pakistan-based JeM operatives coordinate with south Kashmir–based truck operators to transport these operatives from place to place.

7) On the Pakistani side, two villages—Harar and Monin in the Narowal region of Punjab—act as base camps and launch pads for JeM operatives. This is also allegedly the place where they groom themselves (shave their beards and cut their hair) to take photos for their fake Indian ID cards. This grooming is also done as Islamic scriptures demand that people entering Jannah to meet the seventy-two virgins who await them must be clean-shaven. It is also pertinent to mention here that because of FATF scrutiny, after 2020, Pakistan has dismantled its formal launch pads and training camps. Also, after the surgical strikes and Balakot airstrikes, Pakistan's security establishment suspects that Indian agencies have precise locations of all the training camps and launch pads, which can be targeted in the future; hence, to avoid that, they have dismantled this infrastructure.

8) A few days before the infiltration of a specific group, its operatives meet their families. Before infiltration,

the terrorists are sent to firing practice for two days. Then, JeM throws a farewell party for the infiltrating cadres—sometimes, senior JeM leaders like Mufti Rauf also participate. For Talha Rashid's departure (the son of Masood's sister; Talha was killed in October 2017), several senior leaders, including Mufti Rauf, were present at the farewell party.[111]

9) A series of encounters and seizure of weapons' consignments along the National Highway in the Jammu region in 2020–21, especially in the Nagrota region, have possibly led JeM to shift their logistics to Dhar Road once their operatives enter India. It is pertinent to mention that earlier, Ashaq Nengroo, a veteran JeM militant, who facilitated the infiltration of most militants post-2016, used this route initially. Also, there is effectively a support group available for JeM cadres in the Banihal region, which can help them with logistics.

10) The communication devices used by the four JeM terrorists killed at Jammu's Ban toll plaza on 19 November 2020 have provided a crucial link to establish that Pakistan was behind their infiltration, which occurred on 31 January 2020.[112] Terrorists entered India through a 200-metre tunnel dug from the Pakistani side at Pillar 189, which was used to reach the pick-up point at Jatwal, twelve kilometres from the International Border.[113] The tunnel, forty metres long on the Pakistani side, had enough space for militants to walk and cross into India. For communication, the militants used LMR sets. The serial number on the set used for crossing on 31 January 2020, was 908331P00059, and the number on 19 November was 908331P00058. The sets, named 'Radio

Alias: Freedom Fighter', used p1, p2, p4, p5, p55, g1 call signs on 31 January 2020, and on 19 November, they used p1, p55, p11, and p66 call signs. SFs recovered a Garmin eTrex 20X GPS device and highly sophisticated, Japan-made Icom VHF (Very High Frequency) sets. These instruments require a highly trained man to operate them. The Icom sets were also recovered after the Uri fidayeen attack. In both cases, the militants deleted the location logs to prevent SFs from tracking their locations and infiltration routes. Militants used the following frequencies:

- Digital frequencies: 143.500Mhz, 147.270 Mhz, 149.310 Mhz, 150.230 Mhz, 151.230 Mhz, 155.610 Mhz, 157.220Mhz, 160.430Mhz, 162.340 Mhz, 165.710 Mhz.
- Analog frequencies: 145.100 Mhz, 144.700 Mhz, 143.702 Mhz, 143.548 Mhz and 143.887 Mhz.

Talha Rashid

JeM operative Talha Rashid, along with other operatives, infiltrated from the Hiranagar sector on 25 July 2017 and was accompanied by Muhammad Umar Farooq up to IB on the Pakistan side. He was killed on 6 November 2017 at Aglarkandi in Pulwama district along with Mahmood Bhai and one local operative.

Rashid Billa Group

Rashid Billa and his associates reportedly infiltrated on 17 August 2018 and were accompanied by Muhammad Umar Farooq up to the international border on the Pakistani side. Earlier, Rashid tried to infiltrate with Talha Rashid in July 2017, but failed.

He was killed in an encounter at Pakherpora village in November 2017 in Budgam district.

JeM OGWs

In Kashmir's terror scenario, OGWs, or 'uppers', constitute the core strength of a terrorist group. The success of any group depends on how committed, skilled, loyal and trained their OGWs are.

When JeM was flush with money in its early days, it paid its OGWs generously—much more than the other groups. However, after its ban and the subsequent weakening of its finances, it started paying its OGWs less. Before 2016, most JeM OGWs had a Jamaat-i-Islami background; however, after 2016, JeM minimized the use of OGWs with JI backgrounds. From 2018, it has minimized the use of OGWs in general. They send their own militants to collect weapons. JeM, being a highly secretive organization, does not believe in sharing its OGWs with other terrorist groups, whereas LeT is relatively liberal in sharing its uppers. JeM OGWs work in silos—the information is shared with them on a need-to-know basis. Each OGW maintains contact with one or two militants in a particular locality or district, and is not party to any information or network beyond their two handlers. If SFs kill those militants, the OGW remains an orphan for some time before he is assigned new militants. Post-2019, JeM has stopped using its old OGWs, and reportedly uses girls and minor boys as its uppers. The other categories of OGWs that it recruits include chemical engineers who can be trained as IED experts and government officials with access to the senior bureaucracy and confidential documents. JeM apparently treats its female OGWs very respectfully and hardly indulges in sexual abuse. A Srinagar-based intelligence operative interviewed by me had befriended a JeM OGW and got into a relationship with her. He said that the woman was very religious at home and spoke highly of JeM; however, with him, she indulged in a passionate sexual relationship and broke many rules. She allegedly sent him pictures of JeM militants staying at her place. Recruiting girls as OGWs is helpful as the men in security forces do not rigorously frisk them. They can evoke sympathetic treatment from law enforcers and members of SFs guarding checkpoints.

A typical JeM OGW is hardcore, highly indoctrinated and generally has a very high capacity to bear torture. They are taught that the police can torture them, but cannot kill them; however, if they betray the organization, they will not be spared. JeM is particularly ruthless with informers and traitors. Noor Muhammad Tantrey, who revived JeM in 2016, characterizes an ideal template of an OGW working with the organization.[114] He was a close aide of Ghazi Baba. Arrested in 2003, Tantrey was given a life sentence by a POTA court in 2011. Later, he was released on parole in 2015 after being shifted to Srinagar. Following his release, he jumped parole and dedicated himself to reviving JeM as its OGW. His continued dedication and association with JeM since 2000 speaks volumes of his commitment and indoctrination levels.

In interrogations, JeM OGWs are non-cooperative and prove a tough nut to crack. Compared to them, breaking HM and LeT cadres is easier. JeM prefers to keep a tiny number of OGWs but makes sure they are highly trusted. In many cases, I found that the entire family of the JeM OGW was highly trusted and committed to the jihadist cause, and was in business for at least a decade. Masood Azhar and Mufti Rauf often spoke directly to the OGWs and their family members. If LeT has twenty OGWs in an area, JeM will have only two or three but highly trusted and committed ones. They identify a potential local recruit and send their details to their JeM commanders, who forward them to their bosses in Pakistan. After getting the green signal, the JeM commander will depute some FTs to make the target an active militant; however, the target will never know the identity of the OGW who spied on them. Moreover, the FT deputed to train them and the OGW who provided the information in the first place will never know each other's identity. Once JeM recruits a talented OGW with strong religious commitment and loyalty, it tries its best to protect them and keep their identity secret. However, if they are exposed, they are activated as a proper terrorist and asked to join the JeM ranks.[115]

The latest trends in infiltration, as of September 2022, received by the Indian intelligence agencies, indicate that JeM is training its cadres in gliding for infiltration and they have also purchased eight to ten drones, now located in the Shakargarh area of Pakistan, opposite the Jammu region.[116] Moreover, JeM has started reviving the LoC region for infiltration (Uri–Kupwara area, north Kashmir). Reportedly, Mir Humza—Masood Azhar's cousin—is facilitating the infiltration of new cadres into the Valley, who are under the close control of Mufti Rauf, from Kupwara, and they are camping in Beerwah (central Kashmir) before reaching south Kashmir.[117] This is a new development as central Kashmir has never been a JeM stronghold.

Post-2019, JeM is using its OGWs to collect information about J&K's critical security, civil, transport and aviation infrastructure, and provide the information to ISKP. As far as the collection of the coordinates of vital installations is concerned, it has been confirmed by many other sources interviewed by me; however, supplying it to IS-KP to facilitate its expansion in J&K appears a bit far-fetched. However, it cannot be ruled out because IS-KP has many disgruntled elements from TTP who have historical links with JeM; hence, this claim needs further investigation. Also, in addition to OGWs, JeM maintains an entirely dormant category of assets used purely for intelligence gathering. They live ordinary lives—they are carpenters, students, cobblers, religious clerics and small-time mystics. Almost 90 per cent of carpenters in Kashmir are mainly from Punjab, followed by UP and Bihar. JeM militants speak Punjabi fluently, enabling them to mingle with the common folk. Having discussed JeM's OGW network, Farzan's assessment of JeM's capabilities merits mention as it aptly summarizes the quality and depth of its intelligence network, of which its uppers are the main pillars. While concluding his interview, Farzan said that JeM can conduct a fidayeen strike anywhere in Kashmir at short notice and, with some decent effort, anywhere across the length and breadth of India.

Recruitment and Radicalization

JeM more or less follows the broad recruitment pattern of the larger Deobandi extremist ecosystem, of which it is a part. Its FTs are mainly from the Punjab province—largely from south Punjab, i.e., the area around Bahawalpur and Multan, known as the Saraiki belt. The other major catchment areas for JeM are in KPK, the Karachi region and Balochistan. In the early 1990s, JeM's predecessors—HuM and HuA—had cadres from Sudan, Afghanistan, Somalia, Bangladesh and Turkey. Ayesha Siddiqa had the opportunity to investigate and explore JeM's recruitment methods and approaches in her field research in south Punjab.

Interestingly, her findings on JeM recruitment and training resonated almost entirely with Ajmal Kasab's—the only perpetrator of the 26/11 attacks to be caught alive—testimony to FBI interrogators.[118] She suggests that south Punjab's poverty, failing agricultural system, absentee landlordism, economic stagnation, poor education system, underdevelopment, lack of employment opportunities and the ultimate hopelessness of the population make it a fertile recruitment ground for terrorist organizations.[119] Most traditional elites of the area migrated to urban areas and continued to function as absentee landlords. They could not provide any opportunities for the local youth, which has led to immense frustration among them and, as a result, they become easy prey for terrorist groups. The general pattern is of militants using madrasas and other establishments for radicalization, planning and logistics. Afterwards, candidates are sent to KPK or PoK for advanced commando operations and weapons' handling training. In her detailed exploration of the recruitment strategies and methods used by terror groups, she suggests that in the first stage, young children or men are taken to madrasas, fed well and kept in living conditions better than what they are accustomed to in their homes. She writes, 'This is a simple psychological strategy meant to help them compare their homes with the alternatives offered by militant organizations. The returning children, like the boys I met, then undergo ideological indoctrination in a madrasa. Those who are indoctrinated always bring more friends and family with them. It is a swelling cycle.'[120]

South Punjab madrasas have become a hotbed of jihadism and a threat to global security. Sipah-e-Sahaba Pakistan, LeJ, LeT and JeM are the four leading terrorist organizations drawing recruits from south Punjab. LeT, with its Ahl-i-Hadith influence, is popular among the Punjabi and Urdu-speaking muhajirs,[121] whereas JeM, LeJ, and SSP cadres are mainly from the Saraiki-speaking belt. The favourite recruitment areas of all militant groups in south Punjab are Cholistan in Bahawalpur, Rekh in

Dera Ghazi Khan and the Kacha area in Rajanpur. The first two are poor and underdeveloped desert areas, whereas the last was famous for dacoits. Interestingly, the clerics of Lal Mosque[122] are from the Kacha area. Their influence strengthened after they fought against the dacoity of the area with the police's support.

As early as 1988–89, the militias that won Khost in the Afghan jihad had many fighters from south Punjab working for Afghan warlords like Gulbuddin Hekmatyar and Burhanuddin Rabbani. In 2009, about 5,000 to 9,000 jihadists from the region were fighting in Waziristan.[123] Reportedly, over time, the jihadists from this region became the backbone of terror attacks across Pakistan and Afghanistan planned by Al Qaeda and a range of other groups. Post-1980, the number of seminaries in south Punjab increased manifold. Citing a 1996 government report, Ayesha Siddiqa wrote that there were 883 madrasas in Bahawalpur, 361 in Dera Ghazi Khan, 325 in Multan, and 149 in Sargodha district. The madrasas in Bahawalpur outnumbered all other cities', including Lahore. These numbers relate to Deobandi madrasas only and do not take into account Ahl-i-Hadith, Barelwi, and other sects' madrasas. IB estimates of 2008 show approximately 1,383 madrasas in the Bahawalpur division, which house 84,000 students. Although the highest number of madrasas is in Rahim Yar Khan district (559), followed by Bahawalpur (481) and Bahawalnagar (310), it is Bahawalpur in which the highest number of students (36,000) are enlisted. The total number of madrasa students in Pakistan has reached about one million.[124] According to Tahir Kamran, Pakistan's eminent expert on Deobandi militancy, the number of madrasas increased from 1,320 in 1988 to 3,153 in 2000, about 140 per cent. These madrasas became a crucial supply line of jihadis to the Afghan war in the 1980s. By 2001, the Bahawalpur division alone had about 15,000–20,000 trained terrorists who resettled in the area following the crackdown that Musharraf claimed to have launched against jihadist organizations. Most of the research work focused on FATA and NWFP regions of Pakistan; however, south Punjab—going through what Ayesha Siddiqa refers to as 'Talibanization'—remains largely unnoticed by counterterrorism experts and researchers.

The madrasas convert or induct people into Salafism and Deobandism, and impart such foundational teachings that weaken their resistance to extremist interpretations of Islam. Barelwis or Sufis, lacking the logical and rigorous knowledge of scriptures to counter this interpretation, fail to offer much resistance and, in many cases, come under the influence of fundamentalist Salafis and Deobandis. The students in these madrasas are taught that jihad is the most fundamental duty of Muslims as long as they live. As a result, a large number of these madrasa students end up with terrorist groups. Apart from madrasas, the extremist groups and clerics majorly focus on getting recruits from government schools, and the madrasas also attract a significant number of students from better-quality government schools and radicalize them. Masood Azhar did his initial schooling in a government school and then joined the Binoria town seminary. These children are valued because they are sharper and more educated. They can be trained in handling complex weapons and technological gadgets. They are open to recruitment either because they have already been influenced by their friends adhering to extremist ideologies or because they are disgruntled with their parents.

Ayesha Siddiqa, in her interviews with the US embassy staff, said that most of the boys joining JeM were from government schools, not madrasas.[125] They suffered from despondency, seeing no future for themselves, and they kept their parents in the dark about their intentions and frustrations. JeM offered such youth a way out of their small villages and towns, and gave them a sense of empowerment, religious pride and adventure. The school students are initially subjected to a conversion programme (Daura-i-aam), a twenty-one-day initial training programme in KPK or Pakistan-occupied Kashmir. Those who continue are sent to Daura-i-khas, a special training programme of six months in which they are given commando training, and courses in guerrilla operations and weapons' handling. Those who wish to continue further are sent to more specialized programmes where they are exposed to high-level indoctrination, and their capacity to bear and inflict pain is enhanced. Reportedly, in JeM and LeT's training programmes, Pakistan's army and intelligence officers are involved. The veterans of the Afghan jihad also serve as trainers in these courses.

Ayesha Siddiqa also explores the differences between the jihadis from south Punjab and the Pashtun regions of KPK. Comparatively, south Punjab jihadis are more educated. Many of them go to study at Binoria town mosque in Karachi. Also, they are much more motivated, indoctrinated and difficult to crack as compared to the Pashtuns. The Pashtuns join jihad to avenge the killing of their near and dear ones, whereas the jihadis from south Punjab believe in pan-Islamism. They want to avenge the alleged killing and rapes of Muslim women in Chechnya, Afghanistan, Kashmir, Palestine, Somalia, etc. A large number of fidayeens come from south Punjab; comparatively, they are much more brutal with their victims. Some of the most ferocious Taliban commanders in Waziristan and Swat are from south Punjab.

However, according to Ayesha Siddiqa's research, the state authorities are in deliberate denial of a slow 'Talibanization' of south Punjab because of the following reasons:

1) Most of these extremist groups were created by the ISI as a part of Zia-ul-Haq's drive to Islamize Pakistan 'in essence to fight a proxy war for Saudi Arabia against Iran by targeting the Shia community, and later the Kashmir war'.[126] This is why state authorities do not envision the possibility of them getting out of control. In isolated cases, like that of JeM's splinter group Jamaat-ul-Furqan, which got into the state's crosshairs by plotting to kill Musharraf, they were promptly dumped.

2) They are homegrown, so they are perceived as far away from Afghanistan, and incapable of bringing Talibani norms and social systems to distant south Punjab.

3) Many of them, like LeT and JeM, are the state's strategic assets and force multipliers used to perpetuate terrorism in Jammu and Kashmir, and the Indian hinterland, to offset India's superiority in the conventional war.

4) Finally, there are fundamental disagreements over the definition of the process of Talibanization. Because south Punjab has a history of moderate and permissive Sufi culture, allowing the jihadist leaders and madrasas to co-exist with pirs, drugs and sexual indulgence, the authorities believe that the Sufi/Barelwi traditions are too strong to allow the region to go the Afghanistan way.

However, Ayesha Siddiqa disagrees and argues that the Sufi culture cannot be a robust bulwark against extremism and radicalization because it cannot fight poverty, poor governance and underdevelopment—all the factors that directly or indirectly encourage Talibanization. South Punjab has prominent pir families of Mazaris, Legharis and Gilanis, who failed to address the people's grievances in their constituencies. Even in the constituency of the former president of Pakistan, Farooq Ahmad Leghari, i.e., Dera Ghazi Khan, 'the state of underdevelopment is shocking'.[127] In such a state of underdevelopment, the poor and the dispossessed become targets of terrorist organizations. Also, the Sufi–Barelwi institutions became corrupt, superstitious, ritualistic and exploitative over time, as a result of which the gap created by their loss of credibility was filled by Deobandi and Ahl-i-Hadith madrasas, religious leaders, and groups like Tablighi Jamaat and militant organizations. They claim to offer a clear and consistent view of Islam backed by the scriptures, which the Sufi–Barelwi scholars cannot counter ideologically because of the lack of internal discourse and debate on Islam. Also, the Sufi shrine culture had nothing to offer as solace to a hopeless youth in an underdeveloped society. Ayesha Siddiqa aptly summarizes the situation in the following words:[128]

> Sadly, today, the shrines and Barelwi Islam have little to offer in terms of 'marketing' to counter the package deal offered by the Salafists for life hereafter, especially to a shaheed: 70 *hoors* (virgins), a queen *hoor* (virgin queen), a crown of jewels and forgiveness for 70 additional people. This promise means a lot for the poor youth who cannot hope for change in a pre-capitalist socio-economic and political environment, where power is hard to re-negotiate.

Besides, joining jihadist ranks brings social mobility and recognition to a poor and madrasa-educated youth, which he cannot dream of getting in any other way in his social and economic milieu. In the 1980s, with the support of the Zia government, madrasas registered exponential growth in Punjab and, ultimately, the fundamentalist ideologies of Deobandism,

Wahhabism and Tablighi Jamaat prepared the youth to join militant groups.

Interestingly, in my fieldwork in Kashmir, I found striking resemblances to the conditions that facilitated the spread of extremist Islam in south Punjab.[129] In Kashmir, the Sufi shrine, *etqaadi* Islam,[130] lost credibility because it had allegedly become exploitative, corrupt and superstitious. Its moderate teachings could not satisfy the youth living in a conflict-ridden society and had no opportunity to grow. As a result, Wahhabi groups, like Jamaat-i-Islami and Tablighi Jamaat, filled the vacuum by selling dreams of empowerment and confidence through violent jihad, promising seventy-two virgins after martyrdom and Shariah-based rule to the youths suffering from low self-esteem.[131] Besides, the young generation was lured to doctrines of Wahhabism convincingly disseminated by Saudi-educated and better-qualified clerics through modernized and better-equipped madrasas and social media channels. Also, joining militancy and announcing it on social media brought immediate glory and recognition, and getting killed in encounters brought a celebrity-like status, with thousands thronging to a dead militant's funeral.

Further, discussing the role of the state in this matter, Ayesha Siddiqa has suggested that state support played an instrumental role in the spread of Deobandi and Wahhabi madrasas, and the resultant growth of jihadism, religious extremism and sectarianism in this region. According to the two reports prepared in 1994 by the district administrative chief of Bahawalpur and later by the state government of Punjab, the meteoric rise of madrasas fanned sectarian and ideological hatred and violence in the region. Also, according to the report, the state funded extremist religious seminaries through the zakat funds. Further explaining the nuances of this state support,

Ayesha Siddiqa suggests that the political parties had developed an 'understanding' with militant groups. 'The understanding between the SSP and Benazir Bhutto after the 1993 elections, or the alleged deal between the PML-N and the SSP during the 2008 elections, denotes the relationship between major political parties and the jihadis. Currently, the SSP in south Punjab is more supportive of the PML-N,' she observed.[132] Besides, the state intelligence apparatus supported these groups in acquiring real estate, procuring weapons and in logistics. The intelligence brass protected the terrorist groups, their leaders and their compounds from the scrutiny of local and international journalists and researchers. Reportedly, the intelligence agencies chased away a BBC team investigating JeM's activities.

US embassy cables released by Wikileaks also discuss at length the development of a 'sophisticated jihadi recruitment network' in Multan, Bahawalpur and Dera Ghazi Khan divisions. According to the US cable 08LAHORE302_A titled 'Extremist Recruitment on the Rise in Southern Punjab',[133] the jihadi groups exploit the 'worsening poverty conditions' in these groups to recruit children of the said divisions into Deobandi and Ahl-i-Hadith madrasas, where they are ideologically indoctrinated with an extremist interpretation of Islam and then sent to terrorist training camps in FATA. The charitable activities conducted by the front organizations of extremist groups such as Jamaat-ud-Dawa (JuD), LeT's front organization, Al Khidmat Foundation, Jamaat-e-Islami's front organization, and Al-Rahmat Trust, JeM's front organization, strengthen the social and political credibility, and the influence, of parent terror groups, while marginalizing the traditional Sufi and Barelwi entities and increasing the dependence of the people in the region on them. This 2008 cable further said that in the Saraiki and Baloch-speaking regions of western and southern Punjab, extremist recruitment of children aged eight to fifteen had risen in the last few years.

Recruitment Modus Operandi

Coordinators of the terror outfits' charity organizations identify families with multiple children who are facing hardships due to poverty, crop failure and unemployment, and introduce them to the local Deobandi or Ahl-i-Hadith maulana.[134] The maulana convinces the family that their problems are because they deviated from true Islam, which, in their interpretation, is extremist and fundamentalist. Giving priority to jihad, it has no room for allegedly 'idolatrous' shrine worship, seen as a deviant practice. The maulana convinces them to donate one of their children to jihad as an atonement for their sins. Sometimes, they make payments in return for contributing a family member to jihad, which between 2005 and 2008 was USD 6,500 or PKR 50,000 rupees per person.

Generally, younger children between eight and twelve are favoured. These children are taken to madrasas, four to six hours away from their parental place. Typically, such madrasas are located in isolated areas, and the number of students in one madrasa is only about 100 so as not to invite undue attention. A rough estimate suggested that, in 2008, there were 200 such madrasas.[135] The children in the madrasas are not allowed to contact their families and the outside world. They are imbued with a hatred for non-Muslims, Shias, Ahmadiyyas, Sufis, the Western world and also the Pakistan government if it goes against terror groups. The concept of jihad is injected into their minds as the most fundamental duty of every Muslim. They are told that if they attain martyrdom, their families will also get salvation and God's favour. During their indoctrination, the maulanas visit the children's families, telling them exaggerated tales of their performance and progress. These madrasa graduates are employed as teachers in Deobandi and Ahl-i-Hadith madrasas. Some of them—chosen for further indoctrination and terrorist training, based on their interest and propensity for violence—are sent to KPK and PoK. Older children are generally sent straight to terrorist training in KPK and PoK without extended madrasa education. However, as mentioned earlier, they must undergo a twenty-one-day ideological indoctrination.

Reportedly, the local citizens and Sufi authorities have complained to the government about these indoctrination centres; however, they received no support. Political parties do not take their complaints seriously. Local administrative authorities either provide latent support or want to avoid confrontation with these centres as they considered it 'too dangerous'. Locals have complained that the education bureaucracy is mainly made of appointees of Zia's extremist regime; hence, they have a soft corner for such schools.

JeM uses many other tactics to lure talent. It organizes jalsas—large-scale processions—on occasions such as Kashmir Solidarity Day, Afzal Guru's death anniversary, etc. In such jalsas, Masood Azhar gives arousing and provocative speeches on jihad, referencing the Islamic scriptures and tales.[136] Documentaries and videos depicting Muslims facing atrocities and persecution in Kashmir are shown to the audience. The venue is supposedly abuzz with the chants of anti-India slogans like '*Jaish aayi, Jaish aayi, India teri maut aayi* (JeM will bring death to India)'. After Afzal Guru's hanging, JeM showed provocative documentaries on Afzal Guru at these jalsas and recruited people for the Afzal Guru Squads. After Pulwama, because of Masood's failing health, FATF pressure and government pressure, jalsas have declined in numbers—or perhaps the media is not allowed to cover them. Besides, because of Masood's health, his speeches are now telephonically relayed. In his speeches, in addition to the exaggerated and fabricated tales of the persecution of Muslims in Kashmir, Palestine and other jihadi theatres, he also fabricates stories of miracles happening after the death of jihadis. People are said to participate in these jalsas in large numbers; sometimes, the total number has reached 60,000 to 70,000, it is believed. Many people get inspired here and volunteer to become jihadis. Besides, JeM also finds recruits in its forty-day dauras or religious tours.[137] Akram Bhai, my source, told me that sometimes people with criminal backgrounds are also sent to Kashmir and Afghanistan on the condition that they will be pardoned if they come back alive. Also, while recruiting in Pakistan, young jihadis are told that if they come back alive, they will become Ghazis, which is a highly exalted status in Islam. Apart from jalsas, JeM's provincial and district offices also serve as regular recruitment centres where candidates generally come through a recommendation from some insider.

As mentioned previously, many family members of Masood Azhar have been sent to Kashmir for jihad. JeM sets this example of sacrificing its nearest and dear ones through this. In KPK, Karachi and southern Punjab, religion is a fulcrum of social and political existence. In such a milieu, sacrificing family members in holy war strengthens JeM's credibility as a genuine, committed and sincere jihadist movement in the eyes of the lay people. This enhanced credibility helps the organization attract more recruits. As compared to JeM, this practice is not very prevalent in LeT circles, which is why it carries the impression of a geopolitical tool of the Pakistan Army instead of a genuine jihadist movement.

According to Kashmir-based intelligence and police officers, in its second phase, JeM has majorly focused on finding local

Kashmiri recruits for training in IEDs and explosives. They seek young and educated minds, preferably with chemical engineering degrees, for IED training. It has successfully indoctrinated local boys for fidayeen missions. For such missions, they choose passionate, radical and disgruntled youth nurturing grievances against the Indian government and SFs for personal reasons. However, JeM is extremely careful and vigilant while recruiting such youth due to its inherent distrust of locals. They are kept on a close watch for over a year. During this time, they are given minor tasks like transporting weapons, cash, drugs and grenade lobbing. The FT commander personally supervises the recruitment process of locals as OGWs or terrorists. Also, JeM looks for highly religious local cadres. They have to observe namaz prayers and other Islamic rituals strictly. JeM found a fertile recruitment ground in south Kashmir because JI had already done the groundwork to radicalize people along such extremist lines.[138] JI had made ordinary Muslims familiar with political Islam and indoctrinated them against passive Sufi culture, which allowed JeM to find recruits without much effort.

JI members worked as JeM OGWs and kept watch on young individuals visiting Darul Uloom madrasas. Its cadres and OGWs also joined Darul Uloom prayer meetings in disguise to identify potential candidates that OGWs could then contact. Initially, such new entrants served only as OGWs. They were activated as militants only when required. In the Burhan Wani era of Kashmir militancy, recruits announced their joining of a terror group on social media by posting their pictures in military-styled gear with long hair and weapons. JeM was considered as having six-plus feet tall and hefty Pashtun fighters from KPK in its ranks. The organization used this perception as a marketing strategy and posted pictures of its tall, robust cadres to add glamour to the terror business and lure recruits.[139]

Year-Wise JeM Recruitment in Jammu and Kashmir[140]

Place of recruitment	2005	2006	2007	2008	2009	2010	2011	2012	2013	2014	2015
Kashmir	103	75	106	86	27	12	12	30	25	15	19
Jammu	55	51	32	27	18	07	01	02	01	00	00

From the table above, it can be concluded that in J&K, JeM's maximum recruitment has been in the Valley compared to the Jammu region. In Jammu, a few areas like Doda, Kishtwar, Poonch and Rajouri were once the hotbed of militancy; however, after 2010, militancy was almost wiped out in these districts. Besides, most of the militants in these areas were either Gujjars or Paharis who follow the local version of Sufi Islam, and have resisted the Deobandi and Salafi onslaught. Hence, JeM has inhibitions in trusting people from these areas of Jammu. In Kashmir, the highest local recruitment was between 2005 and 2008. This period also coincides with a large number of successful encounters in which JeM militants died. Hence, it can be argued that increasing local recruitment led to more spying by people working for SFs and the intelligence infiltrating the organization. Local recruitment declined after 2008. In 2010 and 2011, it was the lowest—just twelve recruits. From 2012, it started rising again, which coincides with the organization's revival in Pakistan. However, it never reached the levels seen in the first phase. It recruited a few but highly trusted local boys to function as OGWs and trained the best of them as fidayeens. In the Jammu region, JeM recruitment has been negligible since 2010.

After the abrogation of Article 370, overall recruitment methods have changed in Kashmir. Most of the recruitment is now online, through social media and encrypted communication applications.[141] There is one handler sitting in Pakistan and activating hundreds of local Kashmiris for a specific task, for which they are given a weapon. After executing the job, they must surrender the weapon to a designated OGW. This new category of militants is known as 'hybrid militants'. This phenomenon has blurred the boundary between a terrorist and a civilian. On Facebook, LinkedIn and Instagram, local Kashmiris get hundreds of friend requests.[142] Many of them are handlers of terrorist organizations. They use these channels to identify potential candidates, test their commitment, passion and skills, and then recruit them. Besides, there are groups of highly indoctrinated and radicalized people on encrypted communication applications like WhatsApp, Signal and Telegram. Such groups have members from Kashmir, the Indian hinterland, Pakistan, Afghanistan and radical elements from Western countries. Some more secretive groups have their main administrators across the border and potential recruits in Kashmir. It is also pertinent to mention here that another critical reason for JeM to use social media is that, as compared to other groups like LeT and HM, it does not have a vast network of OGWs, coordinators and other financial resources in Kashmir.

JeM also focuses on regular communication through its print and online publications. Reportedly, *Al Qalam*, or *Khabarnama Rang-o-Noor*, is one of the key periodicals published by JeM.[143] It is like a local paper that claims to counter anti-Islamic propaganda. Masood Azhar has always understood the importance of creating a jihad-supportive discourse through literature and regular periodicals. He often pays tribute to JeM militants who die in Kashmir through his articles written under his pen name 'Sadik-e-Kalam'. JeM publications paid tributes to Sajjad Afghani, Ghazi Baba, Noor Muhammad Tantrey,[144] and Talha Saif—Masood's nephew—killed by SFs in Kashmir.[145]

After the encounter death of Talha Rashid, his favourite nephew, Masood Azhar wrote, 'The martyr's sins are forgiven when the first drop of his blood falls, and he is spared the agony of the grave, the terrors of the day of judgment; he is married to seventy-two virgins; his family granted God's mercy.'[146] Such emotional tributes to jihadis, making them community heroes, made JeM immensely popular among young minds with poor education, facing dignity-related issues in the family, and desperately looking for an identity, adventure and an outlet to the world beyond their small towns and villages. Earlier, these magazines and papers also published advertisements for jalsas, which helped with recruitment. Masood Azhar's magazine focused most of its content on jihad, narrating concocted stories of miracles associated with dead militants—for example, instances of a beautiful fragrance springing forth from the dead bodies of jihadis, or tales of jihadis disappearing during operations and coming to life again after their death.[147] In many of his writings, Masood criticized Musharraf for betraying the jihadist cause. He also criticized other politicians like Nawaz Sharif for taking a soft stand on Kashmir. The issues in the few months before the Pathankot attack were full of anti-India invectives.[148] After the attack, JeM stopped its publication; however, it resumed after eight weeks, providing ample evidence of JeM continuing its ground operations despite the Pakistani government's claims of taking action against it. Allegedly, Masood wrote an article titled '*Muhabbat ka Zamana Aa Gaya Hai*', asking his followers to not be disheartened by the Pakistan government's campaign against armed jihad.[149] Describing his sufferings in the Kot Bhalwal Jail during Musharraf's regime, he wrote that he coined this expression when he was tortured in prison. He also warned the Pakistani government not to continue its campaign against jihadis as they were safeguarding the country against India and

Afghanistan's US-supported hostile regime. The other sections of the magazine covered religion with articles on good conduct, actions and warnings against Western culture.

After the Pathankot and Pulwama attacks, one does not come across overt jihad-related content in the magazine. After the Pathankot attack, its JeM and Pakistan link was established through one of the phone numbers listed in *Al Qalam* advertisements, which made JeM sceptical about overtly publishing jihad content.[150] Also, after Pulwama, JeM has faced pressure from the state to maintain a low profile, as a result of which *Al Qalam* has not published jihad-related content, jalsa advertisements and donation requests since March 2019.

6

Militant Profiles

Understanding JeM Mujahideens and JeM Finances

I STUDIED THE INTERROGATION REPORTS (IRs) OF JEM militants arrested in Kashmir. Based on my analysis of the IRs and interviews with interrogators, my findings about the socio-economic profiles and family backgrounds of the militants are presented below:

1) Most of the FTs—64 per cent—belonged to rural backgrounds, while the remaining 36 per cent were from urban backgrounds. The majority of FTs—about 57 per cent—belonged to the Punjab province of Pakistan, whereas KPK and PoK accounted for an equal proportion of FTs—21.42 per cent each. In the case of local terrorists from India, the majority belonged to rural areas.

2) The economic profile of FTs showed that most belonged to the lower-middle class and the middle class (43 per cent for both), while the remaining 14 per cent belonged to the upper-middle class. In the case of local terrorists, the majority, about 87 per cent, belonged to the middle class, while 13 per cent came from the lower middle class.

3) In the case of FTs, a majority of them came from families that worked as teachers, in the army and as peons in offices, while a few were engaged in farming and labour work. In the case of locals, the majority's families were engaged in farming, small businesses and minor jobs.

4) Education-wise, 36 per cent of FTs had graduated between Class 9 and 12, 29 per cent had dropped out of school between Class 6 and 8, 21 per cent had dropped out between Class 1 and 5, and the remaining 14 per cent had never been to school. In the case of locals too, 37.5 per cent had studied up to Class 9–12, 18.75 per cent had bachelor's- and master's-level education each, and 12.5 per cent had studied up to Class 5 and Class 8 each.

5) Age-wise, the majority of FTs—64 per cent —were between eighteen and twenty-five years old, whereas 29 per cent of FTs were between twenty-six and thirty. Only 7 per cent of FTs were below eighteen years of age. In the case of locals, the majority—50 per cent —were between eighteen and twenty-five years old, while 25 per cent were between twenty-six and thirty. Both age brackets of thirty-one to thirty-five years and forty-one to forty-five years had 12.5 per cent local terrorists.

Generally, JeM targets youth below twenty-five years of age and those who are less educated—who have dropped out of school before Class 10. In south Kashmir, almost every village has a madrasa. About 60 to 70 per cent of JeM militants from here have a madrasa background. As discussed earlier, JeM allegedly has hidden and unofficial ties with Darul Ulooms in south Kashmir. A large number of JeM cadres have come from this background.

The interrogators told me that JeM militants are 'hardcore', mentally strong and radicalized to the extreme, particularly the fidayeens. JeM and LeT militants (both FTs and locals) have a lot of similarities in their social, economic and educational backgrounds because they are recruited pretty much from the same region—south Punjab and Indian Kashmir—through a similar recruitment process and are subjected to more or less similar training. However, there are differences. For example, LeT cadres are younger (seventeen to nineteen years old) than the JeM militants.[1] LeT preys upon the vulnerability of innocence, while JeM preys upon the vulnerability of indoctrination and poverty. Secondly, most LeT cadres are Punjabi speaking, whereas JeM cadres tend to speak Urdu and Saraiki. JeM also had a significant number of Baluchi cadres and Pashtuns from KPK. Urdu-speaking JeM cadres are less flamboyant, professional, and generally polite and serious, whereas Punjabi-speaking LeT cadres exude a casual demeanour. Thirdly, JeM cadres are considered more disciplined and loyal than their LeT peers. In 2008, several LeT cadres deserted their parent organization to join TTP and Al Qaeda.[2] As mentioned previously, JeM too has gone through internal fragmentation and splintering. Fourthly, LeT prefers to display Islamic overtones with the way its cadres dress, whereas JeM cadres tend to dress like most civilians in the areas they are infiltrating. Fifthly, LeT militants may have better knowledge of religious matters, scriptures and rituals, more organized and better quality combat training, and IT skills; however, JeM cadres have very high levels of motivation and indoctrination as compared to them.[3] Some interrogators opined that JeM cadres have poor IQ levels and an extremely narrow worldview as compared to LeT.[4]

LeT cadres also have better knowledge of political issues and international relations, whereas, in the case of JeM, one finds a high degree of focus in its ranks. JeM also has a strong belief in pan-Islamism like LeT; however, in operational matters, they are very focused and stay away from long-standing ideological and strategic issues of pan-Islamism and international relations. For them, the given task—for instance, a fidayeen attack—is all that matters. JeM cadres display a robust religious fervour that aligns with the nature of the organization, as in 2001, Masood explicitly mentioned that their goal is religious and they have nothing to do with politics. In the case of LeT, one often comes across its leaders having lofty political ambitions and engagements.

In interrogations, locals are mostly non-cooperative and they can allegedly bear the torture for days. Generally, FTs of all groups are cooperative and prefer to discuss whatever they know if they are not beaten up. However, compared to LeT, JeM cadres are tough and tend to resist a lot. I was told that they give in after a decent measure of torture; however, they are more vulnerable if the interrogators engage in a religious argument or discussion. In Samrauli, in Udhampur, a fidayeen was arrested and interrogated. I interviewed his interrogator, Vi-Pun (name changed), an inspector in the J&K police. He said that the detained fidayeen was eighteen or nineteen years old. He used to steal his brother's money to gamble. He lost the money and got very depressed. It was then that he met a JeM member who told him that the only way to atone for his sins was to undergo religious education from a madrasa to join jihad. He could not return home out of fear and embarrassment, so he joined the outfit. His interrogator did not counter him when he spoke of the persecution of Muslims in Kashmir, knowing that cadres were trained to argue such questions. Instead, he raised some fundamental religious issues and accused him of betraying the jihadist cause on the following grounds:

1) He smoked cigarettes and charas.
2) He spent bait-ul-maal—jihad fund—to talk to his girlfriends.
3) He did not understand jihad as it requires controlling one's senses and desires.

With nothing to counter these facts, the young man allegedly broke down and cooperated with the investigation.

According to my source, Vi-Pun, typical FTs go to madrasas and terror-training camps at a young age, where they get ideologically indoctrinated to practice hatred and violence towards non-Muslims, Shias, Ahmadiyyas and Sufis. During this period, they have no interaction with members of the opposite sex and have no experience of the simple pleasures of life. When they come to Kashmir, they immerse themselves in drugs, alcohol and women. According to my source, women are their greatest weakness for they have had little to no exposure to them before. Allegedly, the local families who shelter them or their OGWs have also encouraged the women in their families to either sexually entertain these militants or build an emotional relationship with them. For example, Tariq Mir, a JeM OGW, who gave shelter to Pulwama attack masterminds like Muhammad Umar Farooq, Samir Ahmed Dar and others at his home in 2018–19 and helped in arranging logistics, knew about his daughter Insha Jan's affair with Muhammad Umar Farooq.[5] Insha Jan actively helped Muhammad Umar Farooq by passing on information about the movement of SFs.[6] The father-daughter duo helped the terrorists with logistics on at least fifteen occasions. However, in some cases, fear is also a compelling factor. In Qari Yasir's case, the police found a large cache of porn videos and anti-Shia content.[7] However, JeM cadres, due to their impression of being heavily radicalized and motivated, are generally expected to not indulge in the pleasures of life and to focus on religious mission only.

Several JeM militants were killed in encounters allegedly because their girlfriends tipped off the police. Many militants themselves became informers because of their relationships. One such case was of Ashiq Jan Lahori (name changed). He was a senior JeM commander from Pakistan in the Valley. His family had donated him for jihad when he was around eighteen years old. He was a well-trained commando and a highly indoctrinated jihadi. He trained the recruits of JeM's Afzal Guru Squad. However, he fell in love with a Kashmiri girl. The police were already trying to get in touch with him. He did not want to be killed in an encounter and wanted to go back to Pakistan with the Kashmiri girl. So, to avoid a typical militant's fate—an encounter death—he started working for the police. Vi-Pun was his handler. He was kept in a decent safe house in Srinagar. The police, under the leadership of a senior officer, ran a covert operation.

Vi-Pun stayed with him in the safe house. Ashiq was given good food and could meet his girlfriend whenever possible. After a few days, she started living with him. Based on his information, the police was able to track down and kill more than a dozen JeM militants. Over time, Vi-Pun developed a strong emotional bond with Ashiq and his wife. Finally, Ashiq returned to Pakistan and now stays in a big city with his family. Ashiq also shared information on the training and recruitment methods of JeM, and, interestingly, he echoed Ayesha Siddiqa's findings on how the organization targets young men from poor economic and educational backgrounds.

JeM commander Ghazi Baba married a local Kashmiri girl. Hence, it can also be argued that JeM leadership permits marriages with local girls in Kashmir. Many JeM militants like

Mahmood Bhai, Khalid, Aftaab, Abu Sarjeel, Saifullah and Wasim were womanizers and callously had multiple affairs. Many JeM commanders were killed because of their involvement in love affairs, which helped SFs either track their locations through intercepts or monitor their movements by cultivating spies. In several cases, their female partners spied on them and tipped off the police. Saifullah was in a relationship with two sisters from the old town of Baramulla (north Kashmir) and a married woman from Handwara (north Kashmir). After him, Mahmood Bhai was in an intimate relationship with the same married woman from Handwara.

Amanullah Bukhari was a JeM commander in Bandipora (2007–10).[8] The police handlers in touch with him convinced him that the Pakistan government was using him and what he was doing was not jihad. Finally, he consented to work for the police and started giving them information about cadres. However, his conviction in the jihadi cause had already weakened, and before long he was addicted to alcohol and women. During the days when he kept up the dual identity of JeM commander and a police informer, the police made sure he had an unlimited supply of alcohol and women to entertain him. Additionally, he was given INR 1 lakh for each militant he helped capture. His inputs helped the police eliminate eleven JeM terrorists.

I also came across contradictory findings in the case of a female OGW of JeM. Generally, its OGWs are from very orthodox and conservative families having a strong faith in Deobandi or Salafi thoughts on jihad. Though money also plays a critical role in motivating OGWs in Kashmir, generally, JeM ropes in people from families with extremist religious views. Alpha 12, whom I interviewed for this project, had befriended a girl from a JeM OGW family. This extremely orthodox family had decades-old ties with JeM, and family members regularly spoke to leaders like Mufti Rauf and Masood Azhar. JeM terrorists frequented her house. The girl and her sister were very conservative as well. They wore burqas, observed religious injunctions and discipline, and barely spoke to males. However, against all these restrictions, and despite having strong faith in religious values, she was having an affair with a college friend of hers. At the same time, she became physically intimate with Alpha 12, an intelligence operative who faked his identity as a local sales boy. The girl gave him crucial information about the character of JeM militants, their pictures, traits and general behaviours. As per her version, JeM militants were well-behaved with the female family members. Once, she complained to them about some local boys who harassed her, and the JeM militants threatened those boys and came to her rescue.

Hence, it can be reasonably argued that JeM militants have no religious or moral qualms as far as getting into relationships with women is concerned. This practice is not considered un-Islamic. One also witnesses a tacit or even direct approval of relationships and marriages with local girls. It is evident from the examples of Ghazi Baba and Muhammad Umar Farooq. JeM never criticized Ghazi Baba for his marriage to a local girl. In JeM publications, he was revered and continues to be a role model for its present cadres. Likewise, Muhammad Umar Farooq was a nephew of Masood Azhar and a prominent figure in the Azhar family. His relationship with Insha Jan was no secret to his family. His wife allegedly even spoke to Insha Jan.

However, JeM cadres still have reservations about getting involved in love affairs, not due to religious reasons but because of the fear of losing their focus on jihad, and the security risks and vulnerability to espionage that entails such romantic and sexual adventures. But, in the case of drug and alcohol consumption,

JeM militants are strictly against it. Only in the rarest of the rare cases, like that of Amanullah Bukhari, does one find a JeM militant addicted to alcohol. As regards drugs, credible sources tell me that JeM is involved in opium and drug smuggling to raise finances, which its ideological sibling, Taliban, also does. JeM cadres are told that selling drugs to non-Muslims is not irreligious. As far as its consumption is concerned, it is difficult to find rampant drug consumption by JeM cadres. However, as compared to FTs, who are highly indoctrinated and much better trained, one can find some incidents of drug abuse by local JeM militants. Interestingly, in the case of fidayeens, several informed interlocutors confirm that drugs are administered to them before they carry out an attack.

The indoctrination methods of terrorists in Pakistan include showing them videos of Muslim women being raped in India, and Muslim men and children being killed by SFs. The very first thing that they are told is that Indian SFs brutally rape Muslim girls, and that Muslims are oppressed and are not even allowed to pray five times a day. Oftentimes they come to Kashmir to find a different reality playing out. Further, they find Kashmiri society relatively liberal and moderate about the rights of women, relationships, Islamic dressing and alcohol consumption. After such exposure, the terrorists of LeT and other groups soften a bit, and their ideological passion declines and dilutes; however, I have been told that this is not the case with JeM.

Understanding JeM Minds in Their Own Words

In this section, I describe the life stories of a few JeM militants arrested in Kashmir. These stories discuss their family backgrounds, education, motivation to join JeM, and their journey to becoming a terrorist and infiltrating into India. These life stories are based on the detailed testimonies given by the arrested militants to their interrogators. The idea is to give readers a nuanced understanding of JeM cadres' minds and their jihadist journeys.

Sajjad Afghani

Sajjad was the first commander of HuM and then HuA in Jammu and Kashmir. Masood Azhar escorted him to Bangladesh, where he crossed into Indian territory. He was arrested with Masood Azhar at Anantnag and was jailed with him in Kot Bhalwal Jail in Jammu. He was from Rawalakot in the Poonch district of PoK. He was twenty-seven years old at the time of his arrest. He had passed his matriculation exams and, by profession, he was an electrician.

His associates in Pakistan and PoK included:

1) Maulana Sadatullah, emir of HuA
2) Maulana Fazlur Rehman Khalil, naib emir (deputy) of HuA
3) Maulana Muhammad Farooq Kashmiri, emir of HuA for J&K
4) Maulana Abdul Jabbar, military chief, HuA
5) Qari Naved Maqsood Kashmiri, HuA activist
6) Maulana Allah Wasaya Qasim from Punjab (Pakistan), a motivator and Afghan jihad veteran
7) Ustad Mawya, weapons instructor and trainer at Yavar camp at Khost in Afghanistan
8) Mufti Shahjahan, Bangladeshi HuA activist who was active in Afghanistan
9) Mufti Abu Obaida, a Bangladeshi HuA activist, who was active in Afghanistan

Sajjad Afghani was born in 1967 and his father was a small-time shopkeeper. Afghani attended a madrasa at Jamia Mosque. He was very conservative and a staunch follower of Deobandi Islam from his childhood. During his madrasa days, he was inspired by Muhammad Mazhar of Poonch (PoK), who went to Afghanistan for jihad against the Soviets. In his lectures, Mazhar narrated the bravery of mujahideens in Afghanistan. During his school days, Sajjad Afghani trained himself to become an electrician. His close association with Mazhar inspired him to join jihad in Afghanistan. Mazhar, who was also a member of HuM under the leadership of Maulana Mafzal-ur-Rahman of Dera Ismail Khan in NWFP, gave Afghani the address of the HuM office in Miranshah in north Waziristan and asked him to go there. In Miranshah, Afghani was introduced to Maulana Farooq, the then emir of HuM for J&K. That very day, Afghani left for the Yavar training camp at Khost in a Toyota vehicle arranged by HuM. They arrived at Khost in about seventy-five minutes.

The camp belonged to Hizb-e-Islami. Yunus Khalis, Hizb-e-Islami chief in Afghanistan, headed it. Several Afghan trainees resided in the camp. Besides Afghans, there were trainees from Saudi Arabia, PoK, Pakistan, Somalia, Sudan and several other Muslim countries. Then, with Muhammad Mazhar, Afghani was sent as part of the secondary force to assist 2,250 Afghan mujahideen against the Soviets at Spinkai (Khost). The battle experience made Afghani tough and courageous. After the mission, his entire batch was given two days' rest, after which their arms' training began. Abu Usra, a Palestinian, and Mufti Shahjahan, a Bangladeshi, were Afghani's instructors. There were twenty-five trainees in his batch. They were all Pakistanis. They learned to handle pistols, grenades, AK-47s, LMG, rocket launchers, Russian/Chinese-made stick grenades and were taught how to use wireless sets. Besides, they were given training in handling advanced weapons, as discussed earlier. They all underwent a month-long training programme with a rigorous schedule and had to take part in strenuous physical exercise. Besides, they were given indoctrination lessons by discourses and lectures on Quranic themes of jihad. After training, Sajjad Afghani returned home, but concealed his Afghanistan trip from his family. He told them that he went on a religious trip with Tablighi Jamaat. He stayed at home for six months, working as an electrician.

HuM is directly affiliated with the Hizb-e-Islami (Yunus Khalis faction) of Afghanistan. To interrogators, Sajjad Afghani proudly identified himself with Hizb-e-Islami, and said that their beliefs are all about a highly conservative and fundamentalist version of religion. He took pride in the extremist and fanatical nature of the organization, and stated that they were strictly against democracy and secularism, and they aimed to bring Shariah rule.

He also told his interrogators that HuM was a separate wing of HuJI, which Maulana Irshad had formed to fight against the Soviets. In the early days—1979–80—Maulana Irshad, Maulana Alvi from Mang, PoK, Fazlur Rehman Khalil and Qari Saifullah Akhtar went to Afghanistan to fight the Russians. Over time, HuJI spread its network to various parts of Pakistan and got many recruits. In 1984, HuJI split into two factions—one remained with the original HuJI and the other was known as HuM under Fazlur Rehman Khalil. They opened a separate office at Miranshah. With Khalil's hard work, HuM spread fast. The other office-bearers were Maulana Farooq Kashmiri (deputy mir) and Abdul Rashid (military commander). HuM opened offices in Bord (Peshawar), Islamabad, Muzaffarabad and Kotli (PoK).

Giving further details about his organization, he said that there was no hierarchy. There were separate sections with heads like a publicity wing, military wing, finance wing, etc., and there were secretaries for each wing. HuM had only two training camps, he said—one at Kotli and the other one at Yavar. In 1993, HuM and HuJI decided to mend fences and formed an organization called HuA.

Revealing more details about HuA, he said that HuA believed in complete Islamization. He confessed that it was not working entirely on ISI's directives as HuA's ideology is different from that of ISI, which wants Kashmir to secede to Pakistan. In contrast, HuA aims to establish an Islamic and Shariah-compliant rule in the Valley. He also said that Hizb-e-Islami had greater control over HuA than ISI.

All the arms and ammunition were coming from Afghanistan—first to PoK, from where it was sent to Kashmir. Several Afghanistan-based outfits helped HuA. In Afghanistan, HuA, under Jalaluddin Haqqani's leadership, had 8,000 activists. HuA cadres were also present in Tajikistan and other Islamic nations, and rich Muslims from all over the world donated to these groups. As per Sajjad Afghani's statement, HuA had planned to send 15,000 battle-hardened mercenaries to Kashmir.

Discussing the indoctrination of HuA cadres, he said that the clerics convinced them that continuous jihad against the infidels is the only way to salvation and that a single martyr can take seventy sinners to heaven. He also said that their ideology was quite close to Jamiat Ulema-e-Islam (Pakistan); however, they have political ambitions, while HuA's and its cadres' aims and motives are strictly religious.

In 1987, Afghani lied to his parents again, telling them that he was going on a four-month-long TJ religious tour. However, he went to Yavar camp first and then to a transit camp in Liza. He remained in Liza for four months doing odd jobs like cooking, cleaning, and carrying arms and ammunition to mujahideens in forward posts. During his Liza stay, the Afghans took nine Soviet soldiers as prisoners and captured huge amounts of weapons from them, including a tank. The tank was sold to another militia and the booty was distributed. That day, Sajjad Afghani got PKR 3,000. After that, he returned home, where his family learned about his Afghan visits. After fifteen days, his parents sent him to Lahore, where his brother worked as a driver. He stayed there for five months but felt out of place. Between February 1988 and December 1989, he visited the Liza and Bari camps in Afghanistan ten times, and participated in combat roles in the anti-Soviet jihad. At the Bari camp, the HuM leadership decided to send cadres to Kashmir to train local youths who were rising up in arms against India. They asked Sajjad Afghani to establish a HuM office at Muzaffarabad in PoK.

After setting up the HuM office, many youths from PoK and Indian Kashmir enrolled in the organization. By June 1990, HuM had trained 190 boys in Afghanistan for the Kashmir jihad. HuM launch pads to send cadres to India were at Muzaffarabad, Domel, Deolia, Delian and Shahdhara (all in PoK). Other groups like HM, JKLF, People's League and Al-Jihad also had offices in Muzaffarabad. They used to send 50 per cent of their recruits to Afghanistan for training. In June 1990, Maulana Farooq Kashmiri asked Sajjad Afghani to go to Kashmir for the overall assessment of the militant movement, to get a feel of the people's mood and the possibility of sending FTs—Pakistani and Afghani cadres—to the Valley. He was also tasked with finding hideouts and shelters for the militants. HuM gave INR 5,000 to Sajjad Afghani and INR 4,000 to his colleague Abid, along with arms and ammunition. They carried AK-47s, sixteen LMGs, rocket launchers, 367 hand grenades, pistols and a dagger with them.

In Kashmir, Afghani's leadership was crucial in establishing HuM. Several young recruits joined at that time. Afghani used to brainwash and radicalize the local boys for armed jihad against India. In those days, he and his team mostly stayed in the winter in Gujjar *dhoks* (hutments). In Kashmir Valley, HuM established several training camps as mentioned previously.

After doing the groundwork for HuM in Kashmir, Afghani returned to PoK to apprise Maulana Farooq of the ground situation and future possibilities. He directed Commander Shazi and Hayat to organize his exfiltration. They decided to send him with valid travel documents. Muhammad Ashraf Dar of Srinagar arranged travel documents for Sajjad Afghani in February 1992. Notably, he is the same person who later arranged Masood Azhar's journey to Kashmir. Afghani's passport had a fake identity in the name of Muhammad Hameed Khan, s/o Akhtar Hussain, a resident of Lahore. Shazi gave INR 4,000 to Afghani for personal expenses during the journey. Shazi took over as HuM commander in the Valley in his absence. In a taxi from Dal Gate, Srinagar, Sajjad Afghani left for Delhi with Muhammad Ashraf Dar and his four family members. They were not stopped or checked by anyone on the way. In Delhi, Ashraf Dar gave him an ID card of Darul Uloom Deoband in the name of Khaleel Ahmed, r/o Sawai Madhopur in Rajasthan. After two days in Delhi, Ashraf Dar gave him his passport under the name of Hameed Khan and a railway ticket. Sajjad Afghani boarded a Lahore-bound train from Old Delhi Railway Station. From Lahore, he reached Muzaffarabad. There, he found that new groups like Al Umar Mujahideen, Hizb-ul-Momineen, Ikhwan-ul-Musalmeen, Tehreek-ul-Mujahideen, Jamaat-ul-Mujahideen and Al-Barq had also opened offices there.

Fazlur Rehman Khalil and Maulana Farooq had collected huge funds from their foreign travels to several Muslim nations.

They used that money to buy arms and ammunition, which were being sent to Kashmir. Sajjad Afghani successfully convinced Khalil and Maulana Farooq that the people of Kashmir were ready for an armed jihad against India, and they needed to be helped with weapons and better communication systems. In April 1992, Sajjad Afghani went to Kabul to celebrate Afghanistan's freedom. After his return, he took nine Kashmiri youths to Kotli camp for weapons' training. In July 1992, he received a letter from Shazi telling him that HuM was on the verge of disintegration and he needed to come soon. Maulana Farooq gave USD 10,000 to Sajjad Afghani and asked him to go to Kashmir. Masood Azhar, general secretary of HuM, was to help Afghani infiltrate India. Afghani had met Masood Azhar in Karachi previously. Masood went to Bangladesh with Afghani by air. In Bangladesh, local guides helped Sajjad Afghani enter India via a fifteen minute walk through the highly porous border. In ninety minutes, Sajjad Afghani and his guides reached Calcutta, where he stayed in Ameena Hotel. He informed Ashraf Dar of his arrival in Calcutta, who joined him there, and together they flew to Delhi. In Delhi, they stayed in the Chittaranjan Park area. The next day, Sajjad Afghani visited Hazrat Nizamuddin Aulia's shrine. After that, he went to Kashmir and took charge of the situation. Over the next few months, more money and weapons were poured into Kashmir. A group of fourteen Afghanistan-trained militants came with INR 5 lakh, VHF sets and large amounts of ammunition. Meanwhile, Shazi arranged a fake driving licence for Sajjad Afghani so that he could travel freely in Kashmir. In October 1993, twenty militants, including eighteen foreign mercenaries, came with LMGs, rocket launchers, wireless sets, 5,000 rounds and INR 18 lakh. Terrorist activity increased under Sajjad Afghani's leadership. He was a dynamic commander. He used to walk long distances on foot to assess the ground situation. He would send press clippings of their terror attacks to Maulana Farooq in Muzaffarabad to keep him abreast of their activities. Ashraf Dar used to send these clippings through registered post in Delhi. In November 1993, Ashraf Dar informed Sajjad Afghani that HuM and HuJI had merged, giving rise to a new entity, HuA. Sajjad Afghani then redesigned the portfolios in Kashmir for the new outfit, HuA. Amjad Bilal, a HuJI chief, handed over a letter signed by Maulana Sadatullah to Sajjad Afghani, asking him to take over as the chief of the new outfit, HuA, in the Valley. By 1993, there were 1,500 HuA militants in Kashmir, and they had 700 AK-47 rifles, twenty-five LMGs, 100 pistols, eighty-eight rocket launchers, 1,000 grenades, two UBGLs, twenty-five mines, 100 daggers, six binoculars, fourteen wireless transmitter sets and 10,000 rounds.

On 9 February 1994, Sajjad Afghani met Masood Azhar at Darul Uloom Qasimia in Lal Bazaar (Srinagar). Amjad Bilal also accompanied him to the meeting. Masood told him that Maulana Sadatullah and Maulvi Farooq sent him to facilitate coordination between HuJI and HuM, expedite their joint terror activities in Kashmir and assess the ground realities. Sajjad Afghani suggested Masood meet Hurriyat leaders after his proposed Anantnag visit. Then, Sajjad and Masood went to Matigund. They met eighty militants at the Pathribal camp. Out of this number, seventy were foreign militants. Shortly after that, they were both arrested at Matigund in Anantnag.

At the Sharifabad interrogation centre, Col. Dagar (name changed) told Afghani and Masood that HuA had abducted two British nationals in Pahalgam to get the two of them and Nasrullah Langaryal released. However, their plan did not work out and they had to set the captives free without any militants getting released. In September 1994, Sajjad Afghani and Masood were transferred to Kot Bhalwal Jail in Jammu. In October that year, the Al Faran group abducted three British nationals and an American to get Masood, Sajjad Afghani and seven other militants released.

Hakim Naved, another militant in the jail, told Sajjad Afghani that FTs were subjected to the worst kinds of torture in the Joint Interrogation Centre (JIC), Jammu. Naved had tried to escape prison earlier, but the guards had caught him. The escape attempt did not make its way into the news. Naved also discussed a jailbreak plan with Sajjad Afghani; however, he reportedly did not show much interest initially. Later, he was convinced about the jailbreak and planned it with some FTs. Masood and Nasrallah consented to this plan. They dug a tunnel for twenty days with the help of other Kashmiri terrorists. Even within jail, Sajjad Afghani was able to mobilize fellow inmates to create unrest and pushed inmates to pelt stones at the guards. The intelligence agencies wanted to interrogate him; however, he told the jail authorities that he would come with Masood and others after 12 December 1994, as they were planning to escape before that. During the jailbreak attempt, Masood Azhar got stuck in the tunnel and Sajjad Afghani was killed.

Abdul Rahman Mughal, Alias Raja, Shabir, Romeo

He was a resident of Poonch in PoK. He speaks Urdu, Pahari and Punjabi. His father retired as a peon and his mother has always been a housewife. He has three brothers and four sisters. His family owns 20 kanals of land. His uncle, Muhammad Sadiq Khan, had retired from the Pakistan Army. His village had 200–250 households, including Jats, Gujjars and Khans. About 500 to 600 metres from his house was an army post—Shakren. The soldiers deputed there behaved in a high-handed and arrogant manner with the villagers. Abdul Rahman Mughal was sent as a JeM cadre to India to recruit militants and OGWs. He was arrested in 2016 at Hajibal in Baramulla. His motivation to join JeM was religious.

After graduating from Class 8, he left his studies due to a lack of interest and started assisting his father in farming. In 2011, he left home to find a job in Rawalpindi. He found employment at a seven-storey 'New Abbasi Hotel'. There, he worked as a cook and waiter, and earned a monthly salary of PKR 15,000–17,000. He worked there till 2013 and then joined JeM.

In December 2013, a childhood friend, Qari Danish, who was also from his village, met him in Rawalpindi. He was pursuing a religious course in Almiyat at a madrasa in Faisalabad. Qari Danish discussed with him the religious issues of jihad, tabligh (discourses) and the need to fight against Shias. His discussions with Danish radicalized Abdul Rahman and motivated him to join jihad. Then Danish introduced him to JeM officer-bearers at the office at Shivainala, Muzaffarabad. JeM's office was hardly 400–500 metres away from the main city police station of Muzaffarabad. He was introduced to Mufti Asghar Khan Kashmiri. Danish already knew the mufti from his Faisalabad contacts. Mufti Asghar Kashmiri regularly visited the Faisalabad madrasa to give religious lectures. He gave Abdul Rahman a recommendation letter (called an izazatnama or tazkian) for admission into the JeM training camp at Balakot. The letter had the stamp of Al-Rahmat Trust, and it was addressed to Muhammad Ghori, commander of the training camp. Abdul Rahman Mughal thus went to Balakot for training. His training schedule has already been described in the previous chapter.

After his training, he reported at JeM's Muzaffarabad office in PoK. In that office, there were two double-storey buildings with twelve rooms. One of the rooms, 10 feet by 10 feet, was a storehouse of arms and ammunition. There was a massive collection of weapons there. The main office had three gates guarded by armed guards in black Pathani suits. Armed guards were also deployed on the rooftop. LeT's office was barely 500 metres from the JeM office. Abdul stayed in the JeM office working as a cook for about a year.

In May 2015, Abdul and a few others were sent to Kel launch det (launch pad) with a Hadid Hoksar. The group was given a recommendation letter signed by Mufti Asghar Khan Kashmiri, which bore the stamp 'Kashmir Freedom Army'. The letter served as an admission certificate. Mohammad Bhai Pathan was the launch-det commander. There were about twenty militants already stationed there to be launched in the Valley. On 27 November 2015, they began their infiltration journey with one guide and three porters to assist the group of JeM militants. The guide charged PKR 6–7 lakh, and the porters took PKR 60–70,000 each for the trip. The guide and the porters were from the Neelam Valley region, and were familiar with the topography and weather. The porters carried 450 rounds of AK-47s and twenty-five hand grenades. Tango 2 (the code name of the team) carried dry fruits, Kashmiri rotis, coconuts, honey, butter, biscuits and chocolates. They also carried with them an inflatable raft and an air pump. First, they reached Machal Darya, where the guide cut the fence on the LoC in about forty to forty-five minutes. After crossing into Indian territory, they trekked through snow-covered jungles and, finally, on 8 December 2015, the team reached a shrine at Trehgam.

Their team used wireless sets (ICOM) to communicate with their handlers and OGWs. They contacted Control 88, the command control centre, Tuba, Dudhnial. Control 88 was headed by someone code named Hanzala. The codes for the infiltrating party and Saifullah—the OGW who had come to receive them at Trehgam—were Tango 2 and Sierra, respectively.

They travelled twenty minutes from the Trehgam shrine and reached their hideout in the Trehgam forest. The hideout was made between a cluster of trees close to each other, creating a circle-like structure. It had a thatched roof, and was covered on all sides with blankets and branches. The hideout had stored enough rice and pulses to last them three to four months. Saifullah used to fetch vegetables and other essential items from the nearby village of Rang. He had to trek downwards for ninety minutes to reach the village.

Then the group left for the Dewar forests in the Lolab area; before they left, they hid some weapons in a dump near their hideout. At a Dewar forest hideout, they spent three nights with LeT militants. The LeT militants left soon as they had no food, but they were cordoned off by the army and killed. Abdul's Tango 2 team heard the gunshots and escaped. Abdul was separated from his group. He trekked alone for three nights and finally spotted a Jamia mosque at Buhana in the Kupwara district. He spent one night at the mosque, had his lunch in the market the next morning and then, for the next twelve days, he roamed around the forests. Somehow, he managed to contact Control 88, who re-established his contact with Saifullah. At a meeting point fixed by Control 88, he met Saifullah in Kupwara. Saifullah asked him to go to Baramulla to recruit OGWs and militants (twenty-five to thirty individuals) and set up a base for JeM in the district. He was also asked to settle down in Baramulla and help with future infiltrations. Saifullah gave him INR 2,000 to buy a mobile phone and contact Mufti Asghar Khan Kashmiri. Saifullah also introduced him as 'Shabir' to a local contact, Amir, who arranged an Aadhaar card for him. For the next few days, he stayed in Baramulla in the company of Amir and his friend, Ashiq. Then, one day, during their journey to Hajibal village in a Tata Sumo car, the police arrested him.

Finally, he went back to Pakistan after serving a jail tenure of two to three years.

Muhammad Sadiq Gujjar, Alias Muawiya

Muhammad Sadiq Gujjar is a Pakistani national from Sialkot. Born on 1 January 1999, he has six brothers and one sister. His father is a farmer. His village mostly comprised Jats and Gujjar communities. He speaks Urdu, Punjabi and Pahari. He was seventeen years old when he was arrested in February 2016 in Baramulla. At the time of his arrest, the police recovered one AK-47, five magazines, six grenades and one wireless set from him.

After graduating from Class 9 at a government school, he lost interest in his studies and dropped out. Muhammad Sadiq used to attend prayers in the local Hazrat Abu Bakr Siddiqui Mosque, where he listened to religious lectures. The clerics spoke at length about the Muslim persecution in Kashmir, Palestine and Gaza. Those lectures nurtured a hatred in him for non-Muslims and the Western world. Abdul Razzaq, a school friend and a resident of his village, who had already undergone JeM training in 2013, motivated him to join a training camp. Razzaq told him stories about the persecution of Muslims by Indian SFs in Kashmir and convinced him to do his duty of jihad. He introduced Muhammad Sadiq to JeM's regional office at Mundeke Berian in Sialkot.

Sadiq reached Mansehra via Rawalpindi with Abdul Razzaq after a ten-hour journey. From there, they hired a Toyota taxi for a thirty-minute drive to Balakot. The cab dropped them near Balakot. They started trekking through the jungles and reached the camp after nearly three hours. The camp had a barrack and two rooms in an open area. Muhammad Ghori was the camp in-charge. In his IR, Muhammad Sadiq named Arshad from

Karachi, Faizal Shah from KPK, Uzair from KPK and Naved from Karachi as his instructors, and Butt Sahab from Punjab was the cook. The training did not start immediately because there were only three or four other candidates. Usually, a batch includes at least twenty to twenty-five trainees. Sadiq and the rest waited six months, doing household chores and attending religious discourses, for their training to begin. Finally, in January 2015, their six-month-long Al-Ra'ad training commenced with twenty-five trainees.

The schedule they followed daily was:

3 a.m.–5 a.m.: The day began with Tahajjud prayers (the namaz before sunrise)

7 a.m.: Physical training, which included running, long jump, high jump, crawling, rope climbing, push-ups, chin-ups and other stamina-building exercises

11 a.m.: Lunch

After the afternoon prayers, the candidates had their weapons' training classes. Initially, they were given only theory lessons. Then, they were taught to handle AK-47s, pistols, grenades, RPGs and UBGLs. They were also taught how to cut fences in the shortest possible time—to facilitate cross-border infiltration.

After training, four candidates were selected to carry out their first fidayeen attack in India.

They were the best of the lot, and as Muhammad Sadiq told his interrogators, 'they volunteered for the fidayeen'. He was a member of this fidayeen team. The other three he mentioned were Rizwan from Faisalabad, Hussain Pathan from KPK, and a Muawiya from Gujranwala. They were killed in the attack on the Tangdhar army camp.

After completing their training, Muhammad Sadiq and the other three fidayeens paid a visit to their families. He told his father about his intention to volunteer for a fidayeen attack in India. His father tried to dissuade him, but he refused to listen. After his visit home, Muhammad Sadiq and the other three fidayeens reached Kundal Shahi det via Balakot. There, Muhammad Sadiq and his group stayed for two months, and learned to operate GPS devices, Google Earth and wireless sets. They were trained in GPS devices and Google Earth to locate the Tangdhar camp. Besides, they were also taught to lay land mines. At the det, they met three other militants from PoK.

While infiltrating into India, they carried on them INR 50,000, fifteen grenades, an AK-47, five magazines, an ICOM wireless set, cutters and rucksacks. They used GPS sets while trekking and reached the LoC in ten days. They cut the fence in thirty minutes and entered the Indian territory through Neelam Valley. After that, they changed into army fatigues. After reaching the Tangdhar camp, they cut the fence, entered the camp and located the fuel dump,[9] where they placed two mines, which exploded after eighteen minutes. They started firing the moment soldiers arrived. The encounter lasted the whole day and three people died in it. Muhammad Sadiq claims to have emptied all his magazines, fired 150 rounds, lobbed hand grenades and killed many soldiers. In the evening, he collected the magazines of his comrades who were killed in the operation. Then, he slipped into the forests and changed his clothes. He stayed in the woods for two days. After hiding his weapon in the rucksack that he had carried, he reached Tangdhar market in a Tata Sumo vehicle, a public taxi ferrying passengers locally. He bought pheran, some utensils and rice. He continued to stay on in the forest. He befriended an Akbar Bakarwal and revealed his true identity to him. Akbar arranged a fake voter's ID for him from a nearby photostat shop. Sadiq gave INR 1,000 to Akbar to arrange for this document. After that, he went to Baramulla on a public transport bus. He stayed at Rashid Bandey and Sohail Rauf Ghanai's shop. Rashid owned a cosmetics shop. Sadiq hid his weapon there. Intermittently, he also stayed in the nearby mosques. Finally, he decided to go back to Pakistan; however, before that, he went to Rashid's shop to collect his weapon and he was arrested there.

Muhammad Sadiq Ahmed Gujjar

Muhammad Sadiq was born in Haripur, in KPK. Born in 1991, he dropped out of school after Class 10. Before joining JeM, he worked in farming. He came to Kashmir in 2012 after crossing the LoC from the Kalaroos–Lolab region in Kupwara district. He was arrested in the Baramulla–Sopore belt in north Kashmir. His father was an employee of WAPDA (Water and Power Development Authority). His mother had died early and he had two sisters. He is from a well-to-do family having an annual income of PKR 50,00,000. His family had owned 350 kanals of land and seven trucks when he left home and joined JeM.

In 2008, at Farooq-e-Azam Mosque, Sadiq attended the Deen-e-Talim (religious lectures) of Maulvi Khalil-ur-Rahman, along with 150 other students. The classes radicalized and motivated him to join jihad in Kashmir and Afghanistan. Besides, the videos of stone-pelting in Kashmir shown on the PTV and Geo news channels of Pakistan also helped radicalize him. Maulvi Rahman instructed him to prepare for advanced religious training and told him to keep it confidential. Without informing his father, he went with the maulvi to Muzaffarabad via Abbottabad and Mansehra. He stayed in Bilal Mosque in Muzaffarabad. The mosque had twenty-five rooms. He studied religious literature. Sajid, the mosque keeper, gave him an izazatnama on JeM's letterhead and asked him to go to Bahawalpur.

He reached Bahawalpur after a nearly twenty-hour bus journey from Muzaffarabad. In Bahawalpur, he met Mufti Rauf at Markaz Usman-o-Ali. It was a four-storeyed building with a capacity of 10,000 persons. He stayed there for twenty days and studied religious literature. He was given a seven-day 'Daura-e-Tarbiya' training (religious training) in a batch of 750 students. In the training, the main focus was on religious discourses and the justifications for jihad.

After the training, there was a grand gathering of youths from Balochistan, KPK, Sind and Punjab. A group of clerics represented each region. The young participants were asked to volunteer for weapons' training. After the final selection, a group of fifteen youngsters was chosen by Mufti Rauf for training. They reached Mansehra, from where someone called Amir escorted all of them to Batrasi in KPK in a Datsun vehicle. It was an eighteen-hour-long journey. Pathan Bhai headed the Batrasi camp. Upon arrival, the recruits were offered tea, food and a pair of Pathani suits at the camp. Pathan Bhai once again asked them about their interest in weapons' training. Sadiq and nine others agreed to join the training programme. Then, after four hours of trekking, Sadiq and his group reached the arms'-training camp, which lay behind the mountains, surrounded by forests. The camp had two sheds—one for the recruits and the other for the trainers. The two trainers were named Bada Ustad and Chota Ustad. There were forty-two other trainees there, but Sadiq and his group were not allowed to mingle with them.

Training included theory and practical classes in handling AK-47s, .303 rifles, pistols, LMGs, UBGLs and hand grenades. They underwent tough physical training, which included night marches in the forest. Training ended on 12 April 2012. After that, four trainees returned to their homes because their parents forced them to leave. The remaining thirty-eight were divided into two groups of nineteen each. They had to infiltrate into Afghanistan and Kashmir. Sadiq's group was given the Kashmir assignment. He reached Bilal Mosque with his group. Over here, due to health issues, four men dropped out of his group. At Bilal Mosque, Sajid introduced him to a Bilal and Fayaz (both from Haripur, KPK). Sadiq visited his family in KPK with both of them and returned in the third week of April. Then, with Fayaz and Bilal, he went to the Dudhnial launching det and then to the Kel launching det. The former had three rooms and a large compound, while the latter was a two-storeyed structure located in the main market with around twenty-five rooms. At Kel launching det, he met Hasan and Rizwan, who were later killed in Sopore in January 2014. Sadiq and his group stayed in these two launching dets for a few days before infiltration. During this stay, they regularly read religious literature, said their prayers and practiced physical training.

Rashid was their guide in the infiltration attempt. They carried an AK-47, four magazines, three grenades, a wireless set and INR 1,50,000. In July 2012, Sadiq, Hasan and Rizwan attempted to cross into the Kashmir Valley. After four tiring days of travel, they reached Durumath, opposite the Gurez sector of LoC. Due to the strict surveillance by Indian SFs, they waited for a day and then decided to go back to Kel. After four days, they decided to make another attempt. Rashid wanted to use an alternate route; however, due to security reasons, Hasan and Rizwan were unconvinced. After two days, Sadiq started the journey with Rashid alone, leaving Hasan and Rizwan at Kel. After six days of arduous travel from Kel to Ringbal, they reached the border at 1.45 a.m. It was very dark with no visibility. Chilly winds and rain showers made the journey even more challenging. However, Rashid forged ahead and cut the fence in forty-five minutes. Crossing into Indian territory, they moved into the lower reaches of the Kalaroos forest. SFs caught them and cordoned them off; however, they escaped.

Rashid then left for an undisclosed location. After a few days, Sadiq made contact with his handler, Mufti Asgar (code name: Saad baba), the JeM launching commander, through a wireless set and enquired about his receiving party. By then, Rashid had already returned to Kel. As per the instructions, Sadiq met Qari Yasir (JeM chief in Kashmir) in Gagal Khori with two other Pakistani militants, Humza and Abbas, from KPK. Sadiq handed over INR 1,00,000 to Qari Yasir and kept the remaining INR 50,000 with himself. Then, they reached the Varnau forest area in the Lolab region of Kupwara district. There, he learned that Qari Yasir and Humza had also received another group of seven militants—six from LeT and one from JeM—at Kawari (Lolab). The other group also travelled to Varanau and met Sadiq there. In that group, all the LeT cadres were from Punjab and the JeM militants were from Haripur, KPK. They stayed in the forests of Dardpora and Dewar in the Kupwara district until November 2012. They procured food and other essential items from the villages of Dardpora and Dewar. In December, the LeT boys left them to join Hafiz Naveed (code name: Fahadullah), the divisional commander of the group in Kashmir. He was also a Pakistani national.

Sadiq and the six other JeM cadres went to a hideout in the forest area of Marbal in Sopore. It was an underground hideout with the capacity to hold nine to ten people. During his stay at the Marbal hideout and Kupwara forests, Sadiq often communicated with his family members in Haripur over the phone. Qari Yasir was unhappy with his frequent calls and complained to Mufti Rauf. Sadiq also had heated arguments with Qari Yasir on several occasions because, as per his testimony, he was treated like a second-rate militant. After many heated exchanges, Sadiq left the group and arrived at the open forest area of Marbal. He collected food from the houses in the nearby villages. He lived in the Marbal forests till November 2013. On 9 November 2013, Sadiq was arrested while traveling to Marbal village to buy medicines. He was shifted to cargo, an interrogation unit of the J&K police, in Srinagar. After some time, his case was handed over to the Special Investigation Team, Srinagar. Then, after a month of detention at the SIT centre, he started working for the police, and, based on his inputs, SFs neutralized several FTs, including Hasan and Rizwan.

Noor Muhammad Tantrey

His real name was Gulzar Ahmed Butt. He was also known as Pir Baba, Chota Noora and Noor Trali. His code name was 'Owais'. His wireless set code was 'lima 4'. He was born in 1972. At the time of his encounter death in December 2017, he was forty-five years and nine months old. He had studied in a school until Class 10. He visited Pakistan in May 1999 and then Afghanistan in August 1999. He received training in IED and explosives-handling at Rahmania camp near Bagram airport in Kabul, in August 1999. The training compound was fenced with barbed wire and had 2,000 trainees. A person named Dr Zahid (possibly a code name) was the main IED expert at the camp. After training, he went to the JeM office in Poonch in an ISI vehicle. After that, Tantrey came back to Kashmir. With a height of just four feet and three inches, he was unfit for a combat role and his presence was conspicuous. So, he worked as a JeM courier of weapons and cash in his early days after training. He also acted as a key coordinator of JeM's hawala operations. He was arrested in Delhi in Azadpur Mandi in 2003 in an operation masterminded by the IB. At the time of his arrest, the police recovered three AK-47s, fourteen UBGLs, twenty hand grenades, three magazines and 100 rounds on him. His main associates in JeM were a Pakistani national named Abu Qasim, an Assamese man named Abu Zubair, a Sudanese man named Zahid Qureshi, and several OGWs from the Chadora sub-division of Budgam district in central Kashmir.

His initial motivation to join JeM was to earn money, as he was in heavy debt. He used to work as a tailor in Anantnag. During his tailoring days, a pir named Sheikh Muhammad Bakir joined him. It is believed that this pir foresaw his own death and prophesied the day. After his death, Noor Tantrey continued his legend and regularly visited his shrine in Tral, particularly during the month of Ramzan. As a result, Tantrey also came to be known as Pir Baba. As time passed and due to his brother's wedding, Tantrey racked up a debt of about INR 70,000 plus interest. He joined JeM to get rid of that debt. A JeM cadre, Manzoor Sheikh, motivated him to visit Pakistan.

In May 1999, Tantrey was asked to wait at an Awantipora hotel, where a civilian OGW picked him up. The OGW escorted him to Heragarol (Anantnag district), to Zamil Gujjar's house, where he met Shahid Guerilla, JeM's district commander. He told Tantrey to go to Poonch, which he subsequently did through Jammu via public transport. Tantrey then crossed the LoC from Hadi Buda hill in Poonch. In PoK, he was received by ISI handlers. The ISI was also referred to as 'agency' and *'bade bhai'*. An ISI officer named Captain Ali escorted Tantrey in a Toyota to the JeM office at Kahuta. After that, Tantrey visited the JeM office in Rawalpindi, headed by Abu Furqan. Tantrey spent about a month there undergoing religious indoctrination. Then he was sent to the Balakot training camp, along with an Arshalan from Pakistan and Abu Zubair, where he trained with 200 other cadres. They visited JeM's office in Muzaffarabad, Kabul and Khost. Abu Zakaria headed JeM's Kabul office. Then, at Rahmania camp, Dr Zahir trained Tantrey along with four others in IEDs, explosives, detonators, remote fixing, and IED fittings in pipes and trees. During his Afghanistan days, Tantrey wanted to meet Osama bin Laden, but he was not allowed to meet him. Moreover, his height was often a subject of ridicule in Afghanistan. This apparently hardened his resolve to show people his true calibre.

On his return to J&K, Tantrey had six matrix sheets on him and was asked to contact Arshalan (code name: Saifullah) at 144.50 frequency, and meet him in Budgam. After that, he was given the task of ferrying JeM's cash—he proved to be a suitable courier. The money he used to ferry around was to the tune of INR 50,000 to 1,00,000. He received INR 2,000–3,000 per transaction/task. Thanks to his work, he created a strong network in Kashmir and Delhi. Soon, he be came close with Ghazi Baba. In April 2002, he was instructed to shift to Srinagar's Chanapora and live in a rented accommodation there. He was also asked to buy a house for JeM in Srinagar. However, his whereabouts were leaked and SFs raided his Srinagar house. Eventually, he could buy a house for JeM in Sonarkul in Srinagar with some effort. However, this house was also raided by SFs. To elude the police, Tantrey escaped to Sonerwani forests in Bandipora with the help of a guide working for the JeM district commander. He stayed in these forests for about six months and used to get INR 2,000–2,500 for personal expenses.

In November 2002, he was asked to bring cash from Delhi through hawala channels. His code name was 'Rahul' for this mission. He received the money mostly in INR 500 notes. Over three trips to Delhi, he brought INR 10 lakh, INR 15 lakh, INR 24 lakh, and INR 54,000. In December 2002, the district commander of JeM in Pulwama, who played an influential role in setting up its base from south Kashmir to Budgam and

Srinagar—Rashid—proposed to send a weapons consignment to Delhi. Rashid had earlier worked with HuM as district commander in Kupwara in 1993 for about eighteen months, and then he returned.

Tantrey did not have a truck for transporting weapons, so Rashid asked him to give INR 4 lakh from the next hawala deal to a Khursheed Alam, a driver from Pulwama, who purchased a truck for JeM. Khursheed introduced Tantrey to the transport company's staff members as his cousin. From January 2003 to August 2003, Tantrey visited Delhi five times and brought back INR 10 lakh, INR 15 lakh, INR 10 lakh, INR 6 lakh and INR 20 lakh, respectively. In June 2003, he arrived in Delhi to supervise the delivery of the weapons consignment to Habib alias Aslam. In Delhi, Tantrey mostly stayed at Mirza Guest House in the Jama Masjid area. However, in 2003, he was keen to stay somewhere else for security reasons. On his next visit, Tantrey stayed in a rented accommodation with mostly Kashmiri workers. He brought over many FTs to Delhi, often handing them over to handlers in the city and then taking the hawala money back with him to Srinagar.

In the second phase of JeM, Noor Tantrey is said to have single-handedly revived the organization. He was taking direct instructions from Mufti Rauf. He also facilitated the entry of Mufti Waqas into India. In the 2016 agitation in Kashmir, Tantrey lay low. From 2015–17, he focused on building assets and hideouts in the forests, and creating an OGW network. His main tasks included target identification, recces, earmarking locations for fidayeen, and transportation. He was the principal architect of the October 2017 attack on the BSF camp near Srinagar airport and the September 2017 attack on the state's PWD minister, Naeem Akhtar's, cavalcade.[10] A senior police officer of the J&K police, Munir Khan, made the following observations about

Noor Tantrey: 'He identified targets and planned the attacks. All attacks along the highways were designed by him. He used to identify escape routes as well.'[11] Besides, he was also known for identifying his sources and keeping the cadres motivated. Rafiq, the JeM guide whom I interviewed, worked and stayed with Noor Tantrey in the same house for several months. He said that Tantrey was exceptionally perceptive and sharp in reading people, highly aware, and always suspicious of others.

Muhammad Ashiq Baba

Born in 1979, Ashiq was from Shajroo in Reasi district of the Jammu region. At the time of his arrest, he was living in Srinagar. He worked as a supplier of solar lights on a 15 to 20 per cent commission fee. His uncle was a police constable in the J&K police's elite interrogation unit. He had all the legal documents to prove his citizenship, such as an Aadhaar card, voter's ID, PAN card, J&K's state subject certificate and a driver's licence. He was arrested in the Khanyar area of Srinagar, and the FIR was registered under UAPA at the NIA police station in Delhi. He was an OGW, and his associates included Tariq Ahmed Dar from Shopian, Muneer ul Islam from Kupwara, and Umar from Srinagar.

After he dropped out of school in Class 8, he studied the Quran for four years in a Deobandi madrasa—Zia-ul-Uloom—in Poonch. In 1998, he went with the other madrasa students to Ankleshwar district in Gujarat. They did a religious course for two years at the Kharod madrasa and got the degree of Qari (a religious degree in Islam). After returning home, he stayed in Reasi for a year. He visited Tablighi Jamaat's centre in Jammu during this time. Then, he visited Srinagar with TJ cadres, where he met Dr Ashai, TJ's chief. Dr Ashai convinced him to work in his 'bukhari' (a heating device) manufacturing factory in the HMT area of Srinagar. He worked there for five to six months. After that, he became the imam of a local mosque near Umrabad in Srinagar. He worked there for one year at a monthly salary of INR 3,500, after which he became imam at another mosque for two-and-a-half years, where he got INR 4,500 monthly. After his marriage in 2007, he started working in a solar equipment company, selling their lights. In 2013, he bought two plots of land in Jammu and Srinagar. His wife took loans of INR 4,00,000 and 7,00,000. Then he bought a three-bedroom house for INR 30 lakh, borrowing the rest of the money from his brothers.

With his debts mounting, he started looking for alternate ways of earning money. In that pursuit, in 2015, he applied for an LoC trade licence application. This was a sought-after permission as it offered ample opportunities to earn money by transporting contraband items from Pakistan. Ashiq wanted to begin a textile business with Pakistan. He visited Pakistan with the help of Ghulam Muhammad Ghanai, from whom he had purchased the three-bedroom house. Ashiq got the visa by producing Hurriyat leader Syed Ali Shah Geelani's recommendation letter at the Pakistani High Commission in New Delhi. In Pakistan, they met Ghanai's cousin, Imran Yusuf, who had moved to Pakistan in the 1990s, married there and settled down in Shekhopura in Lahore. He hosted Ghanai and Ashiq for eighteen days. Imran was supposed to give them a tour of the Rawalpindi textile market; however, he was called by the ISI and instructed not to leave Shekhopura. During his Lahore stay, Ashiq met many Kashmiris who had shifted to Pakistan in the 1990s. Terror groups and the ISI gave them aid. In fact, the ISI had a separate Muhajir fund. They issued PKR 3,000 per adult and PKR 1,500 per child. In return, they had to work for ISI whenever asked.

In April 2016, he visited Pakistan once again. By then, Ashiq had finished all the LoC trade documentation and had submitted the final request. On his second visit to Lahore, Ashiq went straight to Imran's house. Imran informed the ISI about Ashiq's visit and took their permission to give him a tour of the Rawalpindi textile market. Ashiq also met the United Jihad Council (UJC) chief, Syed Salahuddin, aka Mohammad Yusuf Shah, who inquired about the ground situation in Indian Kashmir.

After his return, Ashiq had to sell his Jammu plot because he had to pay INR 12 lakh to Ghanai as he was pressuring him to complete the payment for the house purchase. Muneer-ul-Islam helped Ashiq find buyers for his Jammu plot. After that transaction, Ashiq Baba continued to meet Muneer-ul-Islam. Muneer was an LoC trader for almost a decade, with business interests in the Jammu region. He traded timber in Jammu with Tariq Ahmed Dar, a Pulwama-based businessman. He told Ashiq that there was no need to wait for the licence. He could simply trade under someone else's licence. Muneer also taught him the subtle ways he could profit in the LoC trade.

Then, Ashiq went to Pakistan for the third time. This time he met Fayaz Ahmed Bhatt in Rawalpindi, whose address he got from Muneer. At his place, someone named Safdar and Dr Aizaz brought JeM's launch-pad commander in the Samba–Kathua region, Abu Talha, and his deputy, Wasim, to meet Ashiq. Following this meeting, they all took Ashiq to meet Qari Zarrar (JeM chief, Jammu region) at his residence. After the meeting, Qari Zarrar, Safdar and Dr Aizaz left, while Abu Talha and Wasim stayed with Ashiq for a day. During dinner conversation, Abu Talha and Wasim discussed the atrocities of Indian SFs in Kashmir in provocative words.

The following day, Qari Zarrar, Wasim and Abu Talha accompanied Ashiq to Muzaffarabad to introduce him to Mufti Azgar (code name: Abu Saad), who was the JeM chief of the Kashmir region. Ashiq stayed there for a night. Mufti Azgar inquired about Kashmir's ground situation and the sentiment of the people. The next day, they arranged to give Ashiq a tour of the city. Finally, he came back to Fayaz's house. He spoke to Muneer, who asked him to come back to Kashmir. He also promised to help him with the LoC trade after his return to India. Before he left Rawalpindi, Wasim gave Ashiq a brand-new Chinese-made mobile phone, which had to be delivered to Muneer. Upon his return, though Ashiq stayed in touch with Muneer, he went back to his solar lights business. Then, one day, he went to Jammu on Muneer's instructions, and received a SIM card from a bespectacled older man named Amir at a local shrine. He delivered the SIM card to Muneer, who used it for WhatsApp-based communication with JeM leaders in Pakistan. Muneer regularly communicated with Wasim. Then, Muneer started persuading Ashiq to help him ferry militants from the Jammu region to the Kashmir Valley.

First, Muneer asked Tariq to accompany him in receiving JeM militants, but the latter refused. So, Muneer took his car without telling him and drove towards Gaghwal, near the Jammu region of the IB. Ashiq accompanied him. They received three Pakistani militants with AK-47s at a nullah near Gaghwal. Ashiq helped the militants in conducting the recce of their route to Kashmir.

On 29 November 2016, Muneer instructed Ashiq to take all the militants in his car to a location near the Nagrota army camp. They started the journey at 10 p.m. The militants forcefully occupied the driver's seat near the Gujjar Nagar bridge. After that, they asked him to get out of the vehicle near the Nagrota petrol pump and hand over the car to them. When Ashiq refused, they threatened him by pointing the gun toward him, harassed him and threw him out. Muneer was calling Ashiq, but the militants had snatched away his phone. After some downward journey, they abused him and continued misbehaving; however, they returned his car and mobile phone. They left for the army camp with their weapons.

Ashiq came back to Srinagar after that with Muneer and Tariq. That night, the militants attacked Nagrota army camp, in which seven people died. For ferrying his first batch of militants, Muneer gave Ashiq INR 25,000. After this incident, Ashiq began avoiding Muneer; however, Muneer offered him INR 10 lakh, so he agreed to bring another batch of militants. In this second batch, he brought Muhammad Umar Farooq, the Pulwama mastermind. Ashiq received another militant at a location given by Muneer, and then drove to Ramban with Umar Farooq and the other militants. From there, Muneer ferried the militants in Tariq's car, and dropped them somewhere near Pampore and Zewan (both in south Kashmir). Muneer's Pakistani contact asked him to open an account at either an ICICI or HDFC bank. Ashiq had an account at HDFC. Muneer's Pakistan-based JeM handlers transferred INR 6 lakh to this account, which was shared between Ashiq and Muneer. According to some sources in the Indian intelligence set-up, Ashiq used to get INR 3 lakh per militant, and the money was transferred through a Qatar-based bank.[12]

After that, Ashiq visited Pakistan and stayed at Fayaz's place, where he met Abu Talha and Wasim once again, and requested them not to tell Muneer about his Pakistan visit. They understood that Ashiq wanted independent dealings with them.

He made four trips to Pakistan between 2015 and 2017 on a valid visa, and crossed through the Wagah border. He got the visas on the recommendation of Hurriyat leaders like

S.A.S. Geelani, Abdul Ghani Bhat and Mirwaiz Mohammad Umar Farooq.[13]

In May 2018, Ashiq was arrested in the Khanyar area of Srinagar. His arrest resulted from a bank robbery. When the primary robber was interrogated, he spilled the details about Ashiq Baba. According to some sources, Ashiq also worked for the Indian agencies; however, others say he was a double agent and was only loyal to JeM.

Momin Basharat

Momin, a local Kashmiri terrorist, is the son of a bedding maker. He is one of four siblings. Momin left his studies in 2010 due to financial problems and was arrested that year for stone-pelting near Baramulla Chowk. He was booked under PSA (Public Safety Act, 1978) after about fifteen days in detention. That year, Momin's elder brother Rafiq, a hardcore stone-pelter, sustained a pellet injury and lost his eyesight. Upon his release, Momin joined Tablighi Jamaat and toured Delhi, Salem and Chennai as part of a religious congregation for forty days.

In August 2019, he helped evacuate a militant, Saifullah, from an encounter site in Old Town Baramulla, in which one other militant was killed.

Momin had a soft corner for militants and was fascinated by militancy. Further, he claimed that Saifullah frightened him into believing that the police would take action against him for helping him escape from the encounter site, and, to avoid being arrested by the police, he had to join JeM. Saifullah gave him a pistol and they stayed together for about six days. In August 2019, Momin and a local JeM OGW named Iqbal secretly boarded a truck heading towards Sopore. When they asked the truck driver to stop near Khushalpora, he got frightened. He suspected them to be thieves and stopped the truck near the army deployment at Khushalpora and sought the help of army personnel. While Saifullah was arrested along with an AK-47, Momin managed to escape.

Before his arrest, Momin had stayed at different locations in Sopore and Baramulla. He had spent most of his time at the residence of his childhood friend Tousif (name changed to protect his identity) and at his aunt Rafia Jaan's house in Sopore. On 5 October 2019, Momin, accompanied by Tousif from Sopore, was going to meet his family in a car arranged by Tousif. As soon as they reached the checkpost, security forces apprehended him and recovered one pistol, one magazine and ten live rounds on him.

Mohammad Dilawar Hussain

Dilawar comes from a middle-class family and was arrested from Kreeri village in Sopore, in March 2020. He was nineteen years old at the time of his arrest. His father, Mohammad Hussain Kakroo, was a garment shop owner in Old Baramulla and was able to educate Dilawar in school until Class 11. Dilawar dropped out after that in 2015 and assisted in the garments' business. He was placed in police detention in 2018 for stone pelting. His proximity to other anti-establishment elements, access to the social media content of militant action and participation in funerals of killed militants (2018–19) fuelled his fascination with the lifestyle of militants. In 2013, local religious activists convinced him to join Tablighi Jamaat. He was impressed with its ideology and became a regular fixture in its meetings at Baramulla.

Dilawar created a Facebook account that he used to support militancy. He also joined the AGuH WhatsApp group (he said he received its invite on Facebook). Later, he received a message from the administrator of the group (with a Pakistani number), who wanted to know if he would be interested in working for militants in Kashmir. Dilawar's reply in the affirmative brought him a WhatsApp contact number—a JeM foreign terrorist whose code name was Sadiq. After contacting him, Dilawar received a reference from a Pakistan-based administrator of the AGuH WhatsApp group. At Sadiq's request, Dilawar created a Telegram account on a Pakistani phone number given by the former. During their association, Sadiq intermittently got Dilawar to provide shelter to militants. Sadiq also introduced him to Zafar, a Kashmir-based militant, and asked the two of them to coordinate plans while receiving militants. In March 2020, Zafar and Dilawar received Junaid, from Pulwama, in Baramulla. Dilawar roped in his childhood friend Muzaffar (of Drangbal, Baramulla) to arrange shelter for Junaid. Muzaffar sheltered Junaid in his house for a night and then shifted him to a local mosque the next night.

Dilawar met Majid (who runs a shop in Baramulla) through Tahir (a common friend) in March 2020. Six pro-militancy Urdu posters titled 'The Resistance Front' were given to Dilawar to put up in different areas of Baramulla town. Later, Tahir contacted Dilawar and asked him to pause putting up the posters. Dilawar then handed over the posters to another friend, Salim, who was a domestic help at the residence of a Baramulla-based family.

In March 2020, Dilawar met Junaid and was told to reach Kreeri, where Rehman, a JeM foreign terrorist, would meet them and induct them into Sadiq's group. On reaching Kreeri, Junaid contacted Rehman on Telegram and informed him of their arrival. According to Rehman's instructions, Dilawar and Junaid waited until 4 p.m., but Rehman did not arrive. At about

6 p.m. that day, Dilawar was apprehended in Budgam while Junaid escaped.

Zaid Ahmed Gani

Zaid Ahmad Gani is a local terrorist from Kashmir. He belongs to a middle-class family. His father, Altaf Ahmad Gani, is engaged in the apple business, while his mother, Afsana Begum, is a housewife. He has two brothers and a sister. After passing his Class 10 exams, he enrolled at Siraj-ul-Uloom (run by Jamaat-e-Islami) in 2018, in Shopian, and completed the one-year course of 'Almiyat' there.

Meanwhile, he continued his academic studies as well and passed his Class 12 exams in 2020. He claimed that he was fed up with his father bashing him for his mistakes and he thought it was better to turn to jihad by joining militancy. He was convinced that jihad is an obligation for Muslims.

In August 2020, his father caught him smoking a cigarette at home and scolded him badly. Subsequently, Zaid left home to join militancy. He decided to go towards south Kashmir, where it would be easy to come into contact with militants. After that, he went to Bijbehara, Anantnag, and stayed there for one night in a hotel. The next day, he went to Shopian in search of someone who could facilitate his entry into a militant group. Upon reaching there, he took out the SIM card from his mobile phone and spent the night in an apple orchard.

On the evening of 24 August 2020, he went to Shopian and spent another night in the nearby apple orchard. After that, Zaid took the cover of a labourer from Baramulla and worked packaging apples in different apple orchards in the Shopian area for about two months, on a daily wage of INR 500. Meanwhile, he used to roam around apple orchards in the late evening to come into contact with militants. However, he could not meet any during these two months.

After that, he moved to Kulgam and worked as a labourer in the apple orchards there for about twenty-five days. Finally, in November 2020, he came in contact with an unidentified militant of JeM in the orchards of Kulgam. Zaid requested him to facilitate his joining into militant ranks, to which the unidentified militant provided him a Telegram ID and told him to contact it to be recruited. Zaid continued to work in Kulgam for another month, but did not gather the courage to switch on his SIM card and contact the Telegram ID.

In the last week of January 2021, he went to a Deobandi mosque in Shopian and stayed there for three days. After that, he returned to Kulgam and worked there for about fifteen–twenty more days. After that, he went back to the Deobandi masque in Shopian, where he met a moulvi named Bilal. Zaid told Bilal about his intention to join militancy and his meeting with the JeM militant. Subsequently, Bilal sheltered him at his friend's residence, Rehan (a butcher) in Shopian. Zaid stayed at Rehan's residence for one-and-a-half months.

In mid-April 2021, Zaid provided Bilal with the Telegram ID and told him to contact the number, which Bilal did. The person on the other end asked for Zaid's photograph, which Bilal sent. In the late evening, the Telegram user introduced himself as Arshid (a code name). Following Arshid's instructions, Bilal took Zaid to Qazigund in a Maruti 800 car, which he had arranged.

Meanwhile, Bilal called another friend, Nisar of Rampora (Kulgam), and asked him to come to Chawalgam. Bilal instructed Nisar to ride on a bike ahead of them so that he could inform Bilal about the presence of SFs on the route. However, the Maruti car was intercepted by the police at a checkpost, where the Kulgam police apprehended them. Later, they were taken to the Special Operations Group camp in Kulgam. The police recovered a hand grenade, a pistol and an AK-47 magazine from these guys in the car.

Ishfaq Al Gojri

Ishfaq Al Gojri belongs to a middle-class family and has studied up to Class 10. After dropping out of school, he started selling vegetables on the outskirts of Baramulla town. His father, Ashfaq Gojri (name changed), is a farmer, and his mother, Nafisa Begum (name changed), is a housewife. Ishfaq has one elder brother. His father is originally a resident of Buchroo, Baramulla. After marrying Nafisa Begum, he shifted to his in-laws' house at Baramulla.

In March 2019, Ishfaq's childhood friend, Adil Ahmad Gojri of Arampora, Old Town, Baramulla, introduced him to Hamid (this is a code name), a JeM OGW. He also handed Ishfaq a Chinese-made mobile phone to keep in touch with him. In mid-2019, Adil joined active militancy. In July 2019, Hamid contacted Ishfaq and asked him to join militancy. Ishfaq agreed, but failed to contact Hamid following the suspension of communication in J&K, post abrogation of Article 370.

In October 2019, on Hamid's direction, an unidentified lady came to Ishfaq's residence, and handed over a pistol with rounds and ten threatening posters. She said that Hamid had directed him to paste these posters and fire shots in Baramulla to create terror among the shopkeepers. In November 2019, Ishfaq went to the market in the evening, put up the posters, and fired a few rounds in the air. After that, he went home directly. Later that same evening, an unidentified boy of about sixteen years of age came to his residence and said that Hamid had called Ishfaq to join militancy. He directed Ishfaq to an electric tower adjacent to

Delina, Sopore, and told him to go there in late November. The boy also told Ishfaq that Hamid had asked him to bring some money. Ishfaq stayed in his house for two days and arranged INR 52,000 from his savings.

On the evening of 25 November 2019, at 6 p.m. sharp, he went to the tower, where he met a man code named Gazi—a local terrorist for JeM. Gazi took him through the orchards to a hideout. Five minutes after their arrival, other militants—namely Sajjad, Hamid and Arshid (all code names)—came to the hideout. The militants greeted Ishfaq and he handed over the money to Hamid.

On 26 November 2019, Ishfaq developed a sudden pain in his chest and requested Hamid to allow him to go back home, but Hamid threatened to shoot him. Ishfaq stayed in the hide from 26 November to 21 December 2019. He was also given one grenade. Ishfaq also disclosed that Hamid and Arshid used to go out daily at around 6.30 p.m. to meet a local OGW, Saifullah (code name), who used to provide essential commodities to the militants. The two would return at 8 p.m.

During Ishfaq's stay in the hideout, he overheard Hamid telling Gazi to target 'outside' trucks (non-Kashmiri trucks from other states of India) by setting them ablaze so that other states would stop sending trucks to Kashmir. However, Gazi opposed this plan to kill drivers. The OGW Saifullah had informed Hamid of FTs infiltrating the Valley. Still, their location was unknown and, due to the suspension of the internet, it was difficult to receive directions from across the border. Hamid contemplated sending Saifullah to Jammu, from where he could contact their Pakistani handlers. During an interaction in the hideout, Ishfaq also learned that another local, named Batwala, was working for the group as an OGW in the area.

On the morning of 27 December 2019, Ishfaq escaped from the hideout, carrying one grenade on him. He went straightaway to the house of his maternal aunt, Ameena Begum (name changed) of Sopore, and requested her to help him surrender before the police. That very evening, he surrendered to the police.

Financing Jaish-e-Mohammed

Higher-ups in the JeM echelons arrange finances in Pakistan through donations and state support. JeM, with its strong and pervasive Deobandi network in the social and religious set-up of Pakistan, manages to collect vast amounts of funds through donations alone. The Deobandi madrasa network in Punjab, Karachi and KPK regions are some of the major sources of collection for annual donations from both locals and foreigners. Concerning donations, terrorist groups are known to adapt quite easily to the changing environment and have brought innovative methods in their money-collection tactics. Gone are the days of donation boxes. Now, particularly in villages, followers are told to generate funds by selling harvested crops.[14] Deobandi and Ahl-i-Hadith charity organizations like JuD, Al Khidmat Foundation and Al-Rahmat Trust play a crucial role in radicalizing and recruiting young and poorly educated persons from poverty-stricken families.[15] According to a US embassy cable, 'Government and non-governmental sources claimed that financial support estimated at nearly 100 million USD annually was making its way to Deobandi and Ahl-i-Hadith clerics in the region from "missionary" and "Islamic charitable" organizations in Saudi Arabia and the United Arab Emirates ostensibly with the direct support of those governments.'[16] Extremist madrasas of south Punjab and terrorist outfits like JeM allegedly receive massive state funding from political parties and the intelligence establishment.[17] Besides, middle- and upper-class business elites of Punjab, mostly traders and merchants, and sometimes farmers, also make significant contributions to these madrasas and militant outfits for social, political and moral reasons. They believe that contributing to jihad funds helps them atone for their sins. Besides, the newly wealthy merchant class uses JeM's socio-political power and influence to negotiate with the old local power structures.[18] Farukh Ilyas Shaji, a JeM militant killed in Kralpora (north Kashmir), was from one such business family. His father donated PKR 1 crore annually to JeM for its jihad fund.[19] In Kashmir, there are some cases when JeM allegedly raised money by extorting local business people and orchard owners. However, such incidents are very few. In 2004, JeM raised money through bank robberies in Kachdoora (Shopian) and Nagbal (Anantnag). Besides, Jamaat-i-Islami also helped JeM raise and move funds.[20] From 2005 onwards, Pakistan strengthened the United Jihad Council (UJC), with Syed Salahuddin as its chief. The money flowed to Kashmiri terror groups centrally from UJC. In India, a veteran militant commander or a highly trusted OGW received the funds and distributed them among various groups—the commanders who did not have proper hideouts preferred to keep the money with the OGWs. However, this model led to mild turf wars between JeM and OGWs over time. JeM's independent and secretive style completely contrasted to LeT's template of getting detailed instructions from Pakistan in everything—ranging from operational matters to the distribution of funds.

As regards the sale and smuggling of drugs for raising funds, there are contrary opinions on the subject. Some of the earliest OGWs suggest that JeM is an orthodox Deobandi group, so it refrained from drug smuggling. However, Akram Bhai, my source, said that JeM, in principle, was not against selling drugs because the Taliban, which is like its sister Deobandi organization, raised money from the opium trade. Reportedly, Masood Azhar's brother Ibrahim mostly remained in Afghanistan and handled JeM's Afghan operations, and also its share in the opium trade. Further, Akram Bhai said that after 2019, JeM was active in the drug business, like other terrorist groups, because other channels like the LoC trade and hawala dealing were closed off by the Government of India. JeM's drugs are smuggled from various routes, such as Tangdhar, Keran (both on the LoC), Samba and Firozpur (Punjab). A large chunk of JeM's drugs are sold in Punjab.

JeM also issues donation requests in magazines and pamphlets. In 2001, it listed its address for correspondence and remittances of funds as P.O. Box Number 1249, GPO Islamabad. Drafts and remittances were to be sent in favour of Mohammad Sajid, c/o ANZ Grindlays Bank, 55 Haider Road, Sadar Rawalpindi (Pakistan). Since 2004, JeM has carried out its transactions through Dubai Islamic Bank, based in the UAE. Reportedly, the account was maintained by two brothers from PoK—Abdul Karim and Ashiq. They were running 'New Al Khyam' restaurant at Muna Bazaar, Dubai. JeM was routing funds through them in the name of Kashmir jihad. Pakistani national Mohammad Hussain (a trans-border operator) worked under JeM commander Qari Saifullah and brought INR 6.5 lakh in January 2006 into India. Reportedly, many other Pakistani nationals and ten JeM OGWs in Kashmir were majorly involved in the transactions of hawala money, SIM cards and communication sets.

In 2009, funding was arranged by JeM higher-ups in Pakistan. JeM commanders in J&K are in touch with Mufti Asgar, the launch-pad commander in PoK, who provided funds and gave general directions to them. Over time, JeM found hawala channels risky and highly unreliable, mainly since the Indian enforcement agencies started tightening the screws against terror financing. Their assessment seems to be based on the fact that the arrest of any one person in the hawala network can disrupt the flow of money and expose the operation. After that, there was no recourse other than finding alternative arrangements. Therefore, they started scouting for new methods of securely moving funds. A report published in *India Today* brought out the following facts about the new ways JeM routes its money with stability and minimum risk:[21]

1) PoK-based JeM commanders have asked their counterparts in Kashmir to find locals with relatives living in the Gulf countries. After taking them into confidence, they were asked to share the bank account details of their relatives based in the Arab world. JeM handlers and financiers would then transfer around INR 1–2 lakh into their accounts, before asking them to start transferring money to the accounts of their relatives in the Valley in small installments. The Valley-based relatives would then transfer the funds to JeM operatives through a courier. This method was effective with minimum risk involved and the recipients got a commission at every stage. In one such case, INR 20,000–30,000 was transferred to the accounts of the Qatar-based relatives of a JeM OGW, Naeem (name changed), in 2015, which was then transferred to his relative's account in India. In another case, INR 60 lakh was transferred to India in nine transactions.

2) JeM handlers contact pre-identified Hajis during their Umrah and Haj travels, and persuade them to help transfer money either in the form of cash or gold.

3) When the Srinagar–Muzaffarabad bus service was operational, JeM often took the help of passengers to transfer funds. JeM operatives contacted such passengers through their trusted OGWs for the task. The passengers transferring (from both sides—PoK and Indian Kashmir) money were given a per cent age share.

4) During the regular congregations of people on both sides of the border at Teetwal, JeM operatives tried to transfer money, drugs and weapons. Trusted OGWs would assist in collecting these and arrange to deliver them to the JeM commanders in the Valley, for which they would get paid.

5) Reportedly, the ISI generously funds JeM. Though the relationship between the two is a bit complex, it is symbiotic. Also, compared to LeT, JeM is less dependent on ISI for funding. It has a massive local base of Deobandi mosques and madrasas, and exists in an ecosystem of Deobandi extremist groups, which enables it to generate enormous amounts of funds. Further, JeM's pan-Islamist objectives and religious goals bring it closer to TTGs like Al Qaeda, which also contributed generously to its finances in its early days. Masood's widespread contacts in the Muslim world—particularly in the Arab world—were immensely helpful in generating a robust supply of funds. On his first African visit to Zambia in 1990, Masood collected between PKR 20–22 lakh; on his second visit, he collected PKR 22 lakh again.[22] From his 1990 Abu Dhabi and Saudi visits, he collected PKR 2–3 lakh from each visit.[23] Reportedly, in 2006, he collected INR 17 crore in the name of Kashmir jihad through donations alone in Pakistan, Afghanistan, Middle Eastern countries and the UK. Deobandi Muslims in southern

Africa, the UK and other parts of Europe also helped the Harkat movement and its outfits, like HuM and JeM, in raising funds.

6) Since 2007, JeM has invested in the commodities market and in real estate.[24] The US State Department's 'Country Report on Terrorism' said that fearing asset seizures by the government, JeM withdrew funds from its bank accounts and invested in legal businesses like real estate, the production of consumer goods and commodity trading. Further, the report mentioned that Al Qaeda provided funds to JeM.[25]

Additionally, JeM also raises money in the large-scale processions it organizes time and again. Though, after the Pulwama fidayeen attack, these jalsas declined for the reasons cited in the previous chapter. Before 2019, such processions were a regular feature. JeM organized one such jalsa on 26 January 2014, titled 'Majlis-e-Wursa-Shuhda-e-Jammu & Kashmir', at Muzaffarabad to pay tribute to Afzal Guru and mark 26 January—Republic Day in India—as a 'Black Day'. The event was addressed telephonically by Masood Azhar. In his speech, he announced that jihad would be revived in the Valley and warned India that the group would avenge the hanging of Afzal Guru. During the rally, a book titled *Aaina*, authored by Afzal Guru in prison, was also released. Mufti Rauf presided over the function. In Afzal Guru's memory, Domail Chowk of Muzaffarabad was renamed Afzal Guru Chowk. Generally, up to 60,000 people attend these processions and they donate money for jihad.

JeM also generates funding from affiliated charity organizations like Al-Rahmat Trust.[26] After JeM's ban, it operated through proxies like this trust. However, the UNSC ordered the seizure of its accounts for its alleged links with Al Qaeda. After

2008, JeM started reviving Al-Rahmat Trust (ART). In 2010, Maulana Ghulam Murtaza Khan was tasked to revive ART.[27] According to an interview given by ART coordinator Maulana Ashfaq Ahmed, by 2011, ART fundraising was in full swing in the Punjab and Khyber Pakhtunkhwa provinces.[28] Besides, JeM publications like *Al Qalam* and *Muslim Ummah* were soliciting advertisements and donations for building mosques and for relief work in case of natural calamities, with all the legal permissions.[29] According to an article published by *Bangalore Mirror* in 2016, JeM's finances were handled by five men from Lahore and Sheikhupura, who had a widespread network across several countries.[30] Those five men were Hafiz Tariq Masood, Qari Ehsaan, Shahbaz Haider of Lahore, Qari Abdul Hafeez and Muhammad Tariq of Sheikhupura. JeM also received large donations of land and gold. In an article published by Taliban's *Dharb-i-Mumin* in 2001, Masood thanked donors for giving large tracts of land in grants.[31] Masood also mentioned women sending gold donations for building Madrasa Sayeed Ahmed Shaheed at Balakot for training jihadis.

Properties and Assets of JeM

Intelligence agencies received inputs in 2014 about Pakistan's security establishment engineering the resurgence of JeM in the Valley by extending politico-military patronage to the organization and redrawing its activities/logistical capabilities for cross-border terrorism. The alleged ISI-sponsored reactivation of JeM was also confirmed by the growing activity at the group's headquarters in Bahawalpur's Model Town area. JeM completed the construction of a new five-storeyed building with more than 100 rooms, a state-of-the-art communications room and a huge basement. This building also housed *Al Qalam*, the JeM mouthpiece. It also opened an office in Rawal kot, which was close to the LoC, opposite Poonch, and an important infiltration area. Besides the offices and camps, JeM boasts of a colossal infrastructure in place—including offices and property registered in the name of local trusts, NGOs and charitable organizations.[32] It also owns a chain of educational institutions under different names and a big hospital in Muzaffarabad.[33]

Indoctrination Methods

The role of Deobandi madrasas and clerics in the radicalization and recruitment of young boys in south Punjab and KPK has already been discussed. However, the radicalization of an individual after his joining JeM is also a crucial element of its indoctrination process—which can be attributed to the cadres' extremism after they finish the training programme and enter Kashmir. In the JeM training camps, the cadres are exposed to a range of radicalization material, which includes discourses and lectures on jihad and other religious issues by clerics and motivators, propaganda videos showing the alleged persecution of Muslims, their killings and the rapes of Muslim women in India, Palestine, Bosnia and other conflict theatres. The trainees must follow a rigorous prayer schedule, including namaz five times a day and a Quran recital. Iftikhar Hussain (name changed), a senior counterterrorism officer with more than two decades of experience in the field, raised the subject of the psychological element of radicalization in his interview with me. He said that young teenagers in Pakistani madrasas are exposed to a very conservative and primitive lifestyle. They are subjected to harsh beatings, not allowed to meet their parents and relatives for months, and kept in isolation from outside influences. There are several examples where children have been the victims of sexual abuse. A probe conducted by the Associated Press (AP) in 2017 provided accounts of rampant paedophilia in Pakistani madrasas.[34] The report also mentioned that it continued unchecked because the victims were from poor and vulnerable families, and madrasas belonged to powerful extremist groups. Such life experiences are likely to fill them with hatred, violence and a contempt for non-Muslims.

Fidayeen recruits are subjected to even more hardcore indoctrination. In Kashmir, fidayeens, once recruited, are kept away from their parents and external influences. Adil Dar, the Pulwama fidayeen, was radicalized for six months. Umar Farooq motivated him by narrating the virtues of Islam and how mujahideens were honoured with the highest status in paradise. As a result, Adil devoted himself to intense religious prayers. He became more and more withdrawn, and stayed away from others. Umar Farooq closely watched him to ensure he did not stray or get scared of death.[35] Mostly confined to Peer Tariq Ahmed Shah's house—a co-conspirator in the Pulwama attack—Adil Dar was subjected to an overdose of the Quran and religious lectures, particularly the discourses on jihad. On the day of the attack, Umar Farooq read all the Quranic verses on jihad to him. He focused on a quote from Surah Al-Baqarah: 'Indeed, those who believed and those who have emigrated and fought in the cause of Allah expect the mercy of Allah. And Allah is forgiving and merciful.'[36] He also passionately narrated stories of mujahideens blowing themselves up in Iraq, Afghanistan and Palestine to kill American soldiers and Israelis.

Compared to other groups like LeT and HM, which focus on Kashmir-centric jihad, JeM indoctrination tapes and other material project a pan-Islamic vision. There is an intense focus and emphasis on the religious element. Masood's lectures preach that living under Hindu rule is a sin for Muslims. The preachers instil in the cadres that jihad is not merely for mujahideens; instead, the holy war is the duty of all non-disabled Muslims. The preachers show them the videos and pictures of Muslim women being raped and killed in Kashmir, and draw their parallels with atrocities committed on Muslims in Palestine, Bosnia and Sudan. It can be argued that they want to make mainstream the narrative of Kashmir being a quintessential part of global jihad.

JeM, as compared to LeT and HM, does not have a vast infrastructure in Kashmir, so it relies a lot on social media for radicalization.[37] With the lack of an extensive OGW network, its network chooses a local issue as an instigator, and provokes people by posting videos, tweets and messages about it. At the same time, they also get the material uploaded from their social media team in Pakistan and whip up emotions in Kashmir through such videos and posts.[38]

My source, Mr Dabwal, opined that in his experience, Deobandi groups like JeM had a much more intense and lethal focus and commitment towards jihad as compared to Ahl-i-Hadith groups. He said groups like JeM are 'off-limits' when it comes to jihad. Groups like LeT, which follow the Saudi line of Ahl-i-Hadith, have to face a series of 'ifs' and 'buts' from their clerics on the issue of jihad. As discussed earlier, the Ahl-i-Hadith leadership in Pakistan is not entirely convinced by LeT because they argue that only an Islamic state can wage jihad, not non-state actors. In Kashmir, except for a small segment of extremists, the Wahhabis/Ahl-i-Hadith leadership follows the Saudi line and prefers to stay away from terrorism because of their political and ideological objections to the concept of jihad as perceived and projected by Pakistan-sponsored Ahl-i-Hadith terrorist groups like LeT.[39] This situation is unlike Jamaat-i-Islami, which openly supported a terrorist group, Hizbul Mujahideen.

On the young jihadists' end, the idea of jihad gives them a sense of purpose and an immediate sense of empowerment as they see themselves as protectors of Muslim women and children in far-off lands such as Kashmir, Palestine and Bosnia. They are also given Arab names to inculcate a sense of historical glory and legacy. However, they are disappointed when they find that in Kashmir, Muslims are allowed to practice their religion, and the stories of persecution are fabricated and exaggerated. In one such case, an LeT militant from Pakistan, Bahadur Ali, told his interrogators when he was arrested in July 2016 that he had infiltrated into Kashmir with the extremist ideological baggage of Muslims being killed and their women being raped by the SFs.[40] However, once, in a north Kashmir jungle, he witnessed soldiers approaching local women. For a moment, he thought they would be raped; however, when he saw the soldiers offering bottled mineral water to them, he was shocked and even remorseful. After that, he even regretted coming to Kashmir for jihad.[41] He gave a detailed account of terror training camps, and Pakistan army personnel visiting in civilian clothes and training them.[42] Later, India's foreign minister, Sushma Swaraj, presented his case to the UN as living proof of Pakistan abetting terrorism in Kashmir.[43]

Masood Azhar's Motivational and Indoctrinating Lectures

Reportedly, Masood Azhar's passionate and provocative audio clips on jihad spewing venom against India play a crucial role in radicalizing JeM recruits. He is known for his unique style of oration, intonation and raising the pitch to high decibels to evoke religious passions. It is well-engineered to psychologically impact impressionable young minds and motivate them to jihad. I carefully studied his 450 audio clips, extracting them from the darknet. Below are the translations of a few clips:

Maulana Masood Azhar—Kashmir Aur Ghazwa—Emotional Bayaan[44]

Translated Summary

Oh, dear Muslims! You bow in front of infidels. In a voice full of complaints and anger, he asks Muslims why they shave their beards and what is wrong with the Prophet's practice of keeping beards? On the roads, one hardly finds anyone with a beard and pagri (an Islamic headgear). Are these people Muslims or slaves of the Britishers? Is it a Christian locality? Sajjad Shahid sacrificed his life in jail but did not allow any violation of the Prophet's sunnah. Today, we need to imbibe and relive the lessons from his life. Oh, Muslims, remember, Allah has chosen the Muslims of Kashmir for a unique sacrifice. I am not here to tell false stories; I will quote from the Hadith. The Prophet had promised to Sahaba (the Prophet's companions) that a small group of my *Ummat* (the global Islamic community) would do jihad in Hindustan, and they would not go to hell. (Masood then cites Islamic sources and Abu Huraira's interaction with the Prophet on jihad in Hindustan.) Huraira asked, 'What should we do in jihad in Hindustan?' The Prophet replied that you sacrifice everything, including your wealth and life. Those who survive will become Ghazis, and those who die will be martyrs in heaven. Then he said:

> My Allah has pardoned hell for two segments of my Ummat—those who will come with Hazrat-e-Isa, i.e., Jesus Christ, and do jihad with him and those who will do jihad in India. India has various places like Jalandhar, Delhi, Tripura, and Manipur; however, Allah chose Kashmir only. Ghazis will rise from Kashmir. It will become the heaven of martyrs in the path of jihad. Kafirs said we will make Kashmir Scotland;

we will open nightclubs in Kashmir, and unleash a culture of sin and promiscuity in Kashmir. Allah said Kashmir would be a centre of jihad camps. Mujahids with long hair and beards would descend on Kashmir. Kashmir would have pious sisters and mothers.

The world lost the battle, and Allah's vision of making Kashmir a heaven of jihadists and martyrs has come true. People say that Kashmiris are dying. They are not dying. Death is inevitable; one should not fear it. It can come in any form. Most people are dying with sins of earning interest money, alcohol consumption, sexual promiscuity and bribery. They will face punishment on Judgment Day.

On the other hand, Kashmiris are lucky to die with the crown of martyrdom and the garland of jihad. Kashmiris are reaching the highest pedestal of martyrdom, and Allah has given them respect, dignity and status. One lakh Indians died in an earthquake. They got a disrespectful death, which had no pride in it. In the last twelve years of Kashmir's militancy, 1 lakh people have not died. And those who become martyrs go down with respect and dignity. Even in their death, they write Allah-u-Akbar and get glory.

The Indian Army gets shocked when they see the funerals of jihadis and Allah-u-Akbar written in their blood. People say that maulvis poisoned the Kashmiri mind, and drove them towards jihad and violence. They ruined their lives. But the fact is that maulvis did not destroy Kashmir. Because of their efforts, the Kashmiri community has protected its identity. Ruined are those who are watching pornography and nude photos and are lying, not Kashmiris. Attempts were made to destroy Kashmiris' faith and belief. They were hardwired to believe their hero was Amitabh Bachchan, Muhammad Azharuddin and Sachin Tendulkar. They were told they must enjoy Lata Mangeshkar's songs and Dilip Kumar's movies. However, my Allah gave jihadi heroes and martyrs like Sajjad Afghani, Afaq, and Bilal (two JeM fidayeens) to Kashmiris, who tied bombs to their bodies.

Kashmir's destiny is martyrdom. Do not waste your time and money in elections in Kashmir. Ghazwa-i-Hind has started, and you are worried about getting your names in election registers and your posters in election campaigns. Instead of wasting 20 lakh in election campaigns, if you had bought weapons and bombs from that money and given it to Kashmir's daughters to fight against the Indian Army, you would have attained merit of religious duty. Kashmir is fragrant with jihad and martyrs, whereas, in Pakistan, Muslims are fighting among themselves. Sufi slogans and rituals are a sin. Why are we fighting amongst ourselves? Why are Muslims watching dirty films in Pakistan and asking their daughters to remove their headscarves? On one hand, the dead bodies of martyrs are coming from Kashmir with a pious fragrance. Here, in Pakistan, we are moving towards sin. In this gathering, parents of martyrs of Kashmir are present, and they are asking you—did our sons make a sacrifice for this? It is an insult to the sacrifices of our sons. Do not give your salutes to the green card and British citizenship. Do not respect the drunkards in those countries. Why are Pakistanis so desperate that they sell their land and cattle to migrate to Britain?

Continuing his motivational and indoctrinating speech, he invites people to volunteer for jihad in the following words:[45]

Oh, dear Muslims and followers of Mohammad-e-Arabi, my great martyr Bilal came to Pakistan and tore that British passport for which an average man here sells his cattle and land. Mujahideens have torn apart their American passports so that they get heaven, they get martyrdom on the pathway to jihad, and their posterity pays gratitude to them. My dear Muslims, you may fight elections, and may Allah give you success, but do not insult the legacy and glorious history of jihad and martyrs in Kashmir. I wish the thought and passion of jihad transform this base camp. Here, there should be love, respect and sympathy for the mujahideen, and people should be pious and full of virtue; they must follow Islam with dedication, emotion and commitment.

He talks about Indian Muslims and says:

The Indian Muslims who are in the Indian SFs, wearing their uniforms and guarding a Hindu temple of idols and a wine shop, are ashamed of their ancestors. If you tell them that you are a Muslim with a name like Abdullah or Umar, then ask them what makes you guard a winery or a temple, he would say that his ancestors were cowards who accepted the slavery of Hindus and made him do the shameful job of protecting a temple or guarding a wine shop.

Oh, dear people, if we do not do jihad today, our children will be forced to guard wineries; they will deviate from Islam and indulge in anti-Islamic, immoral and sinful acts of sexual promiscuity and wine drinking. Imagine, with these sins, how would we face the Prophet and ask him for the holy water of 'hauz-e-kausar', on Judgment Day? How would we show our faces to martyrs? The man from your neighbourhood, Sajjad Afghani, was severely tortured and attained martyrdom in the Indian jails. It is indeed a shame that no one is here to avenge his death. Oh, you people showing bravado in elections, if you show even 10 per cent of this effort and bravery in Kashmir, it will become a free country.

Dear friends, this India is not as brave as we think. In jail, Sajjad Afghani became a martyr; then, these people said that they would not leave anyone alive. After Sajjad, I would be killed and, over time, the graves of jihadis would be in large numbers. However, five young men showed courage [in the IC-814 hijack], and India was on its knees. Then, India said there was no question of talks with Pakistan. We said India would come running for peace talks, provided we take the jihad beyond Kashmir. Some of our boys attacked Delhi and Lucknow, and Vajpayee begged Musharraf for talks. It is just the beginning. In the future, we will conduct more attacks in the Indian hinterland, and they will be desperate for talks and willing to surrender Kashmir. When they do so, we will seek revenge for every drop of blood and the pain inflicted by India. Oh, you trader/merchant, you remember your monetary account; we remember our burnt houses and the blood of the martyrs. If Kashmir does not get freedom, let me tell you, this fire of jihad has already reached Bombay and Delhi, and it will destroy and burn everything in the Indian subcontinent. After seeing the dead bodies of our martyrs, we do not fear death. We know that life's true pleasures will arrive after martyrdom, like good food and drink. We are desperate to leave this world and go to the higher other world of Jannah, so be assured, there will not be any betrayal or compromise on the Kashmir issue from our side.

But today, I would like to ask the elders here why they do not allow their sons to join jihad. They get happy when their sons go to Britain and become a lowly barber or cobbler. They have no shame when their son in Britain drinks and indulges in un-Islamic behaviour. If he wanted to become a hairdresser, he could have done so in Pakistan. And they feel embarrassed if their younger son becomes a maulvi and joins jihad. Oh, elders, listen, if your son becomes a jihadi, it is not a shame. It is a moment when even angels celebrate and send good wishes to you. If you believe in Allah, then listen; Allah has said that jihad is not death; it is life. If you believe in the Prophet, then listen: Jihad is not death; it is life, and the Quran has confirmed it. If your son gets life in jihad, you weep and mourn, and if he goes to Britain to get that sinful life, which is a real death, you feel happy. It is so sad that our life principles have changed and become so irreligious. So, I request all of you to send your children to jihad; especially the elders, to send your children to jihad.

Will you send them or not? Send them and make them chivalrous men. Life will be glorious and worth living when they have an AK-47 in their hands, and their bullets will pierce through the chests of Hindus. They will get the ultimate satisfaction of youth when their bullets kill Hindus. Their current life is bleak. They are desperate to see a naked woman in a film when seventy-two virgins are waiting for them in Jannah. So, leave these petty pleasures and join jihad. Allah will shower his blessings at every stage. Hundreds of people from Kasmir have joined jihad. You should also join the jihad like them and seek martyrdom. Do not worry; it is not death but true life.

Jannat Talwaro ke Saye Me[46]

Translated Summary

You have not seen real Muslims. Our people who meet you are always like supplicants, shivering in front of you and genuflecting. They believe and visualize respect, status and prestige in your lifestyle, language, culture and country. They are the people who dream of progress in your culture and country. They are those Muslims who are desperate for an American green card and British citizenship. They are the people who colonize the minds of their children with Western culture by showing your movies and programmes to them on TVs and VCRs at home. Your Westerners have created a sorry and pathetic picture of Muslims as slaves and beggars based on your interaction, understanding and exposure to such people. You have seen Westernized and soft Muslims who are black slaves of the West. They wear a tie and carry briefcases. You have not seen the ones with grenades.

You have seen people who have forgotten the pious soul of Madina. You have seen the long queue of those Muslims outside your embassies who are desperate for your visas, and only focused on getting a promising career and monetary wealth in the West. Having seen them for years, you mistake them for real Muslims and come to believe that you will scare us with your bombs and fighter aircraft and rule us with your advanced weapons.

You have not seen those people who are poor, surviving on a few breadcrumbs but passionate about religion. You have not seen Yunus, a jihadist commander in Chechnya. He was from Saudi Arabia, living a rich and luxurious life that people generally crave. He abandoned his Saudi passport, which is sought after in Pakistan, and people go there to earn money. He left the riches and luxuries and came to Afghanistan to seek martyrdom. He was looking for Jannah. Allah said that Jannah is with armed jihad. You can find Jannah in AK-47s, mortars, grenades and canons. He crossed various countries and ultimately reached Chechnya for jihad. His hands were hurt. People told him to apply ointment and medicines. He refused the Western drugs and followed what the Prophet did—using honey on the wounds.

Oh, Westerners, will you be able to suppress these people who do not need your clothes and medicines, and who do not like to see your faces? Even their dogs and pigs are more beautiful and of higher morals than you. Damned are those who are in love with white Westerners. We do not consider even spitting on the faces of white people to be a respectable action. They do not deserve even to be spat upon by the Muslims. We believe those whites are full of kufr (disbelief) are worse than pigs.

7

Pathankot and Pulwama: Obsession with the Pleasures of Jannat

THE TALES OF JEM AND ITS BRUTALITY ARE INCOMPLETE without studying its two signature attacks which saw global ramifications—the Pathankot and Pulwama fidayeen attacks. The former announced the revival of JeM and the onset of its second phase with a bang. After that, a series of attacks began that culminated in the Pulwama fidayeen attack. The Pulwama attack significantly changed geopolitical dynamics in South Asia. Before that, India was restrained in its response to some of the bloodiest terror attacks—like 26/11—fearing an escalation and nuclear retaliation from Pakistan. However, when the Pulwama attack took place, India's Hindu-nationalist Narendra Modi–led government was in power. One of the main planks of the party was to implement a tough policy against Islamic extremism and Pakistan-sponsored terrorism. Hence, contrary to the expectations of some expert strategic and intelligence veterans of South Asia, who had long been the votaries of friendship and appeasement towards Pakistan, India conducted airstrikes on JeM's Balakot training camp, allegedly killing 300 of its terrorists.

In retaliation, Pakistan also sent its fighter aircraft into India—Indian pilots shot down one F-16; however, while chasing the Pakistani planes, an Indian plane went down and its pilot was arrested in Pakistan. These skirmishes raised tensions in South Asia, bringing the two nuclear-armed adversaries on the verge of a full-fledged war. However, with a flurry of diplomatic activity involving Washington DC, New Delhi and Islamabad, tensions were diffused for the time being.

Nevertheless, India had called off Pakistan's nuclear bluff and displayed a new strategic doctrine of covert operations deep inside enemy territory. In the future, if JeM conducts another fidayeen attack resulting in double-digit casualties, then a highly aggressive Indian response, not to mention an India–Pakistan war, is a real possibility.

Pathankot Attack

The details of the Pathankot fidayeen attack given below are based on the facts mentioned in the charge sheet submitted under the Unlawful Activities Prevention Act (UAPA), 1967, by the NIA.[1] The fidayeen attack took place on 2 January 2016, in which a heavily armed group of four fidayeens dressed in Indian Army fatigues attacked the Pathankot air force base with the alleged objective of targeting combat planes. The airbase falls under the Western Command of the Indian Air Force. The military operation lasted for three days—from 2 January to 5 January—when the final terrorist was declared dead. In total, eight persons, including seven security personnel, were killed, and thirty-eight others were injured. Though initially, the PoK-based United Jihad Council claimed the attack as its own, the central role of JeM emerged very soon. The four JeM terrorists—Nasir Hussain, Hafiz Abu Bakar, Umar Farooq (different from

Muhammad Umar Farooq, mastermind of the Pulwama attack), and Abdul Qayum crossed the IB on 31 December 2015, from the Pakistani side in the Simbal border post area in the Bamiyal forest area of Gurdaspur district,[2] and entered the Indian side.[3] They were all well-trained JeM cadres. They stopped a taxi driver, Ikagaar Singh, and tried to snatch his car.[4] The driver objected and fought back, and they slit his throat. However, they travelled only a few kilometres before the tyres burst. Then, the terrorists stopped the car of the SP of Dinanagar district, Salwinder Singh, who was traveling with his jeweller friend, Rajesh Verma.[5] They killed Rajesh Verma and abducted Salwinder Singh. Later, as it happened, the police was reluctant to believe in Salwinder Singh's abduction report because of his alleged involvement in unethical conduct in the past. The attackers had accidentally left a walkie-talkie set in Salwinder Singh's car, which allegedly was used for group coordination and internal communication, and to stay in touch with 'someone' at the airport, who was guiding them.[6] Reportedly, the loss of the walkie-talkie delayed the attack by twenty hours.[7] Ample evidence suggests that they used the walkie-talkie to connect with the other two members of the fidayeen team, who were to join them later. When the device was lost, they received several calls from their Pakistan-based handlers on the phone of Rajesh Verma. Likewise, the Pakistani handlers also tried to contact them through the phone of Ikagaar Singh, the taxi driver. During their conversation in the SP's car, they allegedly said that by the next morning, the whole world would know about their act—implying that their original plan might have been to launch the attack right after the infiltration. However, their plans were delayed as the lost walkie-talkie was the only way they could contact the other team of fidayeens. After Salwinder Singh managed to free himself and escape, the police authorities treated the case as an armed robbery and did not sound any alert for several hours. By that time, the terrorists entered the air force base, most likely in separate groups.[8]

According to the NIA's charge sheet, the Pathankot attack was planned in a meeting at Sialkot—a border area city in Pakistan, which is about 41 km away from Jammu.[9]

This meeting was the initiative of a JeM operative, Shahid Latif, who believed the Pathankot air base made for an 'easy' target because forests surrounded it and the base was close to the border.[10] Apart from Shahid Latif, the NIA charge sheet has named Masood Azhar, Mufti Rauf and another JeM operative, Kashif Jan, as the key masterminds of the Pathankot attack.[11] The information revealed by a witness, who was present at the Sialkot meeting and later identified Latif, suggested that Latif showed the attackers the base's Google Maps page. Based on intercepts and witness statements, the charge sheet claimed that Kashif Jan and Shahid Latif guided, equipped and launched the four fidayeens.[12] Further, the witness said that the terrorists involved in the attack were very talkative, and boastfully spoke of their ties with Masood Azhar and the inspiration provided by the latter. One of the terrorists, referred to as 'Major', was in regular communication with someone named 'Ustad ji' from Pakistan.[13] The charge sheet further detailed the conversations between various militants. The militant code named 'Major' said that he and his companions were members of a 'great organization', Jaish-e Mohammed, and that they had been imparted the true knowledge of Islam by Maulana Masood Azhar. They also allegedly repeatedly took the name of Masood Azhar and Mufti Rauf.

On their way to the air base, the terrorists attended a call from a Pakistan number (+92-3453030479), and discussed the route and plan of the attack with 'Ustad ji'. The number was 'associated with the Facebook profile of Kashif Jan with profile

ID 100004609026581'.[14] Kashif Jan's Facebook content revealed his links with JeM members and detailed conversations about the Pathankot attack between JeM members. The registration details and login ID of the Facebook account belonged to Pakistan. Some of the messages connected with the Pathankot attack found on Kashif Jan's Facebook profile are as follows:[15]

> Humza Mehboob Shakir (hereafter referred to as Humza): In Indian news channels, JeM and LeT are being named for the attack. Is the operation over?
>
> Kashif Jan: No
>
> Humza: How many brothers were there for the marriage (code name for the fidayeen attack)?
>
> Humza: Please name the brothers involved in the attack.

In another message, Kashif Jan asked one Adil Bhai to track the news updates on the Pathankot attack situation. More conversations are as follows:

> Muhammad Zia: What is the situation in Pathankot?
>
> Kashif Jan: It is over.

Another conversation:

> Kashif Jan: How did you obtain Nasir's photograph?
>
> Ahmed Zarquari: One person named Wasim had uploaded it; I just shared it.
>
> Kashif Jan: Immediately delete and ask Wasim to do the same.
>
> Ahmed Zarquari: Deleted it. Wasim has also deleted it.

Other messages from Kashif's Facebook profile:

Martyr Saddi Shah: What are the details of the damage?

Maroon Shah: Is the encounter over or continuing?

Muhammad Ashir: Mubarak, congratulations.

Humza: Send the pictures of shaheed. Indian Army is showing photos of their dead bodies.

Kashif Jan: The encounter is still continuing.

Humza: Indian media is reporting that the media persons have been given entry into the base.

The Pakistani number from which the terrorists received the call was also linked to a video messenger, IMO, whose account holder was Kashif Jan. He used an Android phone, QMobile X600, manufactured by QMobile, a Pakistan-based smartphone company.[16] The terrorists also called another Pakistani number, +92-3213132786, which was associated with Al-Rahmat Trust.[17] According to the NIA charge sheet, the number mentioned above was also on the Al-Rahmat Trust information banner on the website rangonoor.com—a JeM mouthpiece.[18] After the attack, Mufti Rauf uploaded the video, in which he took ownership of the attack, on the same website taking ownership of the attack. Further, the audio transcript was also posted on the alqalamonline.com, which, along with rangonoor.com, was linked to a Pakistani landline number. The hosting expenses of the above-mentioned websites were paid through a Pakistani credit card. In addition, the charge sheet detailed various other samples of evidence that sufficiently indicated a Pakistani link to the Pathankot attack. It included Pakistan-manufactured medicines, food packets and shoes found on the attackers. The food packets were discovered in the forest area in the vicinity of the Simbal border outpost from where the terrorists infiltrated. The four painkiller injections recovered after the attack were manufactured by Pakistani pharmaceutical companies like SAMI Pharmaceuticals in Karachi, Schazoo Pharmaceutical Laboratories in Sheikhupura, and Epharm in Karachi. Other materials included a disposable syringe manufactured by Medicare Disposable Industries in Lahore, painkillers by Pfizer Pakistan, and Chinese-made lighters.

About the presence of more than four terrorists, the charge sheet remained inconclusive. The forensic analysis of the burnt bodies and the evidence collected was not sufficient to establish the presence of more than four militants. To probe further, the NIA demanded the UAV footage of the anti-terror operation.

Pulwama Attack

Initially, the case was registered under FIR number 20/2019 dated 14 February 2019, at Police Station Awantipora, Jammu and Kashmir, under sections 302, 307 of Ranbir Panel Code (RPC)[19], Section 3 of the Explosive Substances Act, and Sections 16, 18 and 20 of UAPA 1967. This case was related to a VBIED attack at Lethpura, Pulwama, on a convoy of CRPF vehicles, on its way from Jammu to Srinagar, resulting in heavy casualties. The case was transferred to the NIA on 20 February 2019, as case number RC-02/2019/NIA/JMU and the charge sheet was submitted on 25 August 2020.

The details below are based on the NIA charge sheet prepared and submitted by the Jammu branch of NIA.[20] Rakesh Balwal, IPS, superintendent of police, NIA Jammu branch, was the investigation officer. Once the case was transferred, the charge sheet detailing the case of state (NIA) vs Masood Azhar Alvi and others was filed under Section 173 (2) of the Criminal Procedure Code (CrPC). The investigation's findings are based on the examination of the scene of the crime, examination of eyewitnesses, oral evidence, documentary evidence such as post-mortem reports of the dead, medical reports of the injured, documents related to the identity and the ownership of the Maruti Eeco car (the vehicle used in the IED attack), DNA reports, explosive examination report, disclosures by the arrested accused, mobile scrutiny reports and other digital evidence, call detail records (CDR) analysis and the testimony of the relevant witnesses.

The DNA samples of the accused, Adil Dar, were examined and matched with his father, Ghulam Hasan Dar, at the Biology Division of the Central Forensic Science Laboratory (CFSL) and the report was submitted on 3 August 2019. The explosives examination report was submitted on 14 May 2019 by CFSL. The report discovered and established the presence of nitroglycerine, RDX and ammonium nitrate in the samples collected from the attack spot. Muhammad Umar Farooq's Samsung mobile phone was examined by the CERT-In lab, Ministry of Information and Technology, Government of India.

Facts of the Case

On 14 February 2019, Adil Dar, a Kashmiri JeM suicide bomber from Kakapora in Pulwama district, rammed an explosives-laden car into a CRPF convoy on the Jammu–Srinagar National Highway 44 at Lethpura (near Awantipora) at 3.30 p.m. The vehicle used was a Maruti Eeco car with the identification number JK03C 1886. The car was laden with explosives in the form of two IEDs. Adil Dar was killed instantly in the attack, and it resulted in the deaths of forty CRPF soldiers, while eight were injured.

Early Inputs Regarding the Attack

Indian intelligence agencies had received scattered inputs regarding the planning of IED attacks in Kashmir, which they tried to analyse within the limits of their technical and analytical capabilities, and also circulate among the senior hierarchy. Though the then governor of the state, Satya Pal Malik, blamed an intelligence failure for the attack, whether it actually was this or a lack of coordination among the various intelligence agencies remains a question that needs a separate investigation. However, in the section below, I have discussed various intelligence inputs the agencies received about the Pulwama attack at length. It is based on the many interviews I held with Kashmir-based intelligence officials who worked closely on the Pulwama attack case.

In January 2018, a month before the attack, I interviewed Mustapha, a former LeT terrorist, for my research project on radicalization in Kashmir. Mustapha told me that in the last four months, he was approached by some Srinagar-based LeT OGWs who conveyed a message from handlers in the Kashmir Desk (section 26) of the ISI. He was asked to meet someone at the Pakistan High Commission in Delhi. An official with the code name 'Imran' initially met him in the Chawri Bazar area of Old Delhi, and after that, two more meetings took place at the embassy. Imran asked Mustapha to send video recordings and GPS coordinates of the main civilian and government installations, highways and military camps. During the first week of February, inputs based on technical intelligence brought out the fact that various OGWs associated not only with JeM but also with HM and LeT had been directed to arrange supplies of industrial explosive Super-90 (used in quarrying), and few among them had mentioned that this explosive was specifically for Lethpura. The recovery of detonators from an encounter site at Khrew (Pulwama district) on 26 January further corroborated these inputs. It was further confirmed by technical intelligence based on a conversation between a Kulgam-based key JeM OGW and another OGW based in Samboora, suggesting that a drum had been prepared to store explosives of the IED that was used in the Pulwama fidayeen attack, the photograph of which was shared between them. On 12 February 2019, based on specific intelligence inputs, there was an encounter at Ratnipora area of Pulwama in which a terrorist, Hilal Rather, was killed. However, other terrorists, possibly Kamran and Umar Farooq (both main masterminds of the Pulwama fidayeen attack), managed to escape. The above-mentioned inputs regarding possible IED attacks were shared among security agencies via signal GENPOL. Official brief on the intelligence inputs about the possibility of the IED attacks were sent to the agencies.

After the Attack

On 18 February 2019, inputs were shared regarding the presence of JeM operatives in the Deoband area of West UP. These operatives, namely Shah Nawaz Teli, along with another operative, Shahid, were in contact with Kamran, Usman and Khan Baba (all FTs of JeM). The UP ATS arrested the duo from Deoband and seized some arms and ammunition.[21] Shah Nawaz was also hiding a terrorist, Aqib Malik, who was evading arrest in Kashmir after his accomplice, a foreign terrorist, was killed in an encounter in the Pampore area of Awantipora. Shah Nawaz was in contact with Waleed and was operating a network of JeM terrorists in the Kulgam district of south Kashmir.

On 18 February 2019, three JeM terrorists—two foreign and one local, Hilal Naikoo—were killed in an encounter at Pinglena. On 24 February 2019, based on inputs that JeM operatives in the Kulgam region were planning another VBIED in the Kulgam–Anantnag region, an encounter followed. A local terrorist, Rashid

Sheikh of Shiganpora, Kulgam, who was being trained to carry out a suicide attack by two Pakistani terrorists, Muzammil and Waleed Bhai (aka Cheetah Bhai), was eliminated, and another major attack was averted.

Next, on 27 March 2019, two terrorists—Haris and Sahil Nazar—were killed in Memender in Shopian. Mudasir Khan, who was earlier an OGW of Mufti Waqas and played a crucial role in the Pulwama attack, was killed in Pinglish Tral, on 11 March 2019. Another group of JeM operatives responsible for the Pulwama attack was traced to the Nihama area of Pulwama, and CASO (Cordon and Search Operation) was launched, but they managed to escape. Later, on 28 March 2019, they were tracked down and killed at Suthsoo Kala, Srinagar. The terrorists killed were Muhammad Umar Farooq and Muhammad Kamran Ali, the key masterminds of Pulwama. Muhammad Umar Farooq was the son of Ibrahim Athar, Masood Azhar's elder brother and the mastermind of the IC-814 hijacking (1999).

Key evidence regarding the Pulwama attack was gathered from a mobile device found on Umar Farooq, handed over to the NIA. Munna Bihari, a key JeM operative who was also involved in the Banihal IED attack, was killed on 27 July 2019, at Bonpora in Shopian.

Details of the prime accused named in the charge sheet:

1) Masood Azhar Alvi aka Masood Azhar
   Occupation: Chief of JeM
   Religion: Islam
   Age: 52 years
   Nationality: Pakistani
   Status: Absconding

Current Address: Markaz-Usman-o-Ali, Bahawalpur-Karachi Road, Bahawalpur, Pakistan
Permanent Address: Kausar Colony, Bahawalpur, Pakistan

2) Rauf Azgar Alvi aka Abdul Rauf Azgar (Masood Azhar's brother)
Occupation: Operational head of JeM/Deputy chief of JeM
Religion: Islam
Age: 47 years
Nationality: Pakistani
Status: Absconding
Address: Kausar Colony, Bahawalpur

3) Mohiuddin Aurangzeb Alamgir alias Ammar Alvi, aka Chota Masood, aka Chacha (Masood's brother)
Occupation: Terrorist leader of JeM
Religion: Islam
Age: 45
Nationality: Pakistani
Status: Absconding
Address: Bahawalpur, Pakistan

4) Shakir Bashir aka Abu Huzaifah, S/O Bashir Ahmad Magray
Occupation: Terror associate of JeM
Religion: Islam
Age: 24 years
Nationality: Indian

Status: Arrested on 28 February 2020. Presently in judicial custody
Address: Hajibal Lalhar, Tehsil Kakapora, District Pulwama, J&K

5) Insha Jan aka Insha Tariq, D/O Peer Tariq Ahmed Shah
Occupation: Terror associate of JeM
Religion: Islam
Age: 22 years
Nationality: Indian
Status: Arrested on 3 March 2020, presently in judicial custody
Address: Hakripura, Tehsil Kakapora, District Pulwama, J&K

6) Peer Tariq Ahmed Shah, S/O Muhammad Maqbool Shah
Occupation: Terror associate of JeM
Religion: Islam
Age: 53 years
Nationality: Indian
Status: Arrested on 3 March 2020, presently in judicial custody
Address: Hakripura, Tehsil Kakapora, District Pulwama, J&K

7) Waiz ul Islam aka Waiz Bola, S/O Ghulam Haidar Ghanai
Occupation: Terror associate of JeM
Religion: Islam

Age: 20 years
Nationality: Indian
Status: Arrested on 6 March 2020, presently in judicial custody
Address: Bagh-e-Mahtab, Srinagar District, J&K

8) Mohammad Abbas Rather, S/O Mohammad Ramzan Rather
Occupation: Terror associate of JeM
Religion: Islam
Age: 31 years
Nationality: Indian
Status: Arrested on 6 March 2020, presently in judicial custody
Address: Hakripura, Tehsil Kakapora, District Pulwama, J&K

9) Bilal Ahmed Kuchay, S/O Ghulam Ahmed Kuchay
Occupation: Terror associate of JeM
Religion: Islam
Age: 28 years
Nationality: Indian
Status: Arrested on 5 July 2020, presently in judicial custody
Address: Hajibal, Tehsil Lalhar, District Pulwama, J&K

10) Mohammad Iqbal Rathar, S/O Abdul Khaliq Rathar
Occupation: Terror associate of JeM
Religion: Islam

Age: 25 years
Nationality: Indian
Status: Arrested on 5 July 2020, presently in judicial custody
Address: Futlipura, Tehsil Charar-e-Sharif, District Budgam, J&K

11) Mohammad Ismail Alvi aka Lamboo, aka Adnan, aka Saifullah
Occupation: Terror commander of JeM
Religion: Islam
Age: 25 years
Nationality: Pakistani
Status: Killed
Address: Kausar Colony, Bahawalpur, Pakistan

12) Samir Ahmed Dar, aka Hamza/Hanzala Jihadi, S/O Mohammad Subhan Dar
Occupation: Terror commander of JeM
Religion: Islam
Age: 22 years
Nationality: Indian
Status: Killed
Address: Gundibagh, Tehsil Kakapora, District Pulwama, J&K

13) Ashaq Ahmed Nengroo, S/O Ghulam Ahmed Nengroo
Occupation: Terror associate of JeM
Religion: Islam
Age: 33 years

Nationality: Indian
Status: Absconding
Address (permanent): Hanjin Bala, Tehsil Rajpora, District Pulwama, J&K
Address (present): Pakistan

14) Adil Ahmed Dar aka Waqas Commando, S/O Ghulam Hasan Dar
Occupation: Suicide bomber of JeM
Nationality: Indian
Age: 21 years
Religion: Islam
Status: Killed in the Pulwama fidayeen attack
Address (permanent): Gundibagh, Tehsil Kakapora, District Pulwama, J&K

15) Muhammad Umar Farooq aka Idrees Bhai, S/O Ibrahim Athar
Occupation: Terror commander of JeM
Religion: Islam
Age: 24 years
Nationality: Pakistani
Status: Killed
Address: 108/1260-BVI, Kausar Colony, Bahawalpur, Pakistan

16) Mohammad Kamran Ali aka Mohammad Bhai, aka Ali Bhai
Occupation: Terror associate of JeM
Religion: Islam

Age: 25 years
Nationality: Pakistani
Status: Killed
Address: Pakistan

17) Sajjad Ahmed Bhatt aka Sajjad Maqbool, aka Aarzoo, S/O Muhammad Maqbool Bhatt
Occupation: Terror associate of JeM
Religion: Islam
Age: 19 years
Nationality: Indian
Status: Killed in encounter
Address: Marhama, Tehsil Bijbehera, District Anantnag, J&K

18) Mudasir Ahmed Khan aka MD, S/O Farooq Ahmed Khan
Occupation: Terrorist of JeM
Religion: Islam
Age: 24
Nationality: Indian
Status: Killed in encounter
Address (permanent): Midoora, Awantipora, Pulwama, J&K

19) Qari Yasir aka Fauji Bhai, aka Ghazi
Occupation: Terror commander of JeM
Religion: Islam
Age: Unknown
Nationality: Pakistani
Status: Killed

Address: Pakistan

20) Ishfaq Ahmad Bhatt, S/O Late Abdul Majid Bhatt
Occupation: Suspected terror associate of JeM
Religion: Islam
Age: Unknown
Nationality: Indian
Status: Included in the list of accused persons, but not charge-sheeted
Address: Marhama, Anantnag

Investigation Findings

The NIA's investigation established that the Pulwama fidayeen attack was 'conspired, planned, facilitated and executed'[22] by the operatives of Jaish-e-Mohammed. JeM's Pakistan-based terrorist leaders, commanders, handlers, and the terrorists and terror associates in Kashmir hatched a deep-rooted conspiracy that culminated in this VBIED attack. The Pulwama attack amounted to waging war against the Indian state, threatening its integrity, unity and sovereignty by conspiring, supporting, facilitating and implementing this atrocious terrorist attack. Also, all the accused persons listed above were involved in 'training, recruiting, sending, receiving, transporting, concealing, harbouring, supporting, provoking, exhorting and [...] extending all physical and communicational logistics'[23] to active terrorists of JeM to commit terror acts against the security forces. Even after the attack, the Pakistan-based terrorist commanders and handlers, in association with the Kashmir-based JeM commanders, continued to conspire to launch massive attacks against the Indian state.

The NIA charge sheet also mentions that JeM was trying to 'give an indigenous colour'[24] to its terror operations by recruiting local Kashmiri boys as fidayeen. For example, the organization recruited two local terrorists—Fardeen Ahmed Khandey and Manzoor Ahmed Baba, along with a Pakistani terrorist, in the fidayeen attack on the CRPF group centre in Lethpura on 30 December 2017. Further, the charge sheet suggests that the group's association with Al Qaeda, Haqqanis and the Taliban has enabled it to orchestrate IED-based attacks in Kashmir. The VBIED attack near the Indian embassy in Kabul was similar in execution style and modus operandi to the Pulwama attack, and 'had the imprints of Al Qaeda, Haqqani Network, Taliban and JeM elements present in Afghanistan and Pakistan.'[25]

Further, the findings reveal that Muhammad Umar Farooq, the key mastermind, was trained in assembling IEDs, including VBIEDs, at the Sangin terror training camp in Afghanistan. His skills played a crucial role in Pulwama VBIED assembling. Thus, the attack was an outcome of the association between the jihadi groups based in the Af-Pak region and JeM's leadership operating out of Pakistan.

The terror associates who actively assisted JeM commanders in the Pulwama attack were part of various modules of the organization. They remained covert in their terror-supporting activities related to the Pulwama conspiracy and did not formally join or announce their allegiance to JeM. Interestingly, it is also a strategy of the group to keep its OGWs hidden for as long as possible. Once they are exposed, they are asked to join the group as active militants and continue. In one of the voice notes recovered from Umar Farooq's phone, you can hear him praising Shakir Bashir, saying that he preferred keeping him hidden and would activate him if he was exposed.[26] These different modules acted across various domains. Entrusted with different kinds of responsibilities, they worked in silos, a common practice among JeM terrorists and OGWs. The movement of Muhammad Umar

Farooq and four other Pakistani JeM terrorists from the Jammu region to the Valley immediately after their infiltration into Indian territory in April 2018 was arranged by the 'transportation module' consisting of Mohammad Iqbal Rathar and Ashaq Ahmed Nengroo. The 'logistics module' included Insha Jan, Peer Tariq Ahmed Shah, Mohammed Abbas Rather and Bilal Ahmed Kuchay. They helped in providing shelter, harbour and food, and facilitating the terrorist movement in the Valley. The 'core group', comprising Shakir Bashir, Sajjad Ahmed Bhatt, Waizul Islam and others, arranged the vehicle for the attack. Umar Farooq chose Shakir Bashir, a local, despite his distrust for locals, because of Shakir's passionate dedication to the cause of jihad. He adhered to the fundamentalist Ahl-i-Hadith Islam and was in awe of the mujahideens.[27] Shakir showed sincere dedication and loyalty, and refused to accept money for work. Over time, he became the most trusted OGW of Umar Farooq, who began referring to him as his 'Afzal Guru'.[28] The other JeM FT commanders, like Saifullah, also trusted Shakir Bashir. However, Umar Farooq did not entirely trust Kuchay and found him weak in his commitment to religion due to his overt discomfort in hosting Umar Farooq and his colleagues at his home.[29] The core group was also responsible for ordering, collecting and storing explosives and related material, and surveilling the movement of security forces on the national highway.

The Plot Begins

According to the NIA investigation, the Pulwama conspiracy began with the sending of Muhammad Umar Farooq to Afghanistan to train him in explosives, including assembling and detonating IEDs and VBIEDs. Umar Farooq trained at Sangin camp in the Helmand province in September 2016.

Once his rigorous programme ended, he returned to assist JeM's leadership by training other militants and by facilitating the infiltration of Pakistani JeM terrorists into Indian territory via the IB. Masood Azhar, Mufti Rauf and Ammar Alvi decided to send Umar Farooq to Kashmir with the goal of putting to use his skills acquired in Afghanistan and instructed him to commit terror attacks in Kashmir. Umar, with the support and help of Pakistan Rangers and the JeM leadership, illegally infiltrated into Indian territory through the IB at the Hiranagar sector on the night of 13 April. Taking a riverine route, Umar Farooq, along with four other terrorists, reached National Highway 44 near the Bein bridge on the Pathankot–Jammu highway in the early hours of 14 April 2018. Afterwards, the Ashaq Ahmed Nengroo–led transportation module, assisted by Mohammad Iqbal Rathar, arranged their movement into the Valley in a truck with the registration number JK03G 1621. Mohammad Iqbal Rathar piloted the truck carrying the terrorists in his Fiat Punto car with the registration number JK01Q 4551 from Jammu to Kashmir on 14 and 15 April 2018. After reaching the Valley on the morning of 15 April 2018, Umar Farooq stayed at the home of Ashaq Ahmed Nengroo. Thereafter, he took over the reins of JeM's operations in Kashmir. With the help of Bilal Ahmed Kuchay and Mohammad Abbas Rather, Umar Farooq gained a strong foothold in the Valley. He took over as JeM commander in the Pulwama district. He became associated with other prominent JeM commanders like Mohammad Kamran Ali, Qari Yasir, Mudasir Khan, Samir Ahmed Dar, Adil Ahmed Dar, Usman Haider and later with Mohammad Ismail, aka Saifullah, and others. Saifullah infiltrated and arrived in the Kashmir Valley after Umar Farooq.

Gradually, Umar Farooq started getting active help to hatch the Pulwama conspiracy from accused associates like

Mohammad Abbas Rather, Shakir Bashir, Insha Jan, Peer Tariq Ahmed Shah, Bilal Ahmed Kuchay and others, who helped him and other JeM terrorists in arranging shelter and logistics. Saifullah brought Waiz ul Islam into the JeM fold. Waiz assisted in arranging logistics and procuring incriminating items for JeM terrorists from online shopping portals like Amazon.

VBIED Conspiracy

On 30 October 2018, Masood Azhar's other nephew and Umar Farooq's younger brother, Usman Haider Ibrahim, were killed in an encounter with SFs at Tral. An angry Masood Azhar released an audio clip to pay his condolences. The provocative audio message exhorted the Kashmiri youth to choose the path of martyrdom—shahadat. Adil Ahmed Dar listened to this audio message on Umar Farooq's phone. Inspired by Masood's audio message, Adil Ahmed Dar volunteered as fidayeen in a suicide bombing mission for JeM. This, in effect, kickstarted the real execution part of the conspiracy, which ultimately resulted in the Pulwama fidayeen attack on 14 February 2019.

Adil Ahmed Dar from the Gundibagh area of Pulwama, was a labourer. He joined JeM in March 2018. His father, Ghulam Hassan Dar, filed a missing report at the Kakapora police station for his son on 23 March 2018. This wasn't the first time Adil had been exposed to terrorism—his cousin Manzoor Ahmed Dar, an LeT cadre, was killed by SFs in June 2016. Adil was also inspired by his neighbour Samir Ahmed Dar, who became an active cadre with JeM. From May–June 2018, Adil was continuously in the company of JeM commanders like Umar Farooq, Samir Ahmed Dar and Mohammad Kamran Ali. In a parallel development, JeM commander in the Awantipora–Tral belt, Qari Yasir, had motivated and trained another local JeM cadre, Yawar Ahmed

Nazar, to volunteer for the suicide mission in case Adil Dar failed to execute the VBIED attack.

Procurement of the Explosives and Other Materials for the Attack

The magnitude and the intensity of the blast, were so severe that it left the bus, which took the impact of the blast entirely mangled and made an enormous crater on the highway. CFSL examined the sample exhibits collected from the blast site and the adjacent areas, and prepared the explosives examination report. It found the presence of RDX, nitroglycerine and ammonium nitrate in the sample exhibits.

The investigation revealed that the source of nitroglycerine in the sample exhibits was gelatin sticks. They are used for rock-blasting in mining areas and road construction activities, and are abundantly available in Kashmir. Mudasir Khan collected these gelatin sticks, and Shakir Bashir stocked them at his house. Likewise, calcium and ammonium nitrate, readily available from fertilizer shops, were procured by Shakir Bashir from the Kakapora market and kept at his house. The RDX was brought from Pakistan by the JeM terrorists who had infiltrated into India.

Shakir Bashir used his Alto car bearing registration number JK13B 3196 for collecting explosive material, including RDX and aluminium powder. After that, he stockpiled them on the roof of his house. The blue drum already had explosives, so they also brought a small orange can from Parigam, weighing about 30-40 kg.

On the instructions of Umar Farooq, Shakir Bashir travelled to Srinagar on the morning of 4 February 2019, in his Maruti Alto car and bought two red-coloured Exide batteries from a shop in Karan Nagar and two digital multimeters from a street vendor in Gowkadal. Further, on the instructions of Saifullah another terror associate, Waizul Islam, who used to order materials on online shopping portal Amazon for the JeM terrorists, ordered 4 kgs of aluminium powder from Amazon India and delivered it to Saifullah. This aluminium powder was collected by Shakir Bashir and stocked with other explosive materials. Aluminium powder was used as one of the ingredients and mixed with calcium ammonium nitrate during the preparation of the two IEDs.

Target Reconnaissance and the Blast Site

Shakir Bashir's father owned a timber shop adjacent to National Highway 44 on an approach road at Lethpura. The shop's proximity to NH44 enabled him to keep a continuous watch on the road, monitoring the movement of the convoys of security forces. He sent recorded videos of these movements and vital installations along the national highway to Muhammad Umar Farooq using WhatsApp. He also sent pictures, videos and audio notes of the reconnaissance and the convoy traffic on the national highway in and around what would become the blast site. He played a crucial role in identifying the location where the blast would take place, in proximity to the headquarters of 110 Battalion of CRPF at Lethpura. The geographical features of the place suited a VBIED attack as there was a sharp rise in gradient and a bend on the highway, which caused the convoy to slow down.

The Car Used in the VBIED Attack

Umar Farooq instructed Sajjad Ahmed Bhatt, another terror associate of JeM from Marhama, Anantnag, to procure a car that could be used in the VBIED attack. Sajjad, a student of Darul Uloom, Shopian, was motivated by JeM's ideology and supported terrorist activities. He checked many cars and finally zeroed in on a blue Maruti EECO car bearing registration number JK03C 1886. Sajjad Ahmed Bhatt was also assisted by his cousin Danish Ahmed Lone in purchasing the car. The latter purchased it from a Mudasir Abdullah of Bijbehera, Anantnag, for INR 1,70,000 and sold it to Sajjad Ahmed Bhatt for INR 1,85,000. This car was selected for two reasons—first, it did not have a middle-row seat, leaving ample space to assemble explosive material; second, the car was still in the name of its original owner, Jalil Ahmed Haqqani, as it was never transferred in official records to the subsequent owners, thus mitigating the risk of detection. Shakir Bashir brought this Maruti Eeco from Naman, Pulwama, to his house in the last week of January 2019 and parked it in the front yard of his home. He erased the engine and the chassis number of the Eeco car with an iron filer and sent the video to Umar Farooq.

Viral Video Clip of Adil Dar

Immediately after the attack, JeM released a propaganda video, containing a clip of Adil Ahmed Dar, claiming credit for the suicide attack. The video, released to motivate and recruit more Kashmiri youth to JeM, went viral. It was shot in the house of Peer Tariq Ahmed Shah and Insha Jan through 28 and 29 January. In the video, Adil Dar acted and Samir Ahmed Dar gave the voice-over. Notably, Samir Ahmed Dar had already practiced the script in December 2018. It took many rehearsals to record the clip—the raw versions show him sitting in front of a black almirah with a red border. The final video also features a JeM flag in the background. Later, Insha Jan identified this almirah during a pointing-out exercise in one of the rooms in her house in Hakripura. After recording this video clip, it was sent to JeM leadership in Pakistan through WhatsApp for editing. Umar

Farooq received it in its final form on 4 February 2019, with all the special effects added. It was released immediately after the attack on 14 February 2019. The two-day practice and the final recording of the video happened in the presence and knowledge of Peer Tariq Ahmed Shah and Insha Jan.

Preparation of the Two IEDs

In the third week of January 2019, Umar Farooq, Samir Ahmed Dar, and Adil Ahmed Dar arrived at the house of Peer Tariq Ahmed Shah and Insha Jan with arms and ammunition. They used the house as a hideout frequently. They stayed there until the evening of 5 February 2019. Afterwards, they went to Shakir Bashir's house in his Maruti Alto car. On the night of 5 February 2019, Umar Farooq, Adil Dar, Samir Ahmed Dar and Shakir Bashir started assembling the IEDs in the blue drum and the orange-coloured can. They prepared the two IEDs using the RDX, calcium, ammonium nitrate, aluminium powder, gelatin sticks and the detonators already collected by Shakir Bashir. That very night, they placed the two IEDs in the Maruti Eeco car and joined the wires with a switch near the steering wheel. All this while, Umar Farooq continuously received directions on encrypted communication applications from the Pakistan-based JeM leadership.

Further, the NIA investigation revealed that the original plan was to carry out the VBIED attack on 6 February 2019, at an appropriate time to be decided after carefully studying the convoy movement of security forces on the national highway near Lethpura. However, due to heavy snowfall on the night of 5–6 February, vehicular traffic on the national highway was suspended. Umar Farooq, Samir Ahmed Dar and Adil Ahmed Dar stayed on at Shakir Bashir's home, waiting for the highway to reopen. All this while the Maruti Eeco car—laden with about

200 kgs of explosives, remained parked in the front yard of Shakir Bashir's house.

The IED Attack

On the afternoon of 14 February 2019, Shakir Bashir saw from his shop that the Road Opening Party (ROP) was being deployed on National Highway 44 at Lethpura. He communicated this to Umar Farooq. He also told him that the convoy of security vehicles might be coming from Jammu. Shakir Bashir went to his house after that and, around 3 p.m., Umar Farooq told Adil Ahmed Dar and Shakir Bashir to start immediately in the Maruti Eeco car. Adil Ahmed Dar took a pistol with him in case the IED did not detonate. Shakir Bashir drove the Maruti Eeco car from his house in Hajibal to the Hajibal Bridge on the Jhelum River. After that, Adil Ahmed Dar took the steering wheel of the vehicle laden with explosives. They halted on the link road adjacent to the national highway for about five to ten minutes. As soon as they saw the convoy of security vehicles coming from Jammu, Adil Ahmed Dar started the car and dropped off Shakir Bashir on a link road to the national highway. He started driving towards the Srinagar side of the national highway and, after a minute or two, rammed the Maruti Eeco car into a CRPF bus of the 76th Battalion and detonated the IEDs, causing a huge explosion. It resulted in the complete destruction of the bus; all thirty-nine soldiers in the bus were killed, while eight others in the adjacent buses got injured. One CRPF personnel on ROP (Road Opening Party) duty—ASI Mohan Lal—was also killed in the attack.

Events after the Attack

Umar Farooq circulated the propaganda video on social media and made it viral with the help of his terror associates. He and

Samir Ahmed Dar left the house of Shakir Bashir after the IED attack and went to other hideouts. Further, the investigation revealed that Umar Farooq was instructed by JeM leader Mufti Rauf and others based in Pakistan to delete all his chat history and destroy his Samsung mobile. Umar Farooq and other JeM terrorists involved in this case visited the house of Peer Tariq Ahmed Shah and Insha Jan on 19 February 2019, and kept visiting till late March 2019. Umar Farooq continued his contact with Shakir Bashir as JeM was planning another fidayeen attack. Shakir Bashir once again began surveilling the deployment and movement of SFs. He was asked to be the fidayeen for the next attack, but he wanted to become an active terrorist first and then become a suicide bomber. Waizul Islam continued ordering incriminating material for JeM terrorists on his Amazon account and delivered the same to them. Further, as the NIA investigations unearthed the details of the car used in the VBIED attack, the JeM leadership in Pakistan decided that Sajjad Ahmed Bhatt, who had arranged the car used in the attack, should join the ranks of active terrorists to pre-empt the unveiling of the conspiracy by him.

Continuing the criminal conspiracy to attack security forces, in March 2019, the JeM terrorists and terror associates in the Valley, led by Umar Farooq, planned another VBIED fidayeen attack in collaboration with Mohammad Kamran Ali, Saifullah, Samir Ahmed Dar, Qari Yasir, Shakir Bashir, Waizul Islam and others. Insha Jan, Peer Tariq Ahmed Shah and others continued harbouring and providing shelter to JeM terrorists. The Pakistan-based leadership of JeM had initially communicated to Umar Farooq and other JeM terrorists to delay the attack for some time due to the fierce reaction by Indian security forces after the Pulwama attack. For their second attack, the JeM terrorists had collected the explosives, the vehicle and other materials.

The leadership in the Valley had selected the place of attack and also completed a survey of the route to be taken by the suicide bomber from the hideout on the national highway, with the help of Shakir Bashir and others.

JeM Claims the Attack

Immediately after the attack, Tanveer-ul-Ahad, editor of the Global News Service (GNS), received a WhatsApp call, reportedly from JeM spokesperson Mohammad Hussain. In that conversation, Mohammad Hussain claimed responsibility for the fidayeen attack on the CRPF convoy at Lethpura. Also, immediately after the attack, a video clip featuring the suicide bomber Adil Ahmed Dar, in which JeM owned up to the attack, went viral on social media through WhatsApp. To verify JeM's claims of Adil Ahmed Dar being the suicide attacker, his father Ghulam Hassan Dar's blood sample was collected after obtaining his permission to match it with the DNA profile collected from the tissue and flesh material retrieved from the vehicle remains. The examination done by CFSL established that the samples matched and Adil Dar was the fidayeen in the Pulwama attack.

A team of experts from Maruti Suzuki India Ltd examined the vehicle's remains. Based on studying its crankshaft, they confirmed that the car used was a Maruti Eeco van and that the crankshaft was manufactured on 22 January 2011, and assembled in the Maruti Eeco vehicle on 25 January 2011. According to its records, this Maruti Eeco vehicle was sold to Peaks Auto Pvt. Ltd in Srinagar. Also, during an extensive search of the blast site and its adjoining areas up to the bank of the Jhelum River, the NIA team found one twisted steel key of a vehicle with a number inscribed on it. The key belonged to the Maruti Eeco car, which was registered in the name of Jalil Ahmed Haqqani of Anantnag, in the office of the assistant road transport officer, Anantnag. The chain of possession of this Maruti Eeco car was established up to the day of the execution of the attack. The last owner was Sajjad Ahmed Bhatt of Marhama, Anantnag. Thus, the vehicle used in the VBIED attack was identified as well.

The explosives examination report of CFSL stating the use of explosives based on nitroglycerine, RDX and ammonium nitrate was corroborated by the testimony of one of the IED makers, Shakir Bashir, and the digital evidence retrieved from the mobile phone of Muhammad Umar Farooq.

Encounter of the Key Mastermind Umar Farooq and the Recovery of His Phone

During the first few days of the investigation, after the case was transferred to the NIA on 20 February 2019, despite the agency's best efforts, the results were discouraging as the team could not find any concrete links and substantial evidence. To probe deeper, the NIA team began following the encounters of JeM terrorists in the Valley and the evidence recovered from the encounter sites. During this exercise, the NIA team came to know about the encounter of FTs Umar Farooq and Kamran at Suthsoo Kala, Nowgam in Srinagar on 29 March 2019. Samir Ahmed Dar, who was with them at the time of the encounter, escaped. After the encounter, the investigation officer recovered a mobile phone in a semi-burnt state. According to the charge sheet:[30]

> ... [T]he copy of the extracted data from the seized mobile phone in the above case was collected in the instant case. The scrutiny of the data revealed that the phone belongs to slain terrorist Mohd Umar Farooq. During the further scrutiny of the data, many images, videos, and some voice notes related to the Pulwama case were recovered from the extracted

data. The possession of the mobile phone was taken from the Investigating officer on the order of the Hon'ble Court [sic].

A closer scrutiny of the Pulwama fidayeen attack and its investigation suggests that the data recovered from the mobile phone played an instrumental role in untying the knots of the case. Before that, the NIA was quite clueless—making desperate attempts to establish the necessary connections in the conspiracy. If not for the recovery of the phone, the NIA would not have been able to prove the role of Pakistan with such concrete and irrefutable evidence.[31] Also, the US reportedly helped retrieve the WhatsApp conversations, videos, audio clips and other data from the phone.

Financing the Pulwama Attack

Examination of the digital evidence from Umar Farooq's phone revealed that a total expenditure of INR 5,70,000 was made to finance the Pulwama attack. The money was deposited in to Umar Farooq's accounts in the Pakistan-based Allied Bank and Meezan Bank in the run-up to the attack. While Umar Farooq was in Kashmir, he received PKR 10,43,280 in his bank accounts between 8 January 2019 and 7 February 2019, to meet the expenses incurred on procuring the explosive materials, the car and other attack-related preparations.

A Brief Overview of the Roles Played by Each of the Accused

Masood Azhar

He claimed responsibility for the attack. His audio tape after his nephew Usman Haider's encounter in Kashmir motivated Adil Dar to volunteer as a suicide bomber. In the audio, he encouraged all Kashmiris to choose the path of martyrdom.

The audio message was recovered from Umar Farooq's phone. His role was also proved when JeM's spokesperson took credit for the attack in a telephonic conversation with the editor of the GNS news agency. Also, JeM mouthpieces *Al Qalam* and *Khabarnama Rang-o-Noor* published articles and news items in the third week of February, eulogizing and congratulating Adil Dar. Allegedly, Masood Azhar also wrote an obituary for Adil Dar in *Rang-o-noor*. UN reports on the presence of JeM camps and terrorists in Pakistan and Afghanistan also bring forth his involvement in the Pulwama attack. Besides, a large number of his videos, audio messages and hate speeches recovered from Umar Farooq's mobile phone also provide incriminating evidence of his involvement. In his speech on Kashmir Solidarity Day on 5 February 2019, he said, 'If you google a girl from Pulwama, you will notice the Jaish flag fluttering atop her house with my picture.'[32] Though this statement does not provide conclusive evidence that he knew about the forthcoming Pulwama attack, it indicates that he had a clue, which he was conveying to his audience indirectly.

Mufti Rauf Azgar

Being JeM's deputy chief, he, along with Masood Azhar, was the principal scriptwriter of the Pulwama conspiracy. He was in regular communication with Umar Farooq before and after the attack. As a part of the larger conspiracy, he launched Kamran and Umar Farooq in the Valley to orchestrate attacks on Indian SFs. Also, he financed the attack by transferring the money to Umar Farooq. Several of his images, audio and video messages were recovered from Umar Farooq's phone. Also, he was mentioned in several WhatsApp voice notes exchanged between Umar Farooq, Kamran and Saifullah about the finances of the Pulwama attack and preparations for a future IED attack.

In many of Mufti Rauf's voice notes with Umar Farooq, he enquired about the strikes of JeM terrorists on Indian SFs and the movement of Indian fighter jets in the Kashmir Valley.

Ammar Alvi

JeM's top-ranking leader and younger brother of Masood is held responsible for sending Umar Farooq to Afghanistan for training in explosives and IEDs. He also launched Umar Farooq into India, along with Masood and Mufti Rauf. Besides, he visited several JeM training camps and was in regular touch with Umar Farooq through WhatsApp calls and social media platforms after the Pulwama attack. His voice notes and text messages have been retrieved from Umar Farooq's phone. Also, he gave a provocative speech on 27 February 2019, after the Balakot airstrikes.

Shakir Bashir Aka Abu Huzaifah

Shakir was introduced to JeM terrorists Umar Farooq and Adil Ahmed Dar by Bilal Ahmed Kuchay of Pulwama in mid June 2018. After that, he sheltered Umar Farooq, Adil Ahmed Dar and Samir Ahmed Dar in his house. From December 2018 onwards, he reconnoitred the traffic movement of SFs on the Jammu–Srinagar highway. Also, he kept a continuous vigil on the movement of SFs and the intelligence agents along the highway area from his shop, and identified the place with minimum civilian movement. In addition to moving arms, ammunition and money for JeM terrorists, he also acted as a courier in procuring and bringing chemicals used in making the IEDs and stocked the material at his house. Under Umar Farooq's instruction, in January 2019, he arranged for a blue-coloured Maruti Eeco vehicle, which did not have a middle seat and had a switch near the steering wheel. Shakir Bashir parked the car in the front courtyard of his house. In the first week of February 2019, he removed the engine and chassis numbers with an iron filer. He also purchased two Exide batteries and two digital multimeters for the planned attack. On 5 February, he picked up Umar Farooq, Adil Ahmed Dar and Samir Ahmed Dar from Hakripora, and they assembled the two IEDs to target the convoy of security forces at a pre-scheduled time.

Further, he also assisted the three JeM terrorists in fitting the two IEDs in the Maruti Eeco car. The explosive-laden vehicle remained parked in the courtyard of his house. After he saw the Road Opening Party on the highway on 14 February 2019, he alerted Umar Farooq. Following that, he drove Adil Ahmed Dar to the attack site, where he left, leaving Adil Dar with the explosives-laden vehicle. In WhatsApp exchanges with his JeM handler in Pakistan, Abu Talha, Umar Farooq compared his contribution to that of Afzal Guru.

Insha Jan Aka Insha Tariq

Insha and her father, Peer Tariq Ahmed Shah, were introduced to JeM militants by their neighbour, Mohammad Abbas Rather, in May 2018. Umar Farooq and Kamran came to her house in June 2018. After that, they regularly visited her home, and she was involved in providing shelter, logistics and food to them. JeM militants Umar Farooq, Kamran, Adil Dar and Samir Ahmed Dar stayed in her house, with arms and ammunition, for many days. Insha Jan was also in a relationship with Umar Farooq. Adil Dar's video clip, which went viral after the Pulwama attack, was recorded at her house in her presence between 28–29 January 2019. She had many WhatsApp calls and messages with Umar Farooq on his Pakistani number.

Peer Tariq Ahmed Shah

He was sympathetic towards terrorists because his cousin Manzoor Ahmad Shah of Litter, Pulwama, a militant of the Al-Jihad group, and his nephew Muhammad Altaf Mir of

Awantipora, Pulwama, an LeT terrorist, were killed by SFs in different encounters. Besides providing shelter and food to JeM militants in his house, on the directions of Samir Ahmed Dar, he collected a polythene bag containing three pairs of Indian Army–patterned camouflage uniforms and green belts from a person outside the Falah-e-Millat school at Singu Narbal, Pulwama. Samir Ahmed Dar and Umar Farooq proceeded to wear the uniforms.

He was regularly communicating with Umar Farooq on WhatsApp. He was also present when Adil Dar's video clip was recorded. Three to four days after the Pulwama attack, Umar Farooq, Kamran and Samir Ahmed Dar visited his house to congratulate and thank him for providing material and moral support to them during the attack.

Waiz-ul-Islam

In August 2018, he sheltered three JeM terrorists, including Saifullah and Samir Ahmed Dar, at one of his friend's residences. The terrorists gave him a virtual number starting with +1, along with an OTP to activate that number for WhatsApp communication. He was also asked to open an online shopping account on Amazon. After that, Saifullah started sending him links to procure items such as apple lighters, hiking shoes, cargo pants, head-mounted torches, LED torches, aluminium powder, big knives, laser pointers and mobile covers. He paid either by cash-on-delivery or by using his friend, Inayat Malik's[33] debit card. In January 2019, he received 1kg of aluminium powder, followed by 3 kgs a few weeks later. This powder was used to make the IED for the attack. Most often, he delivered these materials to JeM militants on the Nowgam bypass near Pulwama. Even after the attack, he continued working for JeM. He maintained regular communication with Umar Farooq, as proved by his voice notes, texts and calls from a virtual number to Umar Farooq's mobile.

Bilal Ahmed Kuchay

In addition to providing shelter to the militants, he bought two Samsung mobiles from Gulshan Electronics Mobile Shop in Khanda, Budgam, in August 2018. Umar Farooq exclusively used one of these mobiles for all kinds of communication about the planning, conspiracy and execution of this attack.

Mohammad Iqbal Rathar

He was crucial in Umar Farooq's infiltration into India through the Hiranagar sector of Jammu; moreover, he aided his travel to the Valley on 14–15 April 2018. He was aided by Ashaq Ahmed Nengroo, who is absconding. On Ashaq Ahmed Nengroo's instructions, he came to Jammu in his Fiat Punto car, with the registration number JK01Q 4551 to help and facilitate the movement of five freshly infiltrated JeM terrorists on 13 April 2018. Ashaq Ahmed Nengroo had come in his truck bearing the registration number JK03G 1621. Mohammad Iqbal Rathar then piloted this truck. On 15 April 2018, in the early morning, they reached the house of Ashaq Ahmed Nengroo at Rajpora, Pulwama.

Mudasir Ahmed Khan

He was an active militant of JeM working under the leadership of Qari Yasir in south Kashmir's Tral region. He was also a main accused in the Lethpura CRPF Group Centre attack of October 2018. As a co-conspirator and planner of the Pulwama attack, he maintained regular contact with Umar Farooq. He provided the gelatin sticks used in the manufacturing of the two IEDs that were later fitted in the Eeco car for this attack. SFs killed him in Pinglena village on 10 March 2019.

Qari Yasir

He was a Pakistani terrorist and a JeM commander in the Awantipora–Tral area at the time of the Pulwama attack. As a co-conspirator of the attack, he had even identified another local Kashmiri JeM terrorist as a fidayeen—Yawar Ahmed Najar—as a backup in case Adil Ahmed Dar refused to do the IED attack. His voice notes from Umar Farooq's phone indicate that he was already in an advanced stage of planning another IED attack with Umar Farooq. SFs killed him in an encounter at Hari Parigam, Awantipora, on 25 January 2020.

The Role of Pakistan-Based JeM Leadership

The role of the Pakistan-based leadership of JeM has been discussed in this case study under various heads. Umar Farooq, Kamran and Saifullah were all using Pakistani WhatsApp numbers to communicate with the organization's leadership, handlers, and with other terrorists and terror associates. Also, a few days before the VBIED attack, money was transferred to Umar Farooq's accounts in Allied Bank and Meezan Bank, both in Pakistan. In many voice messages, Umar Farooq is heard informing Pakistani terrorists that the total expenditure on the attack was INR 5,70,000. In a voice note sent by Umar Farooq to his uncle Ammar Alvi after the Pulwama attack, he mentions the financial hurdles he faced, conveying that he had not yet received the money spent by him on making the IED. He also said that he had already informed Mufti Rauf about the expenses incurred on the preparations, procuring the vehicle, etc. Further, he said that his associate, Kamran, had also spoken to Mufti Rauf many times, but had not received money in Kashmir, causing him financial difficulties. The Pakistan-based JeM handlers, Kashif Bhai and Abu Talha, provided Pakistani numbers to all the JeM terrorists based in the Valley.

Adil Dar's video was edited in Pakistan. Further, Umar Farooq's phone had conversations between him and Pakistan-based JeM leaders and handlers about making another video on the Pulwama attack showing mutilated bodies for propaganda and publicity. Abu Talha is heard in another voice note sent to Umar Farooq, asking if there was any audio message of Adil Dar available in the Kashmiri language, which could be edited and used for further propaganda among Kashmiri-speaking people.

Interestingly, on the day of the Balakot strikes—26 February 2019—Umar Farooq was constantly in touch with Mufti Rauf and his family via WhatsApp calls. In a voice note dated 27 February 2019, Kamran told Umar Farooq that Mufti Rauf was asking them to orchestrate another major strike, on the lines of Pulwama, at once. The reason was their immediate frustration and anger due to the Balakot strikes, and the objective was to avenge these strikes. However, later, due to international pressure and scrutiny, the Pakistan-based JeM leaders asked Umar Farooq to lie low for a while and that the next attack was to be done at an 'appropriate time' only. The words, '*Agli karwaai ki izazat bilkul nahi hai abhi* (no permission for the next attack)' are repeated in many voice notes. Besides, there are many voice notes in which, in reply to Mufti Rauf's questions about the movement of Indian fighter jets in Kashmir, Umar Farooq gave a live account of the fighter jets at Koel Airbase, Pulwama. Pakistani intelligence had approached Mufti Rauf to find more information about the movement of fighter jets in India. On several critical dates before and after the attack, Umar Farooq had long WhatsApp calls with JeM leaders in Pakistan, including Mufti Rauf and Ammar Alvi, and handlers like Abu Talha and Kashif Bhai. Further, after the heightened tensions between India and Pakistan following the Pulwama attack, Kamran, Umar Farooq and Saifullah were discussing the possibility of war between India and Pakistan. They appeared very enthusiastic about the idea of JeM jihadis stationed at launch pads taking advantage of the war and infiltrating into India to join the war against India from within its territory.

In a voice note dated 5 March 2019, Abu Talha allayed Umar Farooq's fears about the so-called detention of JeM leaders by the security forces in Pakistan. As per Abu Talha, the message from those in higher positions was that it was all pre-planned and that it was only an eyewash to demonstrate to the world that Pakistan was sincere in its fight against JeM. Further, he said that the supposed detention would last seven or eight days only, and that the discussions between JeM and Pakistani authorities had already happened. In a conversation dated 21 February 2019, Umar Farooq asked Ammar Alvi for permission to attack the BBC team (which included many foreigners) visiting Adil Dar's house after the attack, given the absence of large security detail. Ammar Alvi, in response, said that he should cherish the great mission he had executed; however, the permission to attack the journalists could not be granted due to the increasing tensions between India and Pakistan. Ammar Alvi also denied permission to release another video clip of 'Adil Shaheed's' preparations for the Pulwama attack.

Masood Azhar's video addressing a huge audience holding JeM flags in a rally organized at night in a big open compound in Karachi, on the occasion of Kashmir Solidarity Day on 5 February 2017, was also retrieved from Umar Farooq's phone. Many speakers made provocative speeches to the audience consisting of JeM terrorists and supporters. Many Pakistani JeM leaders and terrorists—Masood Azhar, Ammar Alvi, Saifullah, Umar Farooq and Talha Rashid—can be identified among those who attended this terrorist rally in Karachi.

Notably, the Sangin camp in Afghanistan, where Umar Farooq was trained in IEDs and explosives, was jointly run by Al

Qaeda and Taliban. The members of all the infiltrating groups were given weapons' training and practice at the launch pad before infiltrating into Indian territory from the IB. Shakargarh in Pakistan is a launch pad opposite the Samba sector on the IB. Notably, Shakargarh is the headquarters of the Pakistani Rangers, the border guard force. The location of a JeM launch pad in Shakargarh gives robust indication of the tacit support provided by the Pakistani state to JeM in infiltration and terrorist activities on Indian soil.

Digital Evidence from Umar Farooq's Phone

Pictures, messages and voice messages recovered from Umar Farooq's phone provide the following details about the infiltration of JeM terrorists.

Serial Number	Date of Infiltration	Details of the Infiltrating JeM Group
1	25–26 July 2017	Group of five terrorists
2	17–18 August 2017	Five terrorists led by Badshah Khan
3	23–24 October 2017	Five terrorists led by Talha Rashid
4	18–19 December 2017	Group of five terrorists
5	14–15 January 2018	Group of five terrorists led by Usman Haider
6	13–14 March 2018	A group of five terrorists led by Munna Bihari, aka Munna Lahori
7	13–14 April 2018	Five terrorists led by Muhammad Umar Farooq

The Future of JeM: Masood's Formidable Successors

The second-generation leadership of JeM has shown high levels of motivation, indoctrination and skills in radicalizing, recruiting, planning, managing and executing large-scale terror attacks. As the deputy chief, Mufti Rauf has proved his organizational and operational capabilities by transforming the organization into a highly specialized and lethal fidayeen terror group. In the second phase of JeM, it has mainly been the second-generation commanders from the Masood Azhar family—such as Umar Farooq, Usman Haider, Saifullah and Talha Rashid, who have been at the forefront of leading Kashmir operations. They are motivated, skilled and battle-hardened, and have died in Kashmir in encounters with SFs. JeM's firm entrenchment in the Punjab province of Pakistan and its sprawling madrasa network ensures an uninterrupted supply of cadres.

Regarding finances, JeM continues to have a strong Deobandi support base in addition to the support from the Pakistani state. The return of the Taliban has further strengthened its safe havens and finances. On the weapons and technology front, JeM cadres are continuously improving and innovating with the use of new encrypted communication technology, drones, IEDs, VBIEDs, etc. In Kashmir, its cadres have been found using NATO weapons left by the Americans in Afghanistan, like M4 rifles, steel bullets (armour-piercing bullets) and sophisticated NVDs. Hence, there is no shortage of leadership, motivation, cadre, finances, recruits, weapons, technology and skills.

However, on the other hand, it can be argued that the new generation of the Pakistan Army has witnessed the horrors of terrorism in incidents like the Peshawar army school attack and the brutalities unleashed by organizations like TTP—so they are not as enthusiastic and supportive of terror groups as the previous generation of proxy war veterans, who trained most of the Deobandi terror outfits in Afghanistan in the jihad against the Soviets. However, this change in the newer army officers' attitude will not make any significant difference in the state's attitude towards Kashmir-centric terrorist groups like JeM as they are seen as geostrategic assets of Pakistan to continue this low-intensity and low-cost hybrid war against India—a superior military and economic power. In the past as well, Pakistan has differentiated between 'good' and 'bad' terrorists, thereby nurturing anti-India terrorist groups like LeT, JeM and HM, while simultaneously launching operations against anti-Pakistan terror outfits like TTP. Moreover, JeM, despite its occasionally rebellious instincts, mainly during the Musharraf era, has remained loyal to the Pakistani state. The Pakistani civil society and the army have undergone intense religious radicalization. Christine Fair and Ayesha Siddiqa have provided an evidence-based description of how groups like LeT and JeM recruit from Punjab. This state also supplies an overwhelming number of men to the Pakistan Army. Even if the state decides to withdraw support from terrorist groups, it would be highly challenging for them to stop their activities, particularly in the case of Deobandi groups, as they have a robust social, religious and financial support system that is indigenous, and comprises a home-grown constituency of sympathizers and volunteers.

India's Future Threats from JeM and Its Jihadist Ecosystem

Though Kashmir-centric organizations like JeM, HM and LeT have not been formally integrated into the wider AQ network the way terrorist groups in the MENA region have acceded to AQ as an umbrella organization, there have always been informal operational and ideological links between the groups, as discussed previously. A relevant example of such synergies is Brigade 313,[34] an umbrella organization formed around mid-2002 with members from JeM, LeT, HM, SSP, LeJ, and Al Qaeda. It included those members who were disappointed with Pakistan's support of the US-led GWoT. Reportedly, Brigade 313 was involved in the assassination attempts against Musharraf, Pakistan's PM Shaukat Aziz, Karachi Corps Commander General Ahsan Saleem Hayat, the murder of *Wall Street Journal* reporter Daniel Pearl, sending parcel bombs to the police's anti-terrorist branch, and attacks on the US consulate and Sheraton Hotel in Karachi in 2002.[35] The group allegedly had close connections with AQ and was working under the direction of Khaled Sheikh Mohammad, the AQ mastermind of 9/11. Based on the analysis done in this chapter, counterterrorism experts can contemplate the following possibilities for the future.

Kashmir-centric terror outfits, mainly JeM, are likely to move closer into the fold of TTGs like AQ and their pan-Islamist agenda for several reasons. Pakistan is increasingly facing tremendous pressure from global bodies like FATF to sever ties with groups like LeT, HM, Al Badr and JeM. Three decades of investment and relations with these groups stand exposed, and are likely to create economic hardships for Pakistan in the form of blacklisting and consequent economic sanctions. Notably, the way Pakistan facilitated the return of the Taliban has majorly shattered its image in the eyes of the Western world—particularly the US security establishment, which heavily relied upon Islamabad in its GWoT for the last two decades. Also, Pakistan is already facing political instability, a crumbling economy and a food crisis.[36] Nurturing an array of terrorist groups for decades has boomeranged by creating an ecosystem of religious hatred, narcotics smuggling, anarchy, crime and violence. Pakistan is itself facing massive terrorist violence from groups like TTP. The Taliban's return has already started strengthening the terror ecosystem, including the anti-Pakistan groups. Hence, it may not be feasible for Pakistan to support and nourish these groups as it has done so far, which may induce them to move closer to TTGs like Al Qaeda Taliban, and IS-KP. Further, due to the worsening economy and intense radicalization, there will not be any shortage of recruits. For instance, reportedly, the LeT has about 1,50,000–2,00,000 armed and trained mujahids in Pakistan and Afghanistan.[37] Also, returning Afghan refugees from Pakistan are likely to fill the ranks of terror groups.

If Pakistan's grip loosens over them and they align with pan-Islamist actors, the security scenario in South Asia will be turbulent. JeM, compared to groups like LeT and HM, is more likely to get into TTG's fold because of its stronger historical proximity with them in the ideological and operational domain, and ISI's relatively feeble grip over it compared to LeT and HM. A recent intelligence report (January 2022) from Indian sources mentions:[38]

> ... [T]he group is likely to get a boost from the unravelling situation in Afghanistan following the withdrawal of US forces. Given the Taliban's close strategic and ideological unity with groups like the JeM, the latter will likely acquire much-needed strategic depth to benefit its recruitment and the functioning of its training camps. Pakistan's lack of action against Masood Azhar is an added benefit [sic].

The possibility of strengthening JeM–AQ ties is alarming for the US and the Western world. As discussed earlier, JeM has been instrumental in targeting Western interests. After the Taliban's return, both groups are likely to be safely entrenched in Afghanistan. Once AQ targets Western countries, JeM can emerge as a robust operational partner.

Also, let us suppose that Pakistan's political instability and economic troubles raise the possibility of it turning into a failed state with the institutions of the army and ISI becoming dysfunctional. In that case, the terror nexus running from Afghanistan to Pakistan will have its writ. Such a situation may lead to Pakistan's nukes falling into the hands of dreaded terror outfits like JeM and its TTG cohorts.

AQIS has its gaze on the subcontinent. Time and again, it has raised the Kashmir issue and spoken of it on Islamist lines. In the AQ warning, released by As-Sahab Media, dated 6 June 2022, it has threatened to conduct suicide attacks in Delhi, Mumbai, Gujarat and UP against the alleged insult of Prophet Mohammed by the ruling BJP's spokesperson.[39] In the letter, AQ also referred to Prophet Mohammed's prophecy of Ghazwa-i-Hind (Islamic reconquest of India) and warned of 'death, destruction, hangings, imprisonment and executions' of the rulers of India.

In May 2022, AQ chief Ayman Al Zawahiri released a video in which he compared Kashmir with Palestine and called it a 'recurring tragedy'.[40] Drawing parallels between Indian policies in Kashmir and Israel's policies in Palestine, he categorized the former as the cause of the 'oppressed Muslim ummah that had its natural resources stolen and land divided'. Inciting the Kashmiris, he said that repealing Article 370 is like a 'slap on Kashmir's face', and the masses should rise in revolt against this. The video also praised terrorists like Burhan Wani, Zakir Musa and Adil Dar. In 2017, AGuH had emerged as the AQ's Kashmir affiliate. Its commander, Zakir Musa,[41] stated that they struggled to make Kashmir a Shariah-governed state and part of the Islamic caliphate—making it clear that the fight was not for political freedom but the Islamic cause.

AQ has also established sleeper cells and proxy units in the Indian hinterland. The thirteenth report of the UN Analytical and Sanctions Monitoring Team mentions that AQIS has changed the name of its magazine from *Nawa-i-Afghan Jihad* to *Nawa-i-Ghazwa-e-Hind*, which suggests its renewed focus on the Indian subcontinent.[42] The reports confirm that AQ's relationship with the Taliban continues to be strong and cordial. After the Taliban's return, AQ has consolidated in Afghanistan. The UN report also says that JeM and LeT maintain training camps in Afghanistan. The former has ten camps and three of them are directly under Taliban control. During the recent hijab row in Karnataka, Ayman Al Zawahiri released a video message purportedly to radicalize Indian Muslims on communal lines.[43]

Over the last three decades, religious radicalization among Indian Muslims has been fast and intense, primarily due to an increased awareness of religious knowledge, their exposure to global Islamist movements, the spread of Islamist organizations like PFI, and extremist ideologies like Deobandism and Wahhabism. Additionally, Hindu fundamentalism has also intensified and hastened Muslim radicalization. After PM Modi's Hindu nationalist BJP came to power in 2014, Muslim polarization on communal and extremist lines has picked up at an unprecedented pace. Abetted by global Islamist organizations and Pakistan, rising Hindu nationalism, and a perceived sense of alienation, deprivation and discrimination, a significant segment of India's Muslim leadership and Islamic organizations see the Modi government as anti-Islam and anti-Muslim. Getting into the details of this debate is not the main focus of this study; however, in such a communally polarized socio-political milieu, TTGs like AQ and Taliban are likely to get traction in India. The reason for the renewed interest of Zawahiri and AQIS in India, expressed in some of his recent videos, seems to be the presently fertile environment of Hindu–Muslim communal rivalries. Such fault lines provide a suitable milieu to radicalize misguided and vulnerable youth from India's Muslim minority.

In this task, JeM can be of immense value as it already has robust links with AQ in cooperation and coordination in intelligence sharing, logistics, training and funding. With its local human resource network and sleeper cells, it can help AQIS penetrate and conduct terror attacks in India. The possibility of AQIS outsourcing the task of organizing terror strikes to JeM cannot be ruled out. JeM's pan-India vision has been evident since it began its operations in the country. In the Pulwama fidayeen attack, JeM targeted the convoy of the CRPF, which recruits from across India, not merely Jammu and Kashmir. The objective was to send a message to the entire country. Most recently, two terrorists of a JeM-affiliate group, Lashkar-i-Mustapha, were arrested in Bihar.[44] After the Pulwama attack, JeM was training fidayeen squads for organizing similar fidayeen attacks in various other parts of India.[45] In another instance of JeM's ties with TTGs, after the 7 October 2023 Hamas attacks on Israel, Masood's brother Mufti Rauf was recruiting Indian Muslims for Hamas from Jharkhand, Kashmir, Bengal, Madhya Pradesh and Bangladesh.[46] Reportedly, the organization has sent twelve Indians to Palestine via Afghanistan and Turkey after training them in PoK. He also motivated them to carry out Hamas-styled spectacular attacks in India.

JeM subscribes to the Deobandi ideology, which has followers across the entire Indian country (20 per cent of Indian Muslims follow its doctrines). LeT, on the other hand, follows the Ahl-i-Hadith philosophy, which has not gained much traction in India—out of the 17 crore Muslims in India,[47] only 1.8 million or 18 lakh followed this ideology in 2014.[48] Hence, JeM can penetrate into the consciousness of Indian Muslims more easily—especially given the long history of Deobandism in the country. It can quickly establish sleeper cells in Deobandi pockets, and carry on radicalization and recruitment, apart from orchestrating terrorist attacks in the Indian hinterland. JeM can find safe shelters, recruits, logistics and other kinds of support in the areas of robust Deobandi influence. The August 2022 arrest of Muhammad Nadeem, a JeM terrorist from Saharanpur—the global headquarters of Deoband Islam—by the ATS of the UP police substantiated my assessment.[49] Muhammad Nadeem belongs to Kunda Kala village of Saharanpur district. He was tasked to kill Nupur Sharma, the former BJP spokesperson, who allegedly made insulting remarks about the Prophet. As per the ATS's interrogation, he had been in touch with JeM and TTP leaders based in Pakistan and Afghanistan since 2018 through WhatsApp, Telegram, IMO, Facebook, Clubhouse, etc. During the preliminary investigation, the ATS recovered a PDF document titled 'Explosive Course Fidayeen Force' from his mobile phone. A Pakistani named 'Saifullah' was training him to execute a fidayeen attack on government buildings and police installations. Saifullah was also asking him to visit Pakistan for special training. Most recently, on 26 April 2024, JeM's communication office Maktab-ul-Rabita announced that Masood Azhar would directly answer questions from his followers every morning and afternoon, on WhatsApp, Telegram and text messages.[50] This announcement comes ten years after Masood Azhar's last major public appearance. Many security experts are reading this development as a desperate attempt to find more recruits due to India's tough anti-terror policies in Kashmir. However, it seems that this measure of JeM is more about the Indian hinterland. They want to enhance communication with the lay Muslims of India, who are going through intense radicalization, as mentioned above.

On the Kashmir front, the relative lull in JeM activities after Pulwama led some veteran intelligence officials and counterterrorism scholars to argue in muted tones that the organization no longer poses a threat like it used to. They argued that given India's formidable posturing and retaliation after Pulwama, Pakistan was most unlikely to allow or support JeM to indulge in any misadventures like Pulwama. However, after the Balakot strike, there was hardly any change in Pakistan's state policy of supporting proxy terrorist groups in Kashmir. Instead, after the abrogation of Article 370, the country made several attempts to infiltrate a large number of foreign terrorists and intensify the militancy in the Valley. Secondly, the Balakot strikes emboldened JeM, instead of demoralizing it. Umar Farooq's telephonic conversations suggest that he wished India and Pakistan go to war after Balakot so that he could use that situation to infiltrate a large number of cadres into Kashmir.[51]

Post the abrogation of Article 370, militancy has undergone many strategic and tactical changes. Initially, leading outfits like JeM and LeT created front organizations with secular-sounding names to reduce their exposure in front of global terrorism watchdogs.[52] Taliban's victory in Afghanistan led to tremendous euphoria in Kashmir among ordinary Muslims. Militancy appears to have taken on an Islamist turn. The burgeoning rise of Islamist groups combined with communal polarization in the Indian mainland and Hindu nationalism's high-pitched rhetoric in mainstream electronic media and social media, along with academic, social, cultural, religious and political spaces, has given a fillip to the process of deeply entrenched religious radicalization in Kashmir. It has encouraged terrorist groups to exploit people's vulnerability and incite violence on religious lines. The militants are killing members of the Hindu-minority Kashmiri Pandits, which include ordinary civilians like teachers, clerks and business persons. In May 2022, militants killed a local Muslim film artist, Amreen Bhat.[53] Reportedly, she was killed for working in films, which is considered un-Islamic. The enhanced interest of the pan-Islamist agenda of AQ and Taliban may accentuate these Islamist tendencies. In the tactical domain, the militants have shifted to hybrid militancy in which civilians like students, professionals and workers are given small weapons—like a pistol—by OGWs to commit an act of terror and then merge into the crowd.[54] Reportedly, thousands of pistols have been distributed in Kashmir. This model is being implemented because it is challenging to find and eliminate hybrid militants as they are civilians who commit such one-off acts of terror. If they are killed later, civilians agitate against SFs.

On the conventional front, militancy is on the rise. After the abrogation of Article 370, 493 militants have been killed in encounters between 5 August 2019 and 26 January 2022.[55] JeM's activities have been on the rise. Its front organizations, People's Anti-Fascist Front (PAFF), followed by Kashmir Tigers, have conducted some of the most brutal fidayeen attacks over the last two years, which signals a revival of the suicide bombing trend. Unfortunately, SFs have not been successful in containing attacks by these front groups, particularly PAFF, due to a lack of HUMINT and a change in tactics by terrorists. In the future, there is a strong possibility of JeM and its proxies planning IED, VBIED and drone-based attacks on police, civil and military installations, and convoys of SFs.

There is chatter about JeM roping in female suicide bombers from south Kashmir.[56] However, those who don't think it will say that it has projected itself as highly conscientious and committed on issues such as drugs and women—vis-à-vis other groups like HM and LeT. Because of this image, there is a general belief among SFs and intelligence circles that JeM is unlikely to use girls. However, the facts state otherwise. Pulwama mastermind Umar Farooq was thinking of using Insha Jan, a co-conspirator, as a messenger and courier for transporting weapons and cash. He had even considered grooming Insha Jan as a suicide bomber; however, his weakness for her prevented him from doing so. Apart from Insha Jan, Umar Farooq also developed a liking for her cousin and started grooming her as a suicide bomber. He motivated her by narrating stories of Muslim women participating in jihad in Syria and Iraq, about the Black Widows of Chechnya and the active role played by female jihadis in the terrorist attack on Beslan school in Russia. As a result, Insha Jan's cousin became a devout follower and offered herself up as a suicide bomber. Hence, it is likely that in future JeM fidayeen attacks, women, mainly from south Kashmir, will volunteer.

Apart from this, JeM, with its robust base in south Punjab (Pakistan) and expertise in infiltration from the Punjab–Jammu region, can render substantial support to Khalistani terrorists in infiltration, narcotics and weapons smuggling, and in the general reviving of their activities. It aligns with the ISI's strategy of uniting Kashmir and Punjab terrorism.

According to a recent media report,[57] the Taliban has released 100 members of JeM from Afghan prisons after its return to power. The report says that all the members returned to the organization's fold, and Masood Azhar has urged them to intensify attacks in India—particularly in Jammu and Kashmir. Before that, Masood Azhar celebrated Taliban's victory in his write-up titled 'Manzil ki Taraf'.[58] Indian intelligence agencies have encountered similar exhortations on JeM-related social media sites and through their human assets in the JeM congregations in the Bahawalpur complex.[59] Also, between 17–19 August 2021, Masood Azhar and Mufti Rauf met Abdul

Ghani Baradar and other top-level leaders, where he requested the Taliban's help in JeM's Kashmir operations. He also promised full support to Taliban in its operations targeting India. Notably, Indian experts and agencies raised fears about Afghanistan becoming the epicentre of jihad after the Taliban's revival, resulting in an increasing militancy in Kashmir.[60]

However, at least until the time of writing this chapter, the Taliban has not displayed much interest in targeting India. It has said that Kashmir is a 'bilateral' and 'internal' matter of India.[61] Haqqani Network leader Anas Haqqani, in an interview with CNN-News18, said that Kashmir is not a part of their jurisdiction; hence, any interference would be against its policy.[62] He also assured the interviewer that Taliban seeks good relations with India and would not allow its soil to be used for terror attacks against the nation. Indian security expert Tara Kartha also echoed Anas Haqqani's thoughts and said that Taliban leaders like Mullah Baradar, Mullah Yakub and their mid-level leaders have no genuine interest in India. In the immediate future, they would mostly be engaged in settling scores and feuds.[63] Moreover, India's massive aid and development programme can help nurture cordial relations with the Taliban. Likewise, former R&AW chief and Kashmir expert Dulat also expressed his reservations about the Taliban dancing to the tune of ISI and fomenting militancy in Kashmir.[64] Further, he said that the Taliban needs global recognition, including from India, so they are less likely to support terrorist groups in the Valley.

However, barely a few days after the 'bilateral' and 'internal' comment, Taliban spokesperson Suhail Shaheen, in a BBC Urdu interview, said that the group has the right to raise its voice for the concerns of Muslims across the world, including Kashmir.[65] A month before that, in August 2021, a member of Imran Khan's Pakistan Tehreek-i-Insaaf party claimed that the

Taliban would help them in liberating Kashmir.[66] Hence, at this juncture, the Taliban might have moderated its stance because it needs recognition from India. However, in the future, once it settles firmly into power, it is likely to pursue its extremist agenda by covertly supporting groups like AQ and JeM in their anti-India operations, and also provide shelter to them in Afghanistan—as it did in the 1990s. Though many experts prefer to believe that Taliban 2.0 has moderated from its 1990s version, the recent Taliban strictures and Shariah-based restrictions on women[67] expose the hollowness of such claims, and indicate that its ideology and agenda continue to be the same, driven by archaic religious extremism and medieval values. Hence, given the backdrop of JeM and Taliban sharing the umbilical cord of Deobandi Islam and their similar vision of Shariah-based governance, the possibility of Taliban supporting terror groups in the Valley is strong.

On the infiltration front, intelligence reports from January 2020 say that 300 militants, including many Afghan veterans, were being trained in launch pads in PoK for infiltration into India.[68] In January 2022, Indian Army chief, Gen. M.M. Naravane, said in a press conference that 400 terrorists were stationed in the PoK launch pads.[69]

In the future, there is a possibility of a violent mass uprising in which pan-Islamist actors are likely to play an important role. A recent report by Disinfo Lab says that after the abrogation of Article 370, the Muslim Brotherhood has also found a foothold in Kashmir, mainly through local Islamist organizations like Jamaat-i-Islami.[70] If Muslim Brotherhood becomes active in Kashmir, the uprising will likely have robust international connections. In the worst case, it may exhibit some features typical of West Asian civil disturbances and revolts witnessed in Syria, Libya, Palestine, etc. Such an uprising can include a range of elements like suicide bombings, targeted killings, violent demonstrations and drone attacks with the involvement of foreign terrorist cadres. JeM, on account of its strong ties with pan-Islamist groups like AQ and Taliban, and its robust grassroots base in Kashmir, has the potential to play a crucial role in spearheading and leading such an uprising. Also, ISI's tenuous control over JeM will make it even more dangerous, elusive and difficult to control in such a situation of mass upheaval.

To address the emerging threats discussed above, India's intelligence must enhance its surveillance and monitoring capabilities. Constant vigil over JeM activities in the Indian hinterland, movements in Deobandi strongholds, and links between Kashmiri terrorists, Islamist organizations and Islamic extremist groups of the Indian hinterland will have to be maintained. While continuing with the necessary political, security and intelligence measures to deal firmly with terrorist and radical Islamist groups, the Indian state will have to ensure that Muslims, in general, do not feel cornered or pushed against the wall. It is essential to mention this because despite the government's precautions and sincere intent to implement its reforms, global Islamist networks have always portrayed an incorrect picture of India's internal developments through their information and propaganda war. They will likely continue to do so in the future to disturb India's communal peace and harmony; hence, a strict vigil is needed. State intelligence departments, which are in bad shape with highly unsatisfactory performance and awareness levels, will have to be overhauled to improve their efficiency and understanding of the jihadi threat. On the kinetic front, India will have to deploy an array of harsh covert and overt measures to curb Islamist organizations, terrorist groups, and their sympathizers, financiers and coordinators within the country. With Pakistan, India will have to continue its formidable posture on the terror issue, and categorically signal that terror and talks cannot go together. It must ensure that any future attack originating from or tracing back to Pakistan on Indian assets in India or on foreign soil will be dealt with firmly, with heavy retaliatory action.

Acknowledgements

WRITING THIS BOOK HAS BEEN AN INCREDIBLE JOURNEY. It is not just about the field trips I took to the remote conflict areas of Kashmir during the rigorous communication and security lockdown imposed after the abrogation of Article 370, but also about the enlightening mental journey of discovering myself as a human being, researcher, writer, philosopher, spiritualist and a peacemaker.

To begin with, I would like to express my heartfelt gratitude and dedicate this work to my Sadgurudev Param Pujya Gulwani Maharaj Ji, Gurudev Param Pujya Prabhu Baa and Jodhpuriya Bawji. Without their blessings and spiritual guidance, completing this massive project—which involved working under life-threatening situations—would have been impossible.

I thank Dr Anita Jain, my colleague at Usanas Foundation, my father S.C. Pandya, mother Maya Pandya, Preeti Khenta, my colleague, and Swati Chopra from HarperCollins India for their support. I extend my heartfelt gratitude to my PhD supervisor, Dr Pankaj Jha, a professor at Jindal University, to my mentor, C.D. Sahay, the former R&AW chief, and to Tejendra Khanna, the former lieutenant-governor of Delhi. I also thank Tahir Ashraf (code name) and Dr Suneem Khan, a doctor with CRPF (Srinagar) and an expert on Kashmir affairs, for his crucial support in this research project. His insights on the ground situation helped me understand the complexities of terrorist organizations in the Valley.

Lastly, I sincerely thank all my expert interlocutors from diverse backgrounds who rendered several eye-opening insights on the subject from their grassroots experience and knowledge. Their names cannot be mentioned here for security reasons, but this work could not have been complete without their support.

Abbreviations

AGuH: Ansar Ghazwat-ul-Hind
AQ: Al Qaeda
AQIS: Al Qaeda in the Indian Subcontinent
ART: Al-Rahmat Trust
ATS: Anti-Terrorism Squad
AUM: Al Umar Mujahideen
BSF: Border Security Force
CASO: Cordon and Search Operation
CBI: Central Bureau of Investigation
CDR: Call Detail Records
CFSL: Central Forensic Science Laboratory
CrPC: Criminal Procedure Code
CRPF: Central Reserve Police Force
FATA: Federally Administered Tribal Areas
FATF: Financial Action Task Force
FiF: Falah-e-Insaniyat Foundation

FT: Foreign Terrorist

FTG: Foreign Terrorist Groups

FTO: Foreign Terrorist Organization

GWoT: Global War on Terror

HM: Hizbul Mujahideen

HuA: Harkat ul-Ansar

HuJI: Harkat-ul-Jihad-al-Islami

HuM: Harkat-ul-Mujahideen

HuMA: Harkat-ul-Mujahideen Al-Alami

HUMINT: Human Intelligence

IAF: Indian Air Force

IB: Intelligence Bureau

IB: International Border

IDSA: Institute of Defence Studies and Analysis

IED: Improvised Explosive Device

IIF: International Islamic Front

IM: Indian Mujahideen

INR: Indian Rupee

IR: Interrogation Reports

IS: Islamic State

ISI: Inter-Services Intelligence

ISJK: Islamic State of Jammu and Kashmir

IS-KP: Islamic State–Khorasan Province

IST: Indian Standard Time
J&K: Jammu and Kashmir
JeM: Jaish-e-Mohammed
JI: Jamaat-i-Islami
JKLF: Jammu-Kashmir Liberation Front
JuA: Jamaat-ul-Ansar
JuF: Jamaat-ul-Furqan
JuH: Jamiat Ulema-e-Hind
JuI: Jamiat Ulema-i-Islam
JuM: Jamaat-ul-Mujahideen
KPK: Khyber Pakhtunkhwa
KuL: Khuddam-ul Islam
LeJ: Lashkar-e-Jhangvi
LeT: Lashkar-e-Taiba
LMG: Light Machine Gun
LoC: Line of Control
MEMRI: Middle East Media Research Institute
MENA: Middle East and North Africa
MFN: Most Favoured Nation
NA: Northern Alliance
NIA: National Investigation Agency
NSA: National Security Advisor
NSG: National Security Guards

NVDs: Night Vision Devices
NWFP: North West Frontier Province
OGW: Over-Ground Worker
PAFF: People's Anti-Fascist Front
PD: Police District
PKR: Pakistani Rupee
PoK: Pakistan-Occupied Kashmir
POTA: Prevention of Terrorism Act
Psyop: Psychological Operation
R&AW: Research and Analysis Wing
RCIED: Remote-Controlled IEDs
ROP: Road Opening Party
RPC: Ranbir Penal Code
RPG: Rocket-Propelled Grenade
SATP: South Asia Terrorism Portal
SDGT: Specially Designated Global Terrorist
SF: Security Forces
SIMI: Students Islamic Movement of India
SOG: Special Operations Group
SPO: Special Police Officer
SSP: Sipah-e-Sahaba Pakistan
TAF: Tehreek Al-Furqan
TECHINT: Technical Intelligence

TJ: Tablighi Jamaat

TRF: The Resistance Front

TTG: Transnational Terrorist Group

TTP: Tehreek-e-Taliban Pakistan

UAPA 1967: Unlawful Activities Prevention Act 1967

UBGL: Under Barrel Grenade Launcher

UJC: United Jihad Council

UNSC: United Nations Security Council

UPA: United Progressive Alliance

VBIED: Vehicle-Borne Improvised Explosive Device

VHF: Very High Frequency

Notes

Chapter 1: The Master of Fidayeen Attacks

1 PTI, 'Jaish terrorists attack CRPF convoy', *The Times of India*, 16 February 2019, https://timesofindia.indiatimes.com/india/37-crpf-jawans-martyred-in-ied-blast-in-jks-pulwama/articleshow/67992189.cms, accessed on 11 February 2022.

2 PTI, 'Pulwama attack, seven detained, 80 kg "high grade" RDX used by Jaish terrorists', *DNA*, 16 February 2019, https://www.dnaindia.com/india/report-pulwama-attack-seven-detained-80-kg-high-grade-rdx-used-by-jaish-terrorist-2720490, accessed on 11 February 2022.

3 India Today Web Desk, 'India withdraws most favoured nation status to Pakistan after Pulwama attack', *India Today*, 15 February 2019, https://www.indiatoday.in/india/story/most-favoured-nation-status-for-pakistan-withdrawn-arun-jaitley-after-pulwama-attack-1456678-2019-02-15, accessed on 11 February 2022.

4 Basu, N., 'After Pulwama, India doubles efforts to get Pakistan blacklisted by FATF', *The Print*, 21 February 2019, https://theprint.in/diplomacy/after-pulwama-attack-india-doubles-efforts-to-get-pakistan-blacklisted-by-fatf/196242/, accessed on 11 February 2022.

5 The figure remains disputed. The *Economic Times* report mentions the figure of 300, quoting government sources. See ET Online, 'Indian air strike in Balakot killed 300 militants: Sources', *Economic Times*, 26 February 2019, https://economictimes.indiatimes.com/news/defence/indian-air-strike-

in-balakot-killed-300-militants-sources/articleshow/68165466.cms?utm_source=contentofinterest&utm_medium=text&utm_campaign=cpps, accessed on 11 February 2022. However, some interlocutors say that the number could be higher, up to the range of 350. Italian journalist Francesca Marino has given the figure of 130–170 casualties based on the information received from local sources (India Today Web Desk, 'As many as 170 JeM terrorists killed in Balakot airstrike: Italian journalist', *India Today*, Updated 9 May 2019, https://www.indiatoday.in/india/story/balakot-airstrike-1520097-2019-05-08, accessed on 11 February 2022.

6 Joshi, S., 'How Pakistan planned to hit India back for Balakot — the mission, the fighters, the tactics', *The Print*, 14 September 2019, https://theprint.in/defence/how-pakistan-planned-to-hit-india-back-for-balakot-the-mission-the-fighters-the-tactics/291522/, accessed on 25 March 2022.

7 BBC, 'Abhinandan: Who is the Indian pilot captured by Pakistan?' BBC, 1 March 2019, https://www.bbc.com/news/world-asia-india-47397409, accessed on 25 March 2022.

8 Fair, C.C., *In their Own Words: Understanding Lashkar-e-Tayyaba* (Oxford University Press, New Delhi: 2019), pp. 45–66.

9 ibid.

10 ibid, p. 46.

11 ibid, p. 47.

12 East, C., 'Guerilla warfare', *Pakistan Army Journal*, 1958, vol.1(4), pp. 57–66, accessed on 24 May 2022.

13 Yashee, '44 years of Zulfikar Ali Bhutto's hanging: The man who would "wage a war for 1000 years with India"', *The Indian Express*, 4 May 2023, https://indianexpress.com/article/explained/explained-history/zulfikar-ali-bhuttos-hanging-speech-against-india-8538275/, accessed on 26 April 2024.

14 Siddiqi, A., *A Path for Pakistan* (Pakistan Publishing House, Karachi, Originally from University of Michigan: 1964).

15. ibid.
16. Fair, C.C., *In their Own Words*, p. 50.
17. Carnegie Endowment for International Peace, 'Pakistan's Sanction Waivers: A Summary,' 29 October 2001, https://carnegieendowment.org/2001/10/29/pakistan-s-sanction-waivers-summary-pub-10778, accessed on 24 May 2022.
18. Burr, W., *China, Pakistan and the Bomb: The Declassified File on the US Policy, 1977–97*, NS Archives, 5 March 2004, National Security Archives Electronic Briefing Book No. 114, https://nsarchive2.gwu.edu/NSAEBB/NSAEBB114/, accessed on 13 February 2023.
19. NSA, *The United States and Pakistan's Quest for the Bomb*, G.W. University, 21 December 2010, https://nsarchive2.gwu.edu/nukevault/ebb333/, accessed on 24 May 2022.
20. ibid.
21. Chari, P., 'Nuclear signaling in South Asia: Revisiting A.Q. Khan's 1987 threat', Carnegie Endowment for International Peace, 14 November 2013, https://carnegieendowment.org/2013/11/14/nuclear-signaling-in-south-asia-revisiting-a.-q.-khan-s-1987-threat-pub-53328, accessed on 24 May 2022.
22. Fair, C.C., *In their Own Words*, p. 51.
23. GHQ Rawalpindi is the headquarters of the Pakistan Army.
24. Kasuri, M.K., *Neither a Hawk, Nor a Dove*, (Oxford University Press, Pakistan: 2015).
25. The former R&AW chief requested anonymity because of the June 2021 order of the Indian government, which makes it mandatory for former security officials to seek Central permission before writing or speaking about their former organization's 'domain', and the permission-seeking process can be very tedious and long.
26. As told to the author in a personal interview.

27 Kalita, P., 'IAF planned hit post-26/11 too, but didn't get govt nod', *The Times of India*, 27 February 2019, https://timesofindia.indiatimes.com/india/is-shashi-tharoor-running-out-of-fancy-words/articleshow/68176525.cms, accessed on 25 May 2022.

28 As told to the author. The former R&AW chief was also part of the delegation that negotiated with the Kandahar hijackers.

29 Pandya, A., 'The future of Indo-Pak relations after the Pulwama attack', *Perspectives on Terrorism*, vol. 13(2), 2019, pp. 65–68, https://www.jstor.org/stable/26626866?seq=4.

30 Pandya, A., 'Kashmir militancy after 370: An assessment of Pakistan's proxy war', *CLAWS*, vol. 14, 2021, https://media.neliti.com/media/publications/369741-kashmir-militancy-after-370-an-assessmen-c4df735d.pdf, accessed on 25 May 2022.

31 Rassler, D., 'Al-Qaida and the Pakistani Harakat movement: Reflections and questions', *Perspectives on Terrorism*, vol. 11(6). December 2017, https://www.universiteitleiden.nl/binaries/content/assets/customsites/perspectives-on-terrorism/2017/issue-6/0420176-al-qaida-and-the-pakistani-harakat-movement-reflections-and-questions.pdf, accessed on 20 April 2022.

32 As told to the author by a former R&AW chief who was dealing with Afghanistan and Pakistan in the late 1990s and early 2000s. He told the author that 1999 onwards, i.e., after the formation of JeM, Pakistan-sponsored jihadist groups, most importantly JeM, had intensified their terrorist activities. India was concerned by these developments, and presented its findings with substantial and irrefutable evidence of Pakistan's involvement in Kashmir to the US several times. However, the US dependence on Pakistan, in its Afghan operations against Taliban and AQ, was a limiting factor which made Washington turn a blind eye to Pakistan's support to terror outfits in Kashmir.

33 Based on the author's personal interview with a former R&AW chief who handled Pakistan from 1998 to 2002.

34 Rashid, A., *Descent into Chaos: The United States and the Failure of Nation Building in Pakistan, Afghanistan and Central Asia*, pp. 109–124.

35 Sindhu, K.K., and S. Haq, 'What is TRF? "Lashkar offshoot" behind killing of BJP worker in Kashmir', *India Today*, 15 February 2019, https://www.indiatoday.in/india/story/what-is-trf-lashkar-offshoot-behind-killing-of-bjp-workers-in-kashmir-1736665-2020-10-30, accessed on 11 February 2022.

36 TKW Staff, 'Another militant outfit emerges, fourth in two years,' *The Kashmir Wallah*, 22 January 2021, https://thekashmirwalla.com/2021/01/kashmir-tigers-another-militant-outfit-emerges-fourth-in-two-years/, accessed on 4 July 2021.

37 Bhatt, S., 'Lashkar-i-Mustapha chief Hidayatullah Malik arrested in Jammu', *India Today*, 6 February 2021, https://www.indiatoday.in/india/story/lashkar-e-mustafa-chief-hidayatullah-malik-arrested-in-j-k-shopian-district-1766646-2021-02-06, accessed on 4 July 2021.

38 D'Souza, S.M., 'Mumbai terrorist attacks of 2008', *Britannica*, https://www.britannica.com/event/Mumbai-terrorist-attacks-of-2008, accessed on 4 July 2021.

39 '2001 Parliament attack: When terror struck India's temple of democracy', *Hindustan Times*, 13 December 2020, https://www.hindustantimes.com/india-news/2001-parliament-attack-when-terror-struck-india-s-temple-of-democracy/story-8juWPlu7D7ox6mMyFSjcII.html, accessed on 4 July 2021.

40 Shreekumar, A., 'Uri and Pathankot: Defending India's defense establishments', *The Diplomat*, 24 September 2016, https://thediplomat.com/2016/09/uri-and-pathankot-defending-indias-defense-establishments/, accessed on 4 July 2021.

41 India Today Web Desk, '3 years of Uri terror attack: The day when Indian Army suffered its worst loss in 20 years', *India Today*, 18 September 2019, https://www.indiatoday.in/india/

story/uri-terror-attack-anniversary-the-day-when-indian-army-suffered-its-worst-loss-in-jammu-kashmir-1600436-2019-09-18, accessed on 4 July 2021.

42. CNN Staff, 'Bombing at Kashmir assembly kills at least 29', *CNN World*, 1 October 2001, https://edition.cnn.com/2001/WORLD/asiapcf/south/10/01/india.kashmir/index.html, accessed on 4 July 2021.

43. 'Pulwama attack: What is militant group Jaish-e-Mohammed?' BBC, 15 February 2019, https://www.bbc.com/news/world-asia-47249982, accessed on 4 July 2021.

Chapter 2: The Origins of JeM and Pakistan's Deobandi Ecosystems

1. Swami, P., 'Jaish-e-Mohammed fidayeen story: How Masood Azhar set up his industry of terror in Kashmir', *Firstpost*, 26 February 2019, https://www.firstpost.com/india/the-jaish-e-mohammads-fidayeen-factory-how-masood-azhar-set-up-his-industry-of-terror-in-kashmir-6129311.html, accessed on 20 April 2022.

2. ibid.

3. Siddiqa, A., 'Brothers in arms', *Newsline*, September 2009, https://newslinemagazine.com/magazine/brothers-in-arms/, accessed on 6 June 2022.

4. ibid.

5. Howenstien, N., 'The jihadi terrain in Pakistan: An introduction to the Sunni jihadi groups in Pakistan and Kashmir', Pakistan Security Research Unit, Department of Peace Studies, Bradford: University of Bradford, 5 February 2005, http://hdl.handle.net/10454/2224, accessed on 4 July 2021.

6. Sharma, S. K., and A. Behera, *Militant Groups in South Asia*, Pentagon, Delhi: 2014, https://idsa.in/system/files/book/book_militantgroups.pdf, accessed on 24 June 2004.

7   Masood Azhar was released in return for setting free 155 passengers of IC-814, the Indian airline hijacked by Masood's parent organization HuM in 1999.

8   Rana, M.A., *A to Z of Jehadi Organisations in Pakistan*, Marshal, Lahore: 2004.

9   Bhattacharjee, Y., 'The terrorist who got away', *The New York Times*, March 2019, https://www.nytimes.com/2020/03/19/magazine/masood-azhar-jaish.html, accessed on 4 July 2021.

10 CISAC, 'Jaish-e-Mohammed: Mapping militants profile', Centre for International Security and Cooperation, Stanford University, last updated July 2018, https://cisac.fsi.stanford.edu/mappingmilitants/profiles/jaish-e-mohammed#text_block_19719, accessed on 4 April 2021.

11 Roy, O., 'Islamic radicalisation in Afghanistan and Pakistan', UNHCR: Emergency and Security Service, January 2002, https://www.academia.edu/1453553/Islamic_Radicalism_in_Afghanistan_and_Pakistan, accessed on 11 April 2022.

12 Upadhyaya, V., 'Factional conflicts continue to roil Pakistan administration after PM Khan's ouster', *Epoch Times*, 13 May 2022, https://www.theepochtimes.com/factional-conflicts-continue-to-roil-pakistan-administration-after-pm-khans-ouster_4442559.html, accessed on 21 May 2022.

13 As told to the author by a former HM commander and the R&AW chief who were overseeing these negotiations between the HM and Jamaat, and the Indian security agencies.

14 Gupta, Shekhar and Rahul Pathak, 'Specter of subversion looms over India as Pakistan sponsored arms, mercenaries and funds from Muslim world pour in to destabilise Kashmir', *India Today*, 15 May 1994, https://www.indiatoday.in/magazine/cover-story/story/19940515-specter-of-subversion-looms-over-india-as-pakistan-sponsored-arms-mercenaries-and-funds-from-muslim-world-pour-in-to-destabilise-kashmir-809140-1994-05-15, accessed on 24 April 2022.

15   Based on the author's interview with a former chief of R&AW, who wished to maintain anonymity.

16   Based on the author's conversations in July 2021 with a journalist who did not wish to be named.

17   ibid.

18   Chaudhari, K., 'Passport office clerks, postman to be prosecuted', *Hindustan Times*, 18 September 2010, https://www.hindustantimes.com/mumbai/passport-office-clerks-postman-to-be-prosecuted/story-2aF89eXRUkaSGtry5sMOaN.html, accessed on 2 July 2022.

19   As told to the author by Farzan (name changed), the son of a prominent Jamaat-i-Islami leader with solid penetration in terrorist organizations. Farzan has fallen out with ISI and, currently, he lives in Kashmir.

20   TOI News Service, 'Arrested Pak diplomat linked to IC 814 hijacking', *The Times of India*, 14 April 2001, https://timesofindia.indiatimes.com/Arrested-Pak-diplomat-linked-to-IC-814-hijacking/articleshow/37542180.cms, accessed on 2 July 2022.

21   ibid.

22   ibid.

23   ibid.

24   Unnithan, S., 'Dulat left out crucial details from his book: RK Yadav', *India Today*, https://www.indiatoday.in/mail-today/story/as-dulat-rk-yadav-kashmir-the-vajpayee-years-details-hidden-282224-2015-07-13, accessed on 7 June 2020.

25   ibid.

26   ibid.

27   Based on the author's interview in April 2022 with Praveen Swami, a veteran journalist with about thirty years of experience in covering strategic and security issues, particularly Kashmir.

28   Arni, A., 'Omar Sheikh: If not Daniel Pearl, a trail with links to ISI, 9/11 mastermind and bin Laden', *The Telegraph Online*,

16 April 2020, https://www.telegraphindia.com/opinion/omar-sheikh-if-not-daniel-pearl-a-trail-with-links-to-isi-9-11-mastermind-and-bin-laden/cid/1765443, accessed on 7 June 2022.

29   As told to the author by veteran journalist Praveen Swami in August 2021.

30   ibid.

31   Dhawan, H., 'ISI backed Kandahar hijackers: Plane crisis negotiator Ajit Dowal,' *Economic Times*, 12 July 2018, https://economictimes.indiatimes.com/news/defence/isi-backed-kandahar-hijackers-plane-crisis-negotiator-ajit-doval/articleshow/56558139.cms?from=mdr , accessed on 26 April 2024.

32   News Desk, 'IC-814 hijackers received Strong Pakistani intelligence support', *Express Tribune*, 15 January 2017, https://tribune.com.pk/story/1295698/ic-814-hijackers-received-strong-pakistan-intelligence-support-doval, accessed on 15 April 2022.

33   Swami, P., 'The Kandahar plot', *Frontline*, 5 December 2003, https://authory.com/PraveenSwami/The-Kandahar-plot-ac60fa6d4bccb40b38d142e5429ac0178, accessed on 26 May 2022.

34   ibid.

35   ibid.

36   ibid.

37   ibid.

38   Riedel, B., 'Blame Pakistani spy service for attack on Indian air force base', Daily Beast, 5 January 2016, https://www.thedailybeast.com/blame-pakistani-spy-service-for-attack-on-indian-air-force-base, accessed on 10 June 2022.

39   Rashid, A., *Descent into Chaos*, p. 114.

40   Wikileaks, 'US state department cable—Bahawalpur: Growing militant recruitment in southern Punjab', Wikileaks

41. Abbas, A., 'Tightening the noose', *Herald*, February 2002.
42. As told to the author by a former HuM commander active in Kashmir from 1994–98.
43. 'Maulana Masood Azhar', *Kashmir Herald*, 8. 2002, http://www.kashmirherald.com/profiles/masoodazhar.html, accessed on 12 April 2022.
44. Siddiqa, A., 'Brothers in arms', accessed on 6 June 2022.
45. ibid.
46. ibid.
47. ibid.
48. Riedel, B., 'Blame Pakistani spy service for attack on Indian air force base'.
49. Siddiqa, A., 'Brothers in arms'.
50. Abbas, A., 'Tightening the noose'.
51. ibid.
52. ibid.
53. ibid.
54. Siddiqa, A., 'Jaish-e-Mohammed: Under the hood', *The Diplomat* 3 March 2019, https://thediplomat.com/2019/03/jaish-e-mohammed-under-the-hood/, accessed on 25 April 2022.
55. Rassler, D., 'Al-Qaida and the Pakistani Harakat movement: Reflections and questions'.
56. Honawar, R., 'Jaish-e-Mohammed', Institute of Peace and Conflict Studies, 2005, https://www.files.ethz.ch/isn/100232/IPCS-Special-Report-04.pdf, accessed on 6 April 2022.
57. Siddiqa, A., 'Brothers in arms'.
58. CISAC, 'Jaish-e-Mohammed: Mapping militants profile'.
59. Riedel, B., 'Blame Pakistani spy service for attack on Indian Air force base'.

(Note: Entry 40 continues at top: Producer, 4 February 2009, https://wikileaks.org/plusd/cables/09ISLAMABAD237_a.html, accessed on 5 June 2022.)

60 Fair, C.C., 'Bringing back the dead: Why Pakistan used the Jaish-e-Mohammed to attack an Indian airbase', *Huffington Post*, 12 January 2016, https://www.huffpost.com/entry/bringing-back-the-dead-wh_b_8955224, accessed on 4 July 2022.

61 ibid.

62 Mohananey, A., 'Jaish is ISI's start-up, it is made to compete with Lashkar-e-Taiba for a reason', *India Today*, 22 February 2019, https://www.indiatoday.in/magazine/guest-column/story/20190304-jaish-the-isi-start-up-1461410-2019-02-22, accessed on 4 July 2022.

63 Akbar, M.J., *Tinderbox: The Past and Future of Pakistan* (HarperCollins, New Delhi: 2012).

64 Pandya, A., *Radicalisation in India: An Exploration* (1st ed.), (Pentagon, New Delhi: 2019).

65 Smith, W.C., *Modern Islam in India* (Victor Gollancz Ltd., London: 1946). According to W.C. Smith, Darul Uloom was 'next to the Azhar of Cairo, the most important and respected theological academy of the Muslim World'.

66 Venkat Dhulipala, 'How the Jamiat Ulama-i-Hind Fought against the Partition of India', *The Caravan*, 8 March 2015, https://caravanmagazine.in/vantage/madani-jinnah-muslim-league-partition.

67 A. Pandya, *Radicalisation in India: An Exploration*, Pentagon, 2019. Retrieved: 4 July 2024.

68 Wahhabis do not believe in any human intercession between Allah and the devotee in the form of interpretation of scriptures by eminent religious scholars of Islamic jurisprudence. For details, see: Pandya, A., *Radicalisation in India* (1st ed.).

69 Taqleed means to follow someone and, in Islamic context, it means to follow an eminent scholar on Islamic jurisprudence. For details, please refer to: Saleem Bhimji, 'What is taqleed',

Al-Islam.org, https://www.al-islam.org/articles/what-taqleed-saleem-bhimji, accessed on 26 April 2024.

70 Pandya, A., and S. Westrop, 'Tablighi Jamaat: Missing the mark', Usanas Foundation, 8 October 2020, https://usanasfoundation.com/missing-the-mark, accessed on 29 June 2022.

71 'Tablighi Jamaat', Pew Research Center, 11 April 2022, https://www.pewresearch.org/religion/2010/09/15/muslim-networks-and-movements-in-western-europe-tablighi-jamaat/, accessed on 20 April 2022.

72 Burton, F., and S. Stewart, 'Tablighi Jamaat: An indirect line to terrorism', STRATFOR, 2008, https://worldview.stratfor.com/article/tablighi-jamaat-indirect-line-terrorism, accessed on 29 June 2022.

73 'Tablighi Jamaat', Pew Research Center.

74 Alexiev, A., 'Tablighi Jamaat: Jihad's stealthy legions', Middle East Quarterly, Winter 2005, vol. 12:1, pp. 3–11, https://www.meforum.org/686/tablighi-jamaat-jihads-stealthy-legions, accessed on 11 April 2022.

74 Lewis, P., *Islamic Britain: Religion, Politics and Identity among British Muslims*, (IB Tauris, London: 2002).

76 Bowen, I., 'Hafiz Patel, Influential British Muslim leader dies at 92', BBC, 19 February 2016, https://www.bbc.com/news/uk-35615205, accessed on 11 April 2022.

77 Naqshbandi, M., 'UK mosque statistics/Masjid statistics', MuslimsInBritain.org, 16 September 2017, https://www.muslimsinbritain.org/resources/masjid_report.pdf, accessed on 11 April 2022.

78 Pandya, A. and S. Westrop 'Tablighi Jamaat: Missing the mark'.

79 Doward, J., 'Battle to block massive mosques', *The Guardian*, 24 September 2006, https://www.theguardian.com/society/2006/sep/24/communities.religion, accessed on 11 April 2022.

80 Muhammad-Arif, A., *Salaam America: South Asian Muslims in New York*, (Anthem Press, London: 2002).

81 Burton, F. and S. Stewart, 'Tablighi Jamaat'.

82 Pantucci, R., *We Love Death as You Love Life: Britain's Suburban Terrorists*, (C. Hurst & Company, London: 2015).

83 SATP. (n.d.), 'Petition Filed by Lt Gen. (Retd) Javed Nasir, director-general Inter-Services Intelligence, Pakistan, before the anti-terrorism court, Lahore', South Asia Terrorism Portal, https://www.satp.org/satporgtp/countries/pakistan/document/papers/petition.htm, accessed on 11 April 2022.

84 Alexiev, A., 'Tablighi Jamaat'.

85 Pandya, A. and S. Westrop, 'Tablighi Jamaat: Missing the mark'.

86 SATP, 'Harkat-ul-Jihad-Al-Islami (HuJI), South Asia Terrorism Portal, https://www.satp.org/satporgtp/countries/india/states/jandk/terrorist_outfits/HuJI.htm, accessed on 11 April 2022.

87 Hudson Institute, 'Rising tide of Islamism in Bangladesh', Hudson Institute, 16 February 2016, https://www.hudson.org/national-security-defense/the-rising-tide-of-islamism-in-bangladesh, accessed on 11 April 2022.

88 Chandra, S., *History of Medieval India: From Sultanate to Mughals* (6th ed.) (Har Anand Publications, New Delhi: 2019).

89 ibid, pp. 166-86, 231-67.

90 Kamran, T., 'The genesis, evolution and impact of Deobandi Islam in Punjab: An overview', 2008, https://www.researchgate.net/publication/309917596_The_Genesis_Evolution_and_Impact_of_Deobandi_Islam_on_the_Punjab_An_Overview#:~:text=In%20%E2%80%9CThe%20Genesis%2C%20Evolution%20and,years%20of%20the%20twentieth%20century, accessed on 11 April 2022. This paper was originally written in 2008 but it featured in 2016 as a chapter in a book titled *Faith-based Violence and Deobandi Militancy in Pakistan* (pp. 65–92).

91 ibid.

92 Cohen, S.P., 'The jihadist threat to Pakistan', *Washington Quarterly*, Summer 2003, vol.26, number 3, pp. 5–25, https://

www.tandfonline.com/doi/abs/10.1162/016366003765609543, accessed on 11 April 2022.

93 Gilmartin, D., *Empire and Islam*, (University of California Press, Berkeley: 1992).

94 ibid. Also see: Kamran, T., 'The genesis, evolution and impact of Deobandi Islam on Punjab: An overview'.

95 Rahi, A. *Tazkirah-i-ulema-i-Punjab*, vol. 2, (Maktaba-e-Rahmania, Lahore: 1998).

96 ibid.

97 Kamran, T., 'The genesis, evolution and impact of Deobandi Islam on Punjab: An overview'.

98 For a detailed biographical account of Ubaidullah Sindhi, see 'Maulana Ubaidullah Sindhi', in Mufti Abdul Khaliq Azad, ed., *Khutbat O Maqalat* (Darul Teh qiq Wa Ishaat, Lahore: 2002), pp.19–87.

99 Kamran, T. 'The genesis, evolution and impact of Deobandi Islam on Punjab: An overview'.

100 For details, refer to Maulana Muhammad Ali, *The Ahmadiyyah Movement*, Translated and edited by S. Muhammad Tuffail, (Ahmadiyyah Anjuman Ishaat Islam, Lahore: 1973).

101 For details, see Jan Baz Mirza, *Karwan-i-Ahrar*, vol.1, (Maktaba-i-Tabsara, Lahore: 1975), pp. 81–84.

102 For details see Taj ud Din Ludhyanvi, *Ahrar Aur Tehrik-e-Kashmir 1932* (Maktaba-i-Majlis-e-Ahrar Islam, Pakistan, Lahore: 1968).

103 Kamran, T., 'The genesis, evolution and impact of Deobandi Islam on Punjab: An overview'.

104 Arshad, R.A., *Bees Barrey Musalmaan* (Maktaba-e-Rashidiya, Lahore: 2006).

105 Maulana Muhammad and Maulana Muhammad Abdullah were brothers from Balliawal district, Ludhiana. Abdullah earned considerable acclaim as a scholar. He followed Muhammad assan

Amritsari, Mehmud ul Hassan and Anwar Shah Kashmiri as a disciple of hadith. Rahi A., *Tazkira-i-ulma-i-Punjab*, pp. 346–47.

106 Kamran, T., 'The genesis, evolution and impact of Deobandi Islam on Punjab: An overview'.

107 ibid.

108 Rahman, T., *Denizens of Alien Worlds: A Study of Education, Inequality, and Polarization in Pakistan* (Oxford University Press, Karachi: 2004). From 1988 to 2000, the number of religious schools grew by 236 per cent. The majority of these schools belonged to the Sunni-Deobandi denomination.

109 Nasr, S., 'The rise of Sunni militancy in Pakistan: The changing role of Islamism and the Ulema in society and politics', *Modern Asian Studies*, vol. 34(1), p.142, https://www.jstor.org/stable/313114, accessed on 11 April 2022. The apprehensions of the Arab monarchs were somewhat moderated when Z.A. Bhutto (1926–79) purged his party of left-wing cadres.

110 Kamran, T., 'The genesis, evolution and impact of Deobandi Islam on Punjab: An overview'. Quoted in Saleem Mansur Khalid, *Deeni Madaris Main Ta'leem: Ka'fiyat, Mas'il, Imkanat* (Institute of Policy Studies, Idara-e-Fiqr-e-Islami,Islamabad: 2004), p. 150

111 Nasr, S., 'The rise of Sunni militancy in Pakistan'.

112 Kamran, T., 'The genesis, evolution and the impact of Deobandi Islam in Punjab: An overview'.

113 Burki, S.J., *A Revisionist History of Pakistan* (Vanguard Books, Lahore: 1998).

114 Malik, J., *Colonisation of Islam: Dissolution of Traditional Institutions in Pakistan* (Vanguard Books, Lahore: 1996).

115 Kamran, T., 'The genesis, evolution and the impact of Deobandi Islam in Punjab: An overview'. Quoted in Saleem Mansur Khalid, *Deni Madaris Main Ta'leem: Ka'fiyat, as'il, Imkanat* (Institute of Policy Studies, Idara-e-Fiqr-e-Islami, Islamabad: 2004) p. 145.

116 ibid.

117 Kamran, T., 'The genesis, evolution and the impact of Deobandi Islam in Punjab: An overview'.
118 Siddiqa, A., 'Brothers in arms'.
119 Fair, C.C., *In their Own Words*.
120 Siddiqa, A., 'Brothers in arms'.
121 ibid.
122 ibid.
123 ibid.
124 ibid.
125 FBI, World Trade Center Bombing 1993, https://www.fbi.gov/history/famous-cases/world-trade-center-bombing-1993, accessed in February 2024.
126 This section is primarily based on the factual information given in Ayesha Siddiqa's 'Brothers in arms' and by Stanford's Center for International Security and Cooperation (CISAC) under the 'Mapping Militants' project, https://cisac.fsi.stanford.edu/mappingmilitants/profiles/lashkar-e-jhangvi-lej, accessed on 22 April 2022.
127 Siddiqa, A., 'Terror's training ground', *Newsline*, 9 September 2009, https://chairestrategique.pantheonsorbonne.fr/conferenciers/ayesha-siddiqa, accessed on 11 April 2022.
128 Siddiqa, A., 'Jihadism in Pakistan: The expanding frontier', *Journal of International Affairs*, vol. 63(1), pp. 57–71, http://www.jstor.org/stable/24384172, accessed on 12 February 2024.
129 'Malik Ishaq: Pakistan Sunni militant chief killed by police', *BBC*, 29 July 2015, https://www.bbc.com/news/world-asia-33699133, accessed on 15 February 2024.
130 Siddiqa, A., 'Terror's training ground'.
131 ibid.
132 CISAC, 'Lashkar-e-Jhangvi (LeJ)', Stanford's Center for International Security and Cooperation, https://cisac.fsi.stanford.

edu/mappingmilitants/profiles/lashkar-e-jhangvi-lej, accessed on 11 April 2022.

133 'Pakistan: LeJ behind police academy attack in Quetta', *Al Jazeera*, 26 October 2016, https://www.aljazeera.com/news/2016/10/26/pakistan-lej-behind-police-academy-attack-in-quetta, accessed on 27 April 2024.

134 BBC, 'Malik Ishaq: Pakistani Sunni militant chief killed by the police', *BBC*, 29 July 2015, https://www.bbc.com/news/world-asia-33699133, accessed on 15 February 2024.

135 Fair, C.C., *In their Own Words*; and CISAC, 'Tahreek-e-Taliban, Pakistan', Stanford's Center for International Security and Cooperation, https://cisac.fsi.stanford.edu/mappingmilitants/profiles/tehrik-i-taliban-pakistan, accessed on 11 April 2022.

136 ibid.

137 ibid.

138 ibid.

Chapter 3: Masood Azhar and JeM's Dark Ideological Alleyways

1 'Interrogation report of Masood Azhar', Jammu and Kashmir Police, 1944, accessed on 21 April 2022.

2 Azhar, M.M., *Fat-hul-Jawwad*, translated by P.R. Masood (Maktab Irfan, Lahore: 2012).

3 'Interrogation report of Masood Azhar'.

4 The INTERPOL has issued a red-corner notice for Muhammad Ibrahim Athar Alvi.

5 As told by Masood to his interrogator in 1994: Jehangir and Alamgir were madrasa students then. The details of their current status are unknown.

6 Singh, S.K., 'Masood Azhar: An architect of terror', *DNA*, 7 April 2019, https://www.dnaindia.com/india/report-masood-azhar-an-architect-of-terror-2737045, accessed on 26 April 2022.

7. 'Interrogation report of Masood Azhar'.
8. PTI, 'Jaish chief Azhar has renal failure, being treated at Pak Army hospital', *The Week*, March 2019, https://www.theweek.in/news/india/2019/03/02/del3-terror-azhar.html, accessed on 28 April 2022.
9. ibid.
10. Azhar, M.M., *Fat-hul-Jawwad*.
11. Masood, R. Ahmed, 'Amir-ul-Jihad and Fat-Hul-Jawwad', *Fat-Hul-Jawwad* (English Translation), https://www.fathuljawwad.com/muallif_intro_eng.htm and https://archive.org/details/FathuljawwadEng1/page/n7/mode/2up, accessed on 26 April 2024.
12. Siddiqa, A., 'Jaish-e-Muhammad: Under the hood', *Diplomat*, https://thediplomat.com/2019/03/jaish-e-mohammed-under-the-hood/, accessed on 25 April 2022.
13. A Karachi-centred secular, political group/movement started by Altaf Hussain in 1984 for the protection and promotion of the rights of muhajirs, i.e., Muslim migrants from India, who came to Pakistan after Partition.
14. Jiye Sind/Sindhudesh movement was a Sind-based political movement that advocated Sind's independence from Pakistan.
15. A political movement to make Saraiki region a new province of Pakistan.
16. An Islamist movement in India and Pakistan that aims to establish a Shariah-based society. It draws inspiration from Maulana Maududi, a votary of political Islam. JI is very actively associated with Pakistan-sponsored terrorist groups active in India-administered Kashmir.
17. 'Interrogation report of Masood Azhar'
18. Bowen, I., 'Masood Azhar: The man who brought jihad to Britain', *BBC*, 5 April 2016, https://www.bbc.com/news/magazine-35959202#:~:text=According%20to%20the%20report%20of,on%20the%20issue%20of%20jihad, accessed on 23 April 2023.

19 'Interrogation report of Masood Azhar'.
20 Bowen, I., 'Masood Azhar'.
21 ibid.
22 ibid.
23 Temporary border between India and Pakistan-administered Kashmir in the union territory of Jammu and Kashmir in India.
24 'Interrogation report of Masood Azhar'.
25 CISAC, 'Harkat-ul-Jihad-al Islami', Stanford's Center for International Security and Cooperation, https://cisac.fsi.stanford.edu/mappingmilitants/profiles/harkat-ul-jihadi-al-islami, accessed on 24 April 2022.
26 ibid.
27 Gupta, S., and R. Pathak, 'Specter of subversion looms over India as Pakistan-sponsored arms, mercenaries, and funds from Muslim world pour in to destabilize Kashmir', *India Today*, 15 May 2994, https://www.indiatoday.in/magazine/cover-story/story/19940515-specter-of-subversion-looms-over-india-as-pakistan-sponsored-arms-mercenaries-and-funds-from-muslim-world-pour-in-to-destabilise-kashmir-809140-1994-05-15, accessed on 24 April 2022.
28 Baweja, H., 'Masood Azhar: Inside the mind of a global terror merchant', *Hindustan Times*, 15 March 2019, https://www.hindustantimes.com/india-news/masood-azhar-inside-a-terrorists-s-mind/story-PFALvrZ22ZZn5wdWX7apxL.html, accessed on 24 April 2022.
29 Khajuria, R., '"Still remember the day Masood Azhar was released," recalls former jailor', *Hindustan Times*, 1 May 2019, https://www.hindustantimes.com/india-news/still-remember-the-day-masood-azhar-was-released-recalls-former-jailor/story-Tnbe4lODLSa0JGxLbWkSXL.html, accessed on 24 April 2022.
30 Zargar and Omar Sheikh are discussed in detail later in this book.
31 Khajuria, R., '"Still remember the day Masood Azhar was released," recalls former jailor'.

32. Based on the author's conversations in July 2021 with a journalist who did not wish to be named.

33. Mohananey, A., 'The man who interrogated Masood Azhar recalls the time he sang like a canary', *Economic Times*, 1 May 2019, https://economictimes.indiatimes.com/news/defence/the-man-who-interrogated-masood-azhar-remembers-when-he-sang-like-a-canary/articleshow/68041543.cms?from=mdr, accessed on 25 April 2022.

34. Das, S., 'From jail to Jaish: How Azhar changed the terror narrative', *Mint*, 2 May 2019, https://www.livemint.com/news/world/from-jail-to-jaish-how-azhar-rewrote-terror-narrative-1556818460003.html, accessed on 25 April 2022.

35. Mohananey, A., 'The man who interrogated Masood Azhar recalls the time he sang like a canary'.

36. Swami, P., 'The Kandahar plot', *Frontline*, 5 December 2003, https://authory.com/PraveenSwami/The-Kandahar-plot-ac60fa6d4bccb40b38d142e5429ac0178, accessed on 26 May 2022.

37. Based on the author's conversation with a Jammu-based senior NIA official and another conversation with a key member of the Pulwama fidayeen attack.

38. NIE, 'Masood told Sobhraj about Mumbai plan', *New Indian Express*, 10 December 2008, https://www.newindianexpress.com/nation/2008/dec/10/masood-told-sobhraj-about-mumbai-plan-9603.html, accessed on 25 April 2022.

39. Based on the author's interview with a senior NIA official who worker under Mr R.V. Raju, IPS officer of 1975 batch and the founder of NIA, India's premier counterterrorism agency. See also https://en.wikipedia.org/wiki/Radha_Vinod_Raju#:~:text=His%20first%20appointment%20as%20Superintendent,of%20India's%20National%20Investigation%20Agency, accessed on 26 April 2024.

40. Siddiqa, A., 'Jaish-e-Muhammad'.

41 Mohananey, A., 'The man who interrogated Masood Azhar recalls the time he sang like a canary'.

42 Vinayak, R., 'Abduction of five foreign tourists by militants and blast in Jammu keep Valley on boil', *India Today*, 15 August 1995, https://www.indiatoday.in/magazine/special-report/story/19950815-abduction-of-five-foreign-tourists-by-militants-and-blast-in-jammu-keep-valley-on-boil-807642-1995-08-15, accessed on 25 April 2022.

43 HT, 'IC-814 hijack: 21 years after release, Zargar remains elusive', *Hindustan Times*, 30 December 2020, https://www.hindustantimes.com/cities/ic-814-hijack-21-years-after-release-zargar-remains-elusive/story-KdEtpXFlH9NUFQyzuqjF0J.html, accessed on 25 April 2022.

44 The assets of individuals and companies added to the SDN list are blocked and the US nationals are prohibited from dealing with them.

45 US Department of Treasury, 'Anti-terrorist designations', 4 November 2010, https://home.treasury.gov/policy-issues/financial-sanctions/recent-actions/20101104, accessed on 15 June 2022.

46 PTI, 'China blocks move to declare Masood Azhar a global terrorist at the UN', *The Times of India*, 14 March 2019, https://timesofindia.indiatimes.com/world/pakistan/azhars-unsc-listing-china-hints-it-may-block-move-to-declare-him-global-terrorist/articleshow/68390013.cms, accessed on 26 April 2022.

47 PTI, 'US lauds UN designation of Masood Azhar as global terrorist', *The Week*, 2 May 2019, https://www.theweek.in/news/world/2019/05/02/us-lauds-azhar-designation-global-terrorist-un.html, accessed on 15 June 2022.

48 'Masood Azhar: Jaish-e-Mohammed leader listed as terrorist by UN', *BBC*, 1 May 2019, https://www.bbc.com/news/world-asia-48124693, accessed on 26 April 2022.

49 Baweja, H., 'Masood Azhar'.

50. Siddiqa, A., 'Jaish-e-Muhammad'.
51. Ibid.
52. 'Masood Azhar', 22 May 2019, Global Fight Against Terrorism Funding (GFATF), https://www.gfatf.org/archives/masood-azhar/, accessed on 26 April 2022.
53. ibid.
54. Gupta, S., and R. Pathak, 'Specter of subversion looms over India as Pakistan sponsored arms, mercenaries and funds from Muslim world pour in to destabilise Kashmir'.
55. Firdous, K., 'Militancy in Pakistan', Institute of Strategic Studies Islamabad, 15 March 2009, https://issi.org.pk/militancy-in-pakistan/, accessed on 1 June 2022.
56. Jalal, A., *Partisans of Allah: Jihad in South Asia* (Harvard University Press, Cambridge: 2008).
57. Pandya, A., *Radicalisation in India*.
58. Hussain, R., *Life as a Weapon: Global Rise in Suicide Bombings* (Routledge, London: 2014).
59. Pandya, A., *Radicalisation in India*.
60. Akbar, M., *Tinderbox*.
61. Suroor, H., 'Daft and dangerous: Muslim scholar's plan for a militia to fight global jihad', Firstpost, 25 July 2014, https://www.firstpost.com/world/daft-and-dangerous-muslim-scholars-plan-for-a-militia-to-fight-global-jihad-1634307.html, accessed on 10 May 2022.
62. Baweja, H., 'Masood Azhar'.
63. Guha, R. (@Ram_Guha), 'Masood Azhar "may never have turned his attention to India ... were it not for the demolition of the Babri Masjid"', Twitter, 15 January 2016, https://twitter.com/ram_guha/status/687841431713525760?lang=en, accessed on 28 April 2022.
64. Baweja, H., 'Making of a terrorist: Babri demolition triggered Masood Azhar's jihad', *Hindustan Times*, 14 January 2016,

https://www.hindustantimes.com/india/making-of-a-terrorist-babri-masjid-demolition-triggered-azhar-s-jihad/story-zg6YSKXSjxRk5xo3AlvdfM.html, accessed on 28 April 2022.

65. 'Two arrested for supplying arms to Lashkar-e-Mustafa for terror attacks in J&K', CNN-News 18, 3 July 2021, https://www.news18.com/news/india/nia-arrests-2-people-from-bihar-for-supplying-arms-to-lashkar-e-mustafa-for-terror-attacks-in-jammu-3994709.html, accessed on 28 April 2022.

66. Haqqani, H., 'The gospel of jihad', *Foreign Policy*, 9 November 2009, https://foreignpolicy.com/2009/11/09/the-gospel-of-jihad/, accessed on 29 April 2022.

67. Siddiqa, A., 'Jaish-e-Muhammad'.

68. Based on the author's interview with Farzan, the author's informed interlocutor with deep connections in the ISI.

69. Siddiqa, A., 'Jaish-e-Muhammad'.

70. Baweja, H., 'Masood Azhar'.

71. Azhar, M.M., *Fat-hul-Jawwad*.

72. Masood, R.Ahmed, 'Amir-ul-Jihad and Fat-hul-Jawwad'.

73. ibid.

74. ibid.

75. ibid.

76. ibid.

77. Fair, C.C., 'We asked why Pakistanis support Lashkar-e-Taiba. Results will surprise you', *The Print*, 24 January 2022, https://theprint.in/opinion/we-asked-why-pakistanis-support-lashkar-e-taiba-results-will-surprise-you/809550/, accessed on 30 May 2022.

78. ibid.

79. ibid.

80. Raman, B., 'Harkat-ul-Mujahiddin: An update', South Asia Analysis Group, 20 March 1999, https://www.linas.org/mirrors/

www.saag.org/2001.10.13/papers/paper42.html, accessed on 30 May 2022.
81. ibid.
82. ibid.
83. 'Jaish-e-Muhammad', South Asia Terrorism Portal, https://www.satp.org/terrorist-profile/india-jammukashmir/jaish-e-mohammed-jem, accessed on 30 May 2022.
84. Raman, B., 'Harkat-ul-Mujahiddin'.
85. Verma, R., 'Pakistan and Jaish-e-Muhammad: The unholy alliance', Lowy Institute, 7 July 2017, https://www.lowyinstitute.org/the-interpreter/pakistan-and-jaish-e-mohammad-unholy-alliance, accessed on 30 May 2022.
86. Tiwari, D., 'Pulwama attackers wanted strike to spark India–Pak war: NIA chargesheet', *The Indian Express*, 26 August 2020, https://indianexpress.com/article/india/pulwama-attackers-wanted-strike-to-spark-india-pak-war-nia-chargesheet-6569874/, accessed on 30 May 2022.
87. Rabasa, A., P. Chalk et al., 'Beyond Al Qaeda: The global jihadist movement, Part 1', Rand Corporation, 2006, https://www.26jstor.org/stable/10.7249/mg429af.15?seq=3, accessed on 12 May 2022.
88. 'Pakistan: Voices of jihad', South Asia Terrorism Portal, https://www.satp.org/islamist-extremism/data/Pakistan-Voices-of%20-Jehad, accessed on 29 May 2022.
89. ibid.
90. Rabasa, A., P. Chalk et Al., 'Beyond Al Qaeda'.
91. Fielding, N., 'British Jackal', *Sunday Times*, 21 April 2002, https://www.mea.gov.in/articles-in-foreign-media.htm?dtl/18174/The+British+jackal, accessed on 12 May 2022.
92. ibid.
93. Swami, P., 'India's most wanted', *Frontline*, 19 January 2002, https://authory.com/PraveenSwami/Indias-most-wanted-a086cdd62459a46e1be2a1e735dab3b52, accessed on 25 May 2022.

94 Based on the author's interview with a senior officer from the Intelligence Bureau, India's domestic intelligence agency, and the in-charge of Kashmir's intelligence operations.

95 Bowen, I., 'Masood Azhar'.

96 ibid.

97 Pantucci, R., 'A biography of Rashid Rauf: Al-Qa'ida's British operative', *CTC Sentinel*, vol. 5(7), July 2012, https://ctc.usma.edu/app/uploads/2012/07/CTCSentinel-Vol5Iss74.pdf, accessed on 7 June 2022.

98 ibid.

99 'UK blast suspect met Islamabad church bomber', *Dawn*, 16 July 2016, https://www.dawn.com/news/148080, accessed on 7 June 2022.

100 'Masood's masterstroke: The Afzal Guru Squad', *Bangalore Mirror*, 15 January 2016, https://bangaloremirror.indiatimes.com/news/india/masoods-masterstroke-the-afzal-guru-squad/articleshow/50596854.cms, accessed on 7 June 2022.

101 ibid.

102 ibid.

103 Egan, M., 'Synagogue targeted in NY plot, four charged', *Reuters*, 21 May 2009, https://www.reuters.com/article/latestCrisis/idUSN20523965, accessed on 15 June 2022.

104 Bowen, I., 'Masood Azhar'.

105 ibid.

106 Rana, M.A., *A to Z of Jehadi Organisations in Pakistan*, (Mashal, Lahore: 2006).

107 Rassler, D., 'Al-Qaida and the Pakistani Harakat movement'.

108 Rana, M.A., *A to Z of Jehadi Organisations in Pakistan*, p. 32.

109 'Harkat-ul-Ansar—The Pakistan dimension excised', Unclassified US Embassy Cable, US Government, 1995, https://nsarchive2.gwu.edu//NSAEBB/NSAEBB389/docs/1995-03-29%20-%20Karachi%20HUA%20and%20Haqqani.pdf, accessed on 12 May 2022.

110 Rassler, D., 'Al-Qaida and the Pakistani Harakat movement'.

111 Gorman, E., 'Khost outpost falls to mujahiddin led by foreign fighters', *The Times*, 21 March 1988, accessed on 12 May 2022

112 Rassler, D., 'Al-Qaida and the Pakistani Harakat movement'.

113 Roy, O., and M.A. Zahab, *Islamist Networks: Afghan-Pakistan Connection*, (Columbia University Press, New York: 2004). See also: Sirrs, J., 'Taliban's international ambitions', *Middle East Quarterly*, Summer 2001, pp. 61–71, https://www.meforum.org/486/the-talibans-international-ambitions, accessed on 12 May 2022.

114 Gul, I., *The Most Dangerous Place: Pakistan's Lawless Frontier*, (Penguin, New York: 2009).

115 Stenersen, A., *Al-Qaida in Afghanistan*, (Cambridge University Press, Cambridge: 2017).

116 Rashid, A., *Taliban: Militant Islam, Oil & Islamic Fundamentalism in Central Asia*, (Yale University Press, New Haven: 2001).

117 Mir, A., *The True Face of Jehadis: Inside Pakistan's Network of Terror*, (Roli Books, Delhi: 2006).

118 Rabasa, A., P. Chalk, et Al., 'Beyond Al Qaeda'.

119 ibid.

120 Soufan, A., 'Al-Qa'ida's (mis)adventures in the Horn of Africa', Combating Terrorism Center, 2009, https://ctc.usma.edu/wp-content/uploads/2010/06/Al-Qaidas-MisAdventures-in-the-Horn-of-Africa.pdf, accessed on 12 May 2022.

121 Watson, P., and S. Barua, 'Somalian link seen to Al Qaeda', *Los Angeles Times*, 25 February 2002, https://www.latimes.com/archives/la-xpm-2002-feb-25-mn-29792-story.html, 12 May 2022.

122 Burns, J.F., 'Yemen links to bin Laden gnaw at FBI in Cole inquiry', *The New York Times*, 26 November 2000, http://www.nytimes.com/2000/11/26/world/yemen-links-to-bin-laden-gnaw-at-fbi-in-cole-inquiry.html, accessed on 12 May 2022.

123 Haqqani, H., 'The gospel of jihad', *Foreign Policy*, 9 November 2009, https://foreignpolicy.com/2009/11/09/the-gospel-of-jihad/, accessed on 29 April 2022.

124 Rana, M.A, *Jihad in Kashmir and Afghanistan*.

125 Roy, O., and M.A. Zahab, *Islamist* Networks, p. 30.

126 Ahmad, K., *Sectarian War: Pakistan's Sunni–Shia Violence and its Links to Middle East*, (Oxford University Press, Oxford: 2011).

127 Rana, M.A, *Jihad in Kashmir and Afghanistan*.

128 Azhar, M.M., 'Muhammad Akhtar's journey in the land of jihad' in *Sada-i-Mujahid*, vol. 2(12), pp. 26–28, December 1991, accessed on 12 May 2022.

129 'Harkat-ul-Ansar', Unclassified US Embassy Cable, US Government, 1995.

130 Fielding, N., 'British Jackal'.

131 Burke, J., *Al Qaeda: Casting the Shadow of Terror*, (I.B. Tauris, London & New York: 2004).

132 Sageman, M., *Leaderless Jihad: Terror Networks in the Twenty-first Century*, (University of Pennsylvania, Philadelphia: 2008).

133 Burke, J., *Al* Qaeda.

134 Johnson, J., 'American recalls his 1995 abduction', *Los Angeles Times*, 9 February 2002, http://articles.latimes.com/2002/feb/09/news/mn-27168, accessed on 12 May 2022.

135 Nye, S., 'Al-Qa'ida key operative: A profile of Mohammed Ilyas Kashmiri', *CTC Sentinel*, 1 September 2010, https://ctc.westpoint.edu/al-qaidas-key-operative-a-profile-of-mohammed-ilyas-kashmiri/, accessed on 12 May 2022.

136 Rassler, D., 'Al-Qaida and the Pakistani Harakat movement'.

137 Reuters, 'After the attacks: In Afghanistan; UN officer shot in Kabul after bombing dies; 4 held', *The New York Times*, 23 August 1998, http://www.nytimes.com/1998/08/23/world/after-attacks-

afghanistan-un-officer-shot-kabul-after-bombing-dies-4-held. html, accessed on 12 May 2022.

138 'Three get life term for hijacking Indian plane', *Dawn*, 6 February 2008, https://www.dawn.com/news/288127/three-get-life-term-for-hijacking-indian-plane, accessed on 12 May 2022.

139 Raman, B, 'Amjad Farooqi: The untold story', South Asia Analysis Group, 29 September 2004, http://www.southasiaanalysis.org/paper1129, accessed on 12 May 2022.

140 'Profile: Amjad Farooqi', *BBC*, 27 September 2004, http://news.bbc.co.uk/2/hi/south_asia/3692882.stm, accessed 12 May 2022.

141 Rassler, D., 'Al-Qaida and the Pakistani Harakat movement'.142 Silber, M.D., *The Al-Qaeda Factor: Plots Against the West*, (University of Pennsylvania Press, Philadelphia: 2012).

143 Burke, J., *Al* Qaeda.

144 Mir, H., 'Maulana Allah Wasaya Qasim's Jihad-i-Hind', *Islam*, 6 June 2003, accessed on 12 May 2022.

145 Brown, V., and D. Rassler, *Fountainhead of Jihad: The Haqqani Nexus—1973–2012*, (Columbia University Press, New York: 2013).

146 Rana, M.A, *Jihad in Kashmir and Afghanistan*, p. 37.

147 Rashid, A., *Descent into Chaos*.

148 Mir, A., *The True Face of Jehadis*.

149 Ahmad, K., 'Al Qaeda and Karachi', *Express Tribune*, 12 February 2011, https://tribune.com.pk/story/117942/al-qaeda-and-karachi, accessed on 12 May 2022.

150 ibid.

151 Jaffrelot, C., *Pakistan Paradox: Instability and Resilience*, (Random House, Delhi: 2015).

152 'Al Rashid Trust', South Asia Terrorism Portal, https://www.satp.org/satporgtp/countries/pakistan/terroristoutfits/Al-Rashid_Trust.htm, accessed on 26 April 2024.

153 Rassler, D., 'Al-Qaida and the Pakistani Harakat movement'.
154 Swami, P., 'Head of Al-Qaeda in Indian subcontinent is from Uttar Pradesh', *The Indian Express*, 9 October 2019, https://indianexpress.com/article/india/india-news-india/head-of-al-qaeda-in-indian-subcontinent-is-from-up/, accessed on 14 May 2022.
155 Ahmad, K., 'Al Qaeda and Karachi'.
156 Cooley, K.J., *Unholy Wars: Afghanistan, America, and International Terrorism*, (Pluto Press, London: 2002).
157 Stenersen, A., *Al-Qaida in Afghanistan*, p. 73.
158 Rassler, D., 'Al-Qaida and the Pakistani Harakat movement'.
159 Lawrence, B., ed., *Messages to the World: The Statements of Osama bin Laden*, (Verso, New York: 2005).
160 Lancestor, J., and K. Khan, 'At an Islamic school, hints of extremist ties', *Washington Post*, 13 June 2004, https://www.washingtonpost.com/archive/politics/2004/06/13/at-an-islamic-school-hints-of-extremist-ties/8a43dc9e-e73e-436b-bbd7-3703ddc16e4e/, accessed on 14 May 2022.
161 Stenersen, A., *Al-Qaida in Afghanistan*, p. 73.
162 Al-Sahab, 'Days with the Imam', July–August 2012, https://archive.org/details/Third-Interview/Third-Interview-with-Dr-Ayman_al-Zawahiri.rm, accessed on 14 May 2022.
163 Lancestor, J., and K. Khan, 'At an Islamic school, hints of extremist ties'.
164 Rassler, D., 'Al-Qaida and the Pakistani Harakat movement'.
165 Roy, O., and M.A. Zahab, *Islamist Networks*, pp. 59–60.
166 'Karachi: Ulema call for jihad against the US', *Dawn*, 25 March 2003, https://www.dawn.com/news/89325/karachi-ulema-call-for-jihad-against-us, accessed on 14 May 2022.
167 Coll, S., 'The stand off: How jihadi groups helped provoke the twenty-first century's first nuclear standoff', *The New

       Yorker, 13 February 2006, https://www.newyorker.com/magazine/2006/02/13/the-stand-off, accessed on 14 May 2022.
168 ibid.
169 ibid.
170 Fair, C.C., 'Bringing back the dead: Why Pakistan used the Jaish-e-Mohammad to attack an Indian airbase', *Huffington Post*, 12 January 2016, https://www.huffpost.com/entry/bringing-back-the-dead-wh_b_8955224, accessed on 14 May 2022.
171 Baweja, H., 'Masood Azhar'.
172 'Jaish-e-Muhammad', National Counterterrorism Center, https://www.dni.gov/nctc/groups/jem.html, accessed on 15 May 2022.
173 ibid.
174 Gupta, S., 'Afghan forces intercept Taliban fighters, find Jaish terrorists training for Kashmir', *Hindustan Times*, 16 April 2020, https://www.hindustantimes.com/india-news/afghan-border-clash-with-taliban-exposes-jaish-terror-camps-for-kashmir/story-GyRErS9kvUzbYcq544r6bO.html, accessed on 14 May 2022.
175 ibid.
176 ibid.
177 Mufti Rauf Azgar, de facto chief of Jaish is known as Mufti Rauf, Mufti Abdul Rauf Azgar or Mufti Rauf Asghar.
178 Gupta, S., 'Next wave of 400 Jaish terrorists for Kashmir could be from its Afghan camps', *Hindustan Times*, 5 May 2020, https://www.hindustantimes.com/india-news/next-wave-of-400-jaish-terrorists-for-kashmir-could-be-from-its-afghan-camps/story-MUJTQWvy4LtMC7nLHKVRFL.html, accessed on 15 May 2022.
179 Laskar, H.R., 'Pak's terror groups join Afghan war, India wary', *Hindustan Times*, 11 July 2021, https://www.hindustantimes.com/india-news/paks-terror-groups-join-taliban-war-india-wary-101625942135382.html, accessed on 15 May 2022.
180 ibid.

181 ibid.

182 Ghosh, P., 'Jaish-e-Mohammad leaders met Taliban in Kandahar, discussed J&K: Report', *Hindustan Times*, 28 August 2021, https://www.hindustantimes.com/india-news/jaishemohammad-leaders-met-taliban-in-kandahar-discussed-j-k-report-101630141494850.html, accessed on 15 May 2022.

183 ibid.

184 'Jaish-e-Mohammed chief meets Taliban leadership, seeks "help" in Kashmir: Sources', *India Today*, 27 August 2021, https://www.indiatoday.in/world/story/jaish-e-mohammed-chief-meets-taliban-leadership-seeks-help-in-kashmir-sources-1846167-2021-08-27, accessed on 15 May 2022.

185 'Harkat-ul-Jihad-i-Islami', *Kashmir Herald*, vol. 2, no. 5, October 2002, http://www.kashmirherald.com/profiles/Harkat%20ul-Jihad-i-Islami.html, accessed on 15 June 2022.

186 Robertson, N., and S. Mehsud, 'Al Qaeda promises "war on all fronts" against America as Biden pulls out of Afghanistan', *CNN*, 30 April 2021, https://edition.cnn.com/2021/04/30/asia/al-qaeda-afghanistan-biden-intl-cmd/index.html, accessed on 16 May 2022.

187 Mir, A., 'After the Taliban's takeover: Pakistan's TTP problem', United States Institute of Peace, 19 January 2022, https://www.usip.org/publications/2022/01/after-talibans-takeover-pakistans-ttp-problem, accessed on 16 May 2022.

188 ibid.

189 Haqqani, H., 'Pakistan reaps what it sowed', *Foreign Affairs*, https://www.foreignaffairs.com/articles/afghanistan/2022-05-23/pakistan-reaps-what-it sowed?utm_medium=newsletters&utm_source=fatoday&utm_campaign=How%20to%20Prepare%20for%20the%20Next%20Ukraine&utm_content=20220523&utm_term=FA%20Today%20-%20112017, accessed on 23 May 2022.

190 'UN report claims Taliban and Al-Qaeda remain closely aligned, no changes', *Business Standard*, 5 June 2021, https://www.business-standard.com/article/international/un-report-claims-taliban-and-al-qaeda-remain-closely-aligned-no-changes-121060500089_1.html, accessed on 16 May 2022.

191 Ibid; and Laskat, H.R. (11 July 2021). 'Pak's Terror Group Join Afghan War, India Wary'. *Hindustan Times*, Retrieved: 15 May 2022, https://www.hindustantimes.com/india-news/paks-terror-groups-join-taliban-war-india-wary-101625942135382.html.

192 ibid.

193 Gupta, S., 'Afghan forces intercept Taliban fighters, find Jaish terrorists training for Kashmir'.

Chapter 4: JeM's Organizational Evolution and India Operations

1 Jaleel, M., 'Explaining the history of Masood Azhar's Jaish-e-Mohammad, the mystery of its re-emergence', *The Indian Express*, 17 December 2021, https://indianexpress.com/article/explained/in-fact-history-of-masood-azhars-jaish-the-mystery-of-its-re-emergence-2615926/, accessed on 1 June 2022.

2 Brockes, E., 'British man named as bomber who killed 10', *The Guardian*, 28 December 2000, https://www.theguardian.com/uk/2000/dec/28/india.kashmir, accessed on 29 May 2022.

3 Reidel, B., 'How 9/11 is connected to December 13', Brookings, 11 September 2008, https://www.brookings.edu/opinions/how-911-is-connected-to-december-13/, accessed on 20 April 2022.

4 Bailay, R., 'India says Al Qaeda suspect in custody planned terrorist attack on Parliament', *Wall Street Journal*, 7 December 2001, https://www.wsj.com/articles/SB1007668649674380840, accessed on 29 May 2022.

5 Hersh, S.M., 'The getaway', *The New Yorker*, 20 January 2002, https://www.newyorker.com/magazine/2002/01/28/the-getaway-2, accessed on 14 June 2022.

6. Before 9/11, Pakistan had several hundred ISI agents advising and assisting the Taliban's fight against the Northern Alliance. Besides that, hundreds of former soldiers had joined the Taliban ranks and Pakistani volunteers had joined Al Qaeda legions.
7. Moran, M., 'The "airlift of evil"', *NBC News*, 11 December 2003, https://www.nbcnews.com/id/wbna3340165, accessed on 14 June 2022.
8. Hersh, S.M., 'The getaway'.
9. As told to the author by A.S. Dulat, former R&AW chief.
10. As told to the author by a senior R&AW officer who was involved in the Kandahar hijack negotiations and dealt with Af-Pak affairs from 2000–06. He requested anonymity.
11. Gupta, P., 'To the brink: 2001–02 India–Pakistan stand-off', *Indian Defence Review*, 22 June 2016, http://www.indiandefencereview.com/spotlights/to-the-brink-2001-02-india-pakistan-standoff/, accessed on 29 May 2022.
12. ibid.
13. As told to the author by a senior R&AW officer who was involved in the Kandahar hijack negotiations and dealt with Af-Pak affairs from 2000–06. He requested anonymity.
14. ibid.
15. 'Press availability at New Delhi, India', 10 May 2003, US Department of State Archive, https://2001-2009.state.gov/s/d/former/armitage/remarks/20492.htm, accessed on 29 May 2022.
16. Kalyanraman, S., 'Operation Parakram: An Indian exercise in coercive diplomacy', *Strategic Analysis*, vol. 26, no. 2, pp. 478–492, doi:10.1080/09700160208450063, accessed on 30 May 2022.
17. The organization must engage in terrorist activity, as defined in section 212 (a)(3)(B) of the INA (8 USC § 1182(a)(3)(B)), or terrorism, as defined in section 140(d)(2) of the Foreign Relations Authorization Act, Fiscal Years 1988 and 1989 (22 USC § 2656

f(d)(2)), or retain the capability and intent to engage in terrorist activity or terrorism.

18 Garge, R., and C. Sahay, 'Rise of Jaish-e-Mohammed in Kashmir Valley: An internal security perspective', Vivekananda International Foundation, January 2017, https://www.vifindia.org/sites/default/files/rise-of-jaish-e-mohammed-in-kashmir-valley.pdf, accessed on 30 May 2022.

19 Cronin, A.C., 'Foreign Terrorist Organisations: CRS Report for Congress', Congressional Research Service: Library of Congress, 6 February 2004, https://irp.fas.org/crs/RL32223.pdf, accessed on 30 May 2022.

20 Garge, R., and C. Sahay, 'Rise of Jaish-e-Mohammed in Kashmir Valley'.

21 Popovic, M., 'The perils of weak organization: Explaining loyalty and defection of militant organizations towards Pakistan', in *Studies in Conflict and Terrorism*, vol. 38, no. 11, pp. 919–937, https://doi.org/10.1080/1057610X.2015.1063838, accessed on 30 May 2022.

22 ibid.

23 Gunaratna, R., and S. Kam, *Handbook of Terrorism in the Asia-Pacific*, (Imperial College Press, London: 2016).

24 Garge, R., and C. Sahay, 'Rise of Jaish-e-Mohammed in Kashmir Valley'.

25 Mir, A., 'After they failed to assassinate Musharraf', *Herald*, 14 December 2017, https://herald.dawn.com/news/1153914, accessed on 30 May 2022.

26 ibid.

27 Burman, A., and Diwakar, 'Musharraf is alive, thanks to India', *The Times of India*, 24 February 2004, https://timesofindia.indiatimes.com/Musharraf-is-alive-thanks-to-India/articleshow/517744.cms, accessed on 30 May 2022.

28 AFP, 'Zawahiri targets Musharraf in a new tape', Rediff.com, 26 March 2004, https://www.rediff.com/news/2004/mar/26zawa.htm, accessed on 7 June 2022.

29 ibid.
30 ibid.
31 ibid.
32 ibid.
33 Raman, B., 'Daniel Pearl and the body of evidence', *Hindustan Times*, 8 January 2006, https://www.hindustantimes.com/india/daniel-pearl-and-the-body-of-evidence/story-uefTD8sI6h9SbZNuJMNWvJ.html#:~:text=Shortly%20after%20the%20kidnapping%20of%20Pearl%20and%20before,days%20without%20making%20an%20announcement%20of%20his%20surrender, accessed on 6 June 2022.
34 Popovic, M., 'The perils of weak organization: Explaining loyalty and defection of militant organizations towards Pakistan'.
35 Perlez, J., 'Clinton decides to visit Pakistan, after all', *The New York Times*, 8 March 2000, https://www.nytimes.com/2000/03/08/world/clinton-decides-to-visit-pakistan-after-all.html, accessed on 3 June 2022.
36 ITWD, 'Pervez Musharraf accepts Jaish's involvement in Pulwama attack, but defends Imran Khan', *India Today*, 20 February 2019, https://www.indiatoday.in/india/story/jem-had-tried-to-kill-me-too-but-imran-khan-innocent-pervez-musharraf-to-india-today-1460800-2019-02-20, accessed on 7 June 2022.
37 Verma, R., 'Pakistan and Jaish-e-Muhammad'.
38 Burman, A., and Diwakar, 'Musharraf is alive, thanks to India'.
39 Mohananey, A., 'The man who interrogated Masood Azhar recalls the time he sang like a canary'.
40 Based on the author's interview with Farzan (name changed), an interlocutor with strong connections with Pakistan's Kashmir-centric jihadist ecosystem.
41 'Incidents and statements involving Jaish-e-Mohammed: 1999–2012', South Asia Terrorism Portal, https://www.satp.org/satporgtp/countries/india/states/jandk/terrorist_outfits/jaish_e_mohammad_TL.htm, accessed on 1 June 2022.

42 ibid.

43 ibid.

44 'Airline plot suspect linked with Jaish', *Dawn*, 17 August 2006, https://www.dawn.com/news/206274/airline-plot-suspect-linked-with-jaish, accessed on 3 June 2022.

45 ibid.

46 Kermani, S., 'Pakistan's dilemma: What to do about anti-India militants', *BBC*, 9 March 2019, https://www.bbc.com/news/world-asia-47488917, accessed on 1 June 2022.

47 ibid.

48 Garge, R., and C. Sahay, 'Rise of Jaish-e-Mohammed in Kashmir Valley'.

49 'Incidents and statements involving Jaish-e-Mohammed', South Asia Terrorism Portal.

50 Raman, B., 'Daniel Pearl and the body of evidence'.

51 Arni, A., 'Omar Sheikh: If not Daniel Pearl, a trail with links to ISI, 9/11 mastermind and bin Laden', The Telegraph Online, 16 April 2020, https://www.telegraphindia.com/opinion/omar-sheikh-if-not-daniel-pearl-a-trail-with-links-to-isi-9-11-mastermind-and-bin-laden/cid/1765443, accessed on 7 June 2020.

52 Raman, B., 'Daniel Pearl and the body of evidence'.

53 Indian intelligence sources say that he was kept at Brigadier Ijaz Ahmed Shah's house by the ISI. Later, during his field research in Kashmir, Farzan, the author's interlocutor, confirmed that Omar Saed was kept at Brigadier Shah's house and Brigadier Shah gave him a detailed briefing about his testimony to the police, before making his surrender publicly and handing him over to the police. He also confirmed that Omar Saed was and continues to be a highly trusted asset of ISI.

54 Raman, B., 'Daniel Pearl and the body of evidence'.

55 Gill, M., 'Explained: What is the Daniel Pearl murder case, and who is Omar Sheikh?', *The Indian Express*, 30 January 2021, https://indianexpress.com/article/explained/omar-sheikh-daniel-pearl-murder-case-pakistan-7165493/, accessed on 6 June 2022.

56 ibid.

57 Mishra, A., 'Daniel Pearl's killer being protected by Pak PM Imran Khan's men', *Sunday Guardian*, 2 January 2021, https://www.sundayguardianlive.com/news/daniel-pearls-killer-protected-pak-pm-imran-khans-men, accessed on 7 June 2022.

58 ibid.

59 ibid.

60 Gill, M., 'Explained: What is the Daniel Pearl murder case'.

61 Based on the author's interview of Mushtaq (name changed), a former LeT terrorist from Bandipora, Kashmir. He was trained in Muridke (Punjab, Pakistan) and, due to his intellectual abilities, got a chance to interact with high-profile jihadist figures of Pakistan.

62 Raman, B., 'Daniel Pearl and the body of evidence'.

63 ibid.

64 According to C.D. Sahay, former R&AW chief and a member of the Indian team sent to negotiate with the Kandahar hijackers, the hijackers gave the Indian officers a list of names of thirty-six terrorists on the condition that either India release any seven of them as per their choice or any three from the thirty-six per the hijackers' choice.

65 As told to the author by Farzan (name changed), the author's interlocutor.

66 'Incidents and statements involving Jaish-e-Mohammed', South Asia Terrorism Portal.

67 Siddiqa, A., 'Terror's training ground'.

68 'Incidents and statements involving Jaish-e-Mohammed', South Asia Terrorism Portal.

69   ibid.

70   Agencies, 'Kandahar hijack kingpin may have been nabbed in Chile', *The Indian Express*, 11 April 2011, https://indianexpress.com/article/india/latest-news/kandahar-hijack-kingpin-may-have-been-nabbed-in-chile/, accessed on 11 June 2022.

71   Siddiqa, A., 'Terror's training ground'.

72   'Incidents and statements involving Jaish-e-Mohammed', South Asia Terrorism Portal.

73   The Reuters journalist who attended the event said a telephone was held next to a microphone that broadcasted his comments to loudspeakers. JeM's flags, inscribed with the word 'jihad', were waved around the venue of the gathering. Masood Azhar spoke from an undisclosed location.

74   Subramaniam, N., 'Why Pakistan needs no evidence from India to arrest Masood Azhar', *The Indian Express*, 28 January 2016, https://indianexpress.com/article/explained/why-pakistan-needs-no-evidence-from-india-to-arrest-masood-azhar/, accessed on 11 June 2022.

75   Mackenzie, J., and S. Miglani, 'Explainer: Jaish-e-Mohammad, the Pakistan-based militants, at heart of tension with India', *Reuters*, 15 February 2019, https://www.reuters.com/article/india-kashmir-group-idINKCN1Q41I7, accessed on 5 June 2022.

76   Swami, P., 'Pakistan moves secret Jaish base used for Pathankot attack, reports say', *The Indian Express*, 3 May 2016, https://indianexpress.com/article/india/india-news-india/pakistan-isi-jaish-e-muhammad-pathankot-airbase-attack-2781524/, accessed on 6 June 2022.

77   CISAC, 'Jaish-e-Muhammad'.

78   Routray, B.P., 'Special Report: Patron–client relationship: Pakistani deep state and the Jaish-e-Mohammad', Mantraya 2019, https://mantraya.org/special-report-the-patron-client-relationship-the-pakistani-deep-state-and-jaish-e-mohammad/, accessed on 5 June 2022.

79　CISAC, 'Jaish-e-Muhammad'.
80　US State Department cable, 'Bahawalpur: Growing militant recruitment in southern Punjab', Wikileaks, 4 February 2009, https://wikileaks.org/plusd/cables/09ISLAMABAD237_a.html, accessed on 5 June 2022.
81　ibid.
82　ibid.
83　Siddiqa, A., 'Terror's training ground'.
84　'Incidents and statements involving Jaish-e-Mohammed', South Asia Terrorism Portal.
85　'Extremist recruitment on the rise in southern Punjab', Wikileaks, 13 November 2008, https://wikileaks.org/plusd/cables/08LAHORE302_a.html, accessed on 5 June 2022.
86　Firstpost, 'Property records nail Pakistani lie on Jaish-e-Mohammed HQ in Bahawalpur, finds Firstpost investigation', Money Control, 1 March 2019, https://www.moneycontrol.com/news/india/property-records-nail-pakistani-lie-on-jaish-e-mohammed-hq-in-bahawalpur-finds-firstpost-investigation-3598911.html, accessed on 5 June 2022.
87　Siddiqa, A., 'Terror's training ground'.
88　Swami, P., 'Pakistan moves secret Jaish base used for Pathankot attack, reports say'.
89　ibid.
90　ibid.
91　Firstpost, 'Property records nail Pakistani lie on Jaish-e-Mohammed HQ in Bahawalpur'.
92　ibid.
93　ibid.
94　ibid.
95　Roul, A., 'Jaish-e-Muhammad's charity wing revitalizes banned group in Pakistan', *Terrorism Monitor*, vol. 9, no. 41, 11 November

2011, https://www.refworld.org/docid/4ec248692.html, accessed on 8 June 2022.

96 Firstpost, 'Property records nail Pakistani lie on Jaish-e-Mohammed HQ in Bahawalpur'.

97 Roul, A., 'Jaish-e-Muhammad's charity wing revitalizes banned group in Pakistan'.

98 Firstpost, 'Property records nail Pakistani lie on Jaish-e-Mohammed HQ in Bahawalpur'.

99 Roul, A., 'Jaish-e-Muhammad's charity wing revitalizes banned group in Pakistan'.

100 Al Qalam Online (2011). Retrieved 10 June 2022, from Al Qalam Online: http://www.alqalamonline.com/

101 Routray, B.P., 'Special report'.

102 Hasan, S.S., 'Why Pakistan is "boosting Kashmir militants"?', *BBC News*, 3 March 2010, http://news.bbc.co.uk/2/hi/south_asia/4416771.stm, accessed on 5 June 2022.

103 Mackenzie, J., and S. Miglani, 'Explainer'.

104 Ali, U., 'Pakistan: The rebirth of jihad', *The Diplomat*, 18 August 2016, https://thediplomat.com/2016/08/pakistan-the-rebirth-of-jihad/, accessed on 16 June 2022.

105 Dorsey, J.M., 'Pakistan and its militants: Who is mainstreaming whom?', S. Rajaratnam School of International Studies, 17 October 2018, https://papers.ssrn.com/sol3/papers.cfm?abstract_id=3263124, accessed on 16 June 2022.

106 ibid.

107 Ali, U., 'Pakistan: The rebirth of jihad'.

108 ibid.

109 ibid.

110 'Explained: Who is Mushtaq Ahmed Zargar, declared a terrorist under UAPA?', *Firstpost*, 14 April 2022, https://www.firstpost.com/india/explained-who-is-mushtaq-ahmed-zargar-declared-a-terrorist-under-uapa-10558021.html, accessed on 2 June 2022.

111 Mishra, A., 'ISI activates Mushtaq Zargar: 154 Pak terrorists operating in Kashmir', *Sunday Guardian*, 31 March 2018, https://www.sundayguardianlive.com/news/isi-activates-mushtaq-zargar-154-pak-terrorists-operating-kashmir, accessed on 2 June 2022.

112 'Explained: Who is Mushtaq Ahmed Zargar, declared a terrorist under UAPA?', *Firstpost*.

113 A launching pad is a temporary post/station in Pakistan-administered Kashmir near the Line of Control. Militants are brought to these launching pads after training where they stay for a few days and then they begin their infiltration trek with the help of a 'guide' to enter Indian Kashmir.

114 In Kashmir, militants, OGWs and security personnel generally refer to hideouts as 'hides'.

115 Tanzeem is an Urdu word meaning organization. Here it means a terrorist organization.

116 'Incidents and statements involving Jaish-e-Mohammed', South Asia Terrorism Portal.

117 Jaleel, M., 'Explaining the history of Masood Azhar's Jaish-e-Mohammad, the mystery of its re-emergence'.

118 'Incidents and statements involving Jaish-e-Mohammed', South Asia Terrorism Portal.

119 Ashiq, P., 'Jaish-e-Muhammad: The fountainhead of terror', *The Hindu*, 29 August 2020, https://www.thehindu.com/news/national/the-fountainhead-of-terror/article32475263.ece, accessed on 1 June 2022.

120 'Incidents and statements involving Jaish-e-Mohammed', South Asia Terrorism Portal.

121 After the HuM Kashmir chief Sajjad Afghani died while escaping with Masood in a tunnel in 1999, Jaish decided to use the name Sajjad Afghani as a code name for all its Kashmir operations chiefs. It was done to honour him.

122 Jaleel, M., 'Explaining the history of Masood Azhar's Jaish-e-Mohammad, the mystery of its re-emergence'.

123 SATP, 'Incidents and Statements involving Jaish-e-Mohammed'.

124 Jaleel, M., 'Explaining the history of Masood Azhar's Jaish-e-Mohammad, the mystery of its re-emergence'.

125 Garge, R., and C. Sahay, 'Rise of Jaish-e-Mohammed in Kashmir Valley'.

126 Jaleel, M., 'Explaining the history of Masood Azhar's Jaish-e-Mohammad, the mystery of its re-emergence'.

127 Jaleel, M., 'Afzal Guru and the Jaish's jihad project', *The Indian Express*, 18 February 2017, https://indianexpress.com/article/explained/afzal-guru-and-the-jaishs-jihad-project/, accessed on 9 June 2022.

128 'Incidents and statements involving Jaish-e-Mohammed', South Asia Terrorism Portal.

129 Reuters, 'Deoband fatwa terms terrorism an enemy: All kinds of "unjust violence" rejected', *Dawn*, 2 June 2008, https://www.dawn.com/news/305658/deoband-fatwa-terms-terrorism-an-enemy-all-kinds-of-unjust-violence-rejected, accessed on 1 June 2022.

130 These figures were given by Akram, an OGW for JeM. They do not tally with the official figures from the South Asia Terrorism Portal. According to SATP, 1,013 Jaish militants were killed between 2000 and 2022. In J&K, sometimes militants are killed by SFs during infiltration and encounters; however, they are not recorded for various reasons. Akram, being an insider, said that the number of JeM cadres unofficially killed was very high. Nevertheless, his figure of the 1,500 JeM militants' casualties in ten years from 2000–10, both recorded and unrecorded, is too high to be true.

131 'Incidents and statements involving Jaish-e-Mohammed', South Asia Terrorism Portal.

132 ibid.

133 ibid.

134 ibid.

135 Pandya, A., *Terror Financing in Kashmir*, (Routledge, New Delhi: 2023).

136 HT Correspondent, 'India suspends trade across LoC, says misused for smuggling by Pak groups', *Hindustan Times*, 19 April 2019, https://www.hindustantimes.com/india-news/india-suspends-loc-trade-with-pakistan-says-was-misused-for-arms-smuggling/story-kXsrt9G4Fyx8LwZkjhNCZM.html, accessed on 9 November 2023.

137 'Incidents and statements involving Jaish-e-Mohammed', South Asia Terrorism Portal.

138 Tiwary, D., 'Pulwama attackers wanted strike to spark India–Pak war: NIA chargesheet', *The Indian Express*, 26 August 2020, https://indianexpress.com/article/india/pulwama-attackers-wanted-strike-to-spark-india-pak-war-nia-chargesheet-6569874/, accessed on 30 May 2022.

139 Singh, B., 'Masood's masterstroke: The Afzal Guru Squad', *Bangalore Mirror*, 15 January 2016, https://bangaloremirror.indiatimes.com/news/india/masoods-masterstroke-the-afzal-guru-squad/articleshow/50596854.cms#:~:text=The%20JeM%20immediately%20jumped%20upon%20the%20opportunity%20with,Afzal%E2%80%99s%20book%20about%20his%20days%20in%20Tihar%20jail, accessed on 9 June 2022.

140 ibid.

141 Jaleel, M., 'Explaining the history of Masood Azhar's Jaish-e-Mohammad, the mystery of its re-emergence'.

142 Dixit, S., 'India outraged at Masood Azhar's threat', *The Hindu*, 22 February 2014, https://www.thehindu.com/news/national/india-outraged-at-masood-azhars-threat/article5714394.ece, accessed on 9 June 2022.

143 PTI, 'Jaish-e-Mohammed chief Masood Azhar's address to rally in PoK raises questions: Report', *Economic Times*, 2 February 2014,

https://economictimes.indiatimes.com/news/politics-and-nation/jaish-e-mohammed-chief-masood-azhars-address-to-rally-in-pok-raises-questions-report/articleshow/29778797.cms, accessed on 9 June 2022.

144 Dixit, S., 'India outraged at Masood Azhar's threat'.

145 Riedel, B., 'Blame Pakistani spy service for attack on Indian Air Force base', *Daily Beast*, 5 January 2016, https://www.thedailybeast.com/blame-pakistani-spy-service-for-attack-on-indian-air-force-base, accessed on 10 June 2022.

146 Fair, C.C., 'Bringing back the dead: Why Pakistan used the Jaish-e-Mohammad to attack an Indian airbase', *Huffington Post*, 12 January 2016, https://www.huffpost.com/entry/bringing-back-the-dead-wh_b_8955224, accessed on 14 May 2022.

147 Pakistan's security establishment believes that Kashmir is Pakistan's 'jugular vein'. General Parvez Musharraf, in his 12 January 2002 speech, said, 'Kashmir runs in our blood ... No Pakistani can afford to sever links with Kashmir ... We will never budge an inch from our principled stand on Kashmir. Without Kashmir, Pakistan is incomplete. Accession of Kashmir to Pakistan is quintessential for the two-nation theory of Jinnah, Pakistan's founder. The two-nation theory argues that Hindus and Muslims constitute two different nations, and it was the basis of Pakistan's creation.'

148 Kumar, B., 'Pathankot attack aimed at probing Modi govt's red lines: C. Christine Fair', *Business Standard* 11 January 2016, https://www.business-standard.com/article/current-affairs/pathankot-attack-aimed-at-probing-modi-govt-s-red-lines-c-christine-fair-116010900252_1.html, accessed on 11 June 2022.

149 Pakistan's strategy of using terrorist proxies in tandem with its nuclear shield is not confined to Kashmir only. It is much broader in scope. The country applies this ideal in Afghanistan, Iran and Bangladesh as well. Pakistan-sponsored terrorist groups like JeM and LeT have conducted attacks in other states of India also. In

the Northeast, they teamed up with HuJI to create disturbances. Also, Pakistan seeks false equivalence with India by compelling New Delhi to come to the negotiating table by organizing terror attacks as the country understands that India cannot defeat Pakistan in a short war.

150 Fair, C.C., and S. Oldmixon, 'Let's be clear, the Pathankot attack is not an attempt to derail the Indo–Pak peace process', Scroll, 8 January 2016, https://scroll.in/article/801474/lets-be-clear-the-pathankot-attack-is-not-an-attempt-to-derail-the-indo-pak-peace-process, accessed on 11 June 2022.

151 Fair, C.C., 'Bringing back the dead'.

152 Garge, R., and C. Sahay, 'Rise of Jaish-e-Mohammed in Kashmir Valley'.

153 ibid.

154 PTI, '190 militants killed in Kashmir this year: Army official', *The Indian Express*, 19 November 2017, https://indianexpress.com/article/india/190-militants-killed-in-kashmir-this-year-army-official-4945284/, accessed on 11 June 2022.

155 Garge, R., and C. Sahay, 'Rise of Jaish-e-Mohammed in Kashmir Valley'.

156 Swami, P., 'The dead pool: Key Pulwama perpetrators are dead, but Jaish-e-Muhammad's blood-cult is alive, and killing', *Firstpost*, 3 August 2021, https://www.firstpost.com/india/the-dead-pool-key-pulwama-perpetrators-are-dead-but-jaish-e-muhammads-blood-cult-is-alive-and-killing-9861511.html, accessed on 15 June 2022.

157 Pasagik, A., 'Failed states and terrorism: Justifiability of transnational interventions from the counterterrorism perspective', *Perspectives on Terrorism*, vol. 14, no. 3, June 2020, pp. 19–28, https://www.jstor.org/stable/26918297?seq=1, accessed on 15 June 2022.

158 Singh, B., 'Masood's masterstroke'.

159 Jaleel, M., 'Explaining the history of Masood Azhar's Jaish-e-Mohammad, the mystery of its re-emergence'.

160 Chauhan, N., 'Indian consulate in Mazar-i-Sharif attacked, ITBP engaged with terrorists', *The Times of India*, 4 January 2016, https://timesofindia.indiatimes.com/world/south-asia/Indian-consulate-in-Mazar-i-Sharif-attacked-ITBP-engaged-with-terrorists/articleshow/50431054.cms, accessed on 11 June 2011.

161 Jaleel, M., 'Explaining the history of Masood Azhar's Jaish-e-Mohammad, the mystery of its re-emergence'.

162 Nandy, C., 'Myanmar surgical strike: How former NSCN(K) men helped the army', The Quint, 10 June 2015, https://www.thequint.com/news/india/myanmar-surgical-strike-how-former-nscnk-men-helped-the-army#read-more, accessed on 11 June 2022.

163 PTI, 'Summary of Modi–Sharif talks in Ufa, Russia', *The Indian Express*, 10 July 2015, https://indianexpress.com/article/india/india-others/summary-of-modi-sharif-talks-in-ufa-russia/, accessed on 11 June 2022.

164 Ohri, R., 'Kashmiri youth visiting Pakistan used as terror conduits: Government agency', *Economic Times*, 13 July 2018, https://economictimes.indiatimes.com/news/defence/kashmiri-youth-visiting-pakistan-used-as-terror-conduits-government-agency/articleshow/61620328.cms, accessed on 11 June 2022.

165 ibid.

166 The Anti-terrorism Act (ATA) 1997, SATP, https://www.satp.org/satporgtp/countries/pakistan/document/papers/Anti-TerrorismAct-1997.pdf, accessed on 11 June 2022.

167 TNN, 'Action against Jaish-e-Mohammad will be dangerous for Pakistan', *The Times of India*, 15 June 2016, https://timesofindia.indiatimes.com/india/Action-against-Jaish-e-Mohammad-will-be-dangerous-for-Pakistan-warns-Masood-Azhar/articleshow/50583986.cms, accessed on 12 June 2022.

168 ibid.

169 ibid.
170 ibid.
171 Pandita, R., 'Will the Jaish revival in Kashmir throw it back into chaos?', *Open*, 23 November 2017, https://openthemagazine.com/features/terror/will-the-jaish-revival-in-kashmir-throw-it-back-into-chaos/, accessed on 11 June 2022.
172 ibid.
173 Ehsaan, M., 'J&K's three-feet-tall JeM "commander" who jumped parole killed in Pulwama', *The Indian Express* 27 December 2017, https://indianexpress.com/article/india/three-feet-tall-jaish-commander-who-jumped-parole-killed-in-valley-4999551/, accessed on 12 June 2022.
174 '2017 CRPF group center attack: NIA files chargesheet against four,' *New Indian Express*, 2 August 2019, https://www.newindianexpress.com/nation/2019/Aug/01/2017-crpf-group-centre-attack-nia-files-chargesheet-against-four-2012731.html, accessed on 29 April 2024.
175 Webdesk, 'Sunjuwan terror attack mastermind Mufti Waqas gunned down by army', *The Indian Express*, 5 March 2018, https://indianexpress.com/article/india/sunjawan-terror-attack-mastermind-mufti-waqas-killed-army-5087127/, accessed on 12 June 2022.
176 Based on intelligence reports on JeM's activities in Jammu and Kashmir 2017–21, accessed by the author, on the condition of confidentiality.
177 Webdesk, 'Pulwama terror attack: Timeline of conflict between India and Pakistan', *Gulf News*, 27 February 2022, https://gulfnews.com/world/asia/pulwama-terror-attack-timeline-of-conflict-between-india-and-pakistan-1.1551170592587, accessed on 14 June 2022.
178 Ghosh, D. (ed.), 'Masood Azhar "is in Pakistan", admits foreign minister amid Pulwama outrage', *NDTV*, 1 March 2019, https://www.ndtv.com/india-news/masood-azhar-is-in-pakistan-admits-

shah-mahmood-qureshi-foreign-minister-amid-pulwama-outrage-2001089, accessed on 12 June 2022.

179 Roy, S., and R. Tripathi, 'Pakistan flip-flop: Its army says Jaish does not exist in the country', *The Indian Express*, 7 March 2019, https://indianexpress.com/article/india/pakistan-flip-flop-its-army-says-jaish-does-not-exist-in-the-country-pulwama-jem-5614616/, accessed on 11 June 2022.

180 ibid.

181 ibid.

182 Khan, S., 'Punjab govt takes "administrative control" of Bahawalpur seminary', *Dawn*, 22 February 2019, https://www.dawn.com/news/1465406,accessed on 12 June 2022.

183 ibid.

184 Based on intelligence reports on JeM's activities in Jammu and Kashmir 2017–21, accessed by the author, on the condition of confidentiality.

185 Gupta, S., 'Top Jaish terrorist involved in Pulwama attack gunned down in Kashmir', *Hindustan Times*, 31 July 2021, https://www.hindustantimes.com/india-news/top-jaish-terrorist-involved-in-pulwama-attack-gunned-down-in-kashmir-101627716590991.html, accessed on 29 June 2022.

186 Pandit, M.S., 'Last of Pulwama attackers killed, say security forces', *The Times of India*, 2 January 2022, https://timesofindia.indiatimes.com/india/forces-claim-last-of-pulwama-attack-masterminds-killed/articleshow/88639461.cms, accessed on 29 June 2022.

187 The information provided in this paragraph is based on this author's interview with a senior state-level intelligence officer with about seventeen years of work experience in south Kashmir districts. It is also based on a report from the state-level intelligence agency. My sources requested anonymity so the author has kept their identity confidential.

188 Swami, P., 'Controlled, not crushed: Jaish-e-Muhammad asks Pakistan to lift restrictions on attacks in Kashmir', News 18, 8 September 2020, https://www.news18.com/news/india/controlled-not-crushed-jaish-e-muhammad-asks-pakistan-to-lift-restrictions-on-attacks-in-kashmir-2858023.html, accessed on 11 June 2022.

189 ibid.

190 ibid.

191 ibid.

192 ibid.

193 ibid.

194 Based on intelligence reports on JeM's activities in Jammu and Kashmir 2017–21, accessed by the author on the condition of confidentiality.

195 'Explainer: Who are "Kashmir Tigers" that carried out Srinagar terror attack', *Outlook*, 14 December 2021, https://www.outlookindia.com/website/story/india-news-explained-who-are-kashmir-tigers-that-carried-out-attack-in-srinagar/405079, accessed on 12 June 2022.

196 ibid.

197 ibid.

198 Bhatt, S., 'Lashkar-i-Mustapha chief Hidaytullah Malik arrested in Jammu', *India Today*, 6 February 2021, https://www.indiatoday.in/india/story/lashkar-e-mustafa-chief-hidayatullah-malik-arrested-in-j-k-shopian-district-1766646-2021-02-06, accessed on 12 June 2022.

199 Pandya, A., 'Kashmir militancy after 370'.

200 Shukla, M., 'Jaish terrorist confesses he "recced" NSA Ajit Doval's office, security agencies on high alert', Zee News, 13 February 2021, https://zeenews.india.com/india/jaish-terrorist-conduct-recce-of-nsa-ajit-dovals-office-security-agencies-on-high-alert-2341596.html, accessed on 12 June 2022.

201 Islam, M.U., and P. Shakir, 'Who are Kashmir's hybrid militants ?', *The Diplomat*, 30 November 2021, https://thediplomat.com/2021/11/who-are-kashmirs-hybrid-militants/, accessed on 31 May 2022.

202 As told to the author by Brigadier Pandey (name changed), a sector commander in Kashmir Valley.

203 ibid.

204 ibid.

205 South Asia Terrorism Portal (SATP) data till 1 July 2022, https://www.satp.org/terrorist-groups/fatalities/india-jammukashmir_jaish-e-mohammed-jem, accessed on 22 July 2022.

206 ibid.

207 ibid.

208 ibid.

209 South Asia Terrorism Portal (SATP) data from 6 March 2000 to 1 July 2022, https://www.satp.org/terrorist-groups/explosions/india-jammukashmir_jaish-e-mohammed-jem, accessed on 22 July 2022.

210 'Jaish-e-Muhammad', Global Fight Against Terrorism Funding (GFATF), 3 January 2017, https://www.gfatf.org/archives/jaish-e-mohammad/, accessed on 15 June 2022.

211 As told to the author by Tabriz Sheikh (name changed)—a veteran JeM OGW with eighteen years of experience—and Bashir Assad, a Srinagar-based journalist and the author of *K-File: The Anatomy of Silence*. Tabriz has met JeM chief Masood Azhar four times and attended his lectures several times. He has also met Masood's brother Mufti Rauf.

212 Hussain, Z., 'Freed militant resurfaces', *Associated Press, Karachi*, 5 Jan 2000, https://web.archive.org/web/20000901092056/https://abcnews.go.com/sections/world/DailyNews/militants000105.html, accessed on 28 April 2024 .

213 Based on the author's interview with a senior police officer from J&K who served in the state intelligence from 2005–10.

214 Azhar, M., 'Maulana Masood Azhar—Jihad-e-Kashmir aur Ghazwa-e-Hind', Dailymotion, 2015, https://www.dailymotion.com/video/x2p3wdm, accessed on 15 June 2022.

215 'Incidents and statements involving Jaish-e-Mohammed', South Asia Terrorism Portal.

216 Based on the author's in-person interview with three officers who interrogated Noor Muhammad Tantrey.

217 ibid.

218 Swami, P., 'A circle of hate', *Frontline*, 24 October 2003, https://authory.com/PraveenSwami/A-CIRCLE-OF-HATE-a24ec2569202f4114bd19e8f460281b2c, accessed on 23 June 2022.

219 ibid.

220 ibid.

221 'Incidents and statements involving Jaish-e-Mohammed', South Asia Terrorism Portal.

222 Kaul, S., 'Jaish behind Ayodhya attack, not Lashkar', Rediff, 21 August 2005, https://www.rediff.com/news/2005/aug/21ayodhya.htm, accessed on 8 June 2022.

223 Zee Media, '2005 Ayodhya terror attack case: Four sentenced to life imprisonment, one acquitted', Zee News, 18 June 2019, https://zeenews.india.com/india/2005-ayodhya-terror-attack-case-four-sentenced-to-life-imprisonment-one-acquitted-2212450.html#:~:text=Two%20civilians%20and%20five%20Jaish-e-Mohammed%20terrorists%2C%20who%20carried,Mohammad%20Aziz%20-%20in%20connection%20, accessed on 8 June 2022.

224 Kaul, S., 'Jaish behind Ayodhya attack, not Lashkar'.

225 'Incidents and statements involving Jaish-e-Mohammed', South Asia Terrorism Portal.

226 PTI, 'How terror comes into India', Rediff.com, 3 December 2006, https://m.rediff.com/news/2006/dec/03terror.htm, accessed on 8 June 2022.

227 ibid.

228 'Incidents and statements involving Jaish-e-Mohammed', South Asia Terrorism Portal.

229 Tripathi, R., 'Delhi police say 4 Jaish men held after shootout', *The Indian Express*, 7 February 2007, http://archive.indianexpress.com/news/delhi-police-say-4-jaish-men-held-after-shootout/22550/, accessed on 8 June 2022.

230 ibid.

231 Singh, B., 'Masood's masterstroke'.

232 'Incidents and statements involving Jaish-e-Mohammed', South Asia Terrorism Portal.

233 ibid.

234 ibid.

235 Rabasa, A., P. Chalk et al., 'Beyond Al Qaeda'.

236 'Incidents and statements involving Jaish-e-Mohammed', South Asia Terrorism Portal.

237 ibid.

238 Rabasa, A., P. Chalk et al., 'Beyond Al Qaeda'.

239 ibid.

240 'Incidents and statements involving Jaish-e-Mohammed', South Asia Terrorism Portal.

241 Nanjappa, V., 'Did Bhatkal brothers help dispirited IM plan attacks?', Rediff.com, 1 December 2011, last accessed on 9 June 2022.

242 ibid.

243 Zee Media Bureau, 'Jaish-e-Mohammad "threatens" to blow up railway stations in Punjab, Rajasthan, Uttarakhand', Zee News, 19 April 2019, https://zeenews.india.com/india/jaish-e-mohammad-threatens-to-blow-up-railway-stations-in-punjab-rajasthan-uttarakhand-2196986.html, accessed on 9 June 2022.

244 As told to the author by Alpha 12, a Srinagar-based intelligence operative working in counterinsurgency in central Kashmir. He has interrogated twelve JeM militants in the last four years.

245 Sonawane, A., 'Jaish-e-Mohammad's Masood Azhar releases a threat video to India on the construction of Ram Mandir in Ayodhya', Republic TV, 30 November 2018, https://www.republicworld.com/india-news/general-news/jaish-e-mohammads-masood-azhar-releases-a-threat-video-to-india-on-the-construction-of-ram-mandir-in-ayodhya.html, accessed on 9 June 2022.

246 ibid.

247 Pandya, A., 'Kashmir militancy after 370'.

248 Pandya, A., 'Militancy in Kashmir: A study', Vivekananda International Foundation, March 2019, https://www.vifindia.org/sites/default/files/Militancy-in-Kashmir.pdf, accessed on 31 May 2022.

Chapter 5: JeM and Its Fidayeen Missions: Training and Tactics

1 'How Jaish-e-Mohammad is funding terrorists in J&K', *India Today*, 18 January 2016, https://www.indiatoday.in/india/story/how-jaish-e-mohammad-is-funding-terrorists-in-jandk-304417-2016-01-18, accessed on 17 July 2022.

2 'How Jaish-e-Mohammed funds terror acts. Here's a look at its source of income', Times Now, 28 February 2019, https://www.timesnownews.com/business-economy/economy/article/how-jaish-e-mohammed-funding-terror-acts-heres-a-look-at-its-source-of-income/373997, accessed on 17 July 2022.

3 As told to the author by Dabwal M. (name changed), a senior NIA officer who played a key role in the investigation of the Pulwama fidayeen attack.

4 Sharma, S. K., and A. Behera, *Militant Groups in South Asia*, (Pentagon, Delhi: 2014).

5 ibid.

6 'Jaish-e-Mohammed', South Asia Terrorism Portal.

7 ibid.

8. 'Incidents and statements involving Jaish-e-Mohammed', South Asia Terrorism Portal.
9. As told to the author by Farzan.
10. ibid.
11. ibid.
12. Rana, D., *As Far As the Saffron Fields: The Pulwama Conspiracy*, (HarperCollins, Gurugram: 2022).
13. As told to the author by Farzan.
14. Fair, C.C., *In their Own Words*.
15. Sharan, A., 'Masood Azhar runs JeM like a "family enterprise"', *Mumbai Mirror*, 4 May 2019, https://mumbaimirror.indiatimes.com/mumbai/cover-story/masood-azhar-runs-jem-like-a-family-enterprise/articleshow/69169614.cms#:~:text=Among%20the%20key%20Azhar%20relatives%20in%20decision-making%20roles,an%20Indian%20Airlines%20plane%2C%20IC-814%2C%20in%, accessed on 3 July 2022.
16. Based on the author's interview with the team of intelligence officers of SFs in J&K who investigated and prepared the intelligence assessment of JeM's activities in Jammu and Kashmir since 2017.
17. ibid.
18. Islamic Information Portal, 'The great Shamil, imam of Daghestan and Chechnya, shaykh of Naqshbandi tariqah', Islam.Ru, 27 June 2018, https://islam.ru/en/content/story/great-shamil-imam-daghestan-and-chechnya-shaykh-naqshbandi-tariqah, accessed on 10 July 2022.
19. As told to the author by Farzan.
20. Sharma, S.K., and A. Behera, *Militant Groups in South Asia*.
21. As told to the author by Farzan.
22. Ray, S., 'Who was Maulana Samiul Haq, the slain "father of Taliban"?', The Quint, 4 November 2018, https://www.thequint.com/news/world/who-was-maulana-samiul-haq-the-slain-father-of-taliban#read-more, accessed on 30 June 2022.

23 ibid.

24 As told to the author by Farzan.

25 Ray, S., 'Who was Maulana Samiul Haq, the slain "father of Taliban"?'.

26 As told to author by a senior NIA official who investigated the Pulwama fidayeen attack.

27 As told to the author by Alpha 12.

28 As told to the author by Akram Bhai.

29 As told to the author by Farzan.

30 ibid.

31 Siddiqa, A., 'Brothers in arms'.

32 ibid.

33 Levy, A., and K.S. Clark, *Spy Stories: Inside the Secret World of the RAW and ISI*, (Juggernaut, Delhi: 2021).

34 As told to the author by Dabwal M.

35 As told to the author by Rafiq (name changed), a JeM guide and OGW from Kupwara, who also works covertly with SFs in intelligence gathering. He has helped infiltrate twelve JeM groups over the last ten years.

36 As told to the author by Praveen Swami.

37 ibid.

38 Fair, C.C., 'We asked why Pakistanis support Lashkar-e-Taiba'.

39 As told to the author by Farzan.

40 All Party Hurriyat Conference (APHC), formed in 1993, is a conglomerate of twenty-six political, social, religious and cultural separatist groups in Kashmir. It is a political front of separatists with alleged links with terrorist groups and extremist groups like Jamaat-i-Islami.

41 Jaleel, M., 'Hurriyat: Its history, role and relevance', *The Indian Express*, 31 August 2015, https://indianexpress.com/article/explained/hurriyat-its-history-role-and-relevance/, accessed on 27 June 2022.

42. As told to the author by Akram Bhai.
43. As told to the author by Fayaz Ahmed, a Kashmir-based journalist, in 2021.
44. As told to the author by Akram Bhai.
45. 'Incidents and statements involving Jaish-e-Mohammed', South Asia Terrorism Portal.
46. ibid.
47. Rabasa, A., P. Chalk et al., 'Beyond Al Qaeda'.
48. As told to the author by Akram Bhai.
49. As told to the author by Iftikhar Hussain (name changed), a senior police officer from the Jammu and Kashmir Police. In the last twenty-three years, he has served as a police chief in several districts of the region. He has also served in the state intelligence wing. Besides, he has planned and executed several operations with the Indian Army, which involved infiltrating JeM hierarchy in Kashmir and killing its top leadership.
50. As told to the author by Akram Bhai.
51. ibid.
52. As told to the author by Baseer Khan, former divisional commissioner of Kashmir range during the abrogation of Article 370 (2018–20) and advisor to the lieutenant governor of J&K. Additionally, he has also served as administrative chief of ten districts, mostly in Kashmir Valley, which has seen much militancy. He is an expert voice on separatist and extremist organizations in Kashmir.
53. ibid.
54. JI schools run by FAT are banned in Kashmir as of June 2022.
55. As told to the author by J. Singh (name changed), who has served the police in various capacities in the Kashmir Valley. He has long experience in counterterrorism operations and building intelligence networks.
56. ibid.

57 As told to the author by Farhad Hussain (name changed), a JKPS officer who has served as SDPO in Kulgam. He has led many intelligence-based operations against JeM in south Kashmir, and chased Farukh Nalli and his group for two years.

58 As told to the author by Akram Bhai.

59 Masood, B., 'Mohd Abbas Sheikh killed: Planner, recruiter, militant for 26 yrs, he was most wanted', *The Indian Express*, 25 August 2021, https://indianexpress.com/article/india/mohd-abbas-sheikh-killed-planner-recruiter-militant-for-26-yrs-he-was-most-wanted-7469190/, accessed on 27 June 2022. Abbas Sheikh was one of the oldest surviving militants of HM. He joined HM in 1996. He was arrested in 2004 but released a year later. In 2007, he was again arrested and released after four years. For the next three years, he stayed at home and joined militancy again in 2014. Throughout his career, he kept his ties with militancy alive, either as an OGW or as an active militant; however, he could evade police scrutiny because of his ability to maintain a low profile. Also, he was known for his motivational and recruitment skills.

60 ibid.

61 Zakir Musa was the chief of Ansar Ghazwat-ul-Hind (AGuH), allegedly an Al Qaeda affiliate in Kashmir. Before founding AGuH, he was an HM commander. However, he left HM and started AGuH as he wanted a purely Islamist movement to establish an Islamic caliphate. He was critical of Hurriyat and HM, and called their struggle a political one. He had become a celebrity militant after Burhan Wani.

62 Name changed. Based on the author's interview with a senior police officer posted in south Kashmir.

'Incidents and statements involving Jaish-e-Mohammed', South Asia Terrorism Portal.

63 PTI, 'WikiLeaks: Al-Qaeda operatives used Tablighi Jamaat to get visas', *DNA*, 9 May 2011, https://www.dnaindia.com/world/report-wikileaks-al-qaeda-operatives-used-tablighi-jamaat-to-get-visas-1541227, accessed on 29 June 2022.

64 As told to the author by Gautam Sharma (name changed), who served as a brigadier in the Srinagar-based 15 Corps of the Indian Army.

65 Burton, F., and S. Stewart, 'Tablighi Jamaat'.

66 ibid.

67 Pandya, A., and S. Westrop, 'Tablighi Jamaat'.

68 Wahab, G., 'Dar-ul-Uloom needs to define jihad instead', Force India, https://forceindia.net/firstperson/what-terrorism/, accessed on 30 June 2022.

69 As told to the author by Beta 12, a retired intelligence officer with thirty years of experience in Kashmir. He has visited terrorist training camps in Afghanistan and PoK, and interrogated many JeM, LeT, HuM and HM terrorists. He also studied JeM camps and training in detail.

70 ibid.

71 Assad, B., *K-File: The Conspiracy of Silence*, (Vitasta, New Delhi: 2019).

72 Bhakto, A., 'NIA conducts series of raids in Kashmir, arrests six for ISIS conspiracy to "radicalise impressionable youth"', *Frontline*, 22 June 2022, https://frontline.thehindu.com/dispatches/nia-conducts-series-of-raids-in-kashmir-arrests-six-for-isis-conspiracy-to-radicalise-impressionable-youth/article35273561.ece#!, accessed on 3 July 2022.

73 As told to the author by Bashir Assad.

74 ibid.

75 ibid.

76 Rana, D., *As Far As the Saffron Fields*.

77 Assad, B., *K-File: The Conspiracy of Silence*.

78 ibid.

79 ibid.

80 'Datasheet: Jammu and Kashmir—Yearly suicide attacks', South Asia Terrorism Portal, 2022, https://satp.org/datasheet-terrorist-attack/suicide-attacks/india-jammukashmir, accessed on 3 July 2022.

81 Mufti Waqas was a JeM commander who masterminded the Sunjwan terrorist attack.

82 As told to the author by Beta 12.

83 'Datasheet', South Asia Terrorism Portal.

84 ibid.

85 As told to the author by OGWs of JeM and Muhammad Ashraf (name changed), a veteran police officer who works with state agencies.
After the death of Sajjad Afghani, the first HuM commander in J&K, his name was used as a code for all JeM commanders.

86 Rana, D., *As Far As the Saffron Fields*.

87 ibid.

88 As told to the author by Dabwal M.

89 As told to the author by Mr Mota.

90 ibid.

91 As shared with the author by Beta 12.

92 Umar Farooq, a Pulwama fidayeen mastermind, was trained in explosives and IED at Sangin in Afghanistan, also known as the graveyard of NATO forces.

93 Singh, B., 'Masood's masterstroke'.

94 ET Online, 'Indian air strike in Balakot killed 300 militants: Sources', *Economic Times*, 26 February 2019, https://economictimes.indiatimes.com/news/defence/indian-air-strike-in-balakot-killed-300-militants-sources/articleshow/68165466.cms, accessed on 17 July 2022.

95 As told to the author by Farzan.

96   As told to the author by Beta 12.

97   Based on the interrogation report of Sajjad Afghani accessed by the author.

98   'Incidents and statements involving Jaish-e-Mohammed', South Asia Terrorism Portal.

99   'Who is Abdul Rauf Azgar that China blocked being designated as a global terrorist?', *The Times of India*, 12 August 2022, https://timesofindia.indiatimes.com/india/who-is-abdul-rauf-azhar-that-china-blocked-from-being-designated-a-global-terrorist/articleshow/93512393.cms, accessed on 23 August 2022.

100   'Incidents and statements involving Jaish-e-Mohammed', South Asia Terrorism Portal.

101   Jameel, Y., 'Jaish-e-Muhammad claims responsibility for killing 4 policemen in J&K's Shopian', *Deccan Chronicle*, 29 August 2018, https://www.deccanchronicle.com/nation/current-affairs/290818/4-policemen-killed-in-terror-attack-in-south-kashmirs-shopian.html, accessed on 8 July 2022.

102   As told to the author by Farhad Hussain.

103   'Jaish duo killed SPO, family in Valley', North Lines, 30 June 2021, https://www.thenorthlines.com/jaish-duo-killed-spo-family-in-valley/, accessed on 8 July 2022.

104   As told to the author by Mr Mota.

105   As told to the author by Rafiq.

106   As told to the author by an army officer who was posted in Sopore, north Kashmir, who interrogated Ghazi Umar, a JeM foreign terrorist in 2014. Ghazi Umar was active in Kashmir between 2005 and 2009 and between 2013–14.

107   'How Jaish-e-Mohammad is funding terrorists in J&K', *India Today*, 18 January 2016, https://www.indiatoday.in/india/story/how-jaish-e-mohammad-is-funding-terrorists-in-jandk-304417-2016-01-18, accessed on 17 July 2022.

108   As told to the author by Dabwal.

109 ibid.
110 Gupta, S., 'Gadgets used by Pak's 4 Jaish terrorists help India solve Jan 31 terror strike', *Hindustan Times*, 24 November 2021, https://www.hindustantimes.com/india-news/communication-gadgets-used-by-4-jaish-terrorists-point-to-pak-role/story-dl83SuJ67WIImquimbILEP.html, accessed on 9 July 2022.
111 ibid.
112 'Who is Noor Muhammad Tantrey?', *The Indian Express*, 26 December 2017,https://indianexpress.com/article/who-is/who-is-noor-muhammad-tantray-jaish-e-mohammad-pulwama-encounter-kashmir-militant-4998991/, accessed on 4 July 2022.
113 As told to the author by Akram Bhai.
114 As told to the author by Charlie (name changed), a senior intelligence officer from Military Intelligence, posted in the Kashmir region.
115 ibid.
116 Wikileaks, 'US State Department Cable—Bahawalpur'.
117 Siddiqa, A., 'Terror's training ground'.
118 ibid.
119 Muhajirs are migrant Muslims who came to Pakistan from India after Partition in 1947.
120 Lal Mosque (Islamabad) is famous for its ties with anti-state Deobandi extremist groups and the Lal Mosque siege of 2007 when the Musharraf government conducted a military operation to neutralize the Islamic militants hiding in the mosque.
121 Siddiqa, A., 'Terror's training ground'.
122 ibid.
123 Wikileaks, 'US State Department Cable—Bahawalpur'.
124 Siddiqa, A., 'Terror's training ground'.
125 ibid.
126 ibid.

127 Pandya, A., *Radicalisation in India: An Exploration*.
128 Kashmir's locally prevalent Sufi form of Islam. It is known to be moderate, and is influenced by Buddhism and Shaivism.
129 Pandya, A., 'Militancy in Kashmir'.
130 Siddiqa, A., 'Terror's training ground'.
131 'Extremist recruitment on the rise in southern Punjab', Wikileaks, 13 November 2008, https://wikileaks.org/plusd/cables/08LAHORE302_a.html, accessed on 5 June 2022.
132 ibid.
133 ibid.
134 As told to the author by Praveen Swami.
135 As told to the author by Akram Bhai.
136 Pandya, A., *Radicalisation in India: An Exploration*.
137 As told to the author by Alpha 12.
138 As told to the author by Alpha 12 and the author's analysis of various intelligence reports.
139 As told to the author by J. Singh.
140 ibid.
141 As told to the author by Praveen Swami.
142 *Al Qalam* dedicated an edition, titled 'Khuda ka Banda', to Noor Muhammad Tantrey after his death.
143 As told to the author by Praveen Swami.
144 Swami, P., 'The dead pool'.
145 As told to the author by Alpha 12.
146 Swami, P., 'Jaish-e-Muhammad back with online magazine', *The Indian Express*, 18 March 2016, https://indianexpress.com/article/india/india-news-india/pathankot-masood-azhar-jaish-e-muhammad-journal-al-qalam-back-with-online-magazine/, accessed on 13 July 2022.
147 ibid.
148 As told to the author by Praveen Swami.

Chapter 6: Militant Profiles

1. As told to the author by G.N. Guru (name changed). Mr Guru has served as police chief in the Kashmir range, interrogated several JeM terrorists, and neutralized key members of its top leadership in J&K between 2005 and 2016. He also served as an additional secretary in the National Security Council Secretariat India.
2. As told to the author by Praveen Swami.
3. As told to the author by Mahboob Gilani (name changed), a serving police officer of J&K with twenty-five years of experience in counterinsurgency operations.
4. As told to the author by Ishtiyak Hussain.
5. Sharma, N., 'Pulwama attack: The 23-year-old woman who helped the terrorists', NDTV, 26 August 2020, https://www.ndtv.com/india-news/pulwama-attack-the-23-year-old-woman-insha-jan-who-helped-the-terrorists-2285802, accessed on 13 July 2022.
6. ibid.
7. As told to the author by Ishtiyak Hussain.
8. ibid.
9. Fidayeens are given instructions to do maximum damage for which their first target is the fuel dump. They are asked to prolong the encounter for as long as they can.
10. 'Who is Noor Muhammad Tantrey?', *The Indian Express*.
11. Masoodi, N., and N. Sharma, '4 feet tall terrorist killed in Kashmir today was top Jaish commander', NDTV, 27 December 2017, https://www.ndtv.com/india-news/3-feet-tall-jaish-terrorist-killed-today-was-a-big-headache-for-forces-1792168, accessed on 15 July 2022.
12. As told to the author by M. Poswal, a police officer in J&K who dealt with Ashiq Baba's case.

13. India.com News Desk, 'Jaish, LeT, Hizbul working closely to target India, reveals Srinagar-based operative', India.com, 11 June 2018, https://www.india.com/news/india/jaish-let-hizbul-working-closely-to-target-india-reveals-srinagar-based-operative-3103191/, accessed on 16 July 2022.
14. Siddiqa, A., 'Brothers in arms'.
15. Wikileaks, 'Extremist recruitment on the rise in southern Punjab'.
16. ibid.
17. Siddiqa, A., 'Brothers in arms'.
18. Wikileaks, 'US State Department Cable—Bahawalpur'.
19. As told to the author by Akram Bhai.
20. ibid.
21. 'How Jaish-e-Mohammad is funding terrorists in J&K', *India Today*, 18 January 2016, https://www.indiatoday.in/india/story/how-jaish-e-mohammad-is-funding-terrorists-in-jandk-304417-2016-01-18, accessed on 17 July 2022.
22. Interrogation report of Masood Azhar (1994).
23. ibid.
24. 'Jaish investing in real estate, commodity market: US', *DNA*, 19 November 2013, https://www.dnaindia.com/world/report-jaish-investing-in-real-estate-commodity-market-us-1094085, accessed on 17 July 2022.
25. ibid.
26. Singh, B., 'Masood's masterstroke'.
27. Firstpost, 'Property records nail Pakistani lie on Jaish-e-Mohammed HQ in Bahawalpur'.
28. Roul, A., 'Jaish-e-Muhammad's charity wing revitalizes banned group in Pakistan'.
29. ibid.
30. Singh, B., 'Masood's masterstroke'.

31 ibid.
32 'How Jaish-e-Mohammad is funding terrorists in J&K', *India Today*.
33 ibid.
34 Franklin, L.A., 'Rampant pedophilia in Pakistani madrassas', Gateston Institute–International Policy Council, 20 December 2017, https://www.gatestoneinstitute.org/11564/pakistan-pedophilia, accessed on 17 July 2022.
35 As told to the author by Alpha 12.
36 ibid.
37 As told to the author by Bashir Assad.
38 ibid.
39 Pandya, A., *Radicalisation in India*.
40 As told to the author by Mahboob Gilani.
41 ibid.
42 'Bahadur Ali a living proof of Pak's role in cross-border terror: Sushma', *The Hindu*, 1 November 2016, https://www.thehindu.com/news/national/Bahadur-Ali-a-living-proof-of-Paks-role-in-cross-border-terror-Sushma/article15000741.ece, accessed on 17 July 2022.
43 ibid.
44 Recorded by Masood Azhar, Jaish chief, 'Kashmir aur Ghazwa—emotional bayaan', Youtube, https://www.youtube.com/watch?v=WfkhK7D5QAc, accessed on 17 July 2022.
45 Azhar, M., 'Maulana Masood Azhar—Jihad-e-Kashmir aur Ghazwa-e-Hind'.
46 Azhar, M., 'Jannat talwaro ke saye me', https://archive.org/details/MaulanaMasoodAzharClips/008-NabiKWaris.mp3, accessed on 18 July 2022.

Chapter 7: Pathankot and Pulwama: Obsession with the Pleasures of Jannat

1. Tiwary, D., and R. Tripathi, 'Pathankot attack: Jaish-e-Mohammed plotted attack in 2014 with Google map of airbase, says NIA', *The Indian Express*, 20 December 2016, https://indianexpress.com/article/india/pathankot-air-base-attack-jaish-e-mohammed-nia-charge sheet-maulana-masood-azhar-shahid-latif-4436177/, accessed on 6 August 2022.
2. PTI, 'Pathankot attack: NIA files charge sheet against JeM chief Masood Azhar', *Mumbai Mirror*, 19 December 2016, https://mumbaimirror.indiatimes.com/news/india/pathankot-attack-nia-files-charge sheet-against-jem-chief-masood-azhar/articleshow/56061360.cms, accessed on 6 August 2022.
3. Tiwary, D., and R. Tripathi, 'Pathankot attack'.
4. Dutt, B., 'A cop didn't fight Pathankot terrorists, my brother did', NDTV, 6 January 2016, https://www.ndtv.com/india-news/a-cab-driver-died-fighting-pathankot-terrorists-who-wanted-his-car-1262378, accessed on 6 August 2022.
5. ibid.
6. Sethi, C., 'Did a lost walkie-talkie save the day at Pathankot?', *Hindustan Times*, 9 January 2016, https://www.hindustantimes.com/india/did-a-lost-walkie-talkie-save-the-day-at-pathankot/story-fiJ9lHXEoYvNIysFyPe1yJ.html, accessed on 5 August 2022.
7. ibid.
8. Dutt, B., 'A cop didn't fight Pathankot terrorists, my brother did'.
9. Tiwary, D., and R. Tripathi, 'Pathankot attack'.
10. ibid.
11. ibid.
12. ANI, 'Pathankot attack: Charge sheet filed based on "irrefutable evidences", asserts NIA IG', *India4u.com*, December 2016, https://www.india4u.com/pathankot-attack-charge sheet-filed-

based-on-irrefutable-evidences-asserts-nia-ig/, accessed on 6 August 2022.

13. Tiwary, D., and R. Tripathi, 'Pathankot attack'.
14. ibid.
15. Rana, D., *As Far As the Saffron Fields*.
16. Tiwary, D., and R. Tripathi, 'Pathankot attack'.
17. ibid.
18. ibid.
19. Ranbir Penal Code (RPC) was the main criminal code applicable in the erstwhile state of Jammu and Kashmir. Because of Article 370 giving special status to Jammu and Kashmir, Indian Penal Code (IPC) was not applicable. After 5 August 2019, i.e., after the abrogation of Article 370, RPC ceased to exist with the end of special status.
20. 'NIA charge sheet on Pulwama fidayeen attack: State (NIA) vs Masood Azhar Alvi and others, RC-02/2019/NIA/JMU', (Janipur Courts Complex, Jammu, 25 August 2020), accessed on 12 August 2022.
21. Singh, R.K., 'JeM suspects, arrested by UP ATS from Deoband, had invited "special guest" to hostel: Police', *Hindustan Times*, 25 February 2019, https://www.hindustantimes.com/india-news/jem-suspects-arrested-by-up-ats-from-deoband-had-invited-special-guest-to-hostel-police/story-UOiYVCkF5MIcRhjpzy3vzH.html, accessed on 7 August 2022.
22. 'NIA charge sheet on the Pulwama fidayeen attack'.
23. ibid.
24. ibid.
25. ibid.
26. Rana, D., *As Far As the Saffron Fields*.
27. ibid.
28. ibid.

29   ibid.

30   'NIA charge sheet on the Pulwama fidayeen attack'.

31   As told to the author by Mr Dabwal.

32   Rana, D., *As Far As the Saffron Fields*.

33   Inayat Malik could be Waiz's friend; however, not many details are known about him. The NIA charge sheet on the Pulwama attack only mentions his name.

34   Rabasa, A., P. Chalk et al., 'Beyond Al Qaeda'.

35   ibid.

36   Shakil, F., 'Pakistan facing bankruptcy as the economy crumbles', *Asia Times*, 16 May 2022, https://asiatimes.com/2022/05/pakistan-facing-bankruptcy-as-the-economy-crumbles/?fbclid=IwAR0tPxB9BS_631V7wPKp0kUshFRzbh6crDKz5Tj5DNrD7oACu_NSqSwiQLw, accessed on 16 May 2022.

37   As told by Mustapha, former LeT terrorist, to the author. These figures need to verified. Though Mustapha still has deep contacts in Lashkar and in the ISI, these figures may be exaggerated.

38   As told to the author by sources in the Indian intelligence set-up.

39   Gupta, M., 'Al-Qaeda threatens suicide attacks in Delhi, Mumbai; Sources say "it's to mobilise cadres towards outfit"', News 18, 8 June 2022, https://www.msn.com/en-in/news/other/al-qaeda-threatens-suicide-attacks-in-india-over-prophet-remark-sources-say-they-re-trying-to-mobilise-cadres/ar-AAYchK1?bk=1&ocid=msedgntp&cvid=3db37143faf449d9823d0dc0c36a4de4, accessed on 8 June 2022.

40   Wani, L., 'EXCLUSIVE: Al-Qaeda releases video on Kashmir, Zawahiri calls 370 removal a "slap on Muslims"', Mirror Now, 6 May 2022, https://www.timesnownews.com/mirror-now/in-focus/exclusive-al-qaeda-releases-video-on-kashmir-zawahiri-calls-370-removal-a-slap-on-muslims-article-91371429, accessed on 31 May 2022.

41   Pandya, A., 'Militancy in Kashmir'.

42. 'Terror groups focus from Afghanistan to Kashmir: UN Report', *Daily Excelsior*, 31 May 2022, https://www.dailyexcelsior.com/terror-groups-focus-from-afghanistan-to-kashmir-un-report/, accessed on 31 May 2022.

43. Jha, R., 'In new video, Qaida chief Ayman al-Zawahiri wades into Karnataka hijab row', *The Times of India*, 6 April 2022, https://timesofindia.indiatimes.com/india/in-new-video-qaida-chief-ayman-al-zawahiri-wades-into-karnataka-hijab-row/articleshow/90672577.cms, accessed on 16 May 2022.

44. Arunima, 'Two arrested for supplying arms to Lashkar-e-Mustafa for terror attacks in J&K', CNN-News 18, 23 July 2021, https://www.news18.com/news/india/nia-arrests-2-people-from-bihar-for-supplying-arms-to-lashkar-e-mustafa-for-terror-attacks-in-jammu-3994709.html, accessed on 16 May 2022.

45. Sharma, R. (ed.), 'Planned strike on terror launch pads in Pakistan post 26/11 Mumbai attacks but didn't get government's approval: Retired IAF officer', India.Com., 27 February 2019, https://www.india.com/news/india/planned-strike-on-terror-launch-pads-in-pakistan-post-26-11-mumbai-attacks-but-didnt-get-governments-approval-retired-iaf-officer-3589802/, accessed on 25 May 2022.

46. MHA, 'Intelligence agencies foil "Hamas plan" in India', Tribune India, 25 November 2023, https://sanatanprabhat.org/english/88259.html, accessed on 26 November 2023.

47. This figure may have increased as there is no recent data. Census 2021 could not be held in India because of the COVID-19 pandemic.

48. Nanjappa, V., 'Wahhabis are taking over Indian mosques, spending crores to grow: IB', Rediff.com, 1 August 2014, https://www.rediff.com/news/report/slide-show-1-wahhabis-are-taking-over-indian-mosques-spending-crores-to-grow-ib/20140801.htm#:~:text=The%20current%20number%20of%20Wahhabi%20followers%20in%20India,years%20through%20

funds%20pumped%20in%20from%20Saudi%20A, accessed on 17 May 2022.

49 'Jaish terrorist linked to Pak-based Taliban arrested by UP ATS, was tasked to kill Nupur Sharma', India TV, 13 August 2022, https://www.indiatvnews.com/news/india/nupur-sharma-news-jaish-terrorist-linked-to-pakistan-taliban-arrested-by-up-ats-muhammad-nadeem-2022-08-13-799613, accessed on 13 August 2022.

50 Swami, P., 'Terror commander Masood Azhar resurfaces to launch celeb-style 'ask me anything' online service', *The Print*, 26 April 2024, https://theprint.in/world/terror-commander-masood-azhar-resurfaces-to-launch-celeb-style-ask-me-anything-online-service/2057677/, accessed on 29 April 2024.

51 Based on the Pulwama charge sheet and inputs shared by Mr Dabwal.

52 Pandya, A., 'Kashmir Militancy after 370'.

53 Mir, S., 'J&K artist Amreen Bhat killed: Why did a TV actress become militants' target?', *The Quint*, 20 May 2022, https://www.thequint.com/news/india/jk-artist-amreen-bhat-killed-why-did-a-tv-actress-become-militants-target#read-more, accessed on 31 May 2022.

54 Islam, M.U., and P. Shakir, 'Who are Kashmir's hybrid militants?', *The Diplomat*, 30 November 2021, https://thediplomat.com/2021/11/who-are-kashmirs-hybrid-militants/, accessed on 31 May 2022.

55 '439 militants killed in J-K after Article 370 abrogation: Govt', Kashmirwalla, 2 February 2022, https://thekashmirwalla.com/439-militants-killed-in-j-k-after-article-370-abrogation-govt/, accessed on 31 May 2022.

56 Based on the Pulwama charge sheet and inputs shared by Mr Dabwal.

57 Pandey, D.K., 'JeM planning attacks in India, say reports', *The Hindu*, 26 August 2021, https://www.thehindu.com/

news/national/jem-planning-attacks-in-india-say-reports/article36120687.ece, accessed on 15 June 2022.

58. 'Masood Azhar meets Taliban leadership, seeks "support" in fomenting terrorism in Kashmir: Report', *Times Now News*, 28 August 2021, https://www.timesnownews.com/india/article/masood-azhar-meets-taliban-leadership-seeks-support-in-fomenting-terrorism-in-kashmir-report/804737, accessed on 15 June 2022.

59. Pandey, D.K., 'JeM planning attacks in India, say reports'.

60. Pandya, A., 'How Biden's withdrawal impacts India's stake in Afghanistan', *The National Interest*, 12 June 2021, https://nationalinterest.org/blog/buzz/how-biden%E2%80%99s-withdrawal-impacts-india%E2%80%99s-stake-afghanistan-187591, accessed on 15 June 2022.

61. Roy, A., 'Internal, bilateral: Taliban "clarify" position on Kashmir', *Hindustan Times*, 17 August 2021, https://www.hindustantimes.com/india-news/taliban-kashmir-pakistan-terror-groups-insurgency-afghanistan-security-situation-101629204421516.html, accessed on 15 June 2022.

62. Kotoky, P.D., 'Taliban "won't interfere in Kashmir"; seeks "good ties" with India', *Newsbytes*, 1 September 2021, https://www.newsbytesapp.com/news/world/taliban-won-t-interfere-in-kashmir-anas-haqqani/story#:~:text=Anas%20Haqqani%20said%20Kashmir%20is%20not%20a%20part,Haqqanis%20have%20no%20intention%20to%20interfere%20in%20Kashmir, accessed on 15 June 2022.

63. Kartha, T., 'Taliban leaders like Mullah Baradar have no real interest in Kashmir', *The Print*, 23 August 2021, https://theprint.in/opinion/taliban-leaders-like-mullah-baradar-have-no-real-interest-in-kashmir/720374/, accessed on 15 June 2022.

64. Javeed, A., 'Taliban won't get involved in Kashmir: A.S. Dulat', *Moneycontrol*, 15 July 2021, https://www.moneycontrol.com/news/india/taliban-kashmir-as-dulat-afghanistan-pakistan-

gupkar-alliance-narendra-modi-7174451.html, accessed on 15 June 2022.

65   Ray, M., 'Days after bilateral issue comment, Taliban's new remarks about Kashmir', *Hindustan Times*, 3 September 2021, https://www.hindustantimes.com/world-news/days-after-bilateral-issue-comment-taliban-s-new-remarks-about-kashmir-101630650481173.html, accessed on 15 June 2022.

66   ibid.

67   AFP, 'UN human rights chief decries suppression of women in Afghanistan', *Daily Sabah*, 15 June 2022, https://www.dailysabah.com/world/asia-pacific/un-human-rights-chief-decries-suppression-of-women-in-afghanistan, accessed on 15 June 2022.

68   IANS, 'Intel input reveals 300 terrorists, including Afghans, being trained at PoK launchpads', India TV, 10 January 2020, https://www.indiatvnews.com/news/india/intel-input-reveals-300-terrorists-including-afghans-being-trained-at-pok-launchpads-578234, accessed on 31 May 2022.

69   Sriharsha, P., 'Around 400 terrorists at launchpads in PoK: Gen Naravane', *The Siasat Daily*, 12 January 2022, https://www.siasat.com/around-400-terrorists-at-launchpads-in-pok-gen-naravane-2257254/, accessed on 31 May 2022.

70   'Muslim brotherhood's new startup : Kashmir', Disinfo Lab, January 2022, https://thedisinfolab.org/muslim-brotherhoods-new-startup-kashmir/, accessed on 31 May 2022..

Index

Aaina, Afzal Guru, 157, 324
Abadi, Qazi Ahsan Ahmed Shuja, Maulana 39
Abbasi, Zahir-ul-Islam, Maj. Gen., 92
Abbottabad camp, 135, 238, 299
Abdullah aka Asadullah, 110
Abid, Syed Muhammad, 32
Adil, Mohammad alias Ajmal, 192, 218
al-Adl, Saif, 99
Afghani, Sajjad, 58, 64–65, 69, 72, 74, 150–151, 199, 241–244, 248, 284–292, 332, 334; death of, 72
Afghanistan, 7–8, 35–37, 51, 56, 58–59, 65–66, 87, 93–103, 109–113, 119–120, 122, 129, 131–132, 241, 243, 262–263, 284–288, 356–358, 378–379, 381–386; operations, 8, 202; US invasion of, 105; war, 50, 118, 260
Afghanistan Mazar-i-Sharif, Indian mission in, 164-165
Afghan Taliban, 26, 28–30, 51, 53, 112, 160, 243
Africa, 7, 34, 82, 98, 102, 324

Afroz, Mohammad, 117
Afzal Guru, 152, 157–158, 163–164, 268, 280, 324, 357, 371; execution of, 157, 164; in Tihar Jail, 157
Afzal Guru Squads, 152, 157–158, 163, 268; formation of, 157
Ahl-i-Hadith, 36, 91–92, 210, 214, 219, 223, 259–260, 264, 266–268, 319, 328
Ahl-i-Sunnat Wal Jamaat (ASWJ), 46
Ahmadiyyas, 37, 39–41, 46, 77, 80, 91, 235, 267, 279; agitation against 46
Ahmed, Irshad, 15, 65, 104, 150
Ahmed, Khaled, 47
Ahmed, Mufti Rashid, 66
Ahmed, Murza Ghulam, 41
Ahmed, Nasir, 231
Ahmed, Noor, Maulvi 222
Ahmed, Qari Mansoor, Maulana 199
Ahrar Movement, 39–40
Air India flight IC-814, hijacking, 4, 19, 20–22, 24, 27, 29, 31, 36, 73–74, 83,

473

102, 108, 117–118, 130, 136, 190, 201, 334, 348,; and ISI, 19
Akhtar, Naeem, 306
Akhtar, Qari Saifullah, 15, 65, 104, 107, 286
Akhunzada, Maulvi Hibatullah, 112
Akram Bhai, 143–146, 148, 213, 269, 320–321
Al Badr, 93, 110, 159, 215, 217–218, 236, 380
Al-Barq, 135, 289
Al Faran, 69, 71, 74, 102, 292
Al-Fatah, 135
Al-Furqan as Jamaat Al-Furqan, 28Ali, Ahmed, 41
Ali, Hussain, 38
Ali, Maulana Sher, 30
Ali, Mohammad Kamran, 353, 358–359, 365
Ali, Zulfiqar, 32
Al Khidmat Foundation, 266, 319
All Party Hurriyat Conference (APHC), 69
Al Murabitoon, 148, 202; training conclaves, 165
Al Qaeda (AQ), 7–10, 16–19, 29–30, 35–36, 48, 50–52, 94–99, 102–108, 112–113, 116–117, 119–120, 122–125, 128–130, 132–133, 191–192, 213–214, 220, 237, 323–324, 379–383, 390–391; and Harkat links, 103; Pakistan Intelligence and, 17–31

Al Qaeda in Indian Subcontinent (AQIS), 104, 113, 382–384; pan-Islamist vision, 107; training camp, 101
Al Qalam, 75, 140–141, 167, 176, 202, 272, 274, 325, 369
Al Rahmat Trust (ART), 75, 122, 140142, 166, 201, 266, 293, 319, 324,343, fundraising, 325
Al Rashid Trust, 104
Altaf, Mufti, 177
Altaf Baba, 151, 156, 158
Al Umar Mujahideen (AuM), 135, 144, 168, 206, 289
Alvi, Mohiuddin Aurangzeb Alamgir alias Ammar, 55, 349, 358, 370, 375–376
Al Zarqawi, Abu Musab, 50
Al Zawahiri, Ayman, 104, 123, 382, 383
Americans, 74, 85, 95, 104, 106, 111, 117, 120, 122–123, 128, 175; infidels, 64; jihad against, 105
Ammar Alvi, *See* Alvi, Mohiuddin Aurangzeb Alamgir
Anjuman-i-Khuddam-ud-Din, 40
Ansar Ghazwat-ul-Hind (AGuH), 9, 217, 382; WhatsApp group, 313–314
Ansar-ul-Ummah, 142
anti-India operations, 390
anti-Shiite agenda, 49

INDEX | 475

anti-Soviet jihad, 288
Anti-Terrorism Act (ATA), 166
Anti-Terrorism Squad (ATS), 188, 385
Anwar, Shakeen, 50
Anwar, Ubaidullah, 41
Armitage, Richard L., 120
arms recovery, 183–184
Article 370, abrogation of, 9, 174–175, 177, 182, 196, 217, 271, 317, 386–387, 390
Ashrafi, Maulana Tahir, 28
Ashraf, Mohammad, 154
Assad, Bashir, 222
assassination attempts/plots, 25, 37, 49, 70, 85, 109, 124–127, 207–28, 380
Athar, Ibrahim, 55, 58, 102
Atta, Muhammad, 94
Ayodhya, 80, 149, 187-188, 193; attack in, 187
Azad, Abul Kalam, Maulana, 39, 42
Azad, Ghulam Nabi, 148; assassination plot, 148–149
Azam, Abdullah, 78
Azgar, Abdul Rauf, 55, 101, 349
Azgar, Mufti Rauf, 55, 134, 136, 139–140, 199–201, 204, 253, 256–257, 302, 341, 343, 369–370, 374–375, 378; arrests of, 123; training and, 300
Azhar, Masood, 8, 15–17, 20, 22–30, 55–85, 92–96, 98–102, 107–109, 115–119, 123–30, 134–138, 144, 157–158, 165–168, 173, 184–185, 199–202, 206–207, 272–273, 289–292, 323–325; arrest of, 69; asset to Pakistan, 75; in Bahawalpur Central Jail, 134; birth of, 55; freeing, 29; for Ghazwai-Hind, 85; in Indian jails, 99; India visit, 65–69; and indoctrination, 329–337; jail life, 65–69; as 'Mota,' 72; released from the Mianwali Jail, 129; Mohananey on, 70; Portuguese passport, 63, 67, 69, 72; Raju on, 73; Rashid on, 87–88; release of, 8, 20, 74; rescue attempts, 73–74; scholarly intellectual, 75–87; Swami on, 78; to Tihar, 72; writings, 83
Azhar, Mazhar Ali, Maulana, 39
Azhar, Wali, 110
Aziz, Shaukat, 380; suicide attack on, 128

Baba, Altaf, 151, 156, 158
Baba, Ghazi, 148–149, 151, 169, 199, 216, 230–231, 248, 256, 272, 280, 282; killing of, 146
Baba, Manzoor Ahmed, 169, 356
Baba, Muhammad Ashiq, 307–312
Babri mosque, Ayodhya, 80–83, 184, 194, 241
Badami Bagh cantonment attack, 116, 223
Al-Badr Mujahideen, 135

Bahadur, Hafiz Gul, Maulana 51
Bakr, Abu, 80
Balakot airstrikes, 1–2, 5–7, 172, 176, 238, 252, 338, 370, 375, 386
Balochistan, 44, 100, 150, 159, 198, 231, 258, 300
Balwal, Rakesh, 231, 344
Bangalore, M. Chinnaswamy Stadium, attack 192
Bangladesh, 32, 34, 36, 58, 63, 65, 100, 159, 187–88, 190–92, 214, 242, 250, 258, 284, 290; borders, 65, 189, 247
Baradar, Abdul Ghani, 111, 389
Barelwis, 16, 33–34, 36, , 91, , 235, 260, 261, 263–264,
Barelwi, Syed Ahmad, 83
Barua, Paresh, 191
Basharat, Momin, 312–313
Bashir, Aarzoo, 169
Bashir, Shakir aka Abu Huzaifah, 349, 357, 359–367, 370–371
Basra, Riaz, 47–49
Bengali separatism, 159
Bhai, Kashif, 374–375
Bhai, Waleed (aka Cheetah Bhai), 217, 348
Bhat, Amir Siraj 175
Bhat, Feroz Ahmad, 169, 185
Bhatt, Sajjad Ahmed, 354, 357, 361–62, 365, 367
Bhutto, Benazir, 27, 49, 92, 208, 266; assassination attempt, 51; assassination of, 112; conspiracy to kill, 35
Bhutto, Zulfikar Ali, 3

Bihari, Munna, 348; killing of, 172
Bilal, Amjad, 69, 291
Bilal, Muhammad (aka Asif Sadiq), 94, 102, 116
Billa, Rashid, 170, 251, 254–255
Binalshibh, Ramzi, 133
bin-Laden, Osama, 15–16, 29–30, 78, 84, 93, 96–97, 99, 102–105, 108, 120, 126, 130–131; hijack and, 29; 'Khost Fatwa of Jihad, 98
Binoria mosque seminary (Jamia Uloom Islamia Seminary), 15, 22, 30, 57–59, 61, 65, 100, 103–105, 108, 204, 261–262
Bokhari, Syed Ata Ullah Shah, 39
Border Security Force (BSF), 146, 156, 190, 231; camp, 2017 attack on, 169, 306
Bosnia, 61, 65, 92, 98, 101, 326, 328–329
Bowen, Innes, 62
British Deobandis, 96
Bukhari, Amanullah, 281, 283

camps, 5, 7, 103, 110, 135, 154, 237–238, 242–243, 252, 287–289, 326, 329, 369–370, 381, 383; in Afghanistan, 241; Balakot, 172, 238; Bari, 241, 288; Batrasi, 135, 237, 300; HuM training, 102; jihad, 331; Kotli, 290; mujahideen, 95; in Pakistan and Afghanistan, 243; Rahmania, 303, 305; Taliban, 110; Tangdhar, 298; terror-training, 7, 279; transit, 136, 287; Yavar, 241–242, 284, 287

Central Forensic Science Laboratory (CFSL), 345, 360, 366–367

Central Reserve Police Force (CRPF), 1, 361, 384; attack on of, 356, 366; fidayeen attack on, 1; Laizbal camp attack at, 245

Chaudhry, Fawad, 173

Chechnya, 84, 92, 94, 98, 101, 204, 262, 336, 388

Cheema, Mohammad Arshad alias 'Mac,' 21

Chinar Corps, 153, 161; killing of, 116

CISF vehicle, attack on, 172

Clinton, Bill, Pakistan visit, 124

communal riots, 194

Connaught Place (CP), encounter, 189

cordon and search operations (CASOs), 171

counterinsurgency, 154, 161; 'Mission All-out,' 161

counterterrorism, 54, 73, 158, 161, 166, 197, 221, 248, 261, 326, 380, 386

Cromite, James, 95

Danish, Qari, 293

Dar, Adil Ahmed, JeM fidayeen commando, 1, 172, 224, 327, 345, 353, 358–60, 362–64, 366, 368–372, 374–376, 382; suicide attack, 172

Dar, Ashraf, 67–69, 289, 291

Dar, Ghulam Hassan, 359, 366

Dar, Samir Ahmed, 174, 279, 352, 358–359, 36263, 365, 367, 370–371, 372

Darul-Ifta-e-wal-Irshad, Nazimabad, 30, 62

Darul Uloom Deoband, 32, 38, 45, 62, 67, 152, 220–221, 270, 289, 361

Darul-Uloom Haqqania, 204

Dar-ul-Uloom Qasimiya, 69, 221

Darul Uloom Rahimiya, 221

Daura-i-aam, 262

Dean, Aimen, 96

Dehlawi, Shah Waliullah, 32

Deoband, 32, 37–38, 41, 45, 67, 77, 80, 82, 187, 285, 347

Deobandi: in anti-Ahmadiyya movement, 37; extremist ecosystem, 53, 77, 79, 96, 116, 127, 204, 206–207, 209, 213, 258; institutions, 34–35, 42, 213, 222; leaders, 39, 41–42, 204, 206; madrasa network, 27, 43–46, 53, 222, 260, 307, 319, 326; movement, 17, 30, 32, 38, 62, 79, 205; in Pakistan, 36–40; seminaries, 44, 62, 220–221; terror groups, 27,

46, 52, 73, 91–93, 96, 205, 210; Ulemas, 40–42
Deobandis, 27, 32–37, 39, 44–46, 52–53, 60, 65, 77–79, 91–92, 204, 207, 209–210, 221–223
Deobandism, 18, 77, 108, 214, 261, 264, 383–385
Dera Ismail Khan, suicide bombing, 112
Dhaka, 64–65, 67, 190–191
al-Din, Shah Rafi, 32

Din-e-Elahi, Akbar, 36
donors, Gulf-based, 136
Doval, Ajit, 23–24, 177
drugs, 24, 85, 235, 263, 270, 279, 282–83, 320–21, 323, 337, 387–388
Dujana, Abu, 144
Dulat, A.S., 22, 118, 126

Egypt, 61, 92, 101
Ehsan, Ehsanullah, 52–53
11 September 2001 attacks (9/11), 8, 130
encounter deaths, 9, 143, 150, 158, 162, 217, 273, 280, 303
encounters, 171
Europe, 27, 34–35, 132, 324
extremism, religious, 214–215, 265, 390
extremist groups, 81, 213, 222, 261, 263, 266, 327

Facebook, 272, 313-14, 341, 342, 385

Fadhli, Tariq Nasir, 99
Fair, C. Christine, 2, 10, 28, 30–31, 91, 159–160, 379
Falah-i-Aam Trust (FAT), 216
Farooqi, Amjad, 95, 102, 123
Farooqi, Jamia, 66
Farooqi, Zia-ur-Rahman, Maulana, 40, 46, 48, 60, 65,
Farooq, Muhammad Umar, 202–3, 233, 251, 254, 279, 282, 327340, –348, 353, 356– 357, 367, 377, 386; digital evidences on, 377–379; Pulwama mastermind, 205, 311, 367–368, 388

Fatah-ul-Jawaad, , 57, 75, 84, 87–89, 136
Fazail-i-Jihad, , 76, 83–84, 99
Fazlullah, Mullah, death of, 53
Federally Administered Tribal Areas (FATA), 44, 52–53, 261, 266
fidayeen attack, 1–11, 116, 118–19, 121, 223, 225, 234, 237, 338–339, 342, 365–66, 384–385, 387–388
fidayeen missions, 54, 115–120, 152, 270
Filipino jihadists, 98
Financial Action Task Force (FATF), 1, 10, 110, 176–177, 196, 238, 252, 268, 380
Financing Jaish-e-Mohammed, 319–325
foreign terrorist groups (FTGs), 4, 82, 224, Foreign Terrorist

Organization (FTOs), 11, 18–19, 75, 121, 141, 161
foreign terrorists (FTs), 161, 169–170, 172, 174–175, 231–232, 235, 238, 245–246, 248, 257–258, 275–279, 283, 288, 292, 303, 306, 314, 318
fundraising, 59–60, 67, 82, 130, 141, 186
funds, 192, 213, 320–321

Gandhi, Mahatma, 39
Gandhi, Rahul, 190
Gangohi, Rashid Ahmad, 32, 38
Gani, Zaid Ahmed, 315–317
Ganji, Sadiq, 50
Ghafoor, Asif, Maj. Gen., 173
Ghazi, Khwaja Abdul Rehman, 39
Ghaznavi, Daud, Maulana, 39
Ghori, Muhammad, 239, 293, 296
Gilmartin, 38
global terrorist, 75, 137, 161, 166
Global War on Terror (GWoT), 8, 85, 93, 122, 208, 213, 380
Gojri, Ishfaq Al, 317–319
Guantanamo Bay, desecration of the Quran in, 132
Gujarat riots, 186, 241
Gujjar, Muhammad Sadiq, alias Muawiya, 299
Gujjar, Muhammad Sadiq Ahmed, 299–303
Gulf countries, 322; petrodollars from, 43
Gul, Hamid, 141
Gul, Imtiaz, 97
Gul, Sajjad, 133
Gurdaspur attack, 164–165
Gyanvapi case, 194

Habib-ur-Rehman, 39, 41
Hadi-al-Iraqi, 123
Hai, Abdul, 49
Haider, Usman, 171–172, 202, 358, 378
Hai, Qari Abdul, 49
Hamid, Tahir, 60
Haq, Chaudhry Afzal, 39
Haqqani, Anas, 389
Haqqani, Jalaluddin, 96–97, 287
Haqqani Network, 97, 107, 207, 237, 356, 389
Al-Haramain Foundation, 191–192
Harkat groups, 27, 82, 96–98, 100–103, 106–108, 123; global memberships, 100–107; in Kashmir, 22; leadership, 67; movement, 66, 92, 94, 104, 324; movement with AQ, 96–98; stalwarts, 104; support from Pakistan, 107
Harkat-ul-Ansar (HuA), 15–16, 26–27, 66–67, 69, 74, 79, 96, 99–101, 107, 237, 284, 287, 291
Harkat-ul-Inqalab Islami, 96

Harkat-ul-Jihad-al-Islami (HuJI), 15, 36, 65–67, 69, 96–98, 100, 102–104, 123, 188, 190–191, 214, 286–187, 291; Bangladesh, 190–191; formation of J&K branch, 66; and HuM's Kashmir operations, 82, 98; split, 15, 65, 286

Harkat-ul-Mujahideen (HuM), 8, 15–18, 20, 25, 27, 30–31, 34–36, 46, 57–60, 6267, 69, 74–75, 92, 96–98, 103–104, 125–126, 144, 199, 206, 213–215, 243–244, 284–291; cadres, 57, 97–99, 102, 108, 145, 155, 199; commander, 58, 65, 289; leadership, 26, 30, 58, 288; network, 150, 152, 169, 181, 229–230, 387

Harkat-ul-Mujahideen Al-Alami (HuMA), 16

Hasnain, Syed Ata, Lt Gen., 153

hawala operation, 174, 187, 221, 303, 305

Hayat, Ahsan Saleem, 380

Hidaytullah, Maulvi, 177

high quality of human intelligence (HUMINT), 150

Hissam-ud-din, Sheikh, 39

Hissarvi, Abdul Jabbar, 41

Hizb-e-Islami, 97, 285–87

Hizbul Mujahideen (HM), 9–10, 17–20, 119, 135–136, 145, 148–149, 154, 161–162, 195–196, 213–219, 229–233, 235–236, , 327–328, 379–381, 387

Hizb-ut-Tahrir, 207

Hurriyat Conference, 213

Hurriyat leaders, 291, 311

Hussain, Mohammad Dilawar, 313–315, 321, 366

Ibrahim, Dawood, 137, 187

Ibrahim Athar (Mohammad Ibrahim Athar Alvi), 55, 58, 102, 201, 348

Idara Rahimiya Ulum-i-Qurania, 38

identity, fake, 289, 298, 307

Ikhwan-ul-Musalmeen, 18, 61, 289

improvised explosive device (IEDs), 169, 174, 245–247, 303, 305, 345, 347, 361, 363–364, 370–374, 376, 378; attacks, 247, 345–347, 364–365, 369, 374; training, 270; in Kashmir, 356

India: intelligence, 19, 110, 139, 164, 181, 192, 212, 257, 346, 388; militants crossed into, 145; Muslims, 194, 333–335, 383–384

Indian-administered Kashmir: 2016 unrest in, 143; attack in, 1

Indian Air Force (IAF), 2, 5, 339

Indian Mujahideen (IM), 5, 192, 214, 218

Indian National Congress, 42

INDEX | 481

India–Pakistan ceasefire, 178, 217
India–US nuclear deal, 6
indoctrination, 10, 220, 225, 232, 256, 259, 262, 267–68, 277, 283, 286–387, 326–329
infidels, 33, 78, 81, 85, 105, 287, 330
infiltration, 152, 154–156, 160–161, 178, 181, 200–201, 203, 228–229, 233, 236, 249–254, 257, 294–295, 301, 357–358, 376–377, 386, 388; routes, 156, 215, 249–250, 254; strategy, 251–254
insurgency, 28, 31, 34, 54, 56, 113–114, 153–154, 174–175, 196, 198, 229–230, 234, 236
international border (IB), 154, 251, 253–254
International Islamic Front (IIF), 130
Inter-Service Intelligence (ISI), 17–31, 47, 66, 73, 91–92, 106, 108–109, 113–117, 119–120, 124–131, 133–137, 144, 190–192, 195, 208–214, 287, 308–309, 381–382; Doval on, 23; funds JeM, 323; and hijackers, 23
Iqbal, Tamim, killing of, 149
Iran, 133, 241, 263
al-Iraqi, Abd-al-Hadi, 97(
Irshad, 59
Irshad, Maulana, 286
Ishaq, Malik, 48, 50; arrest of, 29

ISI: backed Deobandi terrorist groups, 7, 117; fundings, 119; masterminds, 20, 177, 196
al-Islam, Saif, 99
Islam, Waizul, 357, 361, 365
Islamabad, 2002 church bombing, 95; Marriott bombing, 50
Islamic Front, 135
Islamic State (IS), 9
Islamic State–Khorasan Province (ISKP), 51, 53, 107–108, 257, 381
Islamic State of Jammu and Kashmir (ISJK), 9, 51, 53, 107–108, 257, 381
Islamic state of Pakistan, 42
Islami Riyasat, 92
Ismail, Mufti, 62–63
Issa, Vali Adam, 63, 67
Al-Ittihad Al-Islamiya, 63–64, 99

Jabbar, Abdul, Maulana, 109, 121, 123, 130, 134, 199, 284
jailbreak, 20, 74, 199, 292; in Kot Bhalwal Jail, 74, 199
Jaish-e-Muhammad (JeM), 5; attack on training camps of, 1–2, 180; Balakot base, 78; ban on, 126, 134, 136, 148, 243; central office of, 198; commanders, 149–151, 153, 221, 225, 231, 233–234, 245, 248, 257, 281, 356, 358–359; as 'family enterprise,' 201–208; fidayeen attacks, 120,

245, 388; financial dealings, 139; as Foreign Terrorist Organization (FTO), 2, 121, 169, 232, 240, 347; formation of, 4, 8, 17, 26, 28, 30, 77, 83, 199; front organization, 83, 140, 266; global ambitions, 184–185; ideology, 83, 361; linked suicide bombings, 121; jihad, 86; leaders, 130, 205, 213, 310, 375–376; militants, 149, 151, 157, 160, 217–218, 229–231, 245–246, 248, 256, 258, 271–272, 275–277, 280–283, 371–372; militants and beheadings, 153, 170; module operating in Bihar, 192; OGW networks, 134, 143, 170, 213, 216, 255–256, 279, 282, 312, 317, 321–322; operatives in J&K, 4, 111, 143–48, 205; origins of, 17–41, 53; pan-India ambitions, 83, 185; pan-India vision, 384; pan-Islamist agenda, 93–96, 323; properties and assets, 325–326; and Taliban linkages, 111; terrorists/cadres, 108, 111, 146–149, 170–172, 228, 231–232, 237–238, 246–247, 253, 276–279, 281–284, 347, 359–361, 365, 370, 377–378; suicide attacks, 227–228*t*; terrorist incidents, 179–184*t*;

training camps, 79, 95, 110, 154, 188, 293, 326, 370
Jalandhar, 38, 41–42, 330
Jamaat-i-Islami (JI), 18–19, 60, 68, 143, 146, 211, 216, 221–223, 265, 270, 320
Jamaat-ul-Ahrar, 110
Jamaat-ul-Ansar, 15
Jamaat-ul-Furqan (JuF), 25, 109–110, 135, 121–122, 127–128, 209, 213, 263
Jamaat-ul-Mujahideen (JuM), 66
Jamal, Arif, 142
Jamali, Gayur Ahmad, 192
Jamia Masjid Subhanallah, 140, 173
Jamia Rashidiya, 41
Jamiat Amal Khairia (Sharjah), 61
Jamiat Ulema-e-Hind, 33, 41–42
Jamiat Ulema-e-Islam (JuI), 27, 33, 42, 60, 65, 104, 204, 287
Jamiat Ulema-e-Islam Sami (JuI-S), 204
Jamiat-ul-Islah (Ikhwan), 60–61
Jamiat-ul-Mujahideen, 135
Jammu and Kashmir (J&K), 1, 8–9, 93, 115, 171, 174, 185, 189, 197, 384, 388; legislative assembly, JeM attack on, 8, 11, 116, 120
Jammu-Kashmir Liberation Front (JKLF), 18, 144, 213, 288
Jan, Insha aka Insha Tariq, 279, 282, 350, 357, 359, 362–363, 365, 371, 388

Jehangir, Mohammad, 55
Jhangvi, Haq Nawaz, Maulana, 40, 46
Jihad/ jihadism, 32, 45, 86, 90, 205, 259, 265, 265–266, 356; Afghan, 8, 15, 18, 20, 44, 46, 58, 62, 204, 210, 260, 262; against American forces, 105; among British Muslims, 62; foreign, 61, 98; funds, 18–19, 64, 140, 320; Kashmir-centric, 15–16, 18, 25, 52, 54, 61, 64, 66, 73, 321, 323, 327; missions to UK, 204; Nawa-i-Afghan, 383; organizations, 45, 137, 203, 261; sexual intimacy and, 147
Al-Jihad, 135, 288
Jihad-bi-Al Saif, 35
Jinnah, Muhammad Ali, 33, 42
Jiye Sindh, 58
Joint Interrogation Centre (JIC), 292
joint operations, 213, 216, 219
Joseph, Ronald, 131
Jullunduri, Faqirullah Raipuri, Maulana, 41
Jullunduri, Khair Muhammad, Maulana, 41–42
Jullunduri, Muhammad Ali, 41

kafirs, 41, 80, 330
Kalimullah, Maulvi, 65–66
Kamran, Tahir, 46, 202, 347, 367, 369, 371, 374–375
Kandahar hijack episode, 16, 22–24, 29, 105, 108–109, 111, 113, 133, 244
Karachi, 30, 48–49, 56–59, 62–63, 65–67, 100, 104–105, 122–123, 140–141, 184, 297, 376, 380
Kargil War, 4, 19, 158
Kartha, Tara, 389
Kashmir-centric terrorist outfits, 18, 51, 135, 141, 161, 379
Kashmir Freedom Army, 294
Kashmir/Kashmiri: invasion, 3; militants, 68, 157, 135; Illyas, 74; Ilyas, 70, 74, 101, 107, 207; Ilyas, death of, 74; Maulana Dawood, 204; Maulana Farooq, 286, 288; Maulana Masood, 65–66; Mohammad Ilyas, 66; Mufti Asghar Khan, 110, 293–295; operations, 66, 111, 129, 134, 195, 206, 212; Pandits, 215
Kashmir Tigers, 10, 174, 177, 182, 196, 387
Kasuri, Khurshid, 5
Katju, Vivek, 23
Kayani, Ashfaq Parvez, Gen., 132, 137, 142, 200, 207
Kent, Shane, arrest of, 95
Kenya, 63–64, 82, 92, 98–100, 103
Khairia, Jamiat Amal, 60–61
Khalil, Fazlul Rehman, Maulana, 15–17, 20, 22, 58–59, 62–63, 65, 96, 98–99, 103–104, 204, 206, 284, 286, 289
Khalis, Maulvi Yunus, 97, 285
Khan, Abdul Qadeer, 4, 133

Khan, Abdul Rias, 21
Khan, Amanullah, 38
Khan, Ayub, 3
Khandey, Fardeen Ahmed, 169, 171, 224, 356
Khan, Ghulam Murtaza, Maulana, 325
Khan, Ghulam Ullah, 38
Khan, Imran, 132, 176, 389
Khan, Ishaq Ahmed, 171–172, 224
Khan, Ishfaq, killing, 171
Khan, Mohammed Siddique, 35, 102
Khan, Mudasir Ahmed, 170–171, 175, 217, 348, 354, 358, 360, 373–374
Khan, Muhammad Sadiq, 292
Khan, Munir, 306
Khan, Shah Nawaz alias Ghazi Baba, 146, 151, 199, 216, 230–231, 248, 256, 272, 282, 305
Khan, Showkat Ahmed, 172
Khan, Zafar Ali, Maulana, 39
Khatme Nabuwwat movement, 39–40, 55, 77
Khilafat Movement, 39
Khomani, Gauhar Aziz, 192
Khost Fatwa, against Jews and Crusaders, 191
Khuddam-ul-Islam (KuL), 25, 109, 121–122
Khyber Pakhtunkhwa (KPK), 52–53, 136, 140, 198, 237–238, 258–59, 262, 268–270, 275, 277, 297, 299–302, 325–26
kidnappings, 20, 49, 69–70, 74, 94, 102
Kim Housego, abduction, 74
Kot Bhalwal Jail, 70, 74, 199, 273, 284, 292
Kotli Jhajhar, encounter, 252
Kuchay, Bilal Ahmed, 351, 357–59, 370, 373
Kumar, Nikhil, 22
Kunduz airlift/'airlift of evil,' 117
Kupwara encounter, 148, 153, 155, 175, 245, 249, 257, 295, 306–307

Lahori, Ahmed Ali, Maulana, 39–40
Lahori, Akram, 48, 123
Lal Masjid, siege, 85, 105, 108, 127, 129, 200
Lambert, Ibrahim, 59
Langaryal, Nasrallah Manzoor, 71, 74
Lashkar-e-Jhangvi (LeJ), 28–29, 33, 45–46, 48–53, 91, 97, 108, 110, 113, 207, 214, 219, 259; ban on, 49; relationship with AQ, 50; split, 49
Lashkar-e-Tayyaba (LeT), 9–11, 30–31, 91–92, 110–111, 123–124, 142–145, 149–154, 159–162, 177–178, 189–192, 195–198, 207–211, 213–216, 218–219, 223–224, 229–233, 235–236, 277–278, 327–329,

379–381; attack on tourist bus and army camp at Kaluchak, 118; cadres, 91, 111, 215, 219, 256, 277, 302; and JeM, 5, 7, 111, 151, 177–178, 190–191, 6, 219, 259, 263, 379
Lashkar-i-Islam, 110
Lashkar-i-Mustapha (LeM), 10, 83, 174, 177, 182, 196, 384
Leghari, Farooq Ahmad, 264
Lethpura CRPF camp, vehicle-borne IED (VBIED) attack at, 169; fidayeen attack at, 171, 224, 344–346, 356, 361, 363–64, 366
al-Libbi, Abu Faraj, 133
Libya, 61, 133, 192, 390
LoC, 65, 72, 151–152, 154–155, 174, 178, 181, 203, 249–250, 294, 298–299, 301, 304, 308–310, 321
London bombings 2005, 95
Ludhianvi, Habib-ur-Rehman Maulana, , 39, 41–42
Ludhianvi, Mufti Rasheed Ahmad Maulana, 30, 104
Ludhianvi, Yousuf Maulana, 204

Mackie, David, abduction, 74
Madaris: proliferation of, 42–46; in Pakistan, *44t*; of various sects, *43t*
Madeh-i-Sahaba movement, 40
Madni, Hussain Ahmed, 42
Madrasa Darul Uloom Numaniya, 41
Madrasai-Khair-ul-Madaris, Jalandhar, 42
Madrasa-i-Numaniya, 38
Madrasa-i-Rashidiya, Jalandhar, 38
madrasas, 59, 61–62, 198, 201, 204, 221–222, 259–261, 263–265, 267, 276, 278–279, 320, 323
Mafzal-ur-Rahman, Maulana, 285
Mahmood Bhai, 170, 254
Mahmud-ul-Hasan, Maulana, 38–39
Mahsud, Baitullah, 52
Majlis-e-Ahrar-e Islam, 39
Majlis-e-Tawan-e-Islami, 30
Maktab-ul-Rabita, 385
Malik, Hidaytullah, 83
Malik, Satya Pal, 346
Malik, Yasin, 144
Mansoor, Mullah Akhtar, 204
Mansoor, Qari Shah, 237
Manzar, Abdullah Shah, 121
Maqbool, Sajad, 222
Marhama, 222, 354–55, 361, 367
Markaz Usman-O-Ali, Bahawalpur, 165, 300
Markaz Usman-o-Ali Establishment (MUAE), 201–2
martyrdom, 25, , 265, 267, 331–36, *see also* suicide bombers
Marzan, Maulvi Ghazi, 60
Masood, Rasheed Ahmed, 57
al-Masri, Abu Hafs, 99, 102

al-Maududi, Abul A'la Maulana, 68, 78, 214
Maulana Hassan Nadwi, aka Ali Mian 68
Mazar-i-Sharif attacks, 164–165
Mazhar, Abdullah Shah, 187
Mazhar, Muhammad, 285
McDonald, Myra, 23
Mehsud, Baitullah, 51
Mehsud, Mufti Noor Wali, 52–53, 112
Mehsud, Qari Hussain, 50
Memon, Tiger, 137
Mir, Hamid, 103
Mir, Khubaib, 229
Mir, Parvez, 169, 185
Mir, Rihan, 229
Mishra, Brijesh, 117
Mitra, A.K., 190
Modi, Narendra, 137, 141, 159–160, 164–165, 167, 194, 338; Lahore visit, 165; meeting Sharif at Ufa, 165; visit to Pakistan, 158
Mohamed, Khalfan Hamis, 102
Mohammad, Abu, 68
Mohammadi, Mohammed Nabi, 96
Mohammad, Khaled Sheikh, 50, 107, 132–133, 380
Mohammed, Maulana Faqir, 51
Mohammed, Prophet, 84, 382
Mohananey, Avinash, 31, 70–71
Moro Islamic Liberation Front, 98
Muawiya, Asmatullah, 112, 119, 199, 248

Mubashir, Mohammad, 149
Mughal, Abdul Rahman, 240–241, 243, 292–293; alias Raja, Shabir, Romeo, 292–296
Mughals, 32, 37, 79
Muhajir Qaumi Movement, 58
Muhammad, Khalid Sheikh, 130
mujahideens, 71–72, 86–87, 94, 185, 198, 222, 285, 288, 327–328, 357
Mukherjee, Pranab, 132
Mumbai: serial blasts, 187, 189; 26/11 terror attacks, 5, 10, 138–139, 258, 338
Murshid-ul-Ikhwan, 61
Musa, Zakir, 217, 382
Musharraf, Pervez, 8–9, 22, 25, 105–106, 108–109, 117–118, 120–123, 125, 127, 131, 133, 136–137, 208–209, 261, 263; assassination plot on, 51, 70, 85, 93, 109, 111, 123–127, 129, 133–134, 207, 213; coup, by 124–125, 158; visit to US, 131
Muslim League, 33, 42, 47, 208
Muslim women, 262, 283, 326, 328–329, 388
Muttawakil, Wakil Ahmed, 24
Myanmar/Burma, 98, 101, 164

Naafil Qurbani fundraising campaign, 166
Nadeem, Muhammad, arrest of, 385
Nadvi, Salman, 80

Nagrota army camp, attack on, 311
Nairobi, 63–64
Nanautai, Muhammad Yaqub, 32
Nannu Mia alias Belal Mandal alias Billal, arrest of, 190
Nanotwi, Muhammad Qasim, 32, 38
Narasimha Rao, 18
Naravane, M.M., Gen., 390
Nasir-al-Bahri, 29, 102
Nasir, Lt Gen., 92
Nasr, Vali, 47
Nasrallah, 71, 72, 74, 111, 291, 292
Nassar, Sajjad, 95
National Democratic Front of Bodoland (NDFB), 191
National Socialist Council of Nagaland, Khaplang (NSCN-K), 164
Nawabuddin, Muhammad Riaz, arrest of, 188
Nawaz, Rab, 28
Nayar, Kuldip, 4
Nazir, Maulvi, 52
Nazir, Osama, 95
Nengroo, Ashaq Ahmed, 253, 352, 357–358, 373
Nepal, 20–21, 188, 190, 192, 214, 247, 250; ISI presence in, 19
night vision devices (NVDs), 178, 378
Non-Cooperation Movement, 39
North West Frontier Province (NWFP), 43, 44, 53, 135, 261, 285

OGWs (over-ground workers), 144–147, 149, 215, 217, 228, 230, 250, 255–258, 270–272, 281, 293–295, 304, 320, 346–347, 356; network base, 119, 145, 162, 171, 175, 233–234, 272, 318, 320, 323, 328
Omar, Mullah, 16, 24, 29, 104, 108–109, 204
Operation Gibraltar (1965), 3
operation Zarb-e-Azaab, 52

Pakistan, 91, 94, 97, 101, 105, 113, 117, 125–126, 159, 161, 163, 207–208, 377–379; ban on JeM, 121, 127–143; evolution of madaris in, 44*t*; intelligence agencies, 200; jihadi ecosystem, 211; nuclear program, 2, 4, 6, 224; Proxy War Strategy, 2–9, 160; revoke of Most Favoured Nation (MFN) status for, 1; security forces, 51, 53; Taliban, 160; Taliban split, 157; terrorist attacks against, 52; terrorists, 110–111, 135, 190–191, 348, 356, 374; trained militants, 186
Pakistan-Administered Kashmir. *See* Pakistan-occupied Kashmir (PoK)
Pakistan Army, 19, 53, 91–92, 106, 108, 122, 124–125, 142–143, 158–159, 200, 203, 207–212, 378–379;

operations, 52; and training, 114; US and, 3
Pakistan Muslim League-Nawaz (PML-N), 47–48, 266
Pakistan-occupied Kashmir (PoK), 7, 44, 60, 64, 66, 123, 129, 134–135, 137, 144–145, 149–150, 154, 201, 237–238, 250, 268, 284–289, 292–293, 321; based commanders, 154; ban on Masood's entry, 129
Pakistan Tahreek-i-Insaaf, 389
Palestine, 84, 93, 242, 262, 269, 296, 326–329, 382, 384, 390
Pandya, Haren, 186
Panging, Mohonto, Group Captain (Retd), 5
Parliament, fidayeen attack on Indian, 2, 5, 8, 11, 103–107, 116–121, 127, 131, 137, 185, 188, 213, 215
Pathan, Adil, 151, 156, 158; killing of, 151
Pathan Kabaili raiders, 3
Pathankot airbase, attack, 93, 139, 158–59, 164–167, 192, 250–251, 273–274, 338–339; masterminds of, 341
Pathan, Mohammad Bhai, 294
Pearl, Daniel, murder of, 102, 123, 130–132, 134, 380
People's Anti-Fascist Front (PAFF), 177, 182, 387
People's Army, 3
Peshawar, Army Public School, TTP attack on, 52, 108, 112, 143, 210, 241, 378

Philippines, 92, 94, 98, 101
pir families, 263
Pir Panjal Peace Forum, 7, 196
police encounter, 49–50, 187
police training facility in Quetta, suicide attack on, 50
Prevention of Terrorism Act (POTA), 169, *see also* Global War on Terror (GWoT)
procurements, 360–361
propaganda videos, 326, 362, 364
proxy war, 2–3, 165, 263; anti-India, 176
Pulwama attack, 6, 155–156, 169, 172–174, 196, 222–223, 250–251, 324, 327, 338, 344–348, 355–356, 359, 365–366, 368–376, 384; conspiracy, 222, 231, 356–358, 369; encounter, 151; financing, 368; mastermind of, 205, 279, 340; VBIED assembling, 356
Pune, German Bakery, bombing of, 192

Qadam, Abu, 149
Qari, Saifullah, death of, 149
Qasim, Abu alias Abdur Rahman, 196
Qasim, Allah Wasaya Maulana, 103, 107, 284
Qasimiya Dar-ul-Uloom, Srinagar, 69, 221
Qasim-ul-Uloom, 40, 45
Qasmi, Isar-ul-Haq, 47–48

Qazi, Javed Ashraf, 116
Quetta, 50–51, 198
Qureshi, Altaf Hussain, 64
Qureshi, Shah Mahmood, 56, 173

Rabtar-e-Islamia (Saudi Arabia), 61
radicalization, 34, 222, 225, 258–259, 263, 326, 328, 379, 381, 383, 385–386; in Kashmir, 19
Rahman, Abdul alias Chota Burmese, 151, 156, 158
Rahman, Akhtar Abdul, Gen., 210
Rahman, Sheikh Abdul, 191
al-Rahman Usmani, Fadhl, 32
Al-Rahmat Trust (ART), 122, 140–142, 166, 201, 266, 293, 319, 324–325, 343
Raipuri, Abdul Rahim, 38
Raipuri, Faqirullah, Maulana, 41
Raju, R.V., 73
Raman, B., 130
Ram Mandir, 193–194
Rana, Muhammad Amir, 16, 99
Rashid, Abdul, 202, 286
Rashid, Ahmed, 29, 99
Rashid, Talha, , 202, 251, 253–254, 273, 376, 378
Al-Rashid Trust, 104
Rashtriya Rifles, 171
Rathar, Mohammad Iqbal, 351, 357–358, 373
Rather, Mohammad Abbas, 351, 358–359, 371

Rauf, Mufti Abdul, 101, 136, 140, 219, 241, 384; Interpol notice on, 136; as MARA, 199
Rauf, Rashid, 95, 128
RDX and ammonium nitrate, 345, 360, 363, 367
recruitment, 94, 98, 138, 141, 194, 198, 201, 204, 258–267, 271, 273, 326–327, 381; in Jammu and Kashmir, 146, 270–271t; Karachi as centre for, 100; modus operandi, 267–274
Reidel, Bruce, 30, 116, 158
Reshi, Manzoor, 170–171
Resistance Force, 196
The Resistance Front (TRF), 7, 10, 133, 177–178, 217, 314
Riedel, Bruce, 28, 30, 116, 158–159
Road Opening Party (ROP), 234, 364, 371
Roy, Olivier, on terrorism, 100

Sabir, Allah Baksh, 55, 140
Sabir Seminary, 140, 173
Sada-i-Mujahid, 58–60, 62, 64, 81, 100
Sadatullah, Maulana, 66
Sadiq, Asif, suicide bomber. *See* Bilal, Muhammad
Sadiq, Muhammad, 296–299
Sadiq, Mustapha, 64
Saed, Omar Sheikh, 130–133, 134, 144, 206, , 436; acquittal of, 132; in jail, 133

Saeed, Hafiz, 143, 157, 161, 214
Sahai, S.M., 248
Sahay, C.D., 24, 26, 119, 126, 133, 161
Sahrai Baba, 148
Al-Saif, Talha, 165–166
Saifi, Saifur Rahman, 78
Saifullah, Abu, 150, 174, 203, 205, 281, 294–295, 312–313, 357–359, 361, 369, 372, 374–376, 378, 385
Salafis, 34, 78–79, 261, 281
Salafism, 261
Salahuddin, Syed, 154, 161, 213–214, 309, 320
Salfi, Rashid Ahmed, 41
Salman, Maulana, 68
Sami-ul-Haq, Maulana, 204
Sanaullah, Rana, 166
Saraiki Movement, 58
Sarhindi, Sheikh Ahmad, 36
Saudi Arabia, 43–44, 55, 60–61, 66, 97, 100–101, 176, 186, 191, 319, 323, 328
Save Kashmir Movement, 213–214
Sayeed Ahmed Shaheed camp, 237
Sayeed, Mufti Mohammad, 148
secrecy, 228–36
sectarian: killings, 28–29, 47, 50–51; violence, 37, 47–49
sectarianism, 214, 265
Security Forces (SFs), 18, 147–150, 152–156, 161–162, 174–175, 180–181, 217–218, 223–225, 227–229, 232, 234–235, 245–246, 254–256, 270–272, 283, 301–303, 305, 370, 387; attacks on, 7, 369, 387; civilians agitation, 387; encounters, 146, 359, 372, 374, 378; Filipino, 98; in Kashmir, 54; killings, 149–150, 359, 373; operations, 148
Servants of Suffering and Humanity International Charity, 191
sexual abuse, 255, 263, 327
Shafi, Mufti Muhammad, 42
Shah, Afaq Ahmad, 116
Shahi Idgah case, 194
Shah, Ijaz Ahmed, Brig, 22, 131–132
Shahjahan, Mufti, 242, 284–285
Shah, Mohammad Yusuf, 161, 309
Shah, Peer Tariq Ahmed, 327, 350, 357, 359, 362–63, 365, 371–372
Shakoor, Abdul, 170
Shamsi, Mujibur-Rahman, 64
Shamzai, Mufti Nizamuddin, 15, 22, 30, 103–105, 108, 204; jihad against America, 105
Shariah laws, 51, 79, 153, 265
Sharif, Nawaz, 47, 92, 131, 158, 160, 166, 273
Sharif, Raheel, Gen., 143
Sharif, Shahbaz, 48
Sheikh, Abdul Latif, 187
Sheikh, Mohammad Abbas, 217

Sheikh, Omar Saed, , 70, 74, 94, 101, 107, 130–133, 144, 206
Sheikh-ul-Hadith Dar-ul Haqqania, 30
Shias, 33, 37, 40, 46–47, 49, 211, 214, 235, 241, 248, 263, 267; Taliban attacks on mosques of, 121; violence against, 48, 91, 108, 211
Shura (tribal group), 51
Sial, Maulana Abdus Samad, 65, 104
Siddiqa, Ayesha, 25, 28, 45, 86, 136, 138, 258, 260–266, 379; assassination plot to kill, 25
Siddique, Aslam, 3
Siddiqui, Mohammed Qateel, 192
Sikander, Abu, 149
Sikhs, 37, 83
Sindh, 38, 44, 100, 159, 198, 300
Sindhi, Ubaidullah, 38–39
Singh, Chanchal, 70
Singh, Jagmeet, 195–196
Singh, Jaswant, 29, 109
Singh, Karnal, 189
Singh, Maharaja Hari, 40
Singh, Manmohan, 5–6
Singh, N.K., 21–22
Singh, Salwinder, kidnap of, 340
Singh, Vikram, killing of, 248
Singh, Yakeer, 21
Sipah-e-Sahaba Pakistan (SSP), 28–29, 33, 44, 45–49, 51–53, 96, 108, 113, 199, 204, 207, 214, 219, 259, 266; formation of, 40
Sirrs, Julie, 97
smuggling, drug, 19, 283, 320
Sobhraj, Charles, 72
Somalia, 61, 63–64, 92, 98–100, 163, 258, 262, 285; jihadists, 99
specially designated global terrorist (SDGT), 161
Specially Designated National list, 75
Special Operation Groups (SOGs), 152, 317
Srinagar, grenade attack in, 214
Srinagar–Muzaffarabad bus service, 323
Stenersen, Anne, 97
Students Islamic Movement of India (SIMI), 5, 189
Sudan, 58, 63, 100–101, 163, 192, 258, 285, 328
Sufis, 20, 36, 49, 78, 225, 235, 261, 263–264, 266–267, 271, 279
Sufyan, Abu, 175
suicide: attacks, 31, 50, 112, 121, 128, 148–149, 157, 171, 192, 223–224, 348; bombers, 102, 111, 116, 122–223, 137, 141, 345, 353, 365–366, 368, 388; bombings, 49, 112, 116, 152, 198, 391; missions, 47, 83, 102, 108, 200, 224–225, 233, 360
Sunni extremist organizations, 214

Sunnis, 32, 40
Swami, Praveen, 78
Swaraj, Sushma, 329

Tablighi Jamaat (TJ), 33–36, 60, 65, 68, 92, 101, 186, 220–223, 264–265, 286–87, 307, 312–313
Tablighis, 35-36, 69, 220–221; cadres, 35; extremists, 35; trained in HuM camps, 36

Tajikistan, 98, 287
Takfiri, 91
Talha, Abu, 251, 309–311, 371, 374–376
Taliban, 7–8, 18–19, 23–25, 50–51, 96–97, 105–113, 117–120, 128–129, 136–137, 207–210, 212–214, 219–220, 356, 377–378, 380–381, 383, 387–391; attacks on Christian centres, 121; Punjabi, 52; regime, 7–8, 49; release of TTP prisoners, 112; return to power, 53–54, 111–112, 243, 381, 383
Talibanization, 261–263
Tankel, Stephen, 10
Tantrey, Noor Muhammad, 156–157, 163, 169–170, 175, 185, 217, 232, 256, 272, 303–307; Gulzar Ahmed Butt as, 303
Tantrey, Noor Muhammad, names of, 169
Tanveer-ul-Ahad, 366
Tanvir, Shehzad, 95

Tanzania, 98, 103
Tariq, Maulana Azam, 28–29, 47–48, 96
technical intelligence (TECHINT), 171, 181, 230, 346–347
Tehreek-al-Furqan (TAF), 141
Tehreek-e-Jihad, 135
Tehreek-e-Taliban Pakistan (TTP), 30, 46, 51–53, 91–92, 107–114, 127, 129, 143, 378–379, 381; formation of, 200
Tehreek-ul-Mujahideen, 135, 289
terror attacks, 5–9, 50, 53, 158, 165–166, 172, 175, 189, 192, 209, 213, 233–334, 388–389; as 7/7, 21/7, 95
terror-funding networks, 162
terror groups, 5–7, 9–11, 18–19, 25, 35–36, 110, 112–113, 118, 125–126, 135–138, 142–143, 176–178, 209–112, 214–115, 217–220, 223–224, 255, 259, 266–267, 378–381
terrorism, cross-border, 325
terrorist groups: in the Af-Pak region, 107; anti-India, 142–143; anti-Pakistan, 143
terrorist operations, 66, 98, 100, 199; targeting Westerners, 102
Thackeray, Bal, 194
Thanvi, Ehtisham-ul-Hassan, 42
Thanwi, Maulana Ashraf, 38

Tomar, Shashi Bhushan Singh, 21
Tonki, Hazrat Maulana Mufti Wali Hasan, 57
tour, religious, 269, 287
training, 26, 94–95, 113–114, 139–140, 187–188, 191–192, 223–228, 236–249, 277, 284–286, 293, 297, 300, 303, 384–385; Al-Ra'ad, 297; Daura-e-Tarbiya, 300, *see also* recruitments
transnational terrorist group (TTGs), 19, 93, 107, 113–114, 323, 380–381, 383–384
Tuhfah-yi sa'adat, Azhar, 83–84
tunnels, 72, 74, 251, 253, 292
Turabi, Maulana Abdur Rasheed, 60
Turkey, 38, 66, 100, 258, 384

UAE, 60–63, 82, 321; Masood visit to, 60
UK, 35, 62–63, 94, 101, 117, 132, 323–324; based Gujarati Deobandi Muslims, 101; jihadist missions to, 82
ul Haq, Ehsan, 126, 131

Under Barrel Grenade Launcher (UBGLs), 150, 240, 291, 297, 300, 303
United Jihad Council (UJC), 141, 178, 213, 309, 320
United Jihad Council, PoK-based, 339
United Liberation Front (ULFA), 191
United Nations Security Council (UNSC), 25, 75, 121, 161, 324
United Progressive Alliance (UPA), 5
Unlawful Activities Prevention Act (UAPA), 307, 339, 344
UN Security Council Resolution, 161
Uri, fidayeen attack, 11, 254, 257
USA: attack on embassies in Africa, 102; ally with Pakistan, 3; banning HuA, 15; banning JeM, 11; bombings of AQ facilities, 102; dependence on Pakistan, 9; GWoT, 109; 'hammer operations' against AQ, 105; led coalition forces, 110; led GWoT, 8, 49, 51, 93, 105, 108, 112, 120, 200, 380; strikes in Afghanistan, 8
Usmani, Mufti Rafi, 66
Usmani, Mullah Akhtar, 24
Usmani, Shabbir Ahmed, 42
Usmani, Zafar Ahmed, 42
Uzbekistan, 92, 98, 100

Vajpayee, Atal Bihari, 92, 118, 137, 167, 185, 334; peace initiatives, 158
Varanasi, serial blasts, 189
Varthaman, Abhinandan, Wing Com., captured alive, 2

VBIED (vehicle-borne IED): attack, 169, 223, 234–235, 344, 347, 355–357, 360–363, 365, 367, 374, 378; Conspiracy, 359–361
Verma, Raj, 125–126

Wagoora power grid attack, 171
Wahab, Abdul, 78
Wahhabism, 18, 33–34, 79–80, 91, 219, , 265, 383
Waiz-ul-Islam, 372–373
Wajid, Sheikh Hasina, attempt assassination, 36
Waleed, Khalid bin, 98, 101, 119, 237
Waliullah, Shah, 78–79
Wani, Burhan, 9, 143, 161–162, 270, 382
Waqas, Mufti alias Abdul Mateen, 169, 170, 172, 225–226, 306, 348; killing of, 171
war: anti-Soviet, 97; fatwas, 104; Kashmir, 263
warfare, irregular, 3–4
Waris, Abdul alias Tauseef, 154
weapons, 3–4, 30, 99, 118, 155–156, 178–79, 186, 192, 240, 242–243, 246, 261–262, 270, 290, 294–295, 300, 306, 377–378, 387–388

WhatsApp, 272, 361–362, 366, 370–372, 375, 385
World Trade Centre bombing, 48

Yadav, R.K., 21–22
Yakub, Mullah Muhammad, 111, 389
Yasir, Qari, 151, 233, 279, 302, 354, 358–359, 365, 373–374
Yusuf, Ramzi, 48

Zafar, Qari Mohammad, 50
Zahab, Mariam A., 100
Zambia, 59–60, 323
Zameel, Maulana, 58
Zarb-e-Azaab military offensive, 160
Zarb-i-Mumin, 93
Zardari, Asif Ali, 132
Zargar, Musarat Hussain alias Firdous, 114, 154
Zargar, Mushtaq Ahmad alias Latram, 23, 29, 70, 74, 133, 144, 206
Zawahiri, Ayman Al, 104–105, 122–123, 191, 382–383
Zia Ansari, 21
Zia-ul-Haq, Muhammad, Gen., 4, 35, 44, 47, 133, 263, 268
Zionists, 103–104
Zubaydah, Abu, 107, 133

About the Author

Dr Abhinav Pandya, a Cornell University graduate in public affairs and a bachelor's-degree holder from St. Stephen's College, Delhi, is the founder and CEO of Usanas Foundation, an India-based foreign policy and security think tank. He has authored two books, *Radicalization in India: An Exploration* (2019) and *Terror Financing in Kashmir* (2023). He has previously advised the former governor of Jammu and Kashmir on security issues during the critical time when Kashmir's special status Article 370 was revoked. He has written extensively for several national and international newspapers and worked with the International Labour Organization, the United Nations.

HarperCollins *Publishers* India

At HarperCollins India, we believe in telling the best stories and finding the widest readership for our books in every format possible. We started publishing in 1992; a great deal has changed since then, but what has remained constant is the passion with which our authors write their books, the love with which readers receive them, and the sheer joy and excitement that we as publishers feel in being a part of the publishing process.

Over the years, we've had the pleasure of publishing some of the finest writing from the subcontinent and around the world, including several award-winning titles and some of the biggest bestsellers in India's publishing history. But nothing has meant more to us than the fact that millions of people have read the books we published, and that somewhere, a book of ours might have made a difference.

As we look to the future, we go back to that one word—a word which has been a driving force for us all these years.

Read.